Right Words, Right Places

Scott Rice
San Jose State University

D0064594

Wadsworth Publishing Company
Belmont, California
A Division of Wadsworth, Inc.

English Editor: *Angela Gantner*
Editorial Assistant: *Patricia Schumacher*
Production Editor: *Vicki Friedberg*
Designer: *Cloyce J. Wall*
Print Buyer: *Barbara Britton*
Permissions Editor: *Jeanne Bosschart*
Copy Editor: *Tom Briggs*
Cover: *Cloyce J. Wall*
Compositor: *Maryland Composition*
Printer: *Malloy Lithographing*

*This book is printed on
acid-free recycled paper.*

Printed in the United States of America

2 3 4 5 6 7 8 9 10—97 96 95 94 93

Library of Congress Cataloging in Publication Data

Rice, Scott.
    Right words, right places / Scott Rice
      p.   cm.
    Includes index.
    ISBN 0-534-16038-7
    1. English language—Rhetoric—Handbooks, manuals, etc.
    2. English language—Grammar—1950–   Handbooks, manuals, etc.
    I. Title.
    PE1408.R556 1992   92-33111
    808'.042—dc20

Credits

pp. 48, 217, 306, 346–347. Copyright © 1990 by The New York Times
Company. Reprinted by permission.
pp. 63–65. © 1991 *The Washington Post*. Reprinted by permission.
pp. 213, 241, 294, 321, 346, 389, 397. Reprinted by permission of
The Wall Street Journal. © 1989/1990 Dow Jones & Company, Inc.
All Rights Reserved Worldwide.
pp. 318–319. Reprinted by permission; © 1986 *The New Yorker* Magazine,
Inc.

Brief Contents

Contents

1 *Grammar*   21

3 *Punctuation*   *351*

4   *MLA Documentation*   *421*

To the Teacher

I compiled this text because I believe that handbooks, in restricting themselves primarily to matters of correctness and usage, have missed a valuable opportunity. Of course, we want our students to produce clean copy, to avoid distracting errors in punctuation, syntax, and idiom, but cleanliness without liveliness equals sterility. If we want to teach lively writing, effective writing, we must first interest our students in the creative options at their disposal. And to accomplish this goal, we must call their attention to the rhetorical and stylistic properties of the words they use, to the power and pleasure inherent in nouns and verbs, in prepositional phrases and relative clauses. I believe that these matters are the natural province of a handbook.

For the title of this text I have adapted Jonathan Swift's description of good style: "proper words in proper places." By "proper words" I do not think that he simply meant precise diction, *propelled* rather than *ejected*, for example. He meant an idea expressed as one part of speech rather than another, as when Joseph Conrad once chose *begrimed* over *grimy*, wanting the passivity in the past participle that was missing in the adjective. By "proper words" he also meant one syntactic grouping over another, like a noun clause or an infinitive phrase rather than a gerund (hence, he would appreciate that "dreaming the impossible dream" does not suggest the potential expressed in "to dream the impossible dream"). And by "proper places" he meant that the propriety of the words was often inseparable from their location in the sentence.

Swift took for granted, however, that judgments of what is proper or "right" grow out of larger rhetorical considerations, considerations of subject and audience and purpose. Word choice and phraseology are in the service of these. But his quote reminds us of the reverse idea, one that we should pursue more aggressively in our writing classes: rhetorical effectiveness also depends on heeding the cues inherent in the language itself; more precisely, on exploiting the properties of the respective parts of speech and the various phrases and clauses. These properties suggest as well as serve rhetorical strategy.

But how do we sensitize our students to these properties, especially when we have only a semester or two to work with them? The answer, I believe, is to treat grammar, rhetoric, and style interchangeably, as extensions of one another. And such treatment requires the study and manipulation of language, beginning with good professional examples and culminating with the students' own work. By these means our students can sharpen the powers of judgment and decision making that James Moffett says are the heart of composition. *Right Words, Right Places*, then, is about revision, about the deliberate cultivation of choices and an informed appreciation of their consequences.

Having said that, I think it is appropriate to explain some of my own choices.

Organization

For reasons of convenience and familiarity, I have organized the text around traditional parts-of-speech grammar. For all of its inconsistencies, it is still the grammar used in most classrooms. In addition to following the parts of speech, the text is also divided into two major parts, "Grammar" and "Rhetoric." The first presents the standard information on forms and usage that some students need to avoid or correct errors. The second explores the rhetorical and stylistic properties of the word classes and structures, properties that accomplished writers exploit instinctively whether or not they ever think consciously about grammar.

Examples

With a few exceptions *Right Words, Right Places* rejects what Francis Christensen called "confected sentences," choosing instead to use live ones, ones taken from published work. Such sentences may lose something from being out of context, but there is still more to be learned from a live sentence taken out of context than from an artificial sentence that never had one. Not having been written to serve a one-dimensional purpose, such sentences also have the benefit of teaching multiple lessons. Furthermore, out-of-context examples invite inferences, a talent our students need to sharpen.

For some of the same reasons that beginning piano students are treated to a little Chopin, I have relied primarily on the work of accomplished writers. I believe that we can learn the most about effective expression from people who love good words, from those who enjoy and cultivate language for its own sake. I have also tried to select quotes that are interesting in themselves, expressing ideas and sentiments that, among other things, will provoke discussion and suggest essay topics. Such material is also more likely to motivate students to do similar justice to their own material.

Not all of the examples come from "literary" sources, however. I have also used material from publications like *Scientific American, Smithsonian, The New York Times*, and *The Wall Street Journal*. I have done this for several reasons. First, such material is similar to the kind of informational writing often required of our students. Second, these sources provide better examples of writing for general audiences than do most academic sources. And third, they often display more rhetorical imagination and stylistic flavor than our profession commonly recognizes. In short, I believe that the distinction between "creative" and "noncreative" writing is often an unwarranted one. Many of the devices we associate with creative writing, from figurative language to experimental narrative techniques, grace the pages of "noncreative" prose. For example, news stories and even occasional scientific articles now use present-tense narrations, a device contemporary fiction writers frequently choose for its immediacy. We do not have to accept the proposition that utilitarian writing must always be flat and colorless and formulaic.

Exercises

The exercises in this text are meant to invite discussion, following a three-step process: evaluating the choices of published writers, paraphrasing or revising, and then weighing the consequences. Their object is to sensitize students to the elements of writing, introducing them to the kind of questions they should be asking of their own work. It is by experimenting with phraseology, by testing different wordings for effects of clarity and emphasis, that they can develop control of their own language.

The exercises are also open-ended. There are no "right" answers, meaning there are many. Even seasoned English teachers will disagree about the effects and advisability of some of the choices. The object is not to arrive at unanimity. Just the contrary. The object of the exercises is to give our students practice with language, experience in manipulating and testing words and phrases that will culminate in the development of their own preferences, their own styles. Vigorous individual styles grow out of confidence in one's personal taste and judgment.

Sentence Work

Good sentences exist in a living environment, flowing out of a rhetorical situation, flowing into and out of other sentences. They should not be studied as static, isolated entities. Viewed in an implied relationship with their setting, they can reveal much about effective choices. Furthermore, they are the product of the same decisions that generate paragraphs and essays—decisions about subject, audience, and purpose, about organization, clarity, and emphasis. In encouraging our students to fine-tune their sentences, we are also helping them develop their rhetorical sense.

Some might dismiss such activity as "tinkering," but tinkering is often the difference between an engine that purrs and one that sputters and misfires. Smooth writing is the sum total of a lot of tinkering, of a lot of small choices competently made.

Paragraph Treatment

In keeping with recent theory, I have tried to avoid treating paragraphs as if they were rigid and self-contained. Like sentences, paragraphs usually operate in a sequence, developing out of and leading into other paragraphs. For this reason, many of the paragraphs are printed with the opening sentence or two of the following paragraph. Furthermore, research indicates that most writers do not deliberately compose in paragraphs. They make instinctive divisions as they write and then tidy up later. For this reason I have tried to focus on paragraphs not as something written but as something revised. And in emphasizing revision, the treatment of paragraphs also adheres to the governing idea of the text.

Student Writing

There is no substitute for working with student writing, but the writing of our own students, not someone else's. Students should see their own sentences on the board and should be working in groups on their own paragraphs and essays. The material in this text is not meant to be a substitute for such work; it is meant to be a prelude.

Besides, what better exercise in carrying coals to Newcastle can there be than printing student writing in a text for writing classes?

A Final Note

This book treats an inexhaustible subject, the rhetorical and stylistic character of grammar. A battery of experienced writing instructors might compile an encyclopedia on it, but our students do not need to read encyclopedias on writing. They need to write. I share some of James Moffett's objections to writing texts, to long, abstract discussions that tell students how they ought to write. Advice is nice, but practice is nicer. What our students need is practical work with language, experience in manipulating and testing words. I think that a handbook is a good tool for such work, allowing for spot use and as-needed consultation as well as sustained study.

In addition to treating an inexhaustible subject, this handbook has also taken some other risks. Traditional handbooks have operated in safer territory, merely summarizing conventions—fixed usages that require or allow little interpretation. But in trying to explore some of the rhetorical and stylistic implications of grammar, and operating where there is little consensus, this text has had to work without clear precedents. If it is sometimes inaccurate, then, or if it happens to contradict the opinions of some users, I believe that it will at least encourage students to think along productive lines, to consider the elements that will enable them to sharpen their own stylistic judgments. My idea was to give students an intensified experience in observing and testing language, to give them a basis for making up their own minds, rather than accepting the stylistic prescriptions and proscriptions of others.

In a text of this nature, the author's own rhetorical preferences are bound to creep in. As much as possible, though, I have tried to base my inferences on empirical evidence, on the work of practicing writers. At the same time, I have tried to avoid that occupational arrogance of writing instructors which represents personal likes and dislikes as "rules" (like Arthur Quiller-Couch, for example, I hate the compound preposition *as to*). Many of us are still trying to shake off artificial prejudices implanted by our own instructors.

In sum, I believe that a handbook should not be simply about accuracy; it should be about observation and experimentation, about exploration and risk taking, about possibility.

Acknowledgments

The integration of grammar, rhetoric, and style is an established if not yet reigning ideal among writing instructors. Hence, many readers will recognize my pedagogical indebtedness to such worthies as Donald Davidson, Francis Christensen, Richard Weaver, Winston Weathers, Otis Winchester, Virginia Tufte, Lewis Milic, Ann Ray, Robert Ray, Edward P. J. Corbett, and Charles Kay Smith, and others whose random insights I have assimilated in my reading.

I have also profited greatly from the suggestions and criticisms of those who reviewed early versions of my manuscript. I was fortunate to have a group of readers who understood so well the spirit and intent of my project: Michael Adams, Albright College; Jean A. Aston, Community College of Allegheny County; Douglas Atkins, University of Kansas; Kathleen Bell, University of Central Florida; Hale Chatfield, Hiram College; Patrick Day, Oberlin College; Sam Dragga, Texas Tech University; Jean M. English, University of Tennessee, Martin; Kim Flachmann, California State University, Bakersfield; Paul Heilker, Texas Christian University; Clayton Holloway, Hampton University; Christine A. Hult, Utah State University; Ted E. Johnston, El Paso Community College; Janet S. Kafka, University of Pittsburgh; Kathleen Ann Kelly, Northeastern University; Ken Kirkpatrick, University of Tulsa; James H. Knickerbocker, Clarion University of Pennsylvania; Jeanette P. Morgan, United States Air Force Academy; Janice Neuleib, Illinois State University; Randell Popken, Tarleton State University; Jonathan L. Price, California State University, Sacramento; Mary P. Richards, Auburn University; Me Me Riordan, City College of San Francisco; Duane H. Roen, University of Arizona; Audrey Roth, Miami-Dade Community College; Jeanne Simpson, Eastern Illinois University; Norman Stroh, Angelo State University; David L. Wallace, Carnegie Mellon University; Vickie Weir, Morehead State University; James D. Williams, University of North Carolina, Chapel Hill; and Thomas Young, California State University, Stanislaus. Also, for their help with the documentation section, I would like to thank Jack Haeger and Jan Patten of the English Department at San Jose State University.

Finally, my special thanks to the two people who gave me the greatest encouragement throughout the four years I spent putting this together: Gabi Rico, my colleague and friend and inspiration; and Angie Gantner, my editor at Wadsworth, whose good humor and patience helped me produce a much better book.

To the Student

his book is not about formulas or paint-by-numbers methods that will enable you to crank out papers effortlessly, almost without thinking. True, there are some familiar and flexible patterns that you can occasionally use, and professional writers master them quickly, but not to avoid thinking. They learn the strengths and limitations of various patterns, then learn to adjust or intermingle them. Human experience, they know, is too extensive and diverse to be reduced to a few static shapes.

Contrary to what some may think or hope, then, learning to write is not a matter of collecting rigid molds into which we can pour our subjects. Rather, it is a matter of accepting the challenge that every writing situation is to some extent a makeshift affair, a mixture of the typical and the unique. Our goal as writers is to allow our subjects to find their best forms, which may or may not resemble those used by earlier writers. The various patterns are simply different ways of exploring and thinking about our subjects, options to be considered, altered, or discarded.

Because of the value of patterns, writing students spend their classroom careers being shown models. But models are not to be worshiped. A model is useful primarily as an example of how another writer solved the problems of expression. What a good example "models" is how to make intelligent choices. The best way to learn from a model, to imitate it, is to make choices in the same spirit. And such informed choosing is the subject of this text.

Language and thought are interdependent; words lead to ideas and ideas lead to words. More particularly, *wording* leads to ideas, and vice versa. To be limited in our wording is to be limited in our thinking. Ultimately, we can only explore and understand and share what we can put into words.

If this book has a single point it is this: every task can be done another way. In selecting and rejecting ways, we learn more about our task, about our subject, and about ourselves.

I wanted to write and I did not even know the English language. I bought English grammars and found them dull. I felt that I was getting a better sense of the language from novels than from grammars.
—*Richard Wright*, Black Boy

Introduction

Grammar, Rhetoric, and Writing

When we say that some people's grammar is "good" or that others' is "bad," we are usually commenting on its "correctness," on how successfully it conforms to the standards of formal spoken or written English. A person whose grammar is "good" avoids expressions like *ain't, between you and I, don't want no, the reason is because,* and *hopefully.* Instead, the person will answer the phone by asking questions like "*Whom* do you want?" and answering, "It is *I.*" Such a person always speaks *well,* but never *good.*

Most of us want our grammar to be "good," or at least good enough to avoid ridicule (although, in many social situations, saying "It is I" is as good a way as any of being ridiculed). Rightly or wrongly, if we want to qualify for many educational and occupational opportunities, such a mastery of language is a social necessity. Mastery of this kind of grammar is principally a matter of avoiding mistakes, of walking without tripping.

There is, however, another kind of "good" grammar, a kind of grammar that allows us not simply to walk without stumbling, but to run and dance (and perhaps even enjoy ourselves while we are doing it). It is the kind of grammar of which Joan Didion speaks when she says, "All I know of grammar is its infinite power." The grammar she means is not the grammar of correctness, but the grammar of effectiveness, a grammar devoted not merely to error avoidance but to forceful expression, a grammar that recognizes the potency of the different parts of speech and of the different kinds of phrases and clauses. This is grammar at its most subtle but also at its most beautiful, a grammar we all recognize if only to a minor extent (when, for example, we find certain expressions memorable: "government of the people, by the people, for the people"). Such grammar is serving **rhetoric**—effective, purposeful expression, or "the art of making truth effective," as Aristotle put it.

1

Good writers, then, are good users of grammar, whether or not they know all the "rules." This statement does not mean, however, that anybody writes by consciously thinking of grammar. To attain just the right emphasis, for example, a writer might decide that it sounds better to say "people *who have cars and money*" rather than "people *with cars and money.*" No writer, though, is on record as ever having thought, "I believe I will opt for the relative clause over the prepositional phrase because it contains a full finite verb and is therefore more emphatic." The sensitive writer simply recognizes that the one kind of structure (which grammarians call a clause) is weightier than the other (which grammarians call a phrase) and that the added weight does more credit to the subject.

But professional writers are not the only people who make such choices. In speech and in writing, with varying degrees of care and success, each of us is constantly making such decisions. Given our understanding of the situation—our subject, our audience, and the effect we want to have on it—we try to select good words and put them in a suitable order. If we are speaking and trying to explain a difficult or sensitive idea, we are likely to restate ourselves frequently, groping for the right combination. If we are writing, at some level of consciousness we are thinking, "Given the sentences around it, this particular sentence would work a little better if it were arranged this instead of that way." Or, more precisely, "This sentence is worded to highlight this, when it should highlight that."

In other words, we all speak and write by "feel," choosing and arranging our words on the basis of instinct and preference and experience. All of these factors can be schooled, can be sharpened and refined until they are more consistent and reliable guides. How do we school them? We school them first by paying particular attention to those who express themselves well. When reading such a writer, for example, we go back and reread the most striking passages. We look for sequences of well-phrased words, and then we turn them over in our minds (and on our tongues).

And, of course, we school our selective instincts by always trying to express ourselves as well as we can, by trying to make our points as clearly and effectively as we are able. Doing the latter means using grammar, grammar without labels. We don't have to be zoologists to know that a bull belongs in a corral or pasture, not in a china shop. At the time we make our initial choices, we are too busy pursuing the flow of our ideas and trying to wrestle them into some kind of acceptable order. We do not want to be distracted by having to tinker with sentences. We only know that we want some general effect. Later, in revising, we can see if we have found all the best means. Next time, though, if we have developed the habit of appreciative reading and close revision, we will be more likely to make more choices in the heat of writing that will stand up to later examination.

But why should anyone want to take all this trouble? Why do serious writers revise and revise until they feel they have gotten the words just right? Why isn't it enough simply "to get our point across"? And why isn't a knowledge of the subject enough?

When we produce well-crafted sentences ("good" sentences), we have done more justice to our intentions, our subject, and our audience. In a major way our sentences are truer, more convincing; they have realized their subject more fully. Their meaning is more apparent; in a manner of speaking, they prove themselves. When we fail or fall short, we have either chosen structures not suited for our topic or arranged them such that they mislead or under- or overemphasize. In any event, we have failed our subject, our audience, and ourselves.

The purpose of this text, then, is to help you make more informed and effective choices. There are very few intrinsically bad or ineffective structures, only poorly chosen and/or ineffectively located ones. The criteria are relative to one's subject, audience, and purpose. The choices, of course, are also a matter of personal taste. The sum total of one's personal preferences, plus one's peculiar sentiments and values, equal one's "style." And finding one's personal style—that signal of the unique contribution we as individuals have to make—is another reason to cultivate our language.

In sum, then, why should all of us work continuously to improve our speech and writing?

▶ so we can better understand the nature and implications of our own ideas

▶ so we can do full justice to our subjects

▶ so people will listen to us and give us the audience we deserve

▶ so we can come closer to saying exactly what we mean and our ideas will be properly received

▶ so we can reveal the best part of ourselves and others will recognize and appreciate our worth

Style

In the broadest sense *style* is simply the way we do something, regardless of how bland and ordinary that may be. Thus, everyone can claim to have a style. Usually, though, when we say that a person "has style" we mean something more—that the person has a distinctive and identifiable manner, often one that shows grace and imagination. This latter notion of style is probably the most useful one to describe what we want to cultivate in our writing. We will think of style, then, as any use of words that sets itself apart from the most ordinary and predictable. Its purpose is to emphasize our ideas, to make them more effective and memorable.

Sometimes style is simply a matter of diction or word choice, such as using a suggestive verb to describe an everyday action:

People at the table laughed and shook their heads as they shovelled up their eggs. —Raymond Carver, "Where I'm Calling From"

Sometimes style is a matter of unusual word order:

Over this rocky area relieved by a few shady tall persimmon trees the graduating class walked.
—Maya Angelou, *I Know Why the Caged Bird Sings*

What his skills were, his acumen, his genius that got him down to Little Rock and into a good job in 1947, I don't know.
—Richard Ford, "Accommodations"

Sometimes style is a suggestive comparison:

Once, when I was a child, I waked from a bad dream to find moonlight pouring into the room, falling across my face like the flashlight of a prowler. —E. B. White, "A Week in April"

His pale pop eyes crawled on her like slugs.
—Wallace Stegner, *Angle of Repose*

Sometimes style is a matter of repetition, either of words or of structures:

They came in wagons from way up in Georgia and they came in truck loads from east, west, north and south.
—Zora Neale Hurston, *Their Eyes Were Watching God*

He could not have landed in a better place at a better time with a better man. —Elting E. Morison, "The Master Builder"

Sometimes style is an unusual manner of connecting items in a series:

Americans are just as likely to be overweight today as they were in the 1960s, according to a new report from the Federal Centers for Disease Control. Not jogging, nor Lean Cuisine, nor health spas, nor Jane Fonda, nor "lite" beer, nor a couple of

decades of nagging from federal health agencies appears to have done much to reduce the national prevalence of fat. —William Booth, *Washington Post*, 22–28 July 1991, natl. weekly ed.

And sometimes style is a rhythmic combination of some of the devices mentioned previously:

It was a clear, picturesque day, a February day without clouds, without emotion or spirit, like a beautiful woman with an empty face. —Annie Dillard, *Pilgrim at Tinker Creek*

We need more coyotes, more mountain lions, more wolves and foxes and wildcats, more owls, hawks and eagles. —Edward Abbey, *Desert Solitaire*

And sometimes style is a short, powerful statement:

Bad news has good legs. —Richard Llewellyn, *How Green Was My Valley*

But always, effective style is a matter of word choice and phraseology, of the right words in the right places:

What the government grasps, the government seeks to keep and hold. —Lewis H. Lapham, "A Political Opiate," *Harper's*, Dec. 1989

In its best sense, then, style is not a triumph over substance, not a distraction, like the gestures of a magician. Good style is a matter of directness and clarity, punctuated by occasional moments of emphasis and intensity. Its purpose is to show our information and ideas to their best advantage, to capture our feelings toward our subject, to make our audience attentive and receptive.

Problems with Style

Writers can offend against style (and therefore against their readers) in any number of ways.

Triteness Language is trite when it is filled with canned, prefabricated, ready-made expressions—usually images and phraseology that have lost their novelty. As the root of *trite* originally meant (worn away), all their shape and color have been eroded by overuse:

like a bolt of lightning
innocent as a newborn babe
madder than a wet hen/a hornet
back to square one
the bottom line

no sooner had I
most are . . . this was no exception
little did I know

The best writers put their individual stamp on what they write. They do not accept worn-out, hand-me-down phraseology.

Pretentiousness   A style is pretentious when the writer is straining to appear overly intelligent or educated or authoritative. The goal of such writing is to present not the subject but the writer to the best advantage, to awe and intimidate rather than to inform and persuade. Such people instinctively select the most obscure or "insider" language. Their vocabulary is filled not with *long* but with *gratuitously polysyllabic* words. They never agree but "answer in the affirmative." They never hear of bad weather, only of "adverse climatic conditions." They never write of crises, only of "crisis situations." Nothing is ever hurtful or damaging; it only "has a negative impact" (or "impacts negatively"). They never receive anything; they are "made recipients of." And their worlds are filled with "parameters" and "interfacing" and "prioritizing."

Wordiness   A style is wordy when it is overly qualified and unnecessarily repetitive, heaping on words that do nothing to clarify or emphasize. Wordy language is cluttered and uneconomical, using phrases and clauses to do the work of single words. Wordiness stifles the subject and the reader, as in the following:

> Is war an internal condition in man or is it external which is to be located outside of man, not within him?   —academic journal

When we ask if something is internal, we are also asking if it is external (it has to be one or the other). And clearly, if it is external to man, it is located outside, "not within him." We can ask this question much more economically:

> Is aggression intrinsic to human nature?

Or:

> Are human beings naturally aggressive?

Of course, put like this, the question has an obvious answer, indicating one motive for both pretentiousness and wordiness: They allow us to disguise the obviousness of our ideas. Or take a longer example:

> However, if survival is to continue through the control of war or its elimination, it is imperative that a new perception of oneself is urgently required.   —academic journal

"If survival is to continue"? *Continue* is what survival does. "The control of war or its elimination"? In this context *control* would probably include elimination. "It is imperative that . . . is urgently required"? An imperative is something necessary or required. In other words, the writer has said that it is necessary that something be necessary. The writer probably meant something like this:

> If we are to control war and survive, we must develop a new perception of ourselves.

Consider another example:

> Consultants must be prepared to find situations **much different from those they have previously observed or experienced.**
> —academic journal

This seventeen-word sentence is cluttered to the brim. To begin with, take "have previously observed or experienced." Observing is one kind of experience, so we don't need both words. Furthermore, "have . . . observed or experienced" is in the *present perfect tense*, a form that takes in everything that has happened up to the present. "Previously," then, is redundant. And finally, we do not need a ten-word phrase to describe something *new, unfamiliar, unprecedented*, as this version shows:

> Consultants must be prepared to encounter unfamiliar situations. (as must everyone else)

Awkwardness A style is awkward or clumsy when the writer has little control over sentence structure, little sense of thematic unity or focus, or of how to achieve them. An awkward sentence may do any of the following:

▶ violate idiom or parallelism

▶ use unnecessary repetition

▶ string together too many prepositional phrases (often with abstract objects)

▶ use the passive voice, often with no clear sense of who or what is acting

And all of these will likely be compounded by wordiness. The following has most of these problems:

> A new perception of a new man using a code of "love for all other men" through self-understanding and the identification of a humanity common to every individual is needed; not a fragmentary humanity. —academic journal

To make the action more precise and concrete, let us start by asking, *Who* needs? The implied answer is humanity: *We* do.

We need . . .

What do we need? The long subject phrase tells us (sort of): "a new perception of a new man . . . to every individual." But we are confused by all the abstractions strung together with prepositional phrases:

A new perception **of** a new man using a code **of** "love for all other men" **through** self-understanding and the identification **of** a humanity common **to** every individual . . .

And much of the connected material is repetitive:

a **new** perception of a **new** man   (a new perception of humanity?)

a new **man** using a code of "love for all other **men**"
(a new sense of justice? charity?)

a humanity **common to every individual**   (a common humanity?)

And, of course, "new perception" overlaps "self-understanding and the identification of a humanity common to every individual." Furthermore, there is the pointless and unparallel qualification thrown in at the end: "not a fragmentary humanity."

How do we fix a sentence with so many problems? If it were an appliance, an honest repair shop would tell us to buy a new one. In cases this extreme, there is nothing to do but give up on the original. We have to back off and do two things: identify a concrete subject for our sentence, then try to express the idea in the clearest language, as if we were speaking to a friend or relative. The following are a few possibilities:

We need a **renewed** sense of our common humanity.

We need to **restore** our sense of community.

(*renew* or *restore* because, of course, these are not new ideas)

This version implies most of what the original writer was straining to express, and in the process packing his sentence with more material than he could manage. Sometimes we can escape with an easy repair, like replacing one unidiomatic word:

That was another case **that** he should have stayed down on the ball.   —sports column

That was another case **when/where** he should have . . .

Other times, we just have to start over and ask, "In ordinary language, without trying to impress anybody, what do I want to say?"

Trying Too Hard   Except for triteness, most of the style problems discussed thus far develop when writers try too hard. Sometimes this effort involves style itself, as when a writer tries self-consciously to be flashy and "literary." Such a writer strains for exotic words and images, then pours them on, as if we could improve a recipe for chocolate chip cookies by adding more and more brown sugar. The following is a good example:

> The monsoon clouds, pregnant with rain, growled and grunted across the swollen pewter sky. The dome of afternoon pressed down on the earth like a soggy blanket, trapping the oppressive humidity and laying low even the most fortitudinous, their bodies robbed of energy, their minds of will.   —historical romance

The novelist has squeezed an entire paragraph out of a familiar and easily evoked experience, relying on two means: **overexplicitness** and cliched imagery. Writing is overly explicit when it spells out what is clearly implied, as if the reader had no experience or imagination. Consider how the first sentence tells us that the monsoon clouds thundered:

> The monsoon clouds, pregnant with rain, growled and grunted across the swollen pewter sky.

Even Westerners know that monsoons are heavy rains. "Monsoon clouds," then, includes the idea of being filled ("pregnant") with rain. And rain clouds are usually shades of gray ("pewter"), and, of course, they are found in the sky. Furthermore, the overexplicitness extends even to a circular statement. The pregnant clouds growl and grunt across a swollen pewter sky? What is swollen and gray? The clouds, of course. Apparently, these clouds growled and grunted across themselves.

And consider the second sentence:

> The dome of afternoon pressed down on the earth like a soggy blanket, trapping the oppressive humidity and laying low even the most fortitudinous, their bodies robbed of energy, their minds of will.

Wet (or soggy) blankets are by nature heavy, and what is heavy presses down. Also, humidity is oppressive by nature—few find it invigorating. Furthermore, if it robs people of energy, by definition it robs them of their will. Energy suggests the inclination as well as the ability to act. The second sentence is as repetitive as the first.

To amplify the scene, the writer also uses figurative language in the form of cliched or ill-considered *similes* and *metaphors*. The idea of pregnant rain clouds is an obvious and old one. And then there is the unfortunate verbal metaphor of growling and grunting, just to escape using *thundered*. The writer then calls the afternoon a "dome," probably meaning the afternoon sky, and compares it to a "soggy blanket." *Soggy* cannot disguise the wet blanket cliche.

As a last touch, the writer uses an artificially formal word to describe the victims of the humidity. It does not lay low the bravest or the most determined, but "the most fortitudinous."

The function of style is to emphasize, to announce that the reader should pay especial attention to our subject, but its use demands restraint. Style is to writing what seasoning is to cooking. Not even the most ornate of writers try to show off in every phrase and clause, knowing better than to dull the reader's sensibility by overloading sentences with special effects. They hold something back, allowing readers to use their imaginations:

The town sweltered beneath the rumbling monsoon clouds.

Or:

Beneath the rumbling monsoon clouds, humidity blanketed the town. (Or something—you try it.)

Not Trying at All The opposite of trying to do too much with the subject is doing nothing at all. Like a cook who simply boils potatoes and then dumps them on someone's plate, some writers make no attempt whatsoever to render their material appetizing. Perhaps not believing in the value of their subject, themselves, or their readers, they make the most obvious and commonplace remarks in the most ordinary language. They start their essays like this:

In many universities students have difficulty expressing their ideas effectively through writing.

Electricity is a form of energy. It is used to produce many forms of energy, such as light and heat.

We might say that these sentiments are worthy of the language, and the language of the sentiments. In any event, neither is worthy of a reader's attention.

Style and Levels of Formality

In classifying writing we sometimes speak of "levels of style," meaning the degree of formality. A given work, then, will fit somewhere on a scale running from formal to informal (or familiar) to colloquial. Each level has its own character and uses, being suitable for some subjects and audiences, but not for others. As a result, such discussions of style usually center on appropriateness.

Formal Style   The *formal style* is the style of academic, scientific, and professional activities. It signals dignity and seriousness and objectivity. If we want to think of style as a tone of voice, we can say that the formal writer sounds like a specialist lecturing to a roomful of fellow specialists. Hence, the vocabulary of formal writing is likely to be technical, preferring long words to short ones and specialized terminology to familiar. The formal writer adheres to a deliberate, logical structure, uses longer sentences, engages in little figurative language, and avoids contractions and pronouns like *I*, *we*, and *you*. In sum, formal writers play impersonal, abstract roles, as the following demonstrates:

> The educator's concern is with providing the conditions, including the guidance of learning activities and materials, under which the individuals in his care may optimally develop.
> —academic journal

Informal Style   The *informal style* is the language of one person speaking to other persons (as opposed to a professional addressing other professionals). It is not only the style we use in writing and speaking to those with whom we are familiar, increasingly it is the style appearing in reviews, personal-opinion pieces, essays on popular topics, and any other writing directed at general readers. Informal writers often stress goodwill along with their technical qualifications, using familiar language, shorter sentences, contractions, pronouns like *I*, *we*, and *you*, and figures of speech (reflecting personal judgments).

The following review of Chet Raymo's collection of essays on science, *The Virgin and the Mousetrap*, captures the flavor of one version of the informal style:

> His essays conjure up an image of those easygoing summertime conversations of yesteryear, when people gathered on a back porch while bugs hovered around the lightbulb and twilight slowly descended into a purple mist.
> —Marcia Bartusiak, *New York Times Book Review*, 18 Aug. 1991

Colloquial Style   The **colloquial style** is the style of daily conversation, the language of private communication. Filled with slang and contractions and a general disregard for what English teachers might think, it is not appropriate for most writing. When the terms are especially apt or colorful, writers occasionally draw on street expressions, but with care. More than formal and informal language, the colloquial depends on immediate context for meaning. Many colloquialisms also have a short life, quickly going out of style and sometimes even "dating" the writer.

Review

Formal	The educator's concern is with providing the conditions, including the guidance of learning activities and materials, under which the individuals in his care may optimally develop.
Informal	As teachers, we obviously want to create a setting where our students can learn the most.
Colloquial	Look, I just think we should give our kids the classrooms where they can do their best.

Audience

Few four-year-olds ask their mothers for something the same way they ask their fathers (or their babysitters, or their friends). Instead, they shape their address and their appeal to fit the individuals from whom they want cooperation. In other words, concern for audience is one of the first social reflexes that humans develop.

Adjusting to Audiences

Effective writers also know to adjust their manner and presentation to suit their **audience**—their readers. Based on their estimate of what the readers know and want, they make choices about style and arrangement and detail. If they are writing for a group of insiders, for example, people who are already well informed and at home with a technical vocabulary, writers know that they can wield certain terminology without stopping to give definitions. Addressing insiders with an understanding of the issues, writers know that they can often plunge right into their subject with a minimum of background preparation. They also know that they can choose between going into great detail (because their audience is well briefed) and taking shortcuts (because they can assume that some information is common knowledge). (See the section "A Tale of Two Openers" in Chapter 11, "The Rhetoric of Nouns.")

Consider the following opener to a critical essay:

> *Major Barbara*, together with *Man and Superman* and *John Bull's Other Island*, forms part of a trilogy of philosophical

comedies, all of which deal with the bankruptcy of nineteenth-century liberalism in the face of the brute facts of sex, nationalism, and poverty.

—Louis Compton, "Shaw's Challenge to Liberalism," *Prairie Schooner*, Fall 1963

The writer enjoys the license of writing for insiders, in this case fellow professors of English. Hence, he can move abruptly into his subject, not bothering to explain that the three works mentioned are plays, all written by an Englishman, George Bernard Shaw. In fact, he does not even mention Shaw in the first sentence. The writer can also use a word like *trilogy*, a technical term for a group of three literary works, and he can assume some historical knowledge of European political thought ("nineteenth-century liberalism"). Most readers will know immediately whether they are part of the writer's target audience.

Sizing up an audience, then, is a matter of estimating its familiarity with the subject: *What do the readers know?* It is also a matter of another kind of familiarity, the distance between writer and reader. We are sometimes offended when certain strangers, such as salespeople, are too familiar with us, when they stand too close. (It is harder to turn down a friend!) Other times, we can be upset when a relative holds us hostage to too much ceremony (like formal thank-you notes after a visit).

Readers also warm or cool to signs of familiarity. When writers are too relaxed, too informal, using the pronouns *I* and *you*, and slang and contractions (*I'll*, *you've*), and taking liberties with organization and accuracy and support, we question their respect for either their audience or their material. When they are too stiff and formal, using the pronoun *one* and unnecessarily technical language and overly detailed explanations, we wonder if they are not more concerned with impressing than with interesting or informing us. (See the section "Pronouns and Formality" in Chapter 12, "The Rhetoric of Pronouns.") Such extremes aside, though, there is a range of acceptable distances between writers and readers.

Consider the distance between writer and audience suggested by the following passages:

Antarctica is a gently domed continent squashed flat, like a dent in the roof of a Chevy, by the weight of its ice. . . . When a tongue of ice flows down a mountain valley, we call it a glacier. When it flows out in all directions from a source point at high elevation, like pancake batter poured on a griddle, we call it a sheet.   —David Quammen, "Strawberries Under Ice"

Isleta, New Mexico, is a Southern Tiwa–speaking pueblo community located some fifteen miles south of the center of downtown Albuquerque. Isleta may be called a community, in that the Isletans vote for, and agree to abide by, the decisions of one common set of governing officials. The pueblo itself, however, is actually an aggregate of five terminologically distinct living areas . . .   —academic journal

Most readers would find the first more friendly and accessible, the second more distant and businesslike. Quammen is writing a familiar essay, one in which it is appropriate to use *I* and *we*. He feels free (and inspired) to indulge his imagination, using similes from familiar experience to describe his subject: Antarctica is like a Chevy (not a Chevrolet) with a dented roof, and an ice sheet spreads like pancake batter. In his tone and treatment the writer is speaking to us as ordinary, inquisitive human beings, suggesting the broad appeal of his subject. He wants to entertain as well as educate us. The reader does not need any special qualifications, not even a studious mood.

Writing for an academic journal, though, the second writer is all business. In a thorough, formal, and dry manner, he explains about the "Southern Tiwa–speaking pueblo community" of Isleta. His assumed audience, of course, knows about Tiwa and about "terminologically distinct living areas." He uses no *I*'s, *we*'s, or *you*'s. He indulges in no colorful comparisons. He is an authority speaking to other serious-minded authorities. He can take need and interest for granted; he does not have to establish them. The writer is not even writing for most of us, and he is standing well back from the audience he has chosen. Even the small targeted body of insiders will read the essay as a task, their professional homework.

Using Audiences

Most of us can remember what it was like to be five years old and have something we urgently wanted to show someone else—a plane writing in the sky, a litter of newborn kittens, an antique car. As adults we even know what it is like to have a bit of news that can be relished by one or two people in particular. Writing can and should be like this. In other words, it is the thought of living, responding human beings that should drive us to write, people with particular needs and interests (environmentalists, psychology majors, taxpayers, readers of Letters to the Editor), but also people with typical human traits—curiosity, sympathy, humor. Recognizing these connections both impels and directs us.

When we write, then, we should not think of our audience simply as people to whom we must adjust ourselves, as a group of finicky eaters daring us to please them. If we signal our goodwill, our intention to do them a service, to appeal to their interests immediate or latent, we can usually assume goodwill on their part. Most readers are willing to meet us part way. For example, they will expect to find unity and significance in our statements and will look for them, drawing a reasonable number of connections and inferences. The more we indicate a willingness to cooperate with our readers by being clear and direct, the more likely they are to cooperate with us. Their imagined presence can even be a source of ideas. Here are some ways we can use our audience:

▶ *By talking to it, by imagining it asking questions:* "Why should this concern us?" "What do you mean by that?" "Aren't you taking some liberties here?" "Could you be a little more specific?"

▶ *By talking to different audiences, not just our prime one.* When we get stuck trying to explain an idea, we can imagine talking to someone other than insiders. For example, in the midst of explaining a lab process or an economic theory, we can think of how we might try to clarify it (and perhaps justify it) to someone in a related field, then to a curious amateur, then to a friend or family member with no technical background. The latter will require us to drop all but the most essential jargon, to address all the problems we have created for ourselves by trying to sound too knowledgeable (we want to win the confidence of our audience by sounding competent, not awe them with our expertise).

This last point is especially important. Much academic writing is so dreary because the writers have defined their audiences too narrowly, thinking of their readers one dimensionally, as entomologists or special educationists or semioticians. The most engaging writers remember the human being behind the specialist.

▶ *By thinking about its special needs and interests.* We rarely inherit a universally receptive audience, a group interested in whatever we will have to say on any subject whatsoever. We usually address a group on a particular occasion and for some timely purpose. They will have some distinguishing need or involvement or background, some established concern, that brings them together and that we can tap.

Erasmus Exercises

In 1512 the Dutch humanist Erasmus published one of the most influential rhetoric texts of the European Renaissance, his *De Copia* ("On command of language/richness of expression"). In one characteristic exercise Erasmus asked students to compose several hundred variations of a single sentence. The object was twofold: to develop a flexible command of sentence structure and, more important, to develop a sense of stylistic judgment. As another Renaissance figure, Pascal, wrote more than a century later, "Words differently arranged have different meanings, and meanings differently arranged have different effects." Erasmus's exercises taught both the different arrangements and an appreciation of the different effects.

To some extent, anyone who has ever revised a sentence has done Erasmus exercises. As we struggle with the phrasing, trying one kind of wording over another, or moving an element from the end of a sentence to the beginning, we are doing what Erasmus taught his students. Many writers, though, in their struggle to put the right words in the right places, have only a limited degree of structural dexterity. They must make do with a handful of options, a small fraction of all the possible meanings and effects. Once they have something on the page, it solidifies, resisting all but the smallest changes.

No writer has to settle for a mere handful of arrangements and effects, however. Using Erasmus exercises, writers at any stage of development can expand their repertoires. They can do it by experimenting with what they already know intuitively, using structures that they at least recognize if not usually employ. And the process does not require any knowledge of grammatical terminology. It requires only that they practice sentence revision, of their own writing or that of others. Beginning with an assessment of where it appears and what task it has to perform, they work variations on a sentence, looking for comparable or even better wording. Each new version should then be referred to the original to see how meaning and effect have changed.

To illustrate the exercise, this text will work with a sentence arbitrarily chosen from a historical novel by Thomas B. Costain, *The Conquering Family*. In vocabulary and structure the sentence is not particularly complicated, but in its context it is effective. It describes the conditions under which a man must make a hazardous horseback ride to London, where he hopes to claim the throne of England:

A sleet was falling which turned the roads into sheets of ice.

This sentence focuses on two pieces of news, the one growing out of the other. It is about discomfort and danger; the rider must endure the cold and wet, and he must worry about his horse's balance. In other words, he is threatened both with freezing and with being crushed beneath a falling horse.

Directions Compose at least ten versions of the Costain sentence above, relying principally upon changes in structure. That is, retain the original vocabulary except where grammar or idiom requires a substitution (*because* a sleet was falling/*because of* a falling sleet). To keep matters simple, you can begin by making one change for each version, then graduate to making several, then to working different combinations. The object is both to exercise your command of sentence structure and to refine your judgment. To accomplish the latter, compare each revision with the original and weigh the differences in focus or emphasis. You might also ask in what circumstances each new version would be most effective.

Variations on this sentence will appear throughout the section on grammar. Taken together, they will represent but a few of the versions possible, which run well past four hundred. So many variations illustrate how much control we can have over our sentences, even without increasing our vocabularies.

Here are just a few possibilities:

1 A sleet was falling, which turned the roads into sheets of ice.

2 A sleet which turned the roads into sheets of ice was falling.

3 A sleet, which turned the roads into sheets of ice, was falling.

4 A sleet was falling; it turned the roads into sheets of ice.

5 A sleet was falling, and it turned the roads into sheets of ice.

6 A sleet was falling and turning the roads into sheets of ice.

7 A falling sleet was turning the roads into sheets of ice.

8 Turning the roads into sheets of ice, a sleet was falling.

9 The roads turned into sheets of ice in the falling sleet.

10 The roads were turned into sheets of ice by the sleet that was falling.

11 Because of a falling sleet, the roads turned into sheets of ice.

12 Because a sleet was falling, the roads turned into sheets of ice.

13 There was a sleet falling that turned the roads into sheets of ice.

14 A sleetfall turned the roads into sheets of ice.

15 It was a falling sleet that turned the roads into sheets of ice.

And we can double the number simply by turning "sheets of ice" into *icy sheets*.

For Openers

At the end of each of the "rhetoric" chapters that comprise Part Two is a section entitled "For Openers" containing opening paragraphs from nonfiction sources like newspapers, magazines, and journals. These paragraphs illustrate some uses of the structures discussed earlier in the chapter, but their principal function is to increase your repertoire of opening strategies. In "Write Before Writing" Donald Murray observes how important it is for a writer to find a good opener or "line." By a line he does not mean a thesis statement, but a good, resonant opener that can "imply a voice, a tone, a pace, a whole way of treating a subject." Newspaper people call this a lead, "that first line—or two or three—which will inform and entice the reader and which, of course, also gives the writer control over the subject."

Getting started on our serious drafts is sometimes our greatest obstacle. Simply knowing what we want to say is not always enough. In fact, it sometimes seems that we have too much to say, too much unruly material to organize effectively. All the information and ideas we have gathered become a shapeless mass; we suffer the anxiety of overchoice. We may even have an idea of how to start, using that old standby the topic sentence or governing generalization. But such beginnings sometimes seem too abrupt, or too sweeping, or too predictable, or they seem to lead nowhere after the first paragraph. And worse, our essay already begins to sound like all the others we have had to write.

What we are looking for is both interest and momentum, a beginning that will "entice the reader" and carry us well into a treatment of our subject. The "For Openers" will illustrate a variety of solutions found by published writers. Some do begin with a generalization, though not one that immediately discloses the main point but rather a provocative one that first establishes the importance or topicality of the subject. Others address the reader directly by asking a challenging question or positing a hypothetical situation ("Suppose you . . ."). Still others may begin narratively by presenting some puzzling ritual (which of course requires explanation), or by presenting an anecdote—a historical episode or a personal adventure that awakened the writer's interest in the subject. And still others may begin with a series of seemingly unrelated details, stimulating immediate curiosity about their connection.

All of these writers understand the importance of courtesy to the reader, of the need to be clear and economical and well organized. And they understand the dangers of beating around the bush or playing games before getting down to business. But they also appreciate that the greatest courtesy of all is to make their material interesting, that it is never a good idea to treat their readers like a captive audience. Hence, they recognize the first job of a good opener: to make the reader want to keep reading. And its second: to help the writer keep writing.

One theme of this book is that there is always another way—another way to word a sentence, organize a paragraph, or start an essay. By considering options and weighing their consequences, we learn more about our language, our subjects, and ourselves. Thinking about possible openers, then, serves the purposes of both discovery and organization. In testing differing beginnings, we view our subject from different angles, consider its various appeals, and get clues to relevant details. And perhaps more important than anything else, a good start gives us confidence.

Grammar

1

Sentences

Definition

The basic English **sentence** is a sequence of phrases like the following:*

In a hole in the ground there lived a hobbit.

This hobbit was a very well-to-do hobbit.

Bilbo's heart jumped into his mouth.

Hobbits have no beards.

To say that Bilbo's breath was taken away is no description at all.

"Let me introduce Bifur, Bofur, Bombur, and especially Thorin!"

The mother of our particular hobbit—what is a hobbit?

---

* The first ten illustrative sentences in this chapter are taken from J.R.R. Tolkien's *The Hobbit*.

"Phrases" is the key word; we do not read, speak, or understand sentences one word at a time, and not since the first grade have most of us read a sentence like this:

> In + a + hole + in + the + ground + there + lived + a + hobbit.

Beginners read word lists; the experienced read like this, in word groups:

> In a hole in the ground   +   there lived + a hobbit.

Someone writing a dictionary once began his definition of *dog* by saying, "Everyone knows what a dog is." Similarly, seasoned readers know what a sentence is, or at least they know one when they see one. For starters, they can recognize a sentence from the way it is printed on the page: It will begin with a capital letter and end with some kind of final punctuation (period, question mark, or exclamation mark). All the preceding examples, including the last one, fit this description. But experienced readers can also recognize when something is not a sentence, even when it does begin with a capital letter and end with concluding punctuation. For example, take the "sentence" that was interrupted to ask a question:

> The mother of our particular hobbit . . .

Or add a word to one of the other sentences:

> **Because** hobbits have no beards.

An experienced reader knows that these can be only parts of sentences; they lack the self-contained quality that experience has led us to expect in "complete" sentences. In a conversation, though, where listeners unconsciously fill in words, such incomplete structures can be functioning "sentences":

> "How do you know that the bearded man is not a hobbit?"
> "Because hobbits have no beards."

The answer contains an understood element: "*I know that the bearded man is not a hobbit* because hobbits have no beards."

What experienced readers usually recognize as a sentence, then, consists of more than an opening capital letter and some final punctuation. What they recognize (and expect) is a reasonably complete sequence of phrases that describes, defines, narrates, asks a question, makes a request, or gives an order. By "complete" we mean that the sequence accomplishes some kind of business: asks a question for someone to answer, makes a request for someone to satisfy, gives an order for someone to obey, or makes a statement for someone to believe. In other words, a complete sentence gives the listener or reader something to do, while *fragments* (parts of sentences), by themselves, do not. Assuming the phrases are not abbreviated answers to specific questions, what can a reader do with "the mother of our particular hobbit" or "because hobbits have no beards"?

In most cases a sentence will also be a two-part structure: a topic and a comment. The part identifying the topic we call the **subject**, and the commenting part we call the **predicate** (from a word meaning "to proclaim"). By itself, the subject is static, a mere name or label, until it is activated by the predicate:

subj   pred
This hobbit   was a very well-to-do hobbit.

The subject is indeed a "subject"—what we are talking about. The predicate contains the *verb*, plus any words it may need to complete its meaning. Together, the subject and predicate create a **clause**, a structure that is sometimes a complete sentence and sometimes only a part of one ("because hobbits have no beards"):

Subject	*Predicate*
This hobbit	was a very well-to-do hobbit.
Bilbo's heart	jumped into his mouth.
Hobbits	have no beards.
To say that Bilbo's breath was taken away	is no description at all.

Subjects

Subjects are also called *noun phrases* because they often consist of a noun and its **modifiers**—details added to make the noun more specific. The noun and its modifiers work together as a unit (as does the predicate, which is sometimes called a **verb phrase**). Structurally, the important thing is that the subject is still a unit, whether it consists of one word, a word and its modifiers, or the various words and phrases and even clauses that can sometimes serve as subjects:

The glade	was evidently a meeting place for wolves.
This glade in the ring of trees	was evidently a meeting place for wolves.

It	was evidently a meeting place for wolves.
Going on from there	was the bravest thing he ever did.
To go on from there	was the bravest thing he ever did.
That he went on from there	was the bravest thing he ever did.
It	was the bravest thing he ever did.

Identifying Subjects and Predicates

Subjects usually appear at the beginning of sentences, before the verb, but the easiest way to identify them is to take the predicate and ask, Who? or What? (*What* was evidently a meeting place for wolves?) And, knowing that verbs have a property called *tense*, we can find the predicate (or verb phrase) by identifying the word or words affected when we change the time of the action or description:

Past   It   **was** evidently a meeting place for wolves.

Present   It   **is** evidently a meeting place for wolves.

Future   It   **will** evidently **be** a meeting place for wolves.

Note: In sentences using the *imperative mood*, the subject is an understood *you*:

"[You] let me introduce Bifur, Bofur, Bombur, and especially Thorin!"

Simple Subjects

In grade school many of us were taught to identify the **simple subject**, a noun subject stripped of its modifiers: "glade" in "this glade in the ring of trees." We need to recognize the simple subject, in part because it will control some words later in the sentence:

Not   This **glade** in the ring of trees **were** a meeting place.

But   This **glade** in the ring of trees **was** a meeting place.

Not   The **ring** of trees had **their** uses.

But   The **ring** of trees had **its** uses.

Except when it has no modifier ("*rings* have their uses"), the simple subject alone is not the full subject of the predicate's statement, and it cannot give an accurate answer to the question Who? or What? It is the simple subject *as modified* that the sentence is about.

Basic Sentence Patterns

Depending on the verb in the predicate—the kind of assertion being made about the subject—there are three basic sentence patterns in English, plus two related patterns. We use these patterns in their simple forms, where each is suited to convey a particular type of news, or we change them into more complicated sentences by adding, dropping, substituting, or rearranging words:

▶ subject + verb + predicate noun/adjective/adverb (usually a detail of location or time):

Cannery Row is a poem.

Cannery Row is poetic.

Cannery Row is in Monterey.

▶ subject + verb:

The icicles dripped.

▶ subject + verb + direct object:

Emily McHugh regretted something.

▶ "there" pattern:

There was an old hippo.

▶ "it" pattern:

It was always pleasant crossing bridges in Paris.

Subject + Verb + Predicate Noun/Adjective/Adverb (Linking Verb Pattern)

This pattern usually comments on the identity, state, or location of the subject.

Subject	*Verb*	*Predicate Noun/Adjective/Adverb*
This hobbit	was	a very well-to-do hobbit.
Cannery Row	is	a poem.
Cannery Row	remains	a poem.
Cannery Row	is	poetic.
Cannery Row	is	in Monterey in California.

■

subj	verb	pred noun	adv
The roads	became	icy sheets	in the falling sleet.

subj	verb	pred adj	adv
The roads	became	icy	in the falling sleet.

subj	verb	pred adv	adv
The roads	were	like sheets of ice	in the falling sleet.

This pattern works best in descriptions and definitions, especially when using the authoritative *be* verb ("The porcupine *is* a herbivore"). But even while the *be* verb sounds so sure of itself, it and most of the other linking verbs still remain relatively bland and undramatic. They do not report actions. Instead, they act more like connectors, "linking" the subject of the sentence to one of the following:

▶ a noun that renames or identifies it

▶ an adjective describing some quality or characteristic

▶ an adverb, usually presenting a detail of time or place

As a result, the real focus of the pattern (its "news") is on the information that comes after the verb. Because the name or quality "completes" the subject in a manner of speaking, it is called a **subjective complement**—completer of the subject.

Cannery Row is . . . what?   Cannery Row is **a poem**.
Cannery Row is **poetic**.

The other kind of detail, usually of time or location, is called either a *predicate adverb* or an *adverbial complement* (an adverb that completes):

Cannery Row is . . . **in Monterey**.

The pattern remains the same even when one of the elements is compounded:

Cannery Row in Monterey   is   a poem,
in California   a stink,
                                  a grating noise,
                                  a quality of light,
                                  a tone,
                                  a habit,
                                  a nostalgia,
                                  a dream

—John Steinbeck, *Cannery Row*

The pattern remains the same when the word order is reversed or rearranged:

pred noun   pred noun   verb   subj
A nostalgia   and   a dream   is   Cannery Row.

verb   subj
**From behind the maid who opened the door   darted   a lovely
little girl of nine who shrieked "Daddy!" and flew up,
struggling like a fish,   into his arms.**
—F. Scott Fitzgerald, "Babylon Revisited"

Subject + Verb (Intransitive Pattern)

This pattern reports an action—physical or mental, literal or figurative—of the subject:

subj   verb
Bilbo's heart   jumped   into his mouth.

subj   verb
The icicles   dripped.

subj   verb
A sleet   fell,   turning the roads into sheets of ice.

The patterns remain the same even when the verb adds modifiers:

subj   verb   adv
The icicles   dripped   rapidly.

subj   verb   adv
**The icicles   dripped   so rapidly that the gravel under
the eaves rattled and jumped.**

The pattern remains the same even when the sentence has an *opener*:

opener   subj   verb   adv
**On the first day   the icicles   dripped   so rapidly that the
gravel under the eaves
rattled and jumped.**

—Marilynne Robinson, *Housekeeping*

This pattern uses what some call a "verb of complete predication"; that is, it takes no complement, making possible a two-word sentence ("Icicles dripped"). With its verb or verb and modifiers in the final position, the pattern focuses on the action or, sometimes more precisely, on the quality or location of the action.

Subject + Verb + Direct Object (Transitive Pattern)

This pattern reports an action of the subject that carries over to someone or something else (a **direct object**):

> subj   verb   dir obj
> **Hobbits have no beards.**

> subj   verb   dir obj
> **Emily McHugh regretted something.**

> subj   verb   dir obj
> **The falling sleet turned the roads into sheets of ice.**

The pattern remains the same even when one of the positions is filled by a phrase or clause:

> subj   verb   dir obj
> **Emily McHugh now very much regretted having taken Constance Pinn into her confidence.**

—Iris Murdoch, *The Sacred and Profane Love Machine*

> subj   verb   dir obj
> **Emily McHugh now very much regretted that she had taken Constance Pinn into her confidence.**

Sometimes the verb in this pattern will also take an **indirect object**, a person or thing to which something is given or for whom something is done:

> subj   verb   ind obj   dir obj
> **Constance Pinn gave Emily McHugh misgivings.**

Sometimes the direct object in this pattern will have an **objective complement**, which will have the same relation to the direct object that a subjective complement has to the subject in the first pattern:

> subj   verb   dir obj   obj comp
> **He considered the things trifling.**

> subj   verb   subj compl
> **The things [were] trifling.**

The pattern remains the same even when the normal word order is changed:

dir objs	subj	verb	obj compl
Broken tongues and singletrees, smashed wheels and splintered axles	he	considered	trifling matters.

—Willa Cather, *Death Comes for the Archbishop*

The transitive pattern is ideal for narratives, focusing both on an action and on whatever it affects.

There are also two other patterns that are variations on the linking verb pattern, named for the words with which they begin—**expletives** ("fillers," words with little actual meaning of their own).

"There" + Be *Verb* + *Subject ("There" Expletive)*

Instead of being about the identity, location, or behavior of the subject, this pattern affirms the very existence of the subject, which is postponed until the emphatic final position:

	expl	verb	subj
In a hole in the ground	there	lived	a hobbit.

expl	verb	subj
There	was	an old hippo.

expl	verb	subj
There	were	long brown mountains.

expl	verb	subj
There	was	a sleet falling that turned the roads into sheets of ice.

This pattern remains the same even when the subject is a long phrase:

expl	verb	subj
There	was	an old hippo that had the bad habit of getting out on the bank and roaming at night over the station grounds.

—Joseph Conrad, *Heart of Darkness*

The pattern also remains the same when it has more than one subject:

expl	verb		subj
There	were	long brown mountains, and a few pines and far-off forests of beech-trees	on some of the mountainsides.

—Ernest Hemingway, *The Sun Also Rises*

In the first three and much more widely used patterns, the sentences focus on the statement about the subject, whose existence is assumed. In the "there" pattern the principal news is the actual existence of the subject. Technically, the "there" has almost no meaning and forms a unit with the *be* verb (*is, are, was, were*, and so on) or a few others (*remain, seem, come, become, live, appear*, and so on).

> *Standard* In a hole in the ground **a hobbit lived.**
> **A hobbit lived** in a hole in the ground.

> *"There"* In a hole in the ground **there lived a hobbit.**

As with the other patterns, the structure is still two-part and the news still falls in the second half:

> There was an old hippo that had the bad habit of getting out on the bank and roaming at night over the station grounds.

Compare:

> An old hippo had the bad habit of getting out on the bank and roaming at night over the station grounds.

This is the difference between the two:

> There was **such** a hippo.

> A hippo did **such** a thing.

The same hippo is in both sentences and taking the same nightly strolls, but the two versions do not highlight the information identically. In the earlier patterns the subject is simply something talked about, the focus being on what it does or on what title or quality attaches to it. In the "there" pattern the subject often appears as something that exists in its own right, as something experienced, not simply discussed, as the following deftly illustrates:

> We came down out of the mountains and through an oak forest and **there were cattle grazing in the forest.**

—Ernest Hemingway, *The Sun Also Rises*

The first clause tells what they did; the second presents—by implication—what they saw in the forest (because it was *there*, to be seen).
Note: In this pattern *there* is not an adverb because it is acceptable in Standard English to say, "There were cattle there." By contrast, it is not acceptable to say, "Here is a cow here."

"It" + Verb + Complement + Subject ("It" Expletive)

This structure exploits the power of **inversion** by placing the verb and complement ahead of the subject:

expl   verb   compl   subj
It   was always   pleasant   crossing bridges in Paris.
—Hemingway, *The Sun Also Rises*

expl   verb   compl   subj
It   is not   often   that someone comes along who is a true
friend and a good writer.
—E. B. White, *Charlotte's Web*

Like the "there" pattern this structure postpones the subject to the climactic final position in the sentence, but like the standard patterns it also makes a statement about the subject. In most sentences, we first encounter the subject, then are curious to learn what will be said of it. In the "it" pattern we first hear the statement, then are curious to learn whom or what it concerns. Reading the pattern is a little bit like hearing the tail end of a choice bit of gossip and at first not knowing whom it concerns.

It was always pleasant . . .

What was always pleasant?

It was always pleasant crossing bridges in Paris.

Rhetorically, the "it" expletive pattern acts much like the following:

They float on the landscape like pyramids to the boom years, all those Plazas and Malls and Esplanades.
—Joan Didion, "On the Mall"

Joan Didion's sentence also exploits the suspense of *delayed revelation*, "they" not being identified until the end of the sentence. What floats on the landscape? All those Plazas and Malls and Esplanades.

We can easily revise the pattern to delete the expletive and create a simple linking verb pattern, but not without changing the news and losing the effects of tension and climax:

Crossing bridges in Paris was always pleasant.

Someone who is a true friend and a good writer does not come along often.

Note: Both expletive patterns are special-effects sentences, devices of emphasis, and their effectiveness—like that of raising our voices—depends on using them in moderation.

Basic Patterns: Some Rhetorical and Stylistic Uses

Linking Verb Pattern

Finn Casperson looks spiffy.   —*Sports Illustrated*, 5 Dec. 1988

Compared to the others, this pattern is relatively static, the verb functioning to equate or connect the subject with something else ("spiffy"). In most cases the equation is literal and provides the common formula for definitions. Other times the equation is figurative or **metaphoric**, comparing two normally incompatible things:

Grammar is a piano I play by ear, since I seem to have been out of school the year the rules were mentioned.
—Joan Didion, "Why I Write"

The whole night had become a poem of moonlight.
—Patrick White, *The Tree of Man*

The center of America seemed to me a huge void between the parentheses of the two populous coasts.
—Gregor Von Rezzori, "A Stranger in Lolitaland"

The eye is the window through which the mind perceives the world around it. It is also a window through which to discern the workings of the brain.
—*Scientific American*, "The Silicon Retina," May 1991

Some other stylistic uses of the linking verb pattern:

The earth seemed unearthly.   —Joseph Conrad, *Heart of Darkness*

Here, the verb links a noun and an adverb deriving from the same root, a device of repetition rhetoricians call **polyptoton**.

The water under the bridge **ran** violent and deep.

—Joseph Conrad, *Under Western Eyes*

The gong **glimmered** pale and huge and yellow, like the moon rising over a southern swamp.   —Lafcadio Hearn, *Letters*

In these examples, "ran" and "glimmered," normally *transitive* or *intransitive verbs*, serve as *linking verbs* ("the water *was* violent and deep"; "the gong *was* pale and huge and yellow"). In the next example the writer uses inversion to place a long series of subjects in the emphatic final position:

Around the cabin are Swede saws, a whipsaw, steel barrels, snowshoes, sheds, a shovel, a rake, a pickaxe, wedges, a crowbar, a hand sledge, axes, traps, the "Alaska Maytag" (basically a tub and plunger), a wall tent, a construction wheelbarrow with inflated tires, and any number of dozens of other things.

—John McPhee, *Coming into the Country*

Try to write (and then read) this sentence without the inversion, placing the subjects in their normal position. Note, too, the logic to McPhee's method of presentation: there must first be a place before something can be or happen there. For this reason many descriptive and narrative sentences begin with details of location or time.

Intransitive Verb Pattern

The highway narrowed.   —Raymond Chandler, *The Little Sister*

This pattern reports an action of the subject, with the focus on the action itself. In cases where there are additional details after the verb, the focus extends to the quality or location of the action:

A trail **leads** from his cabin to his post office through a beautiful grove of aspens.   —John McPhee, *Coming into the Country*

Wilson **sat** on the balcony of the Bedford Hotel with his bald pink knees thrust against the ironwork.

—Graham Greene, *The Heart of the Matter*

In other cases **sentence openers** or introductory details can place the entire pattern in the emphatic location:

Against the pallid background of the mountains and quite close to him—for the mountains themselves seemed but a quarter of a mile away—a moving shape **appeared**.

—C. S. Lewis, *Out of the Silent Planet*

In narrative writing, short, choppy sentences and clauses are sometimes effective. By simply compounding the basic patterns, we can create effects of energy, speed, and even frenzied activity:

> Whistles blew, armour clashed, swords rattled, goblins cursed and swore and ran hither and thither, falling over one another and getting very angry. There was a terrible outcry, to-do, and disturbance. —J.R.R. Tolkien, *The Hobbit*

Repetition of the pattern re-creates a similar outcry and disturbance in the work of a nineteenth-century naturalist and a twentieth-century novelist:

> Wherever I went, dogs barked, children screamed, women ran away, and the men stared as though I were some kind of strange and terrible cannibal monster.
> —Alfred Russel Wallace, *The Malay Archipelago* (1869)

> They screamed, they laughed, they sang, and the dog barked.
> —E. M. Forster, *Howards End*

The structure even works in an opening sentence to an article about air pollution in Eastern Europe:

> The lungs tighten, eyes water, skin stings with the touch of corrosive gases.   —"Science and the Citizen," *Scientific American*, Aug. 1990

Transitive Verb Pattern

> Rose gave him a polite, troubled smile.
> —Anne Tyler, *The Accidental Tourist*

This pattern reports an action that directly involves the subject with someone or something else. Sometimes, when the predicate is compounded, the subject can seem almost heroically active:

> He stops fights, ejects drunks, soothes hysteria, cures headaches, and tends bar.   —John Steinbeck, *Cannery Row*

In the next two sentences the writers compound the predicates and then separate them with repeated *and*'s. The first stresses the monotony of the work; the second, its care and precision:

> They washed windows and swept floors and cleaned lavatories and put jars in to boxes and sealed cardboard boxes in a factory that made malt syrup.
> —Kurt Vonnegut, Jr., *Slaughterhouse-Five*

He flipped the steaks and pressed them down with his spatula
and gathered up the wilting onions and forced them down
into the meat.   —John Steinbeck, *East of Eden*

"There" Pattern

There are other streets in Paris as ugly as the Boulevard
Raspail.   —Ernest Hemingway, *The Sun Also Rises*

Again, this pattern emphasizes the very existence of the subject. In this
sentence Hemingway uses the pattern to create an effect of understatement. (Think of how frequently we hear remarks like, "There are worse
ways to spend an evening.") Some effects of this pattern are achieved
by repetition of the pattern itself:

There were times when they wanted privacy and there was no
privacy.   —Thomas Wolfe, *The Web and the Rock*

Before there was everything to do there was nothing to do.
—James Dickey, *Deliverance*

There was no funeral. There was no music. There was no period of mourning. There were no flowers. There were only silence, quiet weeping, whispers, and fear.
—Richard Wright, *Black Boy*

And from a newspaper account of an angry press conference:

It happened last week: Assembly Speaker Willie Brown vs.
the Capitol press corps. There was shouting. There were insults.
There were tirades and snap retorts. There was rudeness.
—*San Jose Mercury News*, 10 Feb. 1991

Professional writers frequently repeat the "there" pattern in order
to highlight experiences with numerous but also quite distinctive elements. C. S. Lewis demonstrates such use of the device to describe
the wonders of a lavish feast:

But on the table itself there was set out such a banquet as had
never been seen, not even when Peter the High King kept his
court at Cair Paravel. **There were** turkeys and geese and pea-
cocks, **there were** boar's heads and sides of venison, **there
were** pies shaped like ships under full sail or like dragons and
elephants, **there were** ice puddings and bright lobsters and
gleaming salmon, **there were** nuts and grapes, pineapples and
peaches, pomegranates and melons and tomatoes. **There were**
flagons of gold and silver and curiously wrought glass; and the

A Note on Sentence Unity

A sentence presents a sequence of related information to make a single point. This "point" may only contribute to, or be part of, a series of points made in other sentences, but the motive of the writer is to make this point effectively. Long or short, simple or complicated, a sentence must be read as "one thing." If the sentence is properly unified, we should be able to summarize this point in a few words. When sentences lack such unity, we call them *run-ons* or *comma splices*. The C. S. Lewis sentence is not a run-on or a comma splice because all the multiple clauses, with their relationship reinforced by *parallelism*, are about one thing— the banquet. We could summarize it—*tell* what it *shows*—by saying, "There was a great variety of exotic food."

smell of the fruit and the wine blew towards them like a promise of all happiness.   —*Voyage of the Dawn Treader*

"It" Pattern

It is almost a truism among students of architectural history that the use of the arch and the vault began with the Romans.
—"Arches and Vaults in the Ancient Near East," *Scientific American*, July 1989

This pattern reverses the normal focus of a sentence, highlighting not the statement, but the subject of the statement. This pattern also differs from the others in the nature of the subject, often an activity or an idea ("that the use of the arch and the vault began with the Romans"). One value of the "it" pattern is that it allows writers to put long subject phrases after the verb, where they are less taxing on the reader. (See the section "Subjects: Short and Long" in Chapter 10, "The Rhetoric of Sentences.") Consider the following:

To rail against destiny because it has decreed that we shall live in darkness and insensibility is foolish.
—Aldous Huxley, *Beyond the Mexique Bay*

Such a long subject phrase (sixteen words) overpowers the verb, which should be the major news carrier. The long phrase also burdens the memory of the reader, who must retain the entire unit so it can act on the verb. The "it" expletive could streamline Huxley's sentiment:

It is foolish to rail against destiny because it has decreed that we shall live in darkness and insensibility.

Or consider the mammoth subject in the following sentence:

The task of projecting your psychotic image life into the mind of another via telepathy and keeping the hallucinations from becoming sensually weaker is almost impossible.
—Ray Bradbury, *Martian Chronicles*

The "it" pattern could spare the reader having to juggle a twenty-three-word subject while waiting for the verb:

It is almost impossible to project your psychotic image life into the mind of another via telepathy and keep the hallucinations from becoming sensually weaker.

Some other variations:

It was observed from my entrance into the world that I had something uncommon in my disposition, and that there appeared in me very early the tokens of superior genius.
—Samuel Johnson, *Rambler #82*

It is the vice of the vulgar mind to be thrilled by bigness, to think that a thousand square miles are a thousand times more wonderful than one square mile, and that a million square miles are almost the same as heaven. —E. M. Forster, *Howard's End*

It was an eerie feeling too to walk back to the house alone that night down that corridor of darkness with only here and there a frail puddle of light from the street-lamps.
—Lawrence Durrell, *Bitter Lemons*

The "it" expletive can always be deleted, but at the cost of changing the focus. Delete it from the previous three sentences and compare the results with the originals.

Phrases and Clauses

Phrases

Except in their barest forms ("Sleet fell"), sentences consist of **phrases**, word groups acting like units or single parts of speech. This phrase structure enables us to read and make sense of even lengthy sentences, as the following twenty-six-word example illustrates:

> In the late summer of that year we lived in a house in a village
> that looked across the river and the plain to the mountains.
> —Ernest Hemingway, *A Farewell to Arms*

This sentence may be significantly longer than average, but it still has only three major parts or phrases—an adverbial opener telling when the action of the sentence took place, a subject, and a predicate (including another adverb telling where). The following four-word version has the same three-part structure that could answer the question, Where did we live then?

adv	subj	pred
Then	we	lived there.
In the late summer	we	lived in a house in a village
of that year		that looked across the river
		and the plain to the mountains.

And these phrases contain subphrases, and layers of more subphrases:

verb — adv (prep phrases)
lived   in a house in a village that looked across the
river and the plain to the mountains

prep phrase — prep phrase
in a house   in a village that looked across the river
and the plain to the mountains

prep — noun phrase (prep obj)
in   a village that looked across the river
and the plain to the mountains

subj — verb phrase (pred)
that   looked across the river and the plain to the mountains

verb — prep phrase — prep phrase
looked   across the river and the plain   to the mountains

prep — noun phrases — prep — noun phrase
across   the river and the plain   to   the mountains

Note: Grammar is often confusing because so many items have more than one name. For example, grammarians sometimes classify phrases *structurally*, by the central word around which the modifiers cluster: noun, verb, adjective, prepositional, participial, gerund, and infinitive. Other times they will classify phrases *functionally*, by what they are doing in a sentence. Hence, a phrase may be an infinitive by structure (*"to dream* the impossible dream"), but a noun, adjective, or adverb by function:

noun (dir obj)
I try **to dream the impossible dream.**

adj (which time?)
Now is the time **to dream the impossible dream.**

adv (modifying adj "able")
Eventually, you will be able **to dream the impossible dream.**

Clauses

We define clauses *by structure*, as word groups containing a subject and a predicate. There are two kinds: independent (or main) and dependent (or subordinate). **Independent clauses** are the ones we recognize as structurally complete, accomplishing some kind of business by themselves, and thus able to function alone as sentences:

The village looked across the river and the plain to the mountains.

A **dependent clause** is only a part of a sentence, serving either as a noun, adjective, or adverb. For practical purposes, then, when noting sentence components, we can view a dependent clause as simply another kind of phrase—a group of words functioning as a single part of speech:

noun clause (dir obj)
Frederick Henry wrote   that the village looked across the river and the plain to the mountains.

adj clause
He lived in a house in a village   that looked across the river and the plain to the mountains.

adv clause
He lived in that village   because he could look across the river and the plain to the mountains.

Revision note: Dependent clauses can frequently be revised into at least one of several kinds of phrases ("Living in that village, he could look . . ."). Such a revision may be an improvement, depending on whether we want the full weight of a clause with its predicate verb. A clause is generally more emphatic than a phrase, but too many clauses become ponderous.

Dependent Clauses as News Carriers

Dependent clauses are parts of sentences, acting as nouns, adjectives, or adverbs. They are indeed *dependent*, dependent on other structures. Nevertheless, there is one kind of sentence in which the rhetorical focus or principal news is in the dependent clause. Called by some a "cleft sentence," it is structured to highlight the dependent clause, which appears in the final, emphatic position:

> It is nationalism **that tries to check the growth of world civilization.**   —J. B. Priestley, "Wrong Ism"
>
> It was on a Sunday afternoon **that she had her vision.**
> —Flannery O'Connor, "The Displaced Person"
>
> It was Joe Dillon **who introduced the Wild West to us.**
> —James Joyce, "An Encounter"
>
> Those are never lonely **who love the snow and the pines;** never lonely **when the pines are wearing white shawls and snow crunches coldly underfoot.**
> —Tom Whitecloud, "Blue Winds Dancing"

> It was a falling sleet **that turned the roads into sheets of ice.**

Kinds of Sentences

We classify sentences by several different means:

- **clause structure**—simple, compound, complex, compound-complex
- **purpose**—declarative, interrogative, imperative
- **location of main clause**—loose, periodic

Clause Structure

The most familiar but perhaps least helpful way of identifying sentences is by clause structure. This method of classification even misleads because a "simple" sentence is not necessarily as easy and uncomplicated as the label suggests, and a "complex" sentence may not be difficult at all ("I ate because I was hungry" is a "complex" sentence).

Simple Sentences   These sentences contain only one independent or main clause and no dependent clauses. In other words, these are sentences containing one of the basic patterns *with no clausal modifiers*:

> We lived in a house looking across the river and the plain to the mountains.
>
> The barber's pudgy hands moved through his hair, the scissors whirring like a hornet behind his ears.

> A sleet fell, turning the roads into sheets of ice. ■

Compound Sentences   These sentences contain at least two independent clauses and no dependent clauses (two or more of the basic patterns with no clausal modifiers):

> We lived in a house in a village, and it looked across the river and the plain to the mountains.
>
> The barber's pudgy hands moved through his hair, the scissors whirred like a hornet behind his ears.
> —John Dos Passos, *Manhattan Transfer*

> A sleet was falling, and it was turning the roads into sheets ■
> of ice.

Complex Sentences   **Complex sentences** contain one independent clause and at least one dependent clause (a basic pattern plus at least one clausal modifier):

> We lived in a house in a village **that looked across the river and the plain to the mountains.**
>
> **While the barber's pudgy hands moved through his hair,** the scissors whirred behind his ears like a hornet.

> A sleet was falling **which turned the roads into sheets of** ■
> **ice.**   —Thomas B. Costain, *The Conquering Family*
> **Because a sleet was falling,** the roads turned into sheets
> of ice.

Compound-Complex Sentences These sentences have two or more independent clauses and at least one dependent clause (two or more of the basic patterns plus at least one clausal modifier).

It was in the late summer of the year, and we were living in a house in a village **that looked across the river and the plain to the mountains**.

While Bud tried to relax, the barber's pudgy fingers moved through his hair and the scissors whirred like a hornet behind his ears.

A sleet was falling, and it turned the roads into ice **that was like sheets**.

Purpose

We sometimes classify sentences by whether they make a statement, ask a question, or give an order. Each type asks a certain response from the reader or listener.

Declarative Sentences **Declarative sentences** (from a Latin word meaning "to make clear") make statements, like this one, and ask the reader to accept them as true. The great majority of sentences are of this kind. They are punctuated with a period.

Interrogative Sentences **Interrogative sentences** (from a Latin word meaning "to ask"—think of *interrogation*) ask a question and usually expect the listener to respond with information or at least to think about something. Interrogatives are punctuated with a question mark when the question is a direct one.

What is a hobbit?

Could they actually see across the river and the plain to the mountains?

Punctuation note: An *indirect* question is not punctuated with a question mark because it is actually a statement *about* a question:

I sometimes wonder **whether they actually could see across the river and the plain to the mountains**.

We use interrogatives most often in conversation, where we can expect an actual response. In writing, however, they are useful for making transitions and focusing discussions, as Wendell Berry illustrates in a discussion of Peruvian agriculture:

> What I was thinking, then, looking down at the little fields of the Andes, was that the most interesting, crucial, difficult questions of agriculture are questions of propriety. What is the proper size for a farm for one family in a given place? What is the proper size for a field, given a particular slope, climate, soil type, and drainage? What is the appropriate crop for this field? What is the appropriate kind and scale of technology? Andean agriculture is a success—has lasted thousands of years on extremely difficult terrain—because it has so far answered such questions correctly.
>
> —"An Agricultural Journey in Peru," *A Gift of Good Land*

Of course, questions directed to the reader are not meant to elicit actual answers (the writer gets to supply those). They do, however, ask the reader to think more actively about the problem. Questions are also useful in the *prewriting stage*. One good way to brainstorm a topic is to list all the questions it raises, then address the most pertinent or crucial ones. Afterwards, we may even structure our essay around these questions.

Imperative Sentences   **Imperative sentences** (from a Latin word meaning "to command") give an order or request and usually expect the listener to respond with some kind of action. Imperatives have an unstated or "understood" *you* as a subject and are usually punctuated with a period:

> Look at that view of the mountains.
>
> Please be careful with those scissors.
>
> "Let me introduce Bifur, Bofur, Bombur, and especially Thorin!"

Like interrogatives, imperatives appear most often in speech, but they are also useful for writers. Imperatives, we remember, have *you* as the implicit subject, so in using them writers are addressing the reader, asking for some kind of action, if only in the imagination. The imperative may thus help lessen the distance between writer and audience (like a closely related device, the indefinite *you*). As a result, imperatives occur frequently in less formal kinds of writing, like that in popular travel magazines:

> Take it slow. Catch the low autumn light setting the central Sierra aglow as you cruise lightly used roads. Flick a fishing

line into a fork of the Carson River. Pitch a tent under white-
barked boughs. Row across an alpine lake trimmed with gold.
Smell the tang of decomposing leaves in the crisp air as you
walk a forest trail. —"Looking for Sierra Gold," *Sunset*, Sept. 1989

Location of Main Clause

It is sometimes useful to classify sentences by the location of their
modifiers—before or after the main clause. A **loose sentence** begins
with a main clause followed by explanatory, illustrative, or qualifying
remarks. Such structures are also called **cumulative sentences** because
the detail seems to accumulate afterward. In many cases the main clause
makes some kind of broad or general statement, which the succeeding
details then explore or refine. In other words, the sentence follows a
general-to-specifics order. (See the section "General-to-Specific" in Chapter
2, "Paragraphs.")

> **He has aged gracefully**, his hair turning silver, as if on cue
> from some casting director. —David Halberstam, *Summer of '49*

> **They have cleared the final rise**, bringing into view the town,
> its summer cottages and stucco walls a distant splash of white-
> ness against the sea, which is itself a kind of white this hour of
> the early afternoon, catching rays at a gold-flecked angle, so
> that the air above the town, taking its color from some mix of
> sea light and reflected buildings, has a texture of its own, a gos-
> samer, white-blue vibrancy, beneath the larger, deep-sky blue
> above. —James D. Houston, *Continental Drift*

When the main statement is not completed until near the end of
the sentence, it is a **periodic sentence**. The earlier details being prefatory, preparing the way by acting as preconditions, the main clause
can function climactically:

> At length one afternoon a little before sunset, when the
> bright groups of figures, which have for the last hour or two
> enlivened the Ghost's Walk, are all dispersed, and only Sir
> Leicester and my Lady remain upon the terrace, **Mr. Tulking-
> horn appears**. —Charles Dickens, *Bleak House*

> What with the lake and the railroads, and what with blizzards
> and floods and barn fires and forest fires and the general avail-
> ability of shotguns and bear traps and homemade liquor and
> dynamite, what with the prevalence of loneliness and religion

and the rages and ecstasies they induce, and the closeness of families, **violence was inevitable.**

—Marilynne Robinson, *Housekeeping*

From millions of sources all over the globe, through every possible channel and medium—light waves, air waves, ticker tapes, computer banks, telephone wires, television cables, printing presses—**information pours in.**

—Neil Postman, "Learning by Story"

Sentence Confusions: Fragments and Comma Splices

Fragments

A standard English sentence is a sequence of phrases containing at least one subject and one predicate. Even more important, it does not depend on another structure to complete its particular business. But when we punctuate a sentence component as a sentence, we create a **fragment.** We have taken what is only a part and given it the capital letter and period that identify a whole. Any of the phrases and dependent clauses mentioned in previous sections. Appearing separately. Would be fragments.

Intentional Fragments Professional writers occasionally use fragments intentionally, for effect, relying on surrounding structures to make sense of them. In most cases a writer could easily repunctuate the items to include them in adjoining sentences. However, by setting the elements apart, the writer emphasizes them while requiring more active participation from the reader, who must "compose" them into sentences (the same way that a listener automatically does to fragments in conversation).

In an autobiographical passage, for example, Leslie Marmon Silko uses clause fragments to accentuate her feeling of connection with the tribal legends recounted by her aunt:

> What excited me was listening to old Aunt Susie tell us an old-time story and then for me to realize that I was familiar with a certain mesa or cave that figured as the central location of the story she was telling. That was when the stories worked best. **Because then I could sit there listening and be able to visualize myself as being located *within* the story being told,**

within the landscape. Because the storytellers did not just tell their stories, they would in their way act them out.
—"Landscape, History, and the Pueblo Imagination"

Silko's punctuation emphasizes not only the fragments but also the introductory sentence, as we can see by repunctuating them:

That was when the stories worked best, because then I could sit there listening and be able to visualize myself as being located *within* the story being told, within the landscape, and because the storytellers did not just tell their stories, they would in their way act them out.

And not only "creative" writers have learned how to exploit fragments. In the following both a movie critic and a cultural commentator find uses for them:

Daybreak. A cornfield. Two men in evening clothes and a seven-foot lizard on a leash. These components of the final scene of "The Freshman," a witty and enchanted comedy written and directed by Andrew Bergman, will not reveal anything worthwhile about how the film's main plot finally resolves itself. But they may offer some indication of just how sweetly unpredictable and how warmly, enduringly peculiar Mr. Bergman's brand of humor can be.
—film review, Janet Maslin, *New York Times*, 20 July 1990

Clearly, we are swamped by information. **Drowning in it. Overwhelmed by it.** —Neil Postman, "Learning by Story"

Modern writers have added the intentional fragment to their inventory of emphatic devices, something to exploit when even the dash seems too tame. Fragment users write with the faith that the overriding unit of sense is the paragraph, not the sentence, and that readers will assist the writer in constructing meaning. Legitimate rhetorical fragments never remain true fragments, incomplete units abandoned in space. They find their meaning in their relationship with surrounding sentences, but the reader must make the connections.

Warning: In an academic setting, using fragments can be risky. Professional writers, with the authority of editors and publishers and even their own reputations behind them, enjoy the benefit of the doubt: Student writers do not. Their fragments are more likely to be interpreted as signs of ineptitude, as blunders, and not as stylistic effects. Besides, even professionals use them infrequently, seldom more than once or twice in an article or chapter.

Comma Splices

A **comma splice** is usually defined as a compound sentence in which the clauses are joined only by commas:

Wilbur didn't want food, he wanted love.
—E. B. White, *Charlotte's Web*

The frogs were croaking in the garden pools behind the walls, the crickets were announcing tomorrow's heat.
—Anaïs Nin, *Diaries*

The dry starched blue sky whistled around us, there was not a cloud. —Truman Capote, "The Grass Harp"

Low mileage is a form of youth to Florian, it means plenty of mileage to come. —Garrison Keillor, *Leaving Home*

They loved eating on planes, they loved the smallness of plates, knives, and forks.
—Bharati Mukherjee, "The Management of Grief"

His frown deepened, his lips pursed, he shook his head with sharp impatience. —Wallace Stegner, *All the Little Live Things*

He sang, he danced, he was funny, he was dramatic.
—Tom Shales, "Danny Kaye, the Timeless Jester"

Most teachers, editors, and handbooks caution against punctuating independent clauses with commas alone. Instead, they offer these alternatives:

▶ inserting a coordinating conjunction after the comma:

Wilbur didn't want food, **but** he wanted love.
Wilbur didn't want food, **for** he wanted love.

▶ changing the comma to a semicolon:

Wilbur didn't want food; he wanted love.

▶ changing the comma to a period to create separate sentences:

Wilbur didn't want food. He wanted love.

▶ turning one of the independent clauses into a dependent clause:

Wilbur didn't want food **although he wanted love.**
Although Wilbur didn't want food, he wanted love.

And, of course, we can revise the sentence more radically:

Wilbur wanted love, not food.

As the examples from professional writers suggest, however, it might be wiser to define a comma splice by content than by punctuation. Perhaps we can say that a comma splice is a *compound* or *compound-complex sentence* that is about more than one thing, like the following:

I was only four years old when I was first in Paris and talked french there and was photographed there and went to school there, and ate soup for early breakfast and had leg of mutton and spinach for lunch, I always liked spinach, and a black cat jumped on my mother's back. —Gertrude Stein, *Paris France*

A patient and cooperative reader may infer that the black cat jumped on the mother's back one time when the family was having spinach for lunch, but the last two clauses still digress from the governing idea of the sentence. Not even conjunctions and semicolons can justify including the final two clauses; their ideas do not relate sufficiently to what went before. At the end of a list of enjoyable childhood experiences, Stein tacks on one unenjoyable episode. The final two remarks could have been incorporated by parentheses and a dash, but they still would have been digressions (being connected by association, not by logic).

A growing number of professional writers are using "comma splices," but usually when the separate independent clauses are sufficiently related that the reader can easily infer the connection. Take the Stegner example:

His frown deepened, his lips pursed, he shook his head with sharp impatience.

This sentence is about "one thing"—three almost simultaneous actions that express the character's dissatisfaction. The emotion unifies the actions. The other professional examples are similar: they present a sequence of related information to make a single point. The comma suggests the thematic relationship, but a cooperative reader must be prepared to make the inference. In an academic setting, however, you gamble by using such structures. Most writing instructors want their students to master the basic conventions before experimenting too freely with special effects.

Run-On Sentences

Run-on (or *fused*) **sentences** join independent clauses without any conjunctions or punctuation whatsoever:

It was a sunny day the sky was a robin's egg blue.

Not even the boldest innovators are using fused sentences when writing in their own voices. Some novelists, however, will create characters who do. In *Billy Bathgate* E. L. Doctorow uses a school dropout for a *first-person narrator* and, as part of the characterization, fills the boy's language with nonstandard structures, including run-on sentences:

The Park Avenue warehouse was one of several maintained by the Schultz gang for the storage of the green beer they trucked over from Union City New Jersey and points west. **When a truck arrived it didn't even have to blow its horn the warehouse doors would fold open and receive it as if they had an intelligence of their own.**

We can repair fused sentences the same way we repair comma splices. Thus, if Billy had finished high school, he might have punctuated his "sentence" differently:

When a truck arrived it didn't even have to blow its horn; the warehouse doors would fold open and receive it . . .

When a truck arrived it didn't even have to blow its horn. The warehouse doors would fold open and receive it . . .

Subject-Predicate Mismatches

Faulty Predication

Subjects and predicates should be logically compatible. When they are not, we have *faulty predication*, as in the following:

Character is the way a person reacts to his life situations.

Character is not a way; it is a quality of personality that expresses itself in ways.

Revised   Character reveals itself in the way a person reacts to his life situations.

Faulty predication is most common after the *be* verb, which is usually followed by a noun identifying the subject or an adjective describing it. In standard English the *be* verb should not be followed by structures beginning with *when, where,* or *because*:

Not   One kind of faulty predication **is when** the words after a linking verb are incompatible with the subject.

But   A sentence has faulty predication when the words . . .

Or   One kind of faulty predication occurs when . . .

Or   Predication is faulty when . . .

Not   **The reason** I'm going into everything that happened in San Francisco **is because** it ties up with everything else all the way down the line.   —Jack Kerouac, *On the Road*

But   **The reason** I'm going into everything that happened in San Francisco **is that** it ties up with everything else all the way down the line.

Or   I'm going into everything that happened in San Francisco **because** it ties up with everything else all the way down the line.

Mixed Constructions

A sentence has a *mixed construction* when it mismatches sentence elements. This error usually occurs when a writer begins with one kind of structural plan, then in midsentence shifts to another. The most common form of mixed construction uses a modifying phrase or clause as a subject or predicate:

Original   Just because we had a few friends over to watch a football game **is no reason to call the cops.**
(adverb clause acting as subject)

Revised   Just because we had a few friends over to watch a football game, they didn't have to call the cops.

Revised   Our having a few friends over to watch a football game is no reason to call the cops.

Or take another example:

At the end of the year **is when my dream actually came true.**

The sentence is unidiomatic, using a prepositional phrase for a subject and a dependent clause for a complement. We can find a quick repair by simply asking, What happened at the end of the year?

Revised   At the end of the year my dream actually came true.

Revised   It was at the end of the year that my dream actually came true.

Content-Structure Mismatches: Faulty Parallelism

Parallelism uses repeated structures to emphasize a relationship between ideas:

An economy that contains few different niches for people's differing **skills, interests,** and **imaginations** is not efficient.
—Jane Jacobs, "Cities and the Wealth of Nations"

```
                            nouns
for people's differing   skills,
                         interests, and
                         imaginations
```

"Skills," "interests," and "imaginations" are structural equals, being objects of the same preposition. This structural equality underlines their thematic unity, as things wasted in an inefficient economy. The three cover a good deal of ground, but the parallelism suggests that the ground is nevertheless a common one. The effect is concise, symmetrical, and emphatic. Look at the following, however:

Your article about Lofgren stated what we have known for 10 years, that she is a totally dedicated professional with **integrity, acumen, a conscience,** and **caring**.   —letter to the editor

```
         nouns + adj
with   integrity,
       acumen,
       a conscience, and
       caring
```

Meaning and structure collide; the parallelism is faulty. The object of parallelism is to use structure to reinforce a relationship between ideas, but here the ideas are incompatible. The writer has attempted to force a square peg into a round hole, listing three character traits and then a quality of a character trait. A caring person has *compassion*:

with integrity, acumen, a conscience, and compassion

However, even the nouns are not totally parallel; one has an article: "a conscience." The solution is to find a synonym whose idiom does not require the article. We do not have to look far: "integrity" implies the idea of conscience:

> with integrity, acumen, and compassion

Even professional writers occasionally slip into faulty parallelism:

> Off the highway, on what seemed to be the town's main road, a fair was going on: **dinky, pathetic, a handful of booths full of plastic dolls and similar junk, hamburger wagons, and games of chance.**   —Gregor Von Rezzori, "A Stranger in Lolitaland"

Adjective	dinky,
Adjective	pathetic,
Noun Phrase	a handful of booths full of plastic dolls and similar junk,
Noun Phrase	hamburger wagons, and
Noun Phrase	games of chance

We get the idea: the fair is dinky and pathetic, as witnessed by the handful of booths with their junk, the hamburger wagons, and the games of chance. Still, the reader has to find a meaning by wresting it from the structure of the sentence.

2

Paragraphs

Definition

A **paragraph** is a unit of related ideas punctuated as in the following:

> [1]Paragraphs help writers and readers alike. [2]They order our thoughts and make our writing easier to follow. [3]They break our ideas down into manageable units that we can treat efficiently. [4]They let us arrange an essay one step at a time, and they allow readers to follow our thoughts along the stairway we have built for them.
> —Richard Marius, *A Writer's Companion*

Beginning with an indentation and normally ending with a line that falls short of the right margin, a paragraph first strikes the reader visually, as a block of print floating in a sea of white. When read, a paragraph becomes a group of thematically related sentences. In spite of this unity, however, the average paragraph is not independent; it usually serves as a part of a larger organization. Thus, like effective sentences, paragraphs grow into and out of one another. While it is convenient to study paragraphs as self-contained units, then, we must ultimately view them in sequence, noting transitions and weighing their contribution to the larger plan (for this reason, many sample paragraphs in this text are printed with the opening sentence(s) of the next paragraph).

By itself, the preceding sample paragraph illustrates a popular kind of paragraph, one beginning with a **topic sentence**, or statement of its central idea: the mutual benefit of paragraphs to writers and readers. In keeping with this type of paragraph, the remaining sentences all support and develop this idea, culminating with a metaphor: Paragraphs allow the writer to work one step at a time, creating an easy stairway for the reader to follow.

Topic Sentences

Many paragraphs do not have topic sentences, at the beginning or anywhere else, and even those that do are likely to open with introductory or transitional statements. When they do appear, though, topic sentences provide clarity and direction, whether announcing the theme at the beginning or making a summation at the end. What Marius says of paragraphs is even truer of topic sentences: they help writers organize and readers follow. Many teachers promote their use because they require student writers to think more consciously about a plan. To support the practice, these instructors can point to readability studies showing that topic sentences improve the reader's comprehension. By alerting the reader at once to the writer's plans and initiating a pattern of promise and fulfillment, topic sentences are especially valuable as openers.

Topic sentences vary according to the type of writing. In persuasive writing, for example, the topic sentence may state the proposition that the writer intends to support. In informational writing it may make a blanket statement about an object or a class or a condition that the writer will then illustrate. In both cases the topic sentence will often be the most general statement in the paragraph (we express significance with general, abstract words and give support with specific, concrete ones). The following brief example is typical:

[1]**Fossil fuels pose a dilemma for human society.**
[2]**Worldwide, the combustion of coal, oil and natural gas supplies some 88 percent of the energy we purchase and makes much of what we do possible. [3]Yet gases emitted during burning can degrade the environment, perhaps to the extent of altering the climate and threatening the future habitability of the planet.** —"Energy from Fossil Fuels," *Scientific American*, Sept. 1990

Here, the topic sentence makes a statement (*tells*) and the next two restate and explain (*show*). Fossil fuels—more specifically, the combustion of coal, oil, and natural gas—pose a dilemma: they supply most of the world's energy, but also emit gases that damage our environment. The following illustrate some other uses of topic sentences:

[1]**The deserts of southern California, the high, relatively cooler and wetter Mojave and the hotter, dryer Sonoran to the south of it, carry the signatures of many cultures.** [2]Prehistoric rock drawings in the Mojave's Coso Range, probably the greatest concentration of petroglyphs* in North America, are at least three thousand years old. [3]Big-game hunting cultures that flourished six or seven thousand years before that are known from broken spear tips, choppers, and burins† left scattered along the shores of the great Pleistocene lakes, long since evaporated. [4]Weapons and tools discovered at China Lake may be thirty thousand years old; and worked stone from a quarry in the Calico Mountains is, some argue, evidence that human beings were here more than 200,000 years ago.

Because of the long-term stability of such arid environments, much of this prehistoric stone evidence still lies exposed on the ground, accessible to anyone who passes by—the studious, the acquisitive, the indifferent, the merely curious. . . .   —Barry Lopez, "The Stone Horse"

[1]Let us begin with a simple proposition: **What democracy requires is public debate, not information.** [2]Of course it needs information too, but the kind of information it needs can be generated only by vigorous popular debate. [3]We do not know what we need to know until we ask the right questions, and we can identify the right questions only by subjecting our own ideas about the world to the test of public controversy. [4]Information, usually seen as the precondition of debate, is better understood as its by-product. [5]When we get into arguments that focus and fully engage our attention, we become avid seekers of relevant information. [6]Otherwise, we take in information passively—if we take it in at all.

From these considerations it follows that the job of the press is to encourage debate, not to supply the public with in-

* stone carvings
† Stone Age chisels

formation. But as things now stand, the press generates information in abundance, and nobody pays any attention. . . .
—Christopher Lasch, "Journalism, Publicity, and the Lost Art of Argument," *Harper's*, Sept. 1990

In some cases a topic sentence will serve to introduce and connect several paragraphs:

[1]**Genetic studies of Thoroughbreds are particularly timely because of two problems facing the industry.** [2]**First,** Thoroughbreds display disturbingly low fertility: on a global average, only slightly more than 50 foals are produced by every 100 Thoroughbred mares. [3]In the British and Irish population the annual production rate is better—about 67 percent—but even this figure looks very poor compared with those in other single-offspring species, such as cattle, for which a rate of 85 percent is considered normal.

[5]**The other problem** is that contrary to what one would expect from the efforts to breed and train winners, the racing performance of Thoroughbreds is not uniformly improving. [6]The three English classic races are the St. Leger, a 1.75-mile race open to horses of both sexes, and the Oaks and the Derby, 1.5-mile races open to fillies and colts, respectively. [7]Winning times for those races improved from the 1840s up to about 1910 but since then have been relatively static.

A possible genetic explanation for both the infertility and the static performances could be that these problems arise from the fairly small gene pool of the Thoroughbreds. . . .
—"The Genetics of Thoroughbred Horses," *Scientific American*, May 1991

Topic sentences sometimes take the form of questions. For example, a provocative or topical question can be an effective opener. (See the section "For Openers: Sentence Types" in Chapter 10, "The Rhetoric of Sentences.") Later in the body of an essay, when they arise naturally out of a discussion, questions also make convenient and economical transitions. The following paragraph came after a discussion of population density among rats:

[1]**What controls the growth of a rat colony?** [2]When a few rats begin to breed in an area with plenty of food and cover, their rate of increase is slow at first, but it becomes rapid when there are plenty of fecund females; later it slows again. [3]As density increases, several hostile forces can be expected to act progressively against still further increase. [4]Predation by

dogs, hawks and man may become more intense; nest sites for rearing young will be less easily found; infectious diseases may increase. [5]Any of these (or a shortage of food) could put a ceiling on further growth. —"Rats," *Scientific American*, Jan. 1967

As this and the following example illustrate, a question-first paragraph has its own built-in method of development: an answer or explanation, sometimes definite (as in the preceding), sometimes conjectural (as in the following):

[1]**What, then, accounts for the decline of foraging societies?** [2]No one can say definitely, but glimmers of an answer that may have broad application are emerging from studies focusing on the recent changes in the !Kung* way of life. [3]Today young boys no longer learn to hunt, and some of the behavioral codes that gave the society cohesion are eroding. [4]One major catalyst of change appears to have been a sudden easy access to goods. [5]Perhaps a similar phenomenon contributed to the demise of past foraging societies.

It is fortunate that a rather detailed portrait of the !Kung's traditional culture was compiled before the onset of dramatic change. . . .
—"The Transformation of the Kalahari !Kung," *Scientific American*, Apr. 1990

In many cases the topic sentence will serve as a transition statement, taking its bearing from a previous paragraph:

[1]Although it remains unarticulated among us, we Americans share an allegiance to schools, an assumption that schools are the foundation of our meritocracy and the prime requisite to a satisfying existence. . . .

[2]In my classroom at a public high school in an upper-middle class milieu where education is taken relatively seriously, **we read with great purpose precisely those stories that tacitly reaffirm this loyalty to schools:** In *Lord of the Flies* a pack of schoolboys degenerate into killers because no teachers are around to preserve the constraints of civilization. [3]In *To Kill a Mockingbird* the venerable Atticus Finch insists that, for all of its shortcomings—and despite the fact that his daughter, Scout, is best educated by his own good example and by life in the larger web of Maycomb County—Maycomb Elementary is mandatory. [4]*The Catcher in the Rye* is in large part the story of

* a society of people once known as African bushmen

its protagonist's maladjustment to schools, and J. D. Salinger is highly critical of the hypocrisy behind a good education; still he ultimately offers up Mr. Antolini—an English teacher—as Holden Caulfield's last best hope.

—David Guterson, "When Schools Fail Children," *Harper's*, Nov. 1990

In other cases a paragraph may deliver its topic sentence in several stages, even repeating parts of it for emphasis:

[1]To begin with, we must keep in mind that **things do not have "real" names, although many people believe that they do.** [2]A garbage man is not "really" a "garbage man" any more than he is a "sanitary engineer." [3]And a pig is not called a "pig" because it is so dirty, nor a shrimp a "shrimp" because it is so small. [4]There are things, and then there are the names of things, and **it is considered a fundamental error in all branches of semantics* to assume that a name and a thing are one and the same.** [5]It is true, of course, that a name is usually so firmly associated with the thing it denotes that it is extremely difficult to separate one from the other. [6]That is why, for example, advertising is so effective. [7]Perfumes are not given names like "Bronx Odor," and an automobile will never be called "The Lumbering Elephant." [8]Shakespeare was only half right in saying that a rose by any other name would smell as sweet. [9]**What we call things affects how we will perceive them.** [10]It is not only harder to sell someone a "horse mackerel" sandwich than a "tuna fish" sandwich, but even though they are the "same" thing, we are likely to enjoy the taste of tuna more than that of horse mackerel. [11]It would appear that human beings almost naturally come to *identify* names with things, which is one of our most fascinating illusions. [12]But there is some substance to this illusion. [13]**For if you change the names of things, you change how people will regard them,** and that is as good as changing the nature of the thing itself.

—Neil Postman, *Crazy Talk, Stupid Talk*

Expressed all at once, Postman's topic sentence would read like this: "Things do not have real names; nevertheless, what we call things affects how we will perceive them."

---

* the study of meaning

Paragraphs Without Topic Sentences

Topic sentences provide an open, easy, and obvious way of ensuring that the reader knows what is happening. In many cases, however, writers omit such explicit statements of purpose, confident that their intentions are apparent. Some writers also rebel against the rigidity of topic sentence paragraphs, wanting more flexibility in finding appropriate shapes for their thoughts. Besides, unstated topic sentences can have a persuasive advantage: sometimes the best way to make a point is to provide evidence and let the readers draw their own conclusions:

> [1]However much is put down on paper initially to prime the pump or to bring some semblance of order out of the jumble of tumbling thoughts, whenever the act of writing actually begins it is likely not to be a smooth and continual movement through an orderly arrangement of parts, but rather a series of spurts, side-movements, weird reversals—a jerky movement of stop and go that makes for a rather rickety ride. [2]It is in this process that surprises lurk and discoveries are made. [3]We discover thoughts we never suspected we had or could have, and we are surprised by attitudes that we didn't know existed within us. [4]Most experienced writers agree that it is best to drive to the end, even when the end seems some kind of contradiction of the beginning—and this happens more frequently than has been revealed. [5]A first draft will have its rough spots, lapses, paradoxes, outright conflicts—but it will also represent a thinking and muddling through that is invaluable. [6]Run through the mind again with the thought-processes turned on and testing throughout, it can become the basis of a good piece of writing.
>
> —James E. Miller, Jr., *Word, Self, Reality: The Rhetoric of Imagination*

Miller's first sentence remarks on the disorderly, indirect nature of the writing process. As the result of this unevenness, the following sentences go on to say, the process is filled with hidden surprises and discoveries, so experienced writers have learned to "drive to the end" despite the inconsistencies. Out of the muddle and contradictions, writers find their direction. No one sentence summarizes Miller's point; it emerges—clearly and unmistakably—from the six sentences working together.

Writing is a continual process of making choices between being explicit and implicit, of knowing what to put in and what to leave out.

If the explicitness of topic sentences has the advantage of clarity, implicitness has that of inviting and even requiring more reader participation. In fact, one kind of monotonous reading is that which leaves the reader no room to speculate, make connections, or draw conclusions. Put another way, completely explicit writing asks the reader to follow our thinking; tactful use of the implicit invites the reader to think with us.

Writing with Topic Sentences

Whatever way we write, our paragraphs should seem to develop spontaneously out of the first sentence and support some central idea that quickly becomes evident to the reader. Experienced writers instinctively produce such paragraphs, trusting their abilities to point the way with or without visible road markers like topic sentences. Less secure writers may feel safer using them, perhaps inserting them in the revision stage. The one essential rule is that the reader should have confidence in where the discussion is heading. By itself, however, clarity of meaning and organization is not enough. Consider the following:

> **[1]Electricity is fundamental to the quality of modern life.** [2]It is a uniquely valuable, versatile and controllable form of energy, which can perform many tasks efficiently. [3]In little over 100 years electricity has transformed the ways Americans and most peoples of the world live. [4]Lighting, refrigeration, electric motors, medical technologies, computers and mass communications are but a few of the improvements it provides to an expanding share of the world's growing population.
> —"Efficient Use of Electricity," *Scientific American*, Sept. 1990

The preceding is a clear example of a topic-sentence-first paragraph. But is it an effective topic sentence? A good topic sentence should not only reveal the controlling idea of a paragraph; it should identify an idea *that needs and deserves support*, something that is "news." What is the value, then, of spending an entire paragraph supporting the proposition that "Electricity is fundamental to the quality of modern life"? Anyone who can read (and many who cannot) know that electricity is important. This particular topic sentence may have structural and thematic clarity, then, but by being so obvious, by treating as a revelation something that is common knowledge, it also risks offending the reader, especially the reader of *Scientific American*. Being too obvious can be as poor a way of catching the reader's attention as being too subtle.

Having begun an essay so unpromisingly, how is the writer to find a more effective start? Often the answer is simply to discard the first

paragraph and start with the second or the third, as the co-writers of
the article could have done:

> Many analysts believe that regional electricity shortages
> could occur in the U.S. within the next 10 years, perhaps as
> early as 1993. Given the importance of electricity in all sectors
> of the economy, such shortages . . .

Paragraph Length

There is a grammatical inevitability to sentences, to "complete
thoughts" and structurally complete statements, but there is nothing
inevitable about paragraph length or division. A paragraph may contain
a dozen sentences or—sometimes for particular emphasis—only one:

> . . . Ordinariness is sometimes the *status quo*, sometimes the
> slow, unseen movement of a subtle but ineluctable* cycle, like
> a ride on the hour hand of a clock; in any case the Ordinary is
> above all *what is expected*.
> And what is expected is not often thought of as a gift.
> —Cynthia Ozick, "The Riddle of the Ordinary"

The ordinary is "what is expected"—like the idea that paragraphs must
always have more than one sentence.

Length usually depends on how a writer chooses to group ideas for
convenience and emphasis, but this decision may depend on the complexity of the subject, the nature of the audience, or even on the space
available. Consider the following:

> [1]Tired of taking North Carolina's toxic castoffs, South Caro-
> lina passed a law blacklisting wastes shipped from the other
> side of the border. [2]New York threatened to keep out Ohio's
> hazardous wastes after the Buckeye State shut down a major
> landfill, and Ohio countered with threats to embargo munici-
> pal trash from New York. [3]Texas, the nation's largest hazard-
> ous waste generator, imposed a moratorium on construction
> of new disposal facilities, prompting neighboring states to
> erect legal barriers in fear of becoming the toxic dumping
> grounds for Texas. [4]With landfill space dwindling and incinera-
> tors increasingly popular, states' efforts to dispose of their in-
> dustrial waste have ignited a new kind of civil war. [5]On one
> side of the battle are states that have incinerators and landfills
> to handle their waste. [6]On the other side are the "have-not"

* inevitable

states that have dodged the politically sticky task of siting hazardous waste facilities at home, and look beyond their borders for a solution. [7]"What is happening is a destructive daisy chain of retaliatory responses by states that effectively damages the environment and the economic fabric of the nation," says Richard Fortuna, executive director of the Hazardous Waste Treatment Council.

We can argue in support of the unity, coherence, and emphasis of this passage. It follows a *specifics-to-general* order, beginning with three sentences *showing* what some states have done about toxic wastes, then *tells* about the new kind of civil war, identifies the combatants, and ends with a warning about the possible consequences. In sum, it fits the common definition of a paragraph: a group of related sentences on a single topic.

Even if the preceding paragraph were to appear on a standard single-column page, however, most writers and editors would feel more comfortable breaking it into two or three shorter units. The first three sentences form a natural grouping of examples. But what do we do with the fourth sentence?

With landfill space dwindling and incinerators increasingly unpopular, states' efforts to dispose of their industrial waste have ignited a new kind of civil war.

Ordinarily, such a statement would belong at the end of the first paragraph as its topic sentence. But the sentence is not only a concluder, summing up the meaning of the preceding sentences; it is also a transition. By mentioning the "new kind of civil war," it provides a bridge from the three examples to the "sides" identified in sentences 5 and 6. Some, then, would place sentence 4 at the end of the first paragraph, but others would place it at the beginning of the second. As for the quote in sentence 7 about the "destructive daisy chain," it could go at the end of the second paragraph or, for the sake of emphasis, it could serve as a paragraph all by itself.

The article, however, did not appear in a book or other wide-columned publication, but in the narrow 2½-inch columns of a newspaper, where the seven sentences were broken into six paragraphs:

Tired of taking North Carolina's toxic castoffs, South Carolina passed a law blacklisting wastes shipped from the other side of the border.

New York threatened to keep out Ohio's hazardous wastes after the Buckeye State shut down a major landfill, and Ohio countered with threats to embargo municipal trash from New York.

Texas, the nation's largest hazardous waste generator, imposed a moratorium on construction of new disposal facilities, prompting neighboring states to erect legal barriers in fear of becoming the toxic dumping grounds for Texas.

With landfill space dwindling and incinerators increasingly unpopular, states' efforts to dispose of their industrial waste have ignited a new kind of civil war.

On one side of the battle are states that have incinerators and landfills to handle their waste. On the other side are the "have-not" states that have dodged the politically sticky task of siting hazardous waste facilities at home, and look beyond their borders for a solution.

"What is happening is a destructive daisy chain of retaliatory responses by states that effectively damages the environment and the economic fabric of the nation," says Richard Fortuna, executive director of the Hazardous Waste Treatment Council.   —"The War Between the Wastes," *Washington Post*, 18 Mar. 1991

The frequent divisions and the use of **white space** in newspapers and popular magazines are a concession both to appearance and to an understanding of how most people read. Usually we read paragraph by paragraph, with the option of bailing out at any time, like the holders of renewable marriage licenses. This is particularly true of newspaper reading, which is seldom as compulsory as assignments in textbooks. Hence, editors and publishers show especial sensitivity to the convenience and courtesy of frequent paragraphing.

Practically speaking, how long should our paragraphs be? In general terms, a paragraph is long enough when it is developed sufficiently to demonstrate or enforce its idea, when it has made its point clear, emphatic, compelling. Short, choppy paragraphs seldom accomplish this goal; neither do overlong, overloaded ones. Translated into concrete terms, this guideline means that someone thumbing through a student essay should usually see two or three indentations per page.

Writing and Revising Paragraphs

Some writers deliberately compose in paragraphs. From the first sentence they premeditatedly strive to "build" a structure that has unity, coherence, and emphasis. Perhaps they even have a predetermined form in mind, an established pattern of development based on classification, or generalization and illustration, or comparison and contrast. Such writers are often working from detailed outlines, treating paragraphs as separate and discrete stages in their plan, each one of which must be relatively complete and polished before advancing to the next. This process works best when the writer has done the bulk of the research, planning, and intellectual ground-breaking before beginning the draft.

Most writers, however, focus on pursuing their ideas, on creating and maintaining a flow of thought. Postponing concerns about sentence and paragraph form, they plunge on, instinctively making paragraph divisions as they go. They allow their ideas to find their own forms, to assume their most comfortable shapes. Later, in the revision stage, they will tighten up their sentences and paragraphs to ensure the appropriate focus and development, the necessary consistency and continuity. For our purposes, then, we will treat paragraphs not as something written, but as something revised. We will concentrate not on the shapes that our ideas ought to take, but on verifying and strengthening and clarifying the shapes they have taken.

The Shapes of Paragraphs

Paragraphs are the forms that our thoughts take. Just as our thoughts come in different sizes and shapes, so do paragraphs. Some of these shapes are relatively conventional, field-tested methods of exploring their subjects, like comparison and contrast, cause and effect, definition, classification, or process. Most of these methods of development would probably suggest themselves, even if we had no models to follow. In making a generalization like the one in the previous sentence, for example, many would think to follow it with an illustration or an explanation (like this one). In describing a room or a building or a landscape, many would naturally follow a simple spatial order—from left to right, top to bottom, or foreground to background. In other words, subject and purpose often suggest treatment, resulting in certain stereotypic but also elastic forms.

Following are some of the shapes or methods of development that frequently occur in paragraphs. These should not, however, be regarded as paint-by-numbers methods of treating our subjects. They should serve only as flexible models that we can adapt for our own purposes, sometimes even stretching them over several paragraphs. It is the logic driving each method that should concern the writer. Thus, in each case we will consider the generic features of the pattern, then assess its individual application. In other words, we will look upon each as both particular and representative, as *a thing* and *a kind of a thing*.

General-to-Specifics

This method, also described as **deductive** or whole-to-parts, is easily the most popular. The paragraph opens with a broad, general statement, then develops by providing illustrations, details, or other kinds of support. The demand on the writer is to present suitable and convincing specifics; the demand on the reader is to assess their reliability.

[1]Insects include some of the most versatile and maneuverable of all flying machines. [2]Although many show rather simple flight patterns, some insects—through a combination of low mass, sophisticated systems and complex musculature—display astonishing aerobatic feats. [3]Houseflies, for example, can decelerate from fast flight, hover, turn in their own length, fly upside down, loop, roll and land on a ceiling—all in a fraction of a second. [4]Dragonflies, hover flies and lacewings are scarcely less remarkable but in different ways, for with versatility comes diversity. [5]It is now becoming increasingly clear that much of the skill and variety in insect flight results from the subtle and varied constructions of the wings. [6]But just how wing characteristics relate to flight performance has only recently begun to develop from speculation into rigorous science.

As a graduate student in the 1960s working with fossil insects, I became deeply frustrated with the limited range of conclusions that could be safely drawn from the often beautifully preserved material at my disposal. . . .

—"The Mechanical Design of Insect Wings," *Scientific American*, Nov. 1990

This paragraph works a clear variation on the whole-to-parts method of development, beginning with a topic sentence about the versatility and maneuverability of insects as "flying machines." As often happens, the second sentence restates the first on a lower level of generality, explaining which physiological traits allow some insects to perform "astonishing aerobatic feats." Then sentences 3 and 4 keep the specific promise of the opener, illustrating the flying feats of some insects.

In its simplest form a general-to-specifics paragraph contains nothing but a generalization and the supporting illustrations. In this case, however, the paragraph modifies its type. Having already given adequate examples to support the generalization, the paragraph introduces the growing science that studies the construction of insect wings and its relationship to flight performance.

Of concern to writers, though, are not only the forms but also the applications of the methods of paragraph development. Paragraphs "run in packs," existing in larger contexts and serving larger purposes. Sometimes a general-to-specifics paragraph will express the thesis of an entire essay or subsection of an essay. At other times one generalization may function only to introduce a more important one:

[1]Productivity is the holy grail of competitive industries. [2]Corporations whose workers are more productive assemble more cars, etch more microchips or sell more encyclopedias than their rivals. [3]Nations, too, pursue productivity gains and measure their standing by whether their productivity is improving faster or slower than that of others. **[4]But increasing productivity is not as simple as toting another barge or lifting another bale per worker hour.**

[5]Measuring the productivity of a coal miner or steelworker is easy: divide output by hours worked, and if necessary multiply by the price of coal or steel. [6]But how to measure the productivity of people who produce memos?

—"The Analytical Economist," *Scientific American*, June 1990

The first paragraph develops around the generalization "Productivity is the holy grail of competitive industries." It goes on to relate what industries and nations do in pursuit of this sacred goal, ending with the need for evaluation. The second paragraph opens with another generalization, one containing its own mathematical demonstration. Then it concludes with yet another generalization in the form of a question: "But how to measure the productivity of people who produce memos?" In other words, how do we evaluate the performance of those who do not produce something statistically measurable? The point of both paragraphs is to raise this issue, which is the major point of the essay. One use of good generalizations, with or without illustration, is to introduce other and more interesting ones.

Specifics-to-General

Also called parts-to-whole or **inductive,** this pattern begins with details or examples and moves toward an ordering statement. In other words, its topic sentence appears last in the paragraph, serving as a conclusion to a line of demonstration. Such placement has a persuasive advantage: the reader first sees the evidence, then hears the verdict:

[1]What has happened to the American male? [2]For a long time, he seemed utterly confident in his manhood, sure of his

masculine role in society, easy and definite in his sense of sexual identity. [3]The frontiersmen of James Fenimore Cooper, for example, never had any concern about masculinity; they were men and it did not occur to them to think twice about it. [4]Even well into the 20th century, the heroes of Dreiser, of Fitzgerald, of Hemingway remain men. [5]But one begins to detect a new theme emerging in some of these authors, especially in Hemingway: the theme of the male hero increasingly preoccupied with proving his virility to himself. [6]And by mid-century the male role had plainly lost its rugged clarity of outline. [7]Today men are more and more conscious of maleness not as a fact but as a problem. [8]The ways by which American men affirm their masculinity are uncertain and obscure. [9]**There are multiplying signs, indeed, that something has gone badly wrong with the American male's conception of himself.**

—Arthur Schlesinger, Jr., *The Politics of Hope*

Drop the "indeed," and Schlesinger's last sentence, his conclusion, could easily replace the question as a topic sentence opener.

Description

To describe is to picture in words. The more detailed the subject, the more difficult the task, largely because of the strain on the reader's memory. The most common solution is to establish a viewpoint and then present detail in some systematic fashion—from near to far, from one side to the other, from top to bottom. Once a description is under way, a related tactic is then to locate each new detail in relationship to a previous one. In the following a detective (a professional observer) describes what he saw in the entrance hall to a client's mansion:

[1]There were French doors at the back of the hall, beyond them a wide sweep of emerald grass to a white garage, in front of which a slim, dark young chauffeur in shiny black leggings was dusting a maroon Packard convertible. [2]Beyond the garage were some decorative trees trimmed as carefully as poodle dogs. [3]Beyond them was a large greenhouse with a domed roof. [4]Then more trees and beyond everything the solid, comfortable line of the foothills.

[5]On the east side of the hall, a free staircase, tile-paved, rose to a gallery with a wrought-iron railing and another piece of stained-glass romance.*[6]Large hard chairs with rounded red

* allusion to earlier mention of a scene over the hall entrance

plush seats were backed into the vacant spaces of the wall round about. [7]They didn't look as if anybody had ever sat in them. [8]In the middle of the west wall there was a big empty fireplace with a brass screen in four hinged panels, and over the fireplace a marble mantel with cupids at the corners. [9]Above the mantel there was a large oil portrait, and above the portrait two bullet-torn or moth-eaten cavalry pennants crossed in a glass frame. [10]The portrait was a stiffly posed job of an officer in full regimentals of about the time of the Mexican war. [11]The officer had a neat black imperial*, black mustachios, hot hard coal-black eyes, and the general look of a man it would pay to get along with. . . .

—Raymond Chandler, *The Big Sleep*

Chandler presents the descriptive details in climactic order. In the first paragraph he leads the reader's gaze toward the greenhouse, where the detective will later meet his client, General Sternwood. Chandler culminates the second paragraph with the portrait, an imposing figure who turns out to be Sternwood's grandfather. In both cases he challenges the reader to remember and draw conclusions. (Can anyone doubt that the General will also have coal-black eyes?)

The first paragraph follows the natural sweep of the viewer's gaze from near to far, relying on prepositional phrases to get from the French doors "at the back of the hall," then through a series of *beyond*'s to the foothills (mentioned in the first sentence of the chapter). The second paragraph also relies on prepositional phrases to orient the details in relationship to one another: "there was a big empty fireplace . . . over the fireplace a marble mantel . . . above the mantel there was a large oil portrait . . . above the portrait . . ." The repetition creates a natural sequence, reminding of older details even as new ones are introduced (thereby providing descriptive coherence). The tactic works in describing almost any subject.

Chandler is not describing the estate for its own sake, however. In describing Sternwood's home, Chandler depicts its owner. Even more important, because the descriptions come from a novel with a *first-person narrator*, they also help characterize the narrator, detective hero Philip Marlowe. By the details that he includes or excludes, and by the names that he calls things, Marlowe reveals himself. Thus, he is not only the kind to conjecture whether the cavalry pennants are bullet-torn or merely moth-eaten, but he knows what to call the pointed little beard in the portrait (an imperial).

* small, pointed beard

Descriptive method depends on subject matter and theme. When the subject is more complex, and the writer wants to create a dominant impression rather than draw a floor plan or a map, then the relative location of details is less important. Thus, in the following, the writer's object is to depict the character of a Saudi Arabian oasis:

¹The oasis at Al Buraimi, a *locus amoenus** on the edge of the sands, blossoms behind its mud walls. ²This pleasant place, carved out by men, is the product of thought and painstaking. ³*Ghosb* is their Arab word, meaning created "by effort." ⁴The walls, layers of earth stiffened with bricks laid in athwart- ships†, make a palisade against the sand. ⁵Taller than the walls, the castor-oil trees have large star-shaped leaves and fuzzy red flowers, and their skinny boles, reddish brown, are gir- dled like shoots of bamboo. ⁶From the branches of the fry- wood trees, yellow pods hang like tongues depressed for inspection. ⁷Woman's tongue, Arabs call the frywood. ⁸Date gardens, lush green, glorify the oasis. ⁹A gala in the desert, the gardens are flecked with colored lights. ¹⁰The orange lights are mangoes, also bougainvillea. ¹¹Like charity, it covers the walls of the houses, bleached out and scabrous. ¹²Chinese shoe flow- ers, rosy red, grow in plots before the houses. ¹³The ovate green leaves, edged with teeth, are sharp enough to draw blood. ¹⁴Yellow flowers like puff balls hide the dark brown bark of the gum trees, our common acacia. ¹⁵Camels, not choosy, eat the leaves of this tree, prickly with spines, and their drov- ers use the wood for cooking fires.

But the desert, a state of mind, has left its mark on Al Buraimi. It comes up to the walls like Moors coming up from Spain, hell-bent for Tours. Then, without warning, it stops. . . .

—Russell Fraser, "Wadi-Bashing in Arabia Deserta"

The Chandler description leaves the reader with a precise mental picture of the scene. Following his directions, an artist could easily draw a reasonably accurate sketch of Sternwood's hall. By contrast, the Fraser description creates a dominant impression, an oasis literally blossoming behind its mud walls. As for the number, shape, size, and location of specific buildings, these do not matter. What does matter is the overwhelming presence of so much vegetation. It is the cumu- lative impact that Fraser strives to capture, almost as if to answer the

* a charming or "pleasant place"
† crosswise, at a slant

question "What was the place *like?*" And as descriptive writers often do, Fraser supplements the visual details with appeals to other senses ("fuzzy," "prickly").

Narrative

Narration tells a story, a sequence of events unfurling in time, and it often exists separately for its own sake. Whether novels, short stories, or factual accounts, stories occupy much of our reading time. But narration also appears frequently in persuasive and informational writing. The following conjectural narrative, for example, introduces a discussion of the zebra mussel infestation of North American waterways:

> [1]In 1986 or late 1985 a ship leaving a freshwater European port for North America began to take on ballast.* [2]It opened the sea cocks and started the pumps. [3]A thriving population inhabited the harbor from which the ship drew the ballast, and members of that population came aboard along with the water. [4]Alas for North America, one of them was a hardy Asian bivalve named *Dreissena polymorpha*, the zebra mussel, which over a 150-year period had spread from the region of the Caspian Sea into much of Europe, plugging water pipes and clamping onto the hulls of boats as it went. [5]The unknown ship that carried *D. polymorpha* across the Atlantic was headed for the St. Lawrence Seaway. [6]Past Quebec City it sailed, past Montreal, past Toronto, and on through Lake Erie. [7]When the ship finally reached its destination and flushed its ballast, somewhere above Detroit, a founding population of zebra mussels tumbled into Lake St. Clair and a new continent.
>
> Ballast-flushing is by no means a new procedure, so the question of why zebra mussels didn't arrive sooner arises. The answer, biologists surmise, has to do with pollution. For years, they suggest, Europe's major freshwater harbors were so dirty that mussels simply could not survive in them. Environmental clean-ups eventually changed all that. . . .
>
> —Matthew Hart, "Invasion of the Zebra Mussels," *The Atlantic*, July 1990

The events of a story need not always appear in strict chronological order. Except for sentence 4, however, which relates that the zebra mussel had spread from the Caspian Sea, this narrative does follow the order in which the events occurred. Typical of many narratives, it begins by dating the events ("1986 or late 1985"), then proceeds in

---

* water used to stabilize a ship

sequence, pausing only for explanatory material ("a thriving population inhabited the harbor"; the ship "was headed for the St. Lawrence Seaway").

The sixth sentence demonstrates how a skillful narrator can use prepositional phrases to create a sense of movement: "Past Quebec City it sailed, past Montreal, past Toronto, and on through Lake Erie." (See the section "Prepositions and Movement" in Chapter 16, "The Rhetoric of Prepositions.") The repeated *past*'s make the action seem all the more relentless. Then the action culminates in the release of the founding population into the waters of a new continent.

The body of the article goes on to discuss the problems created by the zebra mussels and attempts at eradication.

Process

Just as a standard narrative deals with a one-time and usually unpredictable event, emphasizing its individual character, process writing deals with generalities, reporting the step-by-step development of repeated and predictable events. Its "news" is that something always happens a certain way. The following two paragraphs, for example, present a series of stages in the assembly line construction of a 747 airliner at the Boeing plant near Seattle, Washington:

> [1]Every six days at the Everett plant—usually in the middle of the night, when there are fewer distractions—the Boeing production line moves. [2](A couple of years ago the line moved once every twelve days. [3]This year, with the airlines frantic for new planes, and with last year's Boeing machinists' strike having severely complicated matters, the company doubled the work pace.) [4]In this line there are seven positions, easily recognizable by innocents watching from above on the apartment-sized viewing platform.
>
> [5]At the back great wings are brought in from storage, made into matching pairs, and joined onto what is called a wing-stub box. [6]Then a relatively small section of the fuselage—merely as small as the average house—is attached to the wings. [7]In the third and fourth positions, to which the fetal craft is moved on an arrangement of hydraulic bags and rollers, the rest of the tubular body, the nose (along with the cockpit), and the tail are bolted and glued and riveted and otherwise conjoined. [8]The undercarriage is added, so that the now recognizable plane-to-be can be wheeled around—as indeed it is, to be parked in the remaining three positions at an

angle, to allow more room in the assembly building. [9]In positions five and six much of the interior work, the wiring, and the hydraulics is completed, and at seven the engines are hung. [10]Only then does the 747 head out into the cool and rain for which Everett is famous.

—Simon Winchester, "Leviathans of the Sky," *The Atlantic*, Oct. 1990

Using the present-tense narration common to process writing, the paragraphs relate the seven assembly steps in natural chronological order. Because the stages are enumerated, transition terms like *next* and *then* are unnecessary. The major problem for the writer is to keep the stages separate while maintaining the correct pace, neither too abrupt nor too leisurely. He establishes this pace by varying sentence structure, starting four of the six not with their subjects but with prepositional phrases (a series of subject-first sentences often has an effect of abruptness).

To further maintain the deliberate pace, he also uses various interrupting elements, including dashes, parenthetical remarks, and frequent *and*'s (they may be efficient at Boeing, but they don't exactly throw these things together). And then the paragraph ends with the new 747 being wheeled triumphantly out into the cool and rain of Everett.

Comparison and Contrast

One way to understand something is to compare and contrast it to something else, preferably something related. Comparison and contrast, then, is a form of definition or description. Its method is to point out similarities and differences between two subjects, using them to explain each other. The writer may have an equal interest in the two subjects, or may be interested in one simply to illuminate the other, as is the case in the following example. The principal subject here is Allan Hobson, a Harvard psychiatrist and neuroscientist who has challenged Sigmund Freud's psychoanalytic interpretation of dreams:

[1]On the most general level, Hobson and Freud are in accord. [2]Like Freud, Hobson believes that dreams are psychologically significant. [3]Like Freud, Hobson rejects the dismissive view of one of Freud's scientifically minded predecessors that the dreaming brain is analogous to the "ten fingers of a man who knows nothing of music wandering over the keys of a piano."

[4]But on the specific nature of dreams, Hobson has little use for Freud. [5]Dreams are not obscure but transparent; they are

not censored but unedited; dreaming is not triggered by daily events that resurrect buried memories but is a process as automatic as breathing. [6]Most important, the characteristic strangeness of dreams is not a result of the dreamer's inability to face up to unpleasant memories. [7]The explanation, according to Hobson, is simply that the dreaming brain is working under adverse conditions, deprived of any access to information from the outside world while laboring to fashion a tale from a cascade of internally generated signals.

—Edward Dolnick, "What Dreams Are (Really) Made Of," *The Atlantic*, July 1990

Depending on its length and complexity, a comparison and contrast may occupy a single paragraph or several. Furthermore, a writer may have more interest in one side of the equation than the other. As the topic sentences indicate here, the first paragraph treats the similarities between Hobson and Freud (comparison), and the second their differences (contrast). The first and shorter paragraph accomplishes several purposes, the chief being to "remind" the reader of Freud's principal theories, re-covering familiar territory before getting into the central issue, the new territory explored by Hobson. The tactic is a reliable one: to explain the unfamiliar in terms of the familiar (the primary audience for this article are people who already have some interest and background in the subject).

Dolnick used a comparison with Freud to introduce his real subject, Hobson's contributions to dream theory. The principal "news" was in the contrast. In the following example the writer begins with a brief contrast of two ethnic subtypes, but only to introduce her claim for their overriding similarity. In this case the news is in the comparison. Her treatment exploits one power of comparison and contrast: the greater the differences between two subjects, the more interesting the similarities, and vice versa.

[1]If we were to emulate Giraldus* now we might say that physically **two principal types of Welshmen have emerged** from this complexity, popularly maintained to be derived from separate branches of Celtic-ness, but doubtless really the product of much more involved genetics. [2]One is relatively tall, big-boned, rather patrician† of bearing, quiet and thoughtful of response: the other is short, volatile, vivacious, all too quick to

* twelfth-century historian who wrote about the Welsh
† aristocratic (versus *plebian*—lower class)

answer. [3]The one sometimes seems, with his long thin face and his grey-blue eyes, like a visitor from the past: the other, with his flood of words, his penchant for the comic, the flash and quick chance, is sometimes almost excessively modern. [4]But they have more in common than meets the eye. [5]Both have an element of the sly to their nature, both are easily stirred to emotion, and both are essentially evasive—not necessarily in any malicious sense, not always to gain advantage, but as a matter of profoundest inherited instinct. [6]"Your Frenchman's truth," an American once said, "is like a straight line, but your Welshman's truth is more in the nature of a curve." [7]So it is, for it is only by weaving and winding, by a gift for bemusement and a mastery of romanticization, that the Welsh have managed to stay Welsh at all.   —Jan Morris, *The Matter of Wales*

Whether in one paragraph or more, comparison and contrast takes two general forms. One treats each subject in its entirety; the other treats the two point by point.

Form 1	*Form 2*
Welshman A	Appearance
appearance	Welshman A
demeanor	Welshman B
behavior	Demeanor
Welshman B	Welshman A
appearance	Welshman B
demeanor	Behavior
behavior	Welshman A
	Welshman B

The first method, the one used by Morris to make her contrast, works best when the points of comparison are few and simple; the second, when they are more numerous and complicated.

Morris contrasts the two kinds of Welshmen in her third and fourth sentences. As writers often do in such cases, she uses symmetrical form to reinforce similarity of content:

One is relatively tall, big-boned, rather patrician . . .
the other is short, volatile, vivacious . . .

The one sometimes seems, with his long thin face and his grey-blue eyes, like a visitor from the past:
the other, with his flood of words, his penchant for the comic, the flash and quick chance, is sometimes almost excessively modern.

Within the symmetry, though, there is also variety. In the second part of the comparison and contrast, for example, both clauses are interrupted by a *with* phrase, but the first gives two balanced details of physical appearance ("his long thin face and his grey-blue eyes"), while the second gives two unbalanced details of behavior ("his flood of words, his penchant for the comic, the flash and quick chance"). Morris thus avoids mechanical and predictable similarity, not allowing form to distort content (there is always a temptation to write something that sounds good, even if it is inaccurate).

Analogy

An **analogy** is a comparison, usually a likening of something less familiar to something more familiar. The best analogies are the least obvious, making connections between seemingly incompatible beings. In their simplest forms they are similes. (See the section "Prepositions and Comparisons" in Chapter 16, "The Rhetoric of Prepositions.") Full-blown analogies, however, make point-by-point comparisons and can extend to a paragraph and beyond. In the following passage a college professor and former infantry officer likens universities to the military:

[1]To this day I tend to think of all hierarchies, especially the academic one, as military. [2]The undergraduate students, at the "bottom," are the recruits and draftees, privates all. [3]Teaching assistants and graduate students are the non-coms, with grades (only officers have "ranks") varying according to seniority: a G-4 is more important than a G-1, etc. [4]Instructors, where they still exist, are the Second and First Lieutenants, and together with the Assistant Professors (Captains) comprise the company-grade officers. [5]When we move up to the tenured ranks, Associate Professors answer to field-grade officers, Majors and Colonels. [6]Professors are Generals, beginning with Brigadier—that's a newly promoted one. [7]Most are Major Generals, and upon retirement they will be advanced to Lieutenant-General ("Professor Emeritus"). [8]The main academic administration is less like a higher authority in the same structure than an adjacent echelon, like a group of powerful congressmen, for example, or people from the Judge Advocate's or Inspector General's departments. [9]The Board of Trustees, empowered to make professorial appointments and thus confer academic ranks and privileges, is the equivalent of the President of the United States, who signs commissions very like Letters of Academic Appointment: "Reposing special trust and confidence in the . . . abilities of ———, I do appoint him,"

etc. [10]It is not hard to see also that the military principle crudely registered in the axiom Rank Has Its Privileges operates in academic life, where there are plums to be plucked like frequent leaves of absence, single-occupant offices, light teaching loads, and convenient, all-weather parking spaces.

—Paul Fussell, "My War"

Since the writer's prime audience is composed of those already familiar with universities, the point of the analogy, the "news," is not the explanation of academic pecking orders. The point is the validity of the comparison itself, the uncomfortable similarity of universities to the military. Universities, after all, are supposed to be much more democratic than the army. They are supposed to be places, for example, where people are encouraged to take initiatives, and where authority and tradition yield to truth. And, of course, students and teachers are not supposed to be so conscious of rank and status.

A good analogy, then, is not only a way to explain the unfamiliar. It is a way to put the familiar in a new and more revealing light, one that challenges us to reexamine what we take for granted and therefore no longer see.

Classification (Division)

One way we can investigate a subject is to break it into its kinds or parts. Out of a consideration of the parts comes a more usable perception of the whole or the class. The following brief paragraph, for example, divides heat engines into two categories:

[1]Heat engines, which convert heat into useful mechanical work, are of **two broad types:** those in which combustion operates directly on the piston and those in which it operates indirectly by way of an intermediary known as the working fluid. [2]**The first type** is an internal-combustion engine, of which the gasoline engine is the obvious example: when fuel is burned, the gaseous combustion products expand directly against a piston. [3]**The second type** is an external combustion engine. [4]One example is the steam engine, in which water is the working fluid. [5]First a fuel—coal, say—vaporizes the water; then the steam is introduced into a cylinder and expands against the piston.

Another example of an external-combustion engine is one that was introduced in Scotland in 1816 by the Reverend Robert Stirling. Originally its working fluid was air. . . .

—"The Amateur Scientist," *Scientific American*, Jan. 1990

To keep the reader clearly informed of the divisions, the writer uses repetition (of "type") and parallelism ("The first type is"/"The second type is"). At the same time, like Morris in the previous example, the writer avoids a mechanical symmetry. He uses only one sentence to discuss the internal-combustion engine but three to discuss the external-combustion one. The reason is that he is more interested in the latter, intending to give directions for constructing one—the rest of the article goes on to explain how to build a backyard version of the Stirling engine.

Cause and Effect

We use cause-and-effect structures when we wish to explore one of two questions: Why does something happen? or, What are the consequences of something? Cause and effect may be intimately connected, but to understand one is not necessarily to understand the other. Scientists, for example, know a great deal about what happens during ice ages, but they have yet to agree on the causes. The following paragraph illustrates how to introduce a tentative explanation:

> [1]Eight times within the past million years, something in the earth's climactic equation has changed, allowing snow in the mountains and the northern latitudes to remain where it had previously melted. [2]The snow compacted into ice and the ice built up into glaciers and ice sheets. [3]Over tens of thousands of years, the ice sheets reached thicknesses of several kilometers; they planed, scoured and scarred the landscape as far south as central Europe and the midwestern U.S. [4]And then each glacial cycle came to an abrupt end. [5]Within a few thousand years, the ice sheets shrank back to their present-day configurations.
>
> Within the past 30 years, evidence has mounted that these glacial cycles are ultimately driven by astronomical factors: slow, cyclic changes in the eccentricity of the earth's orbit and in the tilt and orientation of its spin axis. . . .
> —"What Drives Glacial Cycles?" *Scientific American*, Jan. 1990

The first sentence alludes to the unknown cause: "something in the earth's climactic equation." The remaining sentences narrate the coming and going of ice ages, the process initiated by the "something." (See the section "Pronouns and the Rhetoric of Vagueness" in Chapter 12, "The Rhetoric of Pronouns.") Seeking to arouse the reader's curiosity about the unidentified cause, the paragraph concentrates for the time being on the effects. What could have been responsible for creating and setting loose glaciers several kilometers thick that "planed, scoured and scarred" the northern halves of Europe and North America?

Since the scientific community is well informed about the nature of ice ages, the task of the cause-and-effect paragraph here is to remind readers of the issue and reawaken their curiosity about an explanation. In other contexts such paragraphs would not be prefatory but would carry the weight of explanation.

Revising Paragraphs

As noted earlier, most writers do not premeditatedly compose in paragraphs, deliberately constructing each one according to blueprint. Most writers, at least in the drafting stage, focus on getting their ideas down, and paragraph more or less spontaneously, by instinct. In the revision stage they return to see if their paragraphing is logical and does justice to their subject. Then they look to tightening up their paragraphs for clarity and effectiveness. In other words, most writers do not "build" paragraphs; they remodel them.

In remodeling paragraphs, what qualities should one strive for? There is a century-old formula that still works as well as any. It states simply that an effective paragraph (or sentence or essay) has three overlapping qualities: *unity, coherence,* and *emphasis.*

Unity

A paragraph has unity when it is "about one thing," when all of its sentences serve a governing purpose. In many cases a topic sentence will spell out this purpose; other times this purpose will be so clear that such a statement of thesis is unnecessary. In any event, the opening sentence will orient the reader and lead naturally into the sentences that follow. This unity, a consistency of subject and theme, is reinforced principally by the following:

▶ the repetition of key words and phrases

▶ the use of synonyms and related words

▶ pronouns with common antecedents

Consider the unity of the following paragraph about the "buffs" whose hobby is attending court trials:

> ¹Anyone who regularly conducts business in the criminal courts of New York City grows accustomed to seeing buffs seated in the back of the room. ²Many shortsighted lawyers

think of court buffs as part of the furniture, and ignore them. ³But enlightened and resourceful lawyers regard knowledgeable buffs as juror's jurors. ⁴On occasion, during trial recesses, they seek the buffs' counsel. ⁵Attention of this sort pleases a buff. ⁶Just because one buff tells another that an inept lawyer is stinking up a courtroom with his performance, it doesn't mean that he wants the lawyer in question to know he thinks so. ⁷A lawyer who solicits a buff's opinion usually hears words of reassurance. ⁸It is in a buff's interest to massage a lawyer's ego. ⁹Lawyers call witnesses to testify, and courtroom testimony is often amazing. ¹⁰The way a buff sees it, lawyers deserve encouragement; they book a lot of free entertainment. ¹¹"I'd pay a dollar to see a good trial, I really would," Shine [a court buff] has said—grateful, just the same, that he doesn't have to. ¹²"Some of these buffs, though, I think if you charged only fifty cents you'd lose quite a few."

—Mark Singer, "Court Buff"

In this paragraph each sentence focuses directly on the subject of court buffs and their frequent interaction with lawyers, either illustrating or explaining it. Because of the continual interaction of the two parties, and the alternating attention the writer gives to each, either *buff(s)* or *lawyer(s)* appears at least once in every sentence. In support of this repetition are other words associated with their world: *criminal courts, jurors, trial recess, testify, testimony, courtroom,* and *witness.* The frequency of *buff(s)* and *lawyer(s)* reduces the need for pronouns like *they* and *them.*

Coherence

Something is coherent when it "sticks together," when it is logical, consistent, and intelligible. Applied to a paragraph, **coherence** means that its sentences flow easily into and out of one another while developing the unifying idea. In a coherent paragraph sentences depend on one another for meaning. The effect of coherence is to direct the reader's attention in two directions, backward and forward. For even as we are developing an idea, moving forward, we are building on what went before. Momentum (moving forward) depends on memory (looking back). Coherence performs this double task by several means:

❱ transition terms (explicit logical connections)

❱ implicit logical connections

❱ similarity in sentence structure

▶ pronouns (See the section "Pronouns and Coherence" in Chapter 12, "The Rhetoric of Pronouns.")

▶ demonstrative words (*this*, *these*, *such*, and so on)

The following paragraph achieves coherence in a number of ways:

> [1]Porcupines use their quills only *in extremis** for strategic defense, after other methods have failed. [2]The animals are easy to see at night, for they bear the black-and-white pattern that stands out best in the dark. [3]They are easy to hear, for they produce an ominous, shivery tooth clacking as you approach. [4]They are easy to smell, for they emit a goaty, pungent signal scent, probably from a special hairless region of skin, exposed when the tail is lifted. [5]Ignore these three warnings, and you dare the quills.

—review of *The North American Porcupine*, by Uldis Roze, *Scientific American*, June 1990

The paragraph opens with a topic statement (porcupines use their quills only when their lives are threatened). The next three sentences then describe the other methods of defense that minimize the need for quills, using parallel structure to underscore their common purpose:

> The animals are easy to see . . . for they . . .
>
> They are easy to hear . . . for they . . .
>
> They are easy to smell . . . for they . . .

The writer could have introduced these illustrative sentences with a transition term like *for example*, but their function is too obvious to require such an open connection. Their logical relationship is implicitly clear.

The word *porcupines* appears once at the beginning; after this the writer refers to them by a broader term ("the animals"), then by the repeated pronoun *they*. Each pronoun calls the reader back to its antecedent even as it moves its own sentence forward. The last sentence also uses a *demonstrative adjective* to summarize the illustrations: "Ignore *these* three warnings . . ." And finally, the writer ends the paragraph by returning to *quills*. Bracketed between the two "quills" are the alternatives. From opening topic sentence to conclusion, the reader knows precisely what is happening. The paragraph is unified and coherent.

---

* at the point of death

Transition Terms and Paragraph Coherence   One term often used for coherence is *continuity*, or "continuousness." A coherent paragraph must continue, must have momentum, must flow. It flows when there are clear logical relationships between the ideas expressed in the sentences. Sometimes these relationships are so evident that the writer needs only to imply them. Other times the writer will need to keep the reader on track by marking the way with transition or linking terms.

The relationships between ideas cannot be reduced to a rigid formula, but following are the most common ones and some of the common transition terms that identify them:

Addition	and, again, also, first, likewise, similarly, second, third
Illustration	for example, for instance, namely, that is
Alternative	but, although, or, nor, however, yet, still, on the other hand, nevertheless
Location	above, below, farther, opposite
Time	after, before, during, later, next, then
Cause	if, so, consequently, since, because
Conclusion	thus, hence, in short, that is, as a result, accordingly, therefore

Without transition terms and with too many sentences beginning with subjects, coherence fades, as in the following revision:

> [1]Precisely how Islamic mechanical technology entered Europe is unknown. [2]There may be instances of ideas being inherited directly from the Greco-Roman tradition into medieval Europe. [3]We cannot rule out cases of reinvention. [4]Some elements of the rich vein of Islamic mechanical engineering were probably transmitted to Europe when allowances have been made.

Lacking transition words and structural variety, this paragraph reads almost like a series of independent statements. It jerks instead of flows, and the reader must labor to make some of the connections. The writer of the original, however, understood the importance of continuity:

> [1]Precisely how Islamic mechanical technology entered Europe is unknown. [2]**Indeed,** there may be instances of ideas being inherited directly from the Greco-Roman tradition into medieval Europe. [3]**Nor** can we rule out cases of reinvention.

[4]**When allowances have been made, however,** it seems proba-
ble that some elements of the rich vein of Islamic mechanical
engineering were transmitted to Europe.

Any **such** technological borrowing would probably have
been mediated by contacts between craftsmen, by the inspection of existing machines working or in disrepair and by the
reports of travelers. . . .

—"Mechanical Engineering in the Medieval Near East," *Scientific American*,
May 1991

Without the opening "Indeed," the second sentence could itself be
a topic sentence, a reasonably independent statement. *Indeed,* however,
signals a comment on the previous sentence. In the same way, the
opening "nor" of the third sentence announces a statement that parallels
the one it follows. In fact, sentences 2 and 3 cooperate to express possible alternatives to the transmission of Islamic mechanical engineering
to Europe. These are the "allowances" mentioned in the opening qualifier of the final sentence: "When allowances have been made . . ." And
then the "however" reinforces the relatedness of the final statement to
the foregoing. Together, the opening qualifier and the "however" make
the last sentence both a conclusion and a circling reaffirmation of the
paragraph's first sentence. The paragraph holds together even as it
moves, the transition terms ensuring that the sentences rely on one
another to create meaning.

Exercise

In the following paragraph find the devices that create unity and coherence, that is, the words and expressions that hold the sentences
together.

[1]Radioactivities emerge as ambassadors from a distant
world, the nucleus of an atom. [2]The nucleus sends forth a flash
of energy, a couple of protons, a few neutrons or other particles. [3]Each of these ambassadors carries a particular message.
[4]Most often they announce the decay of a nucleus from an energetic, unstable state to a less energetic, more stable one.
[5]Radioactivities also reveal subtle clues about nuclear structure.
[6]By piecing these clues together, investigators have created detailed models of the nucleus. [7]These models not only account
for most nuclear phenomena but also predict many new types

of radioactivities. [8]The triumph of the past decade has been the discovery of several of these new nuclear fragments.
—"New Radioactivities," *Scientific American*, Mar. 1990

Coherence Between Paragraphs   If a paragraph is a sequence of related sentences, an essay or article or chapter is a sequence of related paragraphs. And if these larger units are to be coherent, there must be transitions between as well as within paragraphs. To illustrate, the following are a series of paragraph openers from an essay on the growing commercialization of American movies (Mark Crispin Miller, "Hollywood: The Ad," *The Atlantic*, Apr. 1990):

> Later, dining with his wealthy clients, Candy pours a can of Diet Coke into a brandy snifter of ice cream. . . .
> Such subliminal tactics are certainly not peculiar to the mighty cola rivals. . . .
> These are two examples of Hollywood's new commercialism at its most grotesque, and there are many others. . . .
> Such bald intrusions into dialogue are no longer rare. . . .
> And when shoved right into the spotlight, the product doesn't just upstage the actors but actually stops the narrative. . . .
> Meanwhile, as more and more admen direct films, more and more filmmakers are directing television ads. . . .
> Such is now the norm of cinema. . . .

The presence of transition terms often identifies groupings of related paragraphs, just as their absence often signals the beginning of new sections:

> Even if, armed with some marvelous zapping gizmo, you could sit and blast away every obvious product as it passed through the frame or glowed in a close-up, today's Hollywood movie would still seem like an ad. . . .

The lack of transition terms announces that this paragraph is relatively self-contained and will not rely so closely on earlier paragraphs to make sense.

One step in revision, then, is to check for the presence of appropriate transition terms between as well as within paragraphs.

Overuse of Transition Terms   Writers can also give too many directions to their readers. When they overload their paragraphs with transition terms, labeling even the most obvious of connections, their prose becomes overly deliberate, self-conscious, mechanical. Transition terms, which are supposed to smooth our ride, become speed bumps. The problem worsens when writers rely on transition terms alone, neglecting demonstrative words, related pronouns, and parallel sentence structure to signal connections between ideas. Look what happens to a paragraph when every sentence contains a transition term:

> [1]There are no pure states of mankind. [2]**As a result,** happiness is never more than partial. [3]**Furthermore,** whatever happiness may be, it is neither in having nor in being, but in becoming. [4]**Thus,** what the Founding Fathers declared for us as an inherent right, we should do well to remember, was not happiness but the *pursuit* of happiness. [5]What they might have underlined, **in addition,** could they have foreseen the happiness-market, is the cardinal fact that happiness is in the pursuit itself, in the meaningful pursuit of what is life-engaging and life-revealing, which is to say, in the pursuit of *becoming.* [6]**In short,** a nation is not measured by what it possesses or wants to possess, but by what it wants to become.

The logical relationships between the sentences are clear enough without such markers, as the writer understood:

> [1]Happiness is never more than partial. [2]There are no pure states of mankind. [3]Whatever happiness may be, it is neither in having nor in being, but in becoming. [4]What the Founding Fathers declared for us as an inherent right, we should do well to remember, was not happiness but the *pursuit* of happiness. [5]What they might have underlined, could they have foreseen the happiness-market, is the cardinal fact that happiness is in the pursuit itself, in the meaningful pursuit of what is life-engaging and life-revealing, which is to say, in the pursuit of *becoming.* [6]A nation is not measured by what it possesses or wants to possess, but by what it wants to become.
> —John Ciardi, "Is Everybody Happy?"

Emphasis

Emphasis comes from a word meaning "to show." If our readers had photographic memories, if they accepted on faith everything we said, and if they did not have to understand the basis for any of our beliefs, we would not have to "show" (prove, demonstrate) anything; we could get away with simply "telling." In other words, our writing would be a sequence of unsupported statements, of topic sentences.

To convince our readers of both the truth and the value of what we write about, though, we must linger over our subject a while. We must describe a scene or narrate an action vividly enough for the reader to feel like a witness; we must give enough information that the reader can exercise personal judgment; we must provide enough support for our arguments that the reader will at least respect our point of view. In sum, we must dwell on our subject long enough for it to "take."

Putting aside understatement, which is a kind of emphasis in its own right, all but the barest sentences and paragraphs contain some kind of emphasis. In fact, almost any kind of development qualifies as emphasis. Without it, even the clearest of statements can seem weak or pointless. Take the following:

> Crime especially terrorizes the weakest and most vulnerable among us.

Or:

> Children need order.

We might accept the truth of these sentiments immediately, but nothing signals their importance, their urgency. They are not ideas particularly worth remembering or, more important, doing anything about. Within the context of a paragraph, with a little elaboration, they have more force and insistence:

> [1]Crime especially terrorizes the weakest and most vulnerable among us. [2]Three quarters of America's 64 million children live in metropolitan areas, a fifth live in low-income households, at least a tenth come home from school to a house containing no adult, and all are physically immature and incompletely formed in character. [3]These are the people who suffer most when law and order decay. [4]Aside from love and sustenance, there is nothing children need more than order.

This rather businesslike, matter-of-fact statement covers the subject, but it still lacks the insistence its subject deserves. It informs, but it does not move. The actual writer, however, was introducing a persuasive essay on a crucial issue, child safety. He knew how to establish a tone of urgency:

> [1]Crime does not wash over all Americans equally. [2]It especially terrorizes the weakest and most vulnerable among us.

³Three quarters of America's 64 million children live in metro-
politan areas, a fifth live in low-income households, at least a
tenth come home after school to a house containing no adult,
and all are physically immature and incompletely formed in
character. ⁴These are the people who suffer most when law
and order decay. ⁵Children need order. ⁶Aside from love and
sustenance, there is nothing they need more than order.
   Law enforcement is often presented as a conservative issue,
but today there is a powerful bleeding-heart justification for
getting tough on crime: to protect child welfare. . . .
—Karl Zinsmeister, "Growing Up Scared," *The Atlantic*, June 1990

Most readers would find the first version of the paragraph much
less compelling than the second. Why? Because it lacks the devices of
emphasis, especially the repetition.

One of the principal ways we emphasize a point is to restate it, to
put it in different words. A writer's purpose is not always served by
finding the best single wording and using it; restatement and rephrasing
also have a power, the power of cumulative impact. Repeating our
message gives it a better chance to sink in; rephrasing it gives the reader
more ways to think about it. Hence, the writer here begins and ends
by repeating a few basic ideas. To open, he says that "Crime does not
wash over all Americans equally." Then he restates and expands on
his idea by being more specific: "It especially terrorizes the weakest
and most vulnerable among us."

At the end of the paragraph, the writer again restates himself to
underline the urgency of his thesis (that of his entire essay). He does
not simply say that children need order or that next to love and sustenance they need nothing more than order. Instead, "Children need
order. Aside from love and sustenance, there is nothing they need more
than order." One way to ensure that readers take away an idea from
an article is to repeat it: "Children need order. They need order."

Repetition is a way of being explicit, of drumming on our idea to
make sure that the reader gets it. But the writer here also knows how
to make implicit statements. The second sentence says that crime especially victimizes "the weakest and most vulnerable among us," but
does not identify the group. The third sentence, the longest and most
detailed, begins with "Three quarters of America's 64 million children"—these, then, are the weakest and most vulnerable, the children.
At the end of the sentence, the writer reminds us that "all are physically
immature and incompletely formed in character." By implication, this
description explains why they are the weakest and most vulnerable.

In his opener the writer also uses another form of emphasis: metaphor. He could have expressed his idea literally and said that "Crime does not affect all Americans equally." Instead, he states figuratively that "Crime does not *wash over* all Americans equally." "Wash over" suggests that crime is like a rising flood and, by implication, that some Americans are being drowned by it.

So how does a paragraph achieve emphasis? The methods are numerous, but the following are among the most common:

▶ full development of its governing idea, including illustration, explanation, restatement, and so on

▶ repetition (of key words, concepts, and so on)

▶ figurative language (metaphor, simile, and the like)

▶ unusual word order

▶ occasional use of short sentences ("Children need order.")

Exercise

How does the writer achieve emphasis in the following paragraph? You might even consider diluting its argument by removing as many emphatic devices as possible.

[1]What Dr. [Martin Luther] King promised was not a ranch-style house and an acre of manicured lawn for every black man, but jail and finally freedom. [2]He did not promise two cars for every family, but the courage one day for all families everywhere to walk without shame and unafraid on their own feet. [3]He did not say that one day it will be us chasing prospective buyers out of our prosperous well-kept neighborhoods, or in other ways exhibiting our snobbery and ignorance as all other ethnic groups before us have done; what he said was that we had a right to live anywhere in this country we chose, and a right to a meaningful well-paying job to provide us with the upkeep of our homes. [4]He did not say we had to become carbon copies of the white American middle-class; but he did say we had the right to become whatever we wanted to become.

—Alice Walker, "The Civil Rights Movement: What Good Was It?"

A good paragraph, then, one that does justice to its subject, has unity, coherence, and emphasis. It is a sequence of sentences developing a central idea (unity); its sentences depend on one another for meaning (coherence); and it dwells on the central idea long enough to stress its truth and significance (emphasis). In sum, a paragraph is a "formation"—an arrangement or positioning of sentences for some uniform effect. The strength of individual sentences—their contribution to unity, coherence, and emphasis—depends on their *place* and role in the formation.

3

Nouns

Definition

Nouns are words like those boldfaced in the following sentences:

> Perhaps the quickest **way** to understand the **elements** of what a **novelist** is doing is not to read, but to write; to make your own **experiment** with the **dangers** and **difficulties** of **words**.
> —Virginia Woolf, "How Should One Read a Book?"

> **Gilbert Wynant** was two **years** younger than his **sister,** a gangling pale blond **boy** of **eighteen** with not too much **chin** under a somewhat slack **mouth.** —Dashiell Hammett, *The Thin Man*

Nouns are the naming words we use to identify the things we talk about in sentences, whether they are persons or places or objects or qualities or ideas or processes or activities or conditions.

Classes of Nouns

Each noun (often with the help of modifiers) indicates the nature and amount of reality we wish to talk about. This reality may be material or immaterial, general or specific, but there will be a class of nouns to apply to it. On the basis of their meaning—the kind of reality they talk about—nouns fit into at least one of several overlapping classes: *common, proper, concrete, abstract, collective, count*, and *mass*.

Common Nouns

Common comes from a word meaning "shared by all or many." Hence, *common nouns* form the most inclusive class, nouns that by themselves do indeed apply to entire classes, kinds, orders, or groups. Without modifiers or a context, these nouns are deliberately nonspecific— baggy, one-size-fits-all labels. They begin with lowercase letters (except, of course, when they open sentences):

way	years
elements	sister
novelist	boy
experiment	chin
dangers	mouth

Proper Nouns

In contrast with common nouns, **proper nouns** form the most exclusive class, the one that discusses the smallest amount of reality, identifying one specific person, place, or thing at a time. Even if the proper noun is a name shared by many (*Lee, Mary, Bridal Veil Falls*), its normal use is understood to signify but one particular bearer of that name. In addition to the names of people and places, this class includes the titles of books, plays, movies, sculptures, paintings, and pieces of music. Proper nouns begin with capital or uppercase letters:

Virginia Woolf	*The Thin Man*
Mrs. Dalloway	Edward Ellis
Bloomsbury	Asta

Concrete Nouns

Concrete nouns identify only that part of reality that we can experience physically, the part that we can *verify* (make true) by touching or seeing or hearing or smelling or tasting:

novelist   words   sister   chin   mouth

Abstract Nouns

Abstract nouns identify the part of reality that we can only think about, qualities or ideas or other **abstractions** (from a word meaning "to draw or separate from," as we separate the notion of "speed" or "grace" from the actual horse). Because these things exist principally as concepts and cannot be seen, smelled, touched, tasted, or heard, the effective and accurate use of abstract nouns requires that the writer and audience agree on their definition. For example:

way	honesty
dangers	courage
difficulties	patriotism

Collective Nouns

Collective nouns identify groups as groups. They create difficulty because they are singular in form but sometimes plural in meaning. (See the section "Nouns and Number" later in this chapter.) Hence, their **agreement** with verbs and pronouns depends on whether they refer to their groups as units or as collections of individuals taken separately:

Singular   The **team** lost **its** third game.

Plural   The **team** lost **their** towels.

Singular   The **board is voting** for a pay raise.

Plural   The **board are voting** themselves a pay raise.

The natural impulse is to use such words as singular nouns. When we want to use them as plurals, we often have to indicate the intention by reinforcing them with other plural words (*their, themselves*). Other collective nouns:

audience	the clergy	the United States
band	the faculty	the Senate
class	the military	the class of 1996
coven	the electorate	

Count Nouns

Count nouns (as opposed to *mass nouns*) identify things that we count in units. Hence, they form plurals and can be preceded by *many* or *fewer* (as opposed to *much* and *less*). Someone can have *many* dollars and *few* accidents because *dollars* and *accidents* are count nouns, but the person cannot have *many* money and *few* bad luck because *money* and *luck* are mass nouns. Here are a few count nouns:

novelists   elements   words   years   chins   sisters

Mass Nouns

Mass nouns (or *noncount nouns*) identify abstract qualities, *masses*, and other collections that we usually do not think about in specific units. These do not form plurals and can be preceded by *much* and *less*:

calm   content   courage   dough   dirt   luck

Some words operate as either count or mass nouns, words like *danger, insight,* and *sugar*. A person may have faced *many dangers* or *much danger*; someone else may have *much insight* or have *many insights*; sucrose and lactose are a *few sugars*, but your recipe for chocolate chip cookies may have *less sugar* than someone else's.

Noun Determiners

As the Woolf sentence illustrates, nouns may appear alone or in *noun phrases* (word groups functioning as units):

Perhaps the quickest **way** to understand the **elements** of what a **novelist** is doing is not to read, but to write; to make your own **experiment** with the **dangers** and **difficulties** of **words**.

Determiners, or noun signalers, are words that introduce noun phrases. The most common and the ones that will concern us here are *articles* (*a/an/the*). Other words recognized as determiners are *demonstratives* (*this, that, these, those*), *possessives* (*ours, his, hers,* and so on), *interrogatives* (*what, which, whose*), *relatives* (*which, whose, whatever,* and so on), *cardinal numbers* (*one, two, forty-four, ninety-nine,* and so on), and *indefinites* (*all, any, both, each, every, most, several,* and so on). In most cases we can avoid unnecessary complication by treating determiners as another class of noun modifiers or adjectives, except that they always begin a noun phrase:

the quickest way   **whose** quickest way

these quicker ways   **three** quicker ways

its quicker ways   **several** quicker ways

which quicker ways

Articles are either definite (*the*) or indefinite (*a/an*). In most cases the *definite article* is as its name suggests—definite: applied even to a common noun, it identifies one specific individual, unit, or group and assumes a context in which the identity of *the* object is clear or implicit. If someone says, "Take the car," it is understood that the listener will know which car. *The* may appear before either singular or plural nouns.

In normal use *indefinite articles* also operate the way their name suggests, referring to beings that are indefinite or nonspecific. If someone says, "It is time you buy yourself *a car*," the type of car is left open. Indefinite articles appear only before singular nouns, *a* preceding consonants (*a belt, a fold*), and *an* preceding vowels (*an arch, an example*). When a modifier appears between the article and the noun, its beginning sound determines the article: *a black belt* but *an old belt*.

Generic Uses of Articles

In addition to their standard uses, the definite and indefinite articles also have special applications. The definite article usually precedes a common noun and makes it specific; the indefinite usually precedes a common noun and confirms its generic meaning.

def art	+	common noun	=	specific
the		**belt**		**one particular belt**

indef art	+	common noun	=	general
a		**belt**		**any belt**

Sometimes, however, the indefinite and even the definite article can signal more generic or broadly inclusive meanings. In certain contexts *the* (which normally refers to very specific beings) can also refer broadly to an entire class or at least to the typical. For example, one can speak about the damage that *the automobile* has done to our environment, and about *the traffic* in *the city* that makes some imagine that they yearn for *the country*. To know which way *the* is being used, specifically or generically, we must depend on clues, clues given by the context as well as by other words in the sentence.

The definite and indefinite can also signal generic meaning when applied to proper nouns. Albert Einstein was one solitary genius, but someone writing about *the Albert Einsteins* of the world would be referring to an entire (if very small) class. In this case "the" preceded a proper noun in the plural to signal a generic meaning. By the same token, the indefinite article can also be applied to singular proper nouns to communicate a generic notion. Hence, an English teacher with a particularly gifted student might refer to her as *a Virginia Woolf* or *a Joan Didion*.

And finally, we can also signal the generic by using no article at all, especially with abstract and mass nouns (*calm, contentment, peace, weight, sugar*). Without articles concrete nouns can also be generic. Hence, we can observe that *cats* need more protein than *dogs*, or even that *traffic* is a growing problem in today's cities.

Nouns in Sentences

By itself a noun simply names (*noun* derives from a Latin word meaning "name"). Most of the time, though, a noun is not standing alone, like a label on a jar or a name tag on a coat. A noun usually appears in a sentence, doing something, relating to other words. More than simply naming, a noun in a sentence communicates a certain kind of information, identifying some person or object in a specific situation or relationship—the performer or the recipient of an action, for example. To appreciate the versatility of nouns, as well as to understand the sentences in which they appear, we must recognize all the functions nouns can serve, whether they are alone or in phrases.

Subject	**Gilbert Wynant** was two years younger than his sister.
	Gilbert being two years younger than his sister, he was much less mature.
	(what the sentence or verbal is about; usually the doer or the one being identified)
Predicate Noun	Gilbert was a gangling pale blond **boy** of eighteen.
	(follows a linking verb and identifies the subject)
Direct Object	Gilbert slackened his **mouth.**
	Slackening his **mouth,** he . . .
	(the recipient of an action)
Indirect Object	Gilbert sent his **sister** a telegram.
	Sending his **sister** a telegram, Gilbert . . .
	(the recipient or beneficiary of the direct object)
Object of a Preposition	Gilbert sent a letter **to his sister.**
	with not too much chin
	under a somewhat slack mouth
	(member of a modifying phrase related by a preposition to another word in a sentence)

Appositive	Her brother **Gilbert** was only eighteen.
	Her brother was Gilbert, a gangling pale blond **boy** of eighteen.
	(renames or defines an earlier noun in the sentence)
Modifier	Gilbert was two **years** younger than his sister.
	(limits or qualifies the meaning of another word)
Direct Address	"Chin up, **Gilbert!**"
	"**Asta,** off the bed!"
	(the name of the individual spoken *to*, not *about*)

All of these noun functions can also be performed by other structures and parts of speech. (These structures and parts of speech will be discussed in various sections in the chapters to come.) English is flexible, and one measure of that flexibility is the ability of words to step outside their usual roles; for example, we can place an article in front of an adjective and make it a noun:

None but **the brave** deserves **the fair**.

—John Dryden, "Alexander's Feast"

The deeply **fearful** are driven to righteousness, as we know, and they are the most fearsome fools we have.

—William Kittredge, "Who Owns the West?"

Because there is a name (or a noun) for everything, there is a technical term for such role switching when it stretches the normal boundaries of idiom: **anthimeria.** For example, describing the once stately homes around Washington Square in New York, Cynthia Ozick uses an adjective as a noun, but without the conventional article:

Still, they are plainly old, though no longer aristocratic: haughty, last-century **shabbies** with shut eyelids, built of rosy-ripe respectable brick, down on their luck.

—"The First Day of School: Washington Square, 1946"

Annie Dillard uses the same device to describe the weather:

Today is one of those excellent January partly **cloudies** in which light chooses an unexpected part of the landscape to trick out in gilt, and then shadow sweeps it away.

—*Pilgrim at Tinker Creek*

Nouns as Noun Modifiers

Nouns frequently appear before other nouns as modifiers. English is filled with expressions like *fire truck, fire wall*, and *fire alarm; timepiece, time share, time limit*, and *time exposure; rainfall, snowfall*, and *sleetfall*.

■

> A **sleetfall** was turning the roads into **ice sheets**.
> A **sleet** was falling that turned the roads into **sheet ice**.

Unlike most other modifying structures, however, nouns do not work well in a series, perhaps because each asks for emphasis. If we use more than three nouns in a row as modifiers, we risk awkwardness and confusion:

> They have already mailed the **fall faculty welcoming party** announcements.

One solution is to break up the sequence with possessives and prepositional phrases:

> They have already mailed the announcements **for this fall's faculty welcoming party**.

Nouns and Number

Nouns have a property called *number*, the ability to show whether they refer to one (*singular*) or to more than one (*plural*). The common noun form, the one we find listed in the dictionary, is the singular. Most nouns form their plurals by adding -s or -es to the singular, depending on their final sound. Most final sounds go smoothly with -s:

one needle	two needles
the belt	the belts
one year	two years
one fold	several folds

There are some exceptions:

▶ Some final sounds—*ch, s, sh, x*—do not go well with a simple -s and take a whole syllable, -es:

birch/birches	push/pushes
wretch/wretches	fox/foxes
class/classes	lummox/lummoxes

▶ Nouns ending in -*y* preceded by a consonant (or *qu*) change *y* to *i* and add -*es*:

sky/skies   cherry/cherries
beauty/beauties   soliloquy/soliloquies

▶ Nouns ending in -*f* or -*fe* usually change their ending to -*ve* before adding -*s*:

life/lives   hoof/hooves
wife/wives   thief/thieves

▶ Nouns ending in -*o* can end in either -*s* or -*es*. If the -*o* is preceded by a single consonant or by a vowel, the word usually takes an -*s*:

piano/pianos   echo/echoes
solo/solos   lotto/lottoes
trio/trios   tomato/tomatoes
veto/vetoes   potato/potatoes

▶ Some nouns take neither -*s* or -*es* in the plural: a few English words keeping their older form and some words deriving from other languages that still have their original form:

child/children   datum/data
ox/oxen   alumnus(na)/alumni(nae)
mouse/mice   medium/media
tooth/teeth   analysis/analyses
                  criterion/criteria

▶ Most compound nouns—those formed from two or more words—form their plurals according to the rules governing the last word (usually -*s*):

baby sitter/baby sitters   mouthpiece/mouthpieces
motor vehicle/motor vehicles   doghouse/doghouses

But we add -*s* to the first word when it is the key one:

sister-in-law/sisters-in-law   man-at-arms/men-at-arms
attorney-at-law/attorneys-at-law passerby/passersby

❭   We use an apostrophe and an -*s* to form the plurals of letters, numbers, and words used as words:

There are four **i's** and four **s's** in *Mississippi*.

Gilbert got **C's** and **D's** but his sister got **A's** and **B's**.

Nouns and Gender

Nouns also have **gender,** being classified according to the *masculine*
(*man, king, rooster*), *feminine* (*woman, queen, hen*), or *neuter* (*tree, axe,
kindling*). In Old English (circa A.D. 400–1100), as in modern European
languages, nouns were distributed much more evenly through all three
grammatical genders. Since then, English nouns have become greatly
simplified, and most are now neuter. For practical purposes, gender is
the principal concern of *personal pronouns* (*he/she/it*). Nevertheless, some
gender suffixes survive in English: -*man* for the masculine and -*ess* and
-*ette* for the feminine.

Recognizing gendered nouns is less of a problem for most writers
than knowing when and how to use them. At one time writers could
freely use terms like *chairman, congressman, foreman, policeman, mailman,
salesman,* and *weatherman,* and refer to either men or women. Now,
these terms offend many people because they seem to imply that certain
occupations are the exclusive province of men, that gender is a pre-
requisite for some respected careers. Substituting -*woman* for -*man* is
not a fully satisfactory solution because the feminine suffix still calls
attention to gender. Using -*person* as a substitute is not completely satisfactory, either, because it strikes some as condescending (a male member of a fire department will still probably call himself a fireman, and
if he alludes to a "fireperson," he will likely be speaking about a woman).
The best solution is to seek neutral equivalents:

chairman	chair,* moderator
congressman	representative, legislator, member of Congress
fireman	firefighter
foreman	supervisor (but *forewoman* of a jury)
mailman	mail carrier

* To call people "chairs" is not to diminish them to mere pieces of furniture. It is a
legitimate use of a rhetorical device called **metonymy,** naming something, usually a
person, after something associated with it (the president of the United States is "the
White House," Congress is "Capitol Hill," journalists are "the press," military officers
are "brass"). In an institutional setting a chair is a symbol of authority and responsibility.

policeman	police officer
salesman	sales associate/representative
weatherman	weather forecaster, meteorologist

If *-man* offends because it upholds the prejudice that some work, especially respected and dignified work, is the sole property of men, suffixes like *-ess* and *-ette* offend because in some cases they also seem to demean or patronize women (*-ette* is also a suffix indicating that something is small: *statuette*). If a poet is someone who writes poetry, why set apart a woman who writes poetry as a *poetess*?

Some other gender terms are almost intentionally offensive: *lady lawyer, woman driver, little woman* (of course there are a few derogatory terms that apply strictly to males, like *con man* and *whipping boy*). In addition to courtesy and tolerance, there are rhetorical reasons to avoid such language. To communicate with an audience, to establish the necessary connection so our arguments will be received sympathetically, we must show respect for *all* its members.

Nouns and Case

Case is the term used to describe the form that nouns and pronouns take to indicate their function in a sentence. In English there are three cases: *subjective* (or nominative)—for the subjects of verbs and verbals and for subjective complements; *objective*—for the objects of verbs, verbals, and prepositions; and *possessive* (or genitive)—for showing possession or some like relationship. Some modern European languages have up to six cases, requiring six different endings to identify the functional role of nouns. For all practical purposes, however, the modern English noun has but two cases, changing its usual spelling only to indicate "ownership" (adding an apostrophe plus -*s*, or a simple apostrophe if the word ends in an -*s*). Thus, we have *All the King's Men, One Flew over the Cuckoo's Nest, Sophie's Choice, Prizzi's Honor*, but a *Wuthering Heights'* remake and *Star Wars'* sequels.

Pronouns

Definition

Pronouns are words like those boldfaced in the following sentences:

> Most writers share the feeling that the first draft, and **all** of **those which** follow, are opportunities to discover **what they** have to say and how best **they** can say **it**.
> —Donald Murray, "The Maker's Eye: Revising Your Own Manuscripts"

> I never wholly agreed with the LOVE **IT** OR LEAVE **IT** bumper stickers, **which** held that **everybody who** didn't love the flag ought to be thrown out of the country, but **I** wouldn't have minded seeing **them** beaten up. —Russell Baker, "The Flag"

> I know **what** is being said about **me** and **you** can take **my** side or **theirs, that's your** own business.
> —Truman Capote, "My Side of the Matter"

Pronouns are words that either substitute for nouns or function in noun positions. An individual pronoun usually fills in for a specific noun called its *referent* or *antecedent* (from two Latin words meaning "to go before"), whose identity should be clear from the context.

103

Classes of Pronouns

There are eight classes of pronouns, each with its own properties and uses.

Personal Pronouns

Personal pronouns are the most common type of pronoun. Rhetorically, the most important thing about them is that they derive most of their meaning from the words to which they refer (their **antecedents**). Personal pronouns take their name from their ability to change form to indicate a property called *person*, a term indicating whether the pronoun refers to the speaker (*first person—I/we*), the person spoken to (*second person—you*), or the person or thing spoken of (*third person— he/she/it/they*). Personal pronouns also change form to indicate *number* (singular, plural), *case* (function in a sentence), and *gender* (sex of the antecedent).

	Subject	*Object*	*Possessive*
First-Person Singular	I	me	my, mine
First-Person Plural	we	us	our, ours
Second-Person Singular and Plural	you	you	your, yours
Third-Person-Singular			
Masculine	he	him	his
Feminine	she	her	her, hers
Neuter	it	it	its
Third-Person Plural	they	them	their, theirs

ant
When **Martha Hale** opened the storm-door and got a cut of the north wind, **she** ran back for **her** big woolen scarf.

—Susan Glaspell, "A Jury of Her Peers"

Relative Pronouns

Relative pronouns are words that introduce adjective and noun clauses while performing noun functions inside of them. In the preceding sentence, for example, "that" both introduces and is the subject of the clause. The clause introduced by "that" is called an *adjective clause* because it modifies a noun ("words") and a relative clause because it begins with a relative pronoun.

Subject	Object	Possessive
who	whom	whose
that	that	
which	which	whose, of which
what	what	

A man **who** resembles a rodent should never wear tweed.
—Mark Helprin, "The Schreuderspitze"

It was a little Honda **that** responded to wind like a shuttlecock, and on slick pavement the rear end flapped like the tail of a trout. —David Quammen, "Strawberries Under Ice"

When relative pronouns introduce **noun clauses** (dependent clauses functioning as nouns), they have no antecedent:

I write entirely to find out **what** I'm thinking, **what** I'm looking at, **what** it means. —Joan Didion, "Why I Write"

dir objs

I write entirely to find out what I'm thinking,
what I'm looking at,
what it means.

Interrogative Pronouns

Interrogative pronouns introduce questions.

Subject	Object	Possessive
who	whom	whose
which	which	whose, of which
what	what	

"Who have you been seeing?"*
"No one you know." —Ann Beattie, "Snake's Shoes"

Demonstrative Pronouns

Demonstrative comes from a Latin word meaning "to point out." **Demonstrative pronouns**, then, point out specific persons or things, often according to their proximity to the speaker (*this* is here, *that* is

---

* By the standards of formal English, Beattie's character used the wrong case, using *who* instead of *whom*. Even though the word comes first in the sentence, where subjective-case words usually appear, *whom* is the object of seeing ("You have been seeing *whom*").

there). Other times, they refer to previous things or ideas mentioned in the text (see the Russell Baker example below).

Singular	Plural
this	these
that	those

Inanimate objects are classified scientifically into three major categories—**those** that break down, **those** that get lost, and **those** that don't work. —Russell Baker, "The Plot Against People"

The demonstratives here are appositives for "three major categories":

. . . are classified into . . . **those** that break down,
those that get lost, and
those that don't work.

Indefinite Pronouns

> ■ *All I know about grammar is its infinite power.*
> —Joan Didion, "Why I Write"

Indefinite pronouns form the largest class and include a body of words that usually refer to nonspecific or uncertain persons or objects.

Singular	another, anybody, anyone, each, either, everybody, everyone, everything, much, neither, nobody, no one, nothing, one (a person, not a number), other, somebody, someone
Plural	both, few, many, several, others
Either	all, any, enough, more, most, some, such

David became aware that **something** wet and slug-like was lying on top of him. —Iris Murdoch, *The Sacred and Profane Love Machine*

Reflexive Pronouns

Reflexive pronouns appear in sentences where the doer and receiver of an action are the same. In other words, the *reflexive pronoun* serves as a direct object and "reflects" the subject.

	Singular	Plural
First-Person	myself	ourselves
Second-Person	yourself	yourselves
Third-Person	himself, herself, itself, oneself	themselves

Victorians, especially the men, pictured **themselves** as erect, noble, and splendidly handsome.
—Barbara Tuchman, "Mankind's Better Moments"

You let **yourself** in the front door and gingerly unlock the mail box. —Jay McInerny, *Bright Lights, Big City*

Emphatic Pronouns

Emphatic (or intensive) *pronouns* are the same in form as reflexive pronouns, but they serve as appositives to emphasize nouns or pronouns:

The old man next door said these leaping fish were carp. **Himself**, he preferred muskie, for he was a real fisherman and muskie gave him a fight.
—Margaret Laurence, "Where the World Began"

In other words:

He **himself** preferred muskie/He preferred muskie **himself** . . .

Reciprocal Pronouns

Reciprocal pronouns express mutual or "reciprocal" (from the Latin meaning "returning back") action between two or more persons or things:

each other   one another
They had to be together, share with **each other**, fight with **each other**, quarrel with **each other**.
—Virginia Woolf, *Mrs. Dalloway*

Pronouns and Antecedents

More than any other part of speech, pronouns depend for their meaning on other words, the antecedents to which they refer. For pronouns, especially personal pronouns, to work, *they* must refer clearly to a definite word, a trait which makes *them* especially important in establishing continuity and coherence in sentences and paragraphs. The following sentence has eighty-six words, yet it is held together by the string of pronouns clearly referring to the old Washington Park racetrack in Chicago:

Old Man O'Brien spoke of the good old days, gone by, of the Washington Park racetrack, with **its** Derby in the middle of June and the huge crowds it attracted, **its** eighty acres, **its** race course with a gentle slope from east and north that made **it** a faster track than a dead level one, **its** artificial lakes and garden works on the inner sides of the main track, **its** triple deck stands, **its** bandstands at one end of the stand, why, **it** was a dream.   —James T. Farrell, *Young Lonigan*

Notice how Farrell also uses the repetition of structure (parallelism) to reinforce the repetition of the pronouns:

the Washington Park racetrack, with   its Derby . . .
                                       its eighty acres,
                                       its race course with . . .
                                       its artificial lakes . . .
                                       its triple deck stands . . .
                                       its bandstands . . .

Pronoun Agreement

Pronouns must agree with their antecedents (the noun to which they refer) in person, number, and gender:

The **car** ran on merrily with **its** cargo of hilarious youth.
—James Joyce, "After the Race"

Corley was the son of an inspector of police and **he** had inherited **his** father's frame and gait.
—James Joyce, "Two Gallants"

Not   I realize now that because my feelings for **an individual** may not be as strong as **their** feelings for me, **their** feelings still matter and should still be respected.

But   I realize now that because my feelings for **someone** may not be as strong as **that person's** feelings for me, **that person's** feelings still matter . . .

Or   I realize now that because my feelings for **a woman** may not be as strong as **her** feelings for me, **her** feelings . . .

Not   You always told me a **child's** appearance and manners reflect **their** upbringing.

But   You always told me a **child's** appearance and manners reflect **its** upbringing.

Or   You always told me that **children's** appearance and manners reflect **their** upbringing.

However, even professional writers occasionally violate the principle:

There are about four times in a man's life, or a woman's life, for that matter, when unexpectedly, from out of the darkness, the blazing carbon lamp, the cosmic searchlight of Truth shines full upon **them.**

—Jean Shepherd, "The Endless Streetcar Ride into the Night, and the Tinfoil Noose"

The writer was talking about an individual, an individual of either sex but an individual, and that individual's personal moment of insight. Given the opening, the sentence should probably have concluded: "the cosmic searchlight of Truth shines full upon *him* (or *her*)." Can you think of any other solutions? Is this one of those cases where the plural would be inappropriately impersonal? The singular has the advantage of allowing us to focus our attention (and thus sympathy) on one individual rather than to disperse it over an indefinite number.

Compound Antecedents Joined by And

Compound antecedents joined by *and* usually take plural pronouns:

Jack and Jill dropped **their** buckets.

When the compound antecedent is joined by *or* or *nor, either . . . or, neither . . . nor,* or *not only . . . but also,* the pronoun agrees with the nearest part of the compound:

Not only Jack but also Jill dropped **her** bucket.
Not only Jill but also Jack dropped **his** bucket.

Collective Nouns as Antecedents

When the antecedent is a collective noun (*crowd, company, band, coven, team*), it takes a singular pronoun if it is thought of as a unit, a plural if its members are thought of as individuals:

The team took **their** positions in the field.
The team took **its** rightful place atop the standings.

Indefinite Pronouns as Antecedents

Indefinite pronouns are usually singular when serving as antecedents.

The value of **anything** comes to me in **its** use.

—Barry Lopez, "My Horse"

Some indefinite pronouns are plural:

both   few   many   some

Both dropped **their** buckets.

Many do not drop **their** buckets; they drop **their** pails.

And some indefinites can be singular or plural:

all   any   enough   more   most   some   such

Enough of the pie **is** left to feed the team.

Enough of the pies **are** left to feed the team.

Most of the money **is** missing.

Most of the coins **are** missing.

But not:

"Do you know where someone could find a good mechanic,
somebody who knows what **they're** doing?"   —TV commercial

Some indefinite pronouns, though technically singular in meaning
(*everybody, everyone*), still refer to the entirety of a group so in informal
usage they are often treated as plurals:

Everybody in France naturally tells about **their** education.
—Gertrude Stein, *Paris France*

Why is **everyone** comparing **themselves** to Toyota?
—TV commercial

Indefinite Pronouns and Gender

Unlike personal pronouns (*he, she, it*), indefinite pronouns do not indicate gender. Words like *everyone* and *everybody* might refer as easily
to a woman as to a man, although until recently custom dictated that
they should be referred to by a "generic" masculine pronoun:

No one can view the world with complete impartiality; and if
anyone could, **he** would hardly be able to remain alive.
—Bertrand Russell, "Knowledge and Wisdom"

Before you kill **somebody,** make absolutely sure **he** isn't well
connected.   —Kurt Vonnegut, Jr., *Slaughterhouse-Five*

In specific contexts the gender problem may not exist because the sex
of the *someone* or *somebody* may be known, as it is in the passage from
which the Vonnegut sentence is taken. In daily speech and in informal

writing, people frequently avoid the problem by using the plural. In formal writing, though, we must make a choice. The following are some solutions:

▶ Use *he or she*, or *him or her*. Many find this practice clumsy, especially when used repeatedly:

> Can anybody be so naive as to think **he or she** can learn anything about the past from those buxom best-sellers that are hawked around by book clubs under the heading of historical novels? —Vladimir Nabokov, *Lectures on Literature*

▶ Revise the sentence to use the plural:

> Can any readers be so naive as to think **they** can learn anything about the past from . . .

The drawback to this choice, however, is that the plural is more abstract and general than the singular. In some cases we want specifically to cite a hypothetical solitary individual.

▶ If your level of formality permits it, use the indefinite *you* (an increasingly popular choice among professional writers):

> Can anybody be so naive as to think **you** can learn anything about the past from those buxom best-sellers that are hawked around by book clubs under the heading of historical novels?

See if you can revise the sentence so the indefinite pronoun can be avoided altogether. Is anything lost?

Some writers continue to use the traditional masculine pronoun when an antecedent could be a member of either sex, but others are beginning to use the feminine in such cases:

> The true patriot cares little about flags, but instead focuses on working towards a nation of liberty and justice for all. **Her** countrypeople are all equal in **her** eyes, regardless of race, sex, age or personal behavior and beliefs. —letter to the editor

Other writers have found yet another solution: alternating gender references. Hence, in one essay, Annie Dillard refers to the typical writer as both male and female:

> People love pretty much the same things best. A writer looking for subjects inquires not after what **he** loves best, but after what **he** alone loves at all.
>
> Only after the writer lets literature shape **her** can **she** perhaps shape literature. —*The Writing Life*

We are going through a period of evolution and accompanying self-consciousness about gender references in our language. Time will ultimately sort out a commonly accepted practice. Until then, no single solution will satisfy everyone. Our best policy is to know our audience and proceed accordingly.

Pronoun Reference

By their very nature, most pronouns depend for their meaning on the words to which they refer. If pronouns are to be effective, if they are to be clarifiers instead of confusers, their references must be clear and appropriate:

> The Dallas Cowboys beat the Broncos by 17 points in **their** first Super Bowl appearance in 1978.   —sportscaster

Unless we knew that the Cowboys were in an earlier Super Bowl before playing the Broncos, we could take "*their*" to refer to either team. Here's another one:

> If a teacher knows the student understands the material, yet **he** blows a few assignments, **he** will be more lenient in assigning a grade.

The reader should know immediately to whom the second "he" is referring, but doesn't learn until half way into the clause.

Relative Pronoun Reference

Relative pronouns (the words that introduce adjective clauses) must fit their antecedents. *Who, whom,* and *whose* refer to persons:

> I have rarely known a man, **who**, with a smile and a shrug, could easily acknowledge being wrong.
> —Barbara Tuchman, "An Inquiry into the Persistence of Unwisdom in Government"

Which refers to animals or things:

> A typical aphid, **which** feeds entirely on plant juices tapped off from the vascular system of young leaves, spends winter dormant and protected, as an egg.
> —David Quammen, "Is Sex Necessary? Virgin Birth and Opportunism in the Garden"

> I left him to this thoughts, **which** were probably as small, ugly and frightened as the man himself.
> —Raymond Chandler, *The Little Sister*

And *that* usually refers to animals or things but can refer to people:

> **Wooden-headedness is a factor that plays a remarkably large role in government.**
> —Barbara Tuchman, "An Inquiry into the Persistence of Unreason in Government"

> **Nebraska Crane was a fellow that he liked.**
> —Thomas Wolfe, *The Web and the Rock*

Notice that *which* usually appears in clauses set off by commas, and *that* in clauses that are not.

Indefinite Use of You, It, *and* They

In everyday speech and informal writing, we frequently encounter *you, it*, and *they* without clear antecedents:

> **You can't really think hard about what you're doing and listen to the radio at the same time.**
> —Robert M. Pirsig, *Zen and the Art of Motorcycle Maintenance*

> **They say here that great waves reach this coast in threes.**
> —Henry Beston, *The Outermost House*

> **It says in the paper that the drought may last for another year or two.**

In most formal writing, including much of what we do in school, this casual use of *you, they*, and *it* as indefinite pronouns is inappropriate. When we mean to say "everyone in general," the accepted formal usage is the indefinite pronoun *one*, although many find this word too impersonal and academic. Consider the following sentence from a novel:

> **A city becomes a world when one loves one of its inhabitants.**
> —Lawrence Durrell, *Justine*

Compare:

> **A city becomes a world when you love one of its inhabitants.**

Which do you prefer? How much does the change in pronoun change the tone?

If we judge by usage or common practice, the status of the indefinite *you* is changing. The academic writer Jacques Barzun used the word freely in a study published in 1944:

> **The ultimate educational value of knowing a foreign language is that it lets you into the workings of other human minds, like *and* unlike your own. It takes you out of your narrow local self**

and points out ways of seeing and feeling that cannot be perceived apart from alien words that record the perception.
—*Teacher in America*

Current writers are using the indefinite *you* more and more frequently, in part because of the tendency toward less formality and in part because it sidesteps the gender issue. Rhetorically, the indefinite *you* may hang between the indefinite pronoun (*someone/anyone*) and the second-person pronoun we use in direct address (*you*). It both generalizes about "everyone" and particularizes by speaking to the reader. Perhaps the indefinite *you* just means "most of us." Whatever it means, writers use it to shorten the distance between themselves and their readers, especially when addressing a general audience.

Warning: You (the reader) should know that some teachers and editors still disapprove of the indefinite *you*, especially for more formal writing. Again, you must know what your audience considers acceptable.

Broad Use of This, That, and Which

In conversation and informal writing, *this*, *that*, and *which* frequently refer to a previous statement or idea rather than to a specific word. Although the meaning is often clear and the practice is becoming commonplace, many teachers and editors still frown on such use. The concern is that *this* can be vague and confusing:

> I passed all the other courses I took at my university, but I could never pass botany. **This** was because all botany students had to spend several hours a week in a laboratory looking through a microscope at plant cells, and I could never see through a microscope. I never once saw a cell through a microscope. **This** used to enrage my instructor.
> —James Thurber, *My Life and Hard Times*

> When you want to hurry something, **that** means you no longer care about it and want to get on to other things.
> —Robert Pirsig, *Zen and the Art of Motorcycle Maintenance*

> The most exhausting thing in life, I have discovered, is being insincere. **That** is why so much of social life is exhausting; one is wearing a mask.   —Anne Morrow Lindbergh, *Gift from the Sea*

One solution is to follow *this* or *that* with a noun (turning the demonstrative pronoun into a demonstrative adjective):

This failure occurred because of the requirement that all botany students had to spend several hours a week in a laboratory . . .

This inability used to enrage my instructor.

When you want to hurry something, **that** [*your*?] **impatience** means that you no longer care about it . . .

That need to be insincere is why so much of social life is exhausting.

To be safe, use *this* and *that* alone only when their antecedents are clear:

To have walked on the moon, **that** would be nice, but to be able to dance like Fred Astaire, **that** would be heaven.
—Tom Shales, "Fred Astaire, the Poet of Motion"

Ambiguous Pronoun Reference

A reference is ambiguous when the pronoun could have more than one possible antecedent:

If a dog really becomes a man's best friend **his** situation is desperate. —Edward Hoagland, "Dogs, and the Tug of Life"

Are dogs really desperate when they take men for their best friends? Some would say so. Probably, though, Hoagland (who is a fine writer) meant something like this:

If a man has a dog for a best friend, his situation is desperate.

The original version was ambiguous because the antecedent was implied in the modifier "man's." (See the next section, "Pronouns and Implied Reference.")

Or, consider the following from an exciting moment in a baseball broadcast:

"There's a fly to deep center field. Winfield is going back, back. He hits his head against the wall! **It's** rolling back toward second base!"

Presumably, the announcer meant that *the ball* was rolling back toward second base, either that or the Yankees (for whom Dave Winfield still played at the time) suddenly had a pressing need for a new outfielder. Or, take the following from a football broadcaster's commentary after a linebacker had pressured a quarterback:

"The one thing **he** wanted to do was disrupt **his** rhythm."

"He" did not want to disrupt his own rhythm but someone else's. To make matters clear, "his" should be replaced by a noun: *the quarterback's.* Then there is this revised example from a newspaper story:

> The Soviet pilot whose fighter jet crashed and killed a young man in Belgium after **he** bailed out this week appeared at a news conference yesterday to apologize publicly.

Had the sentence been written this way, "he" could refer to either the pilot or the young man (who might have been a passenger). To avoid confusion, the newspaper account used the very repetition of a noun that pronouns are supposed to help us avoid:

> The Soviet **pilot** whose fighter jet crashed and killed a young man in Belgium after the **pilot** bailed out this week appeared at a news conference yesterday to apologize publicly.
>
> —*Los Angeles Times*, 7 July 1989

The most graceful solution is usually to revise the sentence entirely until both the confusion and the repetition are eliminated:

> The Soviet pilot who bailed out of his fighter jet this week before it crashed in Belgium, killing a young man, appeared at a news conference yesterday to apologize publicly.

Of course this version still has a seventeen-word subject phrase, so it could use further revision:

> At an unusual press conference yesterday, a Soviet pilot apologized for bailing out of his fighter jet earlier in the week before it crashed in Belgium, killing a young man.

Pronouns and Implied Reference

In very formal writing pronouns should have a clear and specific antecedent, not one implied by a modifier:

> Although the births of the third and fourth children were unexpected, **they** were loved as much as the first two.

Technically, "they" should refer to "births" and not to the children mentioned in the modifying phrase. This mistake often occurs because we as writers know exactly what we mean and wrongly assume that the reader will, too. On the other hand, does anyone have any difficulty understanding this particular sentence? This principle is one that professionals occasionally ignore, and sometimes to the confusion of their readers. Rather than gamble that their implied reference will be understood, careful writers will revise the sentence.

Reference of Pronouns Ending in -self and -selves

In formal usage pronouns like *myself*, *yourself*, and *herself* should appear only in sentences that contain their antecedents:

> *Not*   Aided by Jeremy, Jason, and **myself**, Bill completed the move to Boulder Creek in one day.
>
> *But*   Aided by Jeremy, Jason, and **me**, Bill completed . . .

To some people's ears, these words sound more emphatic than *me*, *you*, and *she* or *her*, and for this reason we often hear the *-self* forms in speech.

Pronoun Case

Case is the form that a noun or pronoun takes to show its function in a sentence. There are three cases for pronouns in English: *subjective* (or nominative), *objective*, and *possessive*. The pronouns *I*, *we*, *he*, *she*, *they*, and *who* change form for each.

Subjective	*Objective*	*Possessive*
I	me	mine
you	you	yours
he	him	his
she	her	hers
it	it	its
we	us	ours
they	they	theirs
who	whom	whose
whoever	whomever	whosever

Using the Subjective Case

Pronouns are in the *subjective case* when they are being subjects, subject complements, or appositives to subjects:

> <small>subj</small>   <small>subj</small>   <small>subj</small>
> When I write, I like to have an interval before me when I am not likely to be interrupted.
> —William Stafford, "A Way of Writing"

Its/It's

Possessives create few problems, with one major exception: the misspelling of the third-person, singular, neuter possessive *its* as *it's* (it is). The **its/it's** confusion may be the most common and the most noticed of all writing errors. If you have trouble remembering, try to think of *his/hers/its* (not *hi's*, *her's*, *it's*). Or, you can use a playful memory aid credited to Jessica Mitford:

When is it its? When it's not it is. When is it it's? When it is it is.

Some also confuse *your* (possessive) and *you're* (you are), but not nearly so often. Remember: "You're your own editor."

Somebody behind him in the boxcar said, "Oz."

subj compl

That was   I.   —Kurt Vonnegut, *Slaughterhouse-Five*

appos

That was the narrator,   I,   behind him in the boxcar.

The case remains the same even when the pronoun is part of a compound:

EJ and I polished the entire set of silverware.

It was EJ and I who polished the entire set of silverware.

When in doubt, drop the first element of the compound and see if the pronoun sounds all right by itself:

I polished . . .

It was I who polished . . .

Using the Objective Case

Pronouns are in the *objective case* when they are being direct or indirect objects, the objects of prepositions, or appositives to objects:

dir obj

Cars pass us, driving fast as though on their way to somewhere else.   —Margaret Atwood, "The Grave of the Famous Poet"

ind obj

He wouldn't answer when his friend asked **him** what it felt like to be hit by a car. —Raymond Carver, "A Small, Good Thing"

prep obj

None of **them** knew the color of the sea.
—Stephen Crane, "The Open Boat"

Again, the case remains the same even when the pronoun is part of a compound:

dir objs

Not   One night my parents took **my husband and I** out to dinner.

But   One night my parents took **my husband and me** out to dinner.

Not   The room got silent and there was nobody there

prep obj

but he and I.

But   . . . there was nobody there **but him and me.**

Confusion on this issue is responsible for the following popular usage:

Between **you** and I . . .

Users of this expression often think they are being extremely correct, but the pronouns are objects of the preposition "between," so the more accurate form is this:

Between you and **me** . . .

Exception: Grammar would not be any fun if there were no exceptions. There is one instance when a pronoun serving as a subject is in the objective case: when the pronoun is acting as the subject of an infinitive:

Howard told **her to remain calm**, remain calm, and then he called an ambulance for the child and left for the hospital himself. —Raymond Carver, "A Small, Good Thing"

Grammarians consider the infinitive phrase "her to remain calm" to be the direct object of "told," with "her" being the subject of "to remain." The same applies to the following familiar expression:

The Devil made **me** do it.

subj   verb   dir obj

The Devil   made   me do it.

Using the Possessive Case

We use pronouns in the *possessive case* to indicate ownership, literal and figurative (*my* credit, *your* blame). Such possessives are regarded as adjectives (or *determiners*). Other possessives can appear alone:

> If our plan works, the credit is **mine**; if not, the blame is **yours**.

Subjects of Gerunds   When gerunds have "subjects," they are in the possessive case:

> **His** standing there makes the real boys feel strange.
> —John Updike, *Rabbit, Run*

Pronouns After Than or As Comparisons

Comparisons using *than* or *as* are frequently uncompleted (or *ellipted*). When we say, "They are luckier than we," we mean "They are luckier than we *are lucky*." The correct pronoun depends on our meaning:

> They pay the babysitter more than I [*pay the babysitter*].
> They pay the babysitter more than [*they pay*] **me**.

Using Who and Whom

The use of *who* and *whom* and of *whoever* and *whomever* depends on how they function *inside* a clause. *Who* and *whoever* are subjects.

Not   Our meeting finally came, and we both knew <u>**whom the**</u>
      other was.   (the other was *whom?*)

> *But*   Our meeting finally came, and we both knew <u>**who the**</u>
>   **other was.**   (the other was *who*)

The object of "knew" is not *who/whom* but an entire noun clause: "who the other was." Inside this clause *who* is a subjective complement: "the other was who." If you are confused by which form to use, restore normal word order:

> So **who/whom** are you going to believe?
> (You are going to believe *whom*—direct object.)

Do not be misled when the word appears inside of a clause that is itself an object or the object of a preposition:

> A's manager Tony LaRussa has spent a year telling <u>**whomever**</u>
> <u>**would listen**</u> that any of the four playoff games in <u>1988 could</u>
> <u>have gone either way.</u>   —sports column

The indirect object of "telling" is not "whomever" (which would then be in the objective case, but the entire noun clause "whomever would listen." The subject of a clause must be in the subjective case:

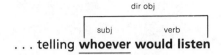

Shifts in Point of View

For the sake of consistency, do not shift abruptly from one point of view to another:

3rd pers   2nd pers

If one didn't do it the right way, **you** got in trouble.

                       2nd pers   1st pers   1st pers

In order not to hurt **your** feet, **we** all wore **our** sneakers into the water.

5

Adjectives

Definition

Adjectives are modifying words like those boldfaced in the following sentences:

> We saw then that we had been following **the** river—**brown, rippled,** and **wrinkled** and **streaked** from **this** height, with **many** channels between **long, thin** islands of green.
>
> —V. S. Naipaul, *A Bend in the River*

> She was so **lovely,** so **ruddy** and **delicate,** she was so **fresh** and **healthy-looking,** and she looked like **a good** child, **eager** and **full** of belief in life, **radiant** with beauty, goodness, and magic.
>
> —Thomas Wolfe, *The Web and the Rock*

Adjectives describe, limit, or otherwise modify nouns or noun substitutes, whether standing before or after the word they modify, or in the predicate position after linking verbs. Used properly, adjectives tighten and clarify nouns, sharpening images and ideas that would otherwise be vague and imprecise. As the previous examples illustrate, adjectives can be either objective or subjective, can either describe verifiable qualities or express the writer's feelings or evaluations. Hence, a good photograph can establish that the river is "brown, rippled, . . . and streaked"; but an unsympathetic onlooker might not find the woman "lovely, . . . fresh and healthy-looking," much less "radiant with beauty, goodness, and magic."

Classes of Adjectives

Most adjectives are *descriptive* and can be preceded by *very* (*brown, rippled, many, lovely, eager*). One subclass of these is the *proper adjective*, formed by adding suffixes to proper nouns (*Arabesque, Elizabethan, Maltese, Johnsonian*). The remaining adjectives fall into the following classes:

Articles		
Definite	the	(*the* river)
Indefinite	a/an	(*a* good child)
Demonstrative	this/these/same	(*this* height)
	that/those/such	(*those* islands)
Indefinite	another, each, both, many, any, either, neither, some, no	(*another* river, *some* channels)
Interrogative	what, which, whose	(*what* river, *which* islands)
Numerical	three, ten, third, tenth	(*one* river, *twenty* islands)
Possessive	my, your, his, her, its, our, their, one's	(*your* river, *their* islands)
Relative	what(ever), which(ever), whose/whosever	(*whichever* island)

Comparison of Adjectives

Descriptive adjectives change endings or take modifiers to express degree: *positive* (*plain*), *comparative* (*plainer*), and *superlative* (*plainest*). There is no simple rule, but generally one-syllable words add *-er* or *-est* to form their comparative and superlative, words of three or more syllables add *more* or *most*, and two-syllable words can do either, though they usually take *-er* or *-est*. There are also a few adjectives (like *good* and *many*) whose comparisons are irregular.

Positive	*Comparative*	*Superlative*
green	greener	greenest
full	fuller	fullest
ugly	uglier	ugliest
cunning	more cunning	most cunning
delicate	more delicate	most delicate
wrinkled	more wrinkled	most wrinkled
good	better	best
many	more	most
bad	worse	worst

Using the Comparative

In formal writing we use the *comparative* to express a greater or lesser degree, or to refer to two in a comparison:

              pos   comp
If the water was green, the vegetation was greener.

   comp   comp
She was fresher and healthier-looking than her gym teacher.

With the word *other* we can use the comparative to refer to more than two:

She was fresher and healthier-looking than the other students.

Using the Superlative

We use the *superlative* in formal writing to indicate the greatest degree or to describe three or more of something in a comparison. Superlatives, however, often represent subjective evaluations, the user's enthusiasm for the subject. Except when they concern measurable qualities, superlatives may reveal more about the attitude of the user than about the nature of the subject:

She is the freshest, healthiest-looking person I have ever seen.

She is the freshest and healthiest-looking of the trio.

Note: Unless we are deliberately striving for comic effect, we should avoid redundant use of the comparative and superlative. We form these with *-er* and *-est*, or with *more* and *most*, not with both.

■   *Predicate and Attributive: The Case of* Fun   ■

In daily speech we often hear *fun* used as an attributive adjective:

We had a fun afternoon.

In formal and even informal writing, however, *fun* should be used only as a predicate adjective:

The afternoon was fun.

Not   Our tabby is **more dumber** than our Siamese.

But   Our tabby is **dumber** than our Siamese.

Not   You are the **most contrariest** child.

But   You are the **most contrary** child.

Shakespeare could get away with "this was the *most unkindest* cut of all"; we cannot.

Adjectives in Sentences

Depending on their location in a sentence, most adjectives are either *attributive* or *predicative*.

Attributive and Predicate Adjectives

Attributive adjectives appear just before or after the words they modify ("a *good* child, *eager* and *full* of belief in life"). *Predicate adjectives* follow a linking verb and modify the subject ("She was so *fresh* and *healthy-looking*"). As a rule, because they are in the emphatic, news-carrying part of the clause, predicate adjectives are more emphatic than plain attributive adjectives, which usually play only a supporting role in a noun phrase. Compare:

The hills across the Ebro were long and white.
—Ernest Hemingway, "Hills Like White Elephants"
Across the Ebro were long, white hills.

Note: Some grammars also identify a third class, *appositive adjectives*, those which are set off from their nouns with commas:

Her eyes, cold and expressionless, remained on his eyes.
—John Steinbeck, *East of Eden*

This use of the term is not consistent with other uses of *appositive*, which usually identifies a structure that renames and can substitute for another. We should probably reserve the term for those occasions when adjectives are performing the usual appositive function:

> There was a **blurry** moon up, **pale** and **watery,** in the gently moving branches of the trees.   —Patrick White, *The Tree of Man*

"Pale" and "watery" are in apposition to "blurry." The adjectives pass the substitution test that usually identifies appositives.

Adjectives as Nouns

In some instances adjectives can also function as nouns. To transform an adjective into a noun, we precede it with an article:

> . . . but there are, I think, few styles of any kind that do not gain new strength from a passionate hatred of unreality, of **the wooly** and **the nebulous, the indefinite** and **the imprecise.**
> —F. L. Lucas, *Style*

Punctuation of Adjectives

For the sake of punctuation, we distinguish between *coordinate* and *cumulative* adjectives. In addition, we can also use hyphens to turn phrases and even clauses into adjectives.

Coordinate and Cumulative Adjectives

Coordinate adjectives modify a noun separately, so for conventional use we punctuate them with commas like any other series:

> The **clear, cloudless, brilliant** morning opened up.

Cumulative adjectives modify the cluster of words ahead of them, so we do not need to punctuate them:

> I bought a **scratched stainless steel** skillet at a garage sale.

When you are in doubt about whether an adjective series is coordinate or cumulative, apply one of two tests:

▶ Coordinate adjectives can be rearranged:

> The **brilliant, cloudless, clear** morning . . .

But not cumulative:

The steel, stainless, scratched skillet . . .

▶ Coordinate adjectives can be linked by *and*'s:

The clear and cloudless and brilliant morning . . .

But not cumulative:

The scratched and stainless and steel skillet . . .

The morning had opened up, clear and cloudless and brilliant.
—Flannery O'Connor, *The Violent Bear It Away*

Hyphenated Adjectives

Some noun modifiers consist of a series of words acting as a unit. Such modifiers are hyphenated when they come *before* the noun:

Bright-feathered birds screech, snakeskins glitter, as the jungle peels away.   —Bharati Mukherjee, "The Middleman"

But:

The screeching birds were **bright feathered.**

Entire clauses can serve as such compound adjectives:

Shine, who is an adherent of the **ours-is-not-a-perfect-system-but-it's-the-best-one-around** school of thought, says that Roy Cohn is the most effective trial attorney he has ever seen.
—Mark Singer, "Court Buff"

Which school of thought? The ours-is-not-a-perfect-and-so-on school.

Adjectivals

Adjectivals are structures other than adjectives that modify nouns: adjective (relative) clauses, participles, prepositional phrases, and infinitives. Like single adjectives, they can appear within noun phrases or be separated by punctuation.

rel clause
A man **who resembles a rodent** should never wear tweed.
—Mark Helprin, "The Schreuderspitze"

rel clause
That man, **who resembles a rodent,** should never wear tweed.

part phrase
A man **resembling a rodent** should never wear tweed.

prep phrase
A man **with a resemblance to a rodent** should never wear tweed.

inf phrase
If a man has the features **to resemble a rodent,** he should never wear tweed.

Wrong Places: Misplaced Adjectivals

Whether it is an adverb or an adjective, the right place for a modifier is as close as possible to what it modifies. Most writers have little trouble with adjectives themselves, but they will occasionally lose control of an adjectival, as in the following:

> She was wearing a blue dress the same color as her eyes **that her father had brought back from San Francisco.**
> —romance novel

Presumably, her father brought back the dress, not her eyes. In fact, the phrasing even suggests that he may have brought back eyes from other places ("her eyes that her father had brought back *from San Francisco*" [not the ones he brought back from Cleveland]). We can usually avoid such confusion by placing the modifier closer to the word it modifies, but not here:

> She was wearing a blue dress that her father had brought back from San Francisco the same color as her eyes.

The structural problem is two consecutive adjectival clauses modifying the same noun ("a blue dress [*that* was] the same color as her eyes *that* her father . . ."). Sometimes we can link the two with an *and*:

> She was wearing a blue dress that was the same color as her eyes and that her father had brought back from San Francisco.

But this version also sounds awkward. We need to try more drastic measures:

> She was wearing a blue dress, one the same color as her eyes, that her father had brought back from San Francisco.

> She was wearing a blue dress that her father had brought back from San Francisco because it was the same color as her eyes.

Sentences are not democracies. Their words are arranged hierarchically to stress a specific idea or piece of information. The original version was awkward because the writer had not decided which was more important, the fact that the dress was the same color as the character's eyes, or that her father had brought it back from San Francisco. Structural problems often reflect logical ones.

Verbs

Definition

Verbs are words like those boldfaced in the following sentences:

> There **was** not the sensation of the water's raging, but rather that of its alertness and resourcefulness as it **split apart** at rocks, **frothed** lightly, **corkscrewed, fluted, fell, recovered, jostled** into helmet-shapes over smoothed stones.
>
> —James Dickey, *Deliverance*

> A rather large blond cocker spaniel **tore** around the Cadillac, **skidded** a little on the wet concrete, **took off** neatly, **hit** me in the stomach and thighs with all four paws, **licked** my face, **dropped** to the ground, **ran** around my legs, **sat down** between them, **let** his tongue **out** all the way and **started** to pant. —Raymond Chandler, *The High Window*

The Passive Voice

The direct object structure is one of two principal ways we identify the recipient of an action. The other is the *passive voice*, in which the subject is the recipient. In fact, any transitive structure can be revised into the passive by taking its direct object, making it the subject, and changing the form of the verb:

dir obj
The cocker spaniel **licked** my face.

subj
My face **was licked** by the cocker spaniel.

Even though both versions relate the same event, the news changes: the first is about what the cocker spaniel did, the second about what happened to "my face."

Verbs are words that either report actions, or define or present states of being. The asserting, declaring words in predicates, they—more than any other part of speech—bring sentences to life and life to sentences.

Verb Types

There are three types of verbs, depending on the kind of assertion they make in the predicate: *transitive*, *intransitive*, and *linking*.

Transitive Verbs

Transitive verbs carry the action of the subject to a *direct object*, which is a receiver of the action. The "news" is this action and its recipient (and sometimes its time, manner, or location as expressed in an adverbial modifier):

verb dir obj   mod
The cocker spaniel **hit** me in the stomach and thighs.

verb   dir obj
The cocker spaniel **licked my face.**

Intransitive Verbs

Intransitive verbs report complete actions *by themselves* without taking a direct object (although they frequently have adverbial modifiers).

Their news, then, is a simple action and—often—its time, location, or manner:

> The water **split apart, frothed, corkscrewed, fluted, fell, recovered, and jostled.**

mod
> The cocker spaniel **dropped** to the ground.

Linking Verbs

Verbs are often described as "action words," but *linking verbs* do not report actions. Instead, they connect their subjects with noun or adjective complements, which identify or describe them. The news, then, is about the identity or nature of the subject itself rather than about its behavior:

compl   compl   adv mod
> The water **was alert** and **resourceful** as it split apart at rocks, frothed lightly, corkscrewed, fluted, fell . . .

compl
> The excited animal **was** a rather large blond **cocker spaniel.**

Linking verbs can also connect the subject with adverbial details of location, time, or manner:

> The raging waters were **over the banks.**

> The cocker spaniel was **in a near frenzy.**

Common Linking Verbs

appear	remain
be	seem
become	smell
feel	sound
grow	taste
look	

Note: Verbs that are normally transitive or intransitive may sometimes serve as linking verbs:

> The water under the bridge **ran** violent and deep.
> —Joseph Conrad, *Under Western Eyes*
> (The water *was* violent and deep.)

Writers sometimes prefer these more lively and descriptive words to the relatively static and colorless linking verbs. When we encounter such verbs in our reading, we can easily substitute some form of the *be* verb; and in our writing we can be alert for cases where a form of the *be* verb can give way to a more colorful and active verb.

Summary

Transitive	A falling sleet **turned** the roads into sheets of ice.
Intransitive	A sleet **fell,** turning the roads into sheets of ice.
Linking	The roads **became** sheets of ice in the falling sleet.

Tense

> *"Take three tenses."*
> *"Must I?"*
> *"Yes you must. Even a little boy like you has a past, a present and a future. You were a baby, you are a boy, you will be a man."* —Rumer Godden, *Take Three Tenses*

Verbs do not simply express actions or states of being; they express them relative to the moment of speaking or writing—as past, present, or future. This property is called *tense*, and grammarians recognize nine in modern English: the *simple* past, present, and future; the past, present, and future *perfect*; and the past, present, and future *progressive* (also called *aspect*).

Simple Tenses

Present Tense

Singular		Plural	
I	fall, skid, am	we	fall, skid, are
you	fall, skid, are	you	fall, skid, are
he/she/it	falls, skids, is	they	fall, skid, are

Past Tense

Singular		Plural	
I	fell, skidded, was	we	fell, skidded, were
you	fell, skidded, were	you	fell, skidded, were
he/she/it	fell, skidded, was	they	fell, skidded, were

Future Tense

I/you/he/she/it/we/they   will fall, skid, be

A sleet **fell** and **turned** the roads into sheets of ice. ■

Perfect Tenses

Perfect tenses indicate actions that have been completed by a certain time (*perfect* comes from a word meaning "finished, done"). They are a composite, formed by the helping verb *have* and the past participle. They are past, present, or future according to the tense of *have*.

Present Perfect

I/you/we/they	**have** fallen, skidded, been
he/she/it	**has** fallen, skidded, been

Past Perfect

I/you/he/she/etc.	**had** fallen, skidded, been

Future Perfect

I/you/he/she/etc.	**will have** fallen, skidded, been

A sleet **had fallen** that **had turned** the roads into sheets of ice. ■

A sleet **had fallen** and **turned** the roads into sheets of ice.

Progressive Tenses

Progressive tenses indicate simultaneous actions, actions in progress at the same time as something else. Like the perfect tenses, they are a composite, formed by the *be* helping verb and the present participle. They are past, present, or future according to the tense of *be*.

Present Progressive

I	**am** falling, skidding, being
you	**are** falling, skidding, being
he/she/it	**is** falling, skidding, being
we/you/they	**are** falling, skidding, being

Past Progressive

I	**was** falling, skidding, being
you	**were** falling, skidding, being
he/she/it	**was** falling, skidding, being

Future Progressive

I/you/he/she/etc.	**will be** falling, skidding, being

> A sleet **was falling** and **turning** the roads into sheets of ice.

> A sleet **had been falling** and **turning** the roads into sheets of ice.   (past perfect progressive)

Uses of Tenses

The simple past and future tenses express past and future action, but the present tense is more complicated. Action taking place *right now* is sometimes expressed by the present tense but usually by the present progressive:

> The cocker spaniel **is running** around my legs.

> You **are reading** this sentence and **wondering** if you want to be a writer.

> A sleet **is falling** and **turning** the roads into sheets of ice.

In addition to action currently taking place, the present tense expresses these:

❯ habitual action, including many generalizations (see the sections "Process" in Chapter 2, "Paragraphs," and "Present-Tense Narration" in Chapter 14, "The Rhetoric of Verbs and Verbals"):

The large blond cocker spaniel **is** excitable.

As a breed, cocker spaniels **are** excitable.

Sleet often **turns** roads into sheets of ice.

▶ action in plays, novels, movies, and the like (which can always be reexperienced in the present):

Burt Reynolds **plays** the part of Lewis, a self-impressed "survivor," in the film version of *Deliverance*.

In Raymond Chandler's *The High Window*, an overexcited cocker spaniel almost **assaults** the detective hero.

A typical astronomy textbook of the mid-18th century **has** chapters on such topics as time and celestial coordinates, and pages devoted to descriptions of the sun, moon and planets and their orbits.   —*Scientific American*, Feb. 1986

▶ future action if there is an accompanying adverbial detail of time:

In thirty minutes we **put** the dog in the trunk of the Caddy and **take** him to the pound.*

The perfect tenses express an action that has been completed prior to some other time:

▶ The *present perfect* reports action that has been completed before the present or an action that began in the past and continues in the present:

Marlowe **has met** the large blond cocker spaniel.

Reading about the large blond cocker spaniel **has begun** to irritate me.

The falling sleet **has turned** the roads into sheets of ice.   ■

▶ The *past perfect* expresses an action that has been completed prior to some other action in the past:

I **had gotten** tired of the cocker spaniel even before I began reading the section on perfect tenses.

---

* In addition to this form and the future tense, we also express future action two other ways. We use *going to* or *about to*: "We are *going to* take the dog to the pound." Or we use the present progressive and an adverbial of time: "Tomorrow we are taking the dog to the pound."

■   A falling sleet **had turned** the roads into sheets of ice.

▶   The *future perfect* expresses an action that will be completed prior to some other event in the future:

By the time you complete this section, you **will have grown** to hate cocker spaniels.

■   By then the sleet **will have turned** the roads into sheets of ice.

Tense Shift

Unwarranted shifts in tense, like those in point of view, send mixed signals that disorient the reader. The effect is a little like that of following a driver who keeps switching in and out of our lane. Advice for a writer using tenses is the same as for a lane-switching driver: pick one and stay in it. Thus, a narration that begins in the past tense should remain in the past tense.

Not   We no sooner **finished** our meal than he **turns** to me and **asks** if I **minded** paying.   (past to present to past)

But   We no sooner **finished** our meal than he **turned** to me and **asked** if I **minded** paying.

Or Even   We no sooner **finish** our meal than he **turns** to me and **asks** if I **mind** paying.

Some writers become confused when reporting action in novels, plays, movies, and other fictional narratives. Because such action is considered to take place in an eternal present (where we can always reexperience it), the standard practice is to use the present tense.

Not   *The Big Sleep* **opens** with Philip Marlowe visiting the estate of his client, General Sternwood. Before he **could get** his interview, however, Marlowe **was waylaid** and **interrogated** by the General's psychotic younger daughter, Carmen.

But   *The Big Sleep* **opens** with Philip Marlowe visiting the estate of his client, General Sternwood. Before he **can get** his interview, however, Marlowe **is waylaid** and **interrogated** by the General's psychotic younger daughter, Carmen.

For most purposes the only acceptable shifts in tense are those de-
manded by logic, but even then the transitions should be clear. For
example, we use the present tense to report habitual events, and the
past tense to report those that happened only once. But what if we
want to use a routine to establish a setting for a specific incident? We
will need to change tenses.

> Every August my family **rents** a cabin at Loon Lake, and we
> **spend** two weeks there sunbathing, sleeping in, collecting pine
> cones, counting stars, and generally trying not to think about
> our problems. Then, last year, one of our problems **followed** us
> to the lake.

Principal Parts

Every verb has four principal forms or parts: the *infinitive* (the form we
find listed in a dictionary—*be, find, list*), the *past tense* (*was, found, listed*),
the *past participle* (*been, found, listed*), and the *present participle* (*being,
finding, listing*). These, plus the present tense (in most cases the same as
the infinitive except for the third-person singular, which takes an *-s*),
comprise the forms with which we express all the moods and tenses.
When the infinitive and participial forms are actually serving as verbs,
they are accompanied by helping or auxiliary verbs like *be* or *have* (*was
being, had found, have been listed*). Used without the helping verbs, the
infinitive and participial forms are called **verbals,** words serving the
functions of other parts of speech (nouns, adjectives, adverbs) but keeping much of the energy and flexibility of verbs:

gerund noun phrase
He was disturbed by **finding the cocker spaniel in the driveway.**

part adj phrase
He was disturbed **finding the cocker spaniel in the driveway.**

inf adv phrase
He was disturbed **to find the cocker spaniel in the driveway.**

Regular and Irregular Verbs

We also classify verbs according to the spelling of their past tense and
past participial forms. Most verbs are *regular* (weak), so called because
they form their past tense and past participle in a regular and predictable
fashion, adding *-d*, or *-ed* (*recover*[*ed*], *jostle*[*d*], *lock*[*ed*], *trace*[*d*]). About
a hundred verbs, though, are *irregular* (strong). Instead of adding

sounds to create the past and past participle, they undergo less predictable changes of their internal vowels (*begin*, *began*, *begun*). As a result, they sometimes create problems for users, especially when combining with auxiliaries (thus, we hear people stumbling over whether to say things like "has stole" and "has stolen"). To master Standard English, you must learn the forms of each irregular verb separately. Because they are indeed irregular, there are no guiding rules to ease the task. When in doubt, consult your dictionary.

Principal Parts of Some Common Irregular Verbs

Infinitive	Past	Past Participle	Present Participle
(to) arise	arose	arisen	arising
(to) bring	brought	brought	bringing
(to) catch	caught	caught	catching
(to) dive	dived/dove	dived	diving
(to) do	did	done	doing
(to) dream	dreamed/dreamt	dreamed/dreamt	dreaming
(to) drink	drank	drunk/drank	drinking
(to) drive	drove	driven	driving
(to) fly	flew	flown	flying
(to) forget	forgot	forgotten, forgot	forgetting
(to) give	gave	given	giving
(to) grow	grew	grown	growing
(to) hang	hung/hanged*	hung/hanged	hanging
(to) know	knew	known	knowing
(to) lay	laid	laid	laying
(to) lead	led	led	leading
(to) lie (recline)	lay	lain	lying
(to) prove	proved	proved/proven	proving
(to) ring	rang/rung	rung	ringing
(to) see	saw	seen	seeing
(to) set	set	set	setting
(to) shrink	shrank/shrunk	shrunk/shrunken	shrinking

* to execute

Infinitive	Past	Past Participle	Present Participle
(to) sink	sank/sunk	sunk	sinking
(to) sit	sat	sat	sitting
(to) spring	sprang	sprung	springing
(to) steal	stole	stolen	stealing
(to) swear	swore	sworn	swearing
(to) swim	swam	swum	swimming
(to) swing	swung	swung	swinging
(to) wake	woke/waked	waked/woken	waking

Lie/Lay, Sit/Set, Rise/Raise

Writers and speakers often confuse some verbs because they sound alike, such pairs as *lie* and *lay*, *rise* and *raise*, *sit* and *set*. One way to keep them separate is to remember the distinction between *transitive* and *intransitive verbs*, those that take direct objects and those that do not. *Lie* (lie down), *rise* (ascend), and *sit* (sit down) are all intransitive; *lay* (to cause to lie), *raise* (elevate), and *set* (place) are all transitive. Hence, we must start by remembering their principal parts:

Intransitive	*Transitive*
lie/lay/lain	lay/laid/laid
rise/rose/risen	raise/raised/raised
sit/sat/sat	set/set/set

Thus:

We **lie** in bed today.

We **lay** in bed yesterday.

We **have lain** in bed all day.

               dir obj

We **lay** <u>the foundation.</u>

We **laid** <u>the foundation.</u>

We **have laid** <u>the foundation.</u>

Prices **rise.**

Prices **rose.**

Prices **have risen.**

               dir obj

They **raise** <u>the prices.</u>

They **raised** <u>the prices.</u>

They **have raised** <u>the prices.</u>

I **sit** at the table.

I **sat** at the table.

I **have sat** at the table.

               dir obj

I **set** <u>the table.</u>

I **set** <u>the table.</u>

I **have set** <u>the table.</u>

Helping Verbs

To form the simple present and past tenses, we need only a single verb:

I wake.   You wrote.

To form the other tenses and some moods, though, we use a **verb phrase,** a form of the main verb plus at least one other verb:

I was waking.   You will have written.

Verb phrases consist of the infinitive and participial forms plus **helping** or **auxiliary** (from a Latin word meaning "aid") **verbs.** These are either simple or modal.

Note: The term *verb phrase* is sometimes also applied to predicates— verbs plus helpers and any complements or modifiers.

Simple Auxiliaries

Simple auxiliaries are those helping verbs which can also function as main verbs by themselves: *be, have, do* (and sometimes *get*).

▶ *Be (am, is, are, was, were, be, being, been)* helps form the progressive tense *(be* + present participle: *was seeing)* and the passive voice *(be* + past participle: *was seen).*

▶ *Have* helps form the perfect tenses *(have* + past participle: *have seen),* in which an action is completed or "perfect."

▶ *Do* is used to ask questions, make negative statements, and create emphasis:

Does the water **corkscrew, flute, fall,** and **recover?**

Did the cocker spaniel **tear** around the Cadillac and **skid** on the wet pavement?

The water **did not create** a sensation of rage as it rolled over the rather large brown cocker spaniel.

Actually, after sliding on the wet concrete, the cocker spaniel **did not take off** very neatly.

I do like cookies.

Modal Auxiliaries

> ■ *The word* **should** *is a dangerous one to use when speaking of writing. It's a kind of challenge to the deviousness and inventiveness and audacity and perversity of the creative spirit.* —Margaret Atwood

Another group of auxiliary or helping verbs are called *modals* (so called because some express the kind of ideas once expressed more commonly by the subjunctive mood—*mode* and *mood* mean almost the same thing). The modals are *can/could, may/might, shall/should, will/would, must, ought,* and—sometimes—*dare* and *need.* The modals differ as a class from other verbs in having no *-s* in the third-person singular. The modals also lack infinitive and participial forms, seldom occurring alone but only as parts of verb phrases, where they are followed by a principal verb in the infinitive: "Hunger *would make* me weak." In speech, of course, the main verb is often ellipted—omitted but understood:

"Should you give them another try?"

"Yes, we should [give them another try]."

Note: Just as the present tense sometimes serves to report a recurring or habitual action ("He *works out* at the YMCA"), the modal *would* reports recurrent or habitual actions in the past:

There were hours when hunger **would** make me weak, **would** make me sway while walking, **would** make my heart give a sudden wild spurt of beating that **would** shake my body and make me breathless; but the happiness of being free **would** lift me beyond hunger, **would** enable me to discipline the sensations of my body to the extent that I could temporarily forget. —Richard Wright, *Black Boy*

Phrasal Verbs

Most verbs, except when they are using auxiliaries, are single words. There are, however, a significant number that consist of several words, a verb plus an adverb:

The water **split apart** at the rocks.

The large blond cocker spaniel **let out** his tongue.

(or, *let* his tongue *out*)

To illustrate just how many such verbs there are in English, look what we can do with *look*:

look after	tend
look down upon	scorn
look for	seek
look forward to	await eagerly
look in on	visit briefly
look into	investigate
look on	consider
look over	examine

Some of these phrasal verbs are transitive, some intransitive, and some both: "The water *split apart* at the rocks" (intransitive) and "The rocks *split apart* the water" (transitive). When they are transitive, we can use them in the passive voice.

Verb Agreement

In Standard English, subjects and verbs are supposed to "agree," meaning that singular subjects should combine with singular verbs and plural subjects with plural verbs. This requirement usually doesn't cause problems because singular and plural forms of the verb are the same except for the third-person singular, present tense:

I/you/we/they **write.**

But:

He/she/it **writes.**

There are some cases, though, where subject-verb agreement is more complicated.

Compound Subjects

Subjects joined by *and* usually take plural verbs:

My brother and I hang out in the side yard doing handstands until dark.

We at school know **Mr. and Mrs. Cuts** come from a family that eats children.   —Mark Richard, "Strays"

The rule of agreement still applies when the compound subjects are noun clauses:

How long and at what temperature pasta is dried <u>are</u> also important to the quality of cooked pasta.
—Korby Kummer, "Pasta," *The Atlantic*, July 1986
(*How long* [pasta is dried] and *at what temperature* . . .)

Exception: When the subjects joined by *and* refer to the same individual, they take a singular verb:

A wife and mother <u>begins</u> her new life in a new country, and that life is cut short.   —Bharati Mukherjee, "The Management of Grief"

Subjects joined by *or*, *either . . . or*, or *neither . . . nor* usually take a singular verb:

He or his brother <u>does</u> handstands in the sideyard until dark.

We at school know that either **he or she** <u>comes</u> from a family that eats children.

But when one subject is singular and the other plural, the verb agrees with the nearest:

Either he or his **brothers** <u>do</u> handstands in the sideyard until dark.

Neither his brothers nor **he** <u>does</u> handstands any more.

Linking Verbs

Linking verbs (the ones that connect their subjects with identifying nouns or describing adjectives) agree with their subjects, even when their complements are plural. Thus:

sing
The second most popular **fruit** in America <u>is</u> bananas.

pl
Bananas <u>are</u> the second most popular fruit in America.

But not:

The second most popular fruit in America **are** bananas.

This rule sometimes confounds even professional writers:

subj

The only **hint** this is cross-country season <u>are</u> the trees, which have ripened into harvest reds and oranges.

—*Sports Illustrated*, 11 Nov. 1989

(The hint *are* the trees?)

The reporter should have written:

The only **hint** this is cross-country season <u>is</u> the trees, which have ripened . . .

If, as often happens, you find this version jarring if still technically correct, then look for a way to recast the sentence:

The only hint this is cross-country season **is** the color of the trees, which have ripened into harvest reds and oranges.

Or, perhaps better:

Only the color of the trees **hints** that this is cross-country season, having ripened into harvest reds and oranges.

Relative Pronouns as Subjects

When a relative pronoun (*that, which, who*) is the subject of its clause, the verb agrees with the pronoun's antecedent:

Wilbur was merely suffering the **doubts and fears** <u>that</u> often <u>go</u> with finding a new friend.   —E. B. White, *Charlotte's Web*

(doubts and fears [that] *go*)

It is **the dirt** of the world with the sun shining on it <u>that aston-ishes</u> the poet when he is a boy.

—William Saroyan, *Bicycle Rider in Beverly Hills*

(the dirt [that] *astonishes*)

A **sleet** was falling <u>which turned</u> the roads into sheets of ice.   (a sleet [which] *turned*)

This rule of agreement remains true even for an expression like *one of those who*:

Not   He is **one** of those people who <u>chews</u> their grievances like a cud.

But   He is one of those **people** who <u>chew</u> their grievances like a cud.

He was one of those people who can chew their grievances
like a cud. —George Orwell, *Road to Wigan Pier*

However, when *one* is preceded by *the only*, the verb in the *who* clause
is singular because it then agrees with *one* instead of with the plural
object of the preposition:

He is **the only one** of those people who <u>chews</u> his grievances
like a cud.

Inverted Word Order

Verbs continue to agree with their subjects even when the verbs come
first. The practice applies to sentences opening with *there* and *here*:

Across the river <u>were</u> **the broken <u>walls</u> of old houses that
were being torn down.** —Ernest Hemingway, *The Sun Also Rises*

In the middle of the river where it had forked <u>was</u> **a long <u>sand
bar</u>.** —Norman Maclean, *The River Runs Through It*

There <u>were</u> **soft <u>pillows</u> on large couches and <u>walls</u> filled with
books and a <u>rug</u> cut in a thick rose pattern, and <u>iced tea</u> in the
hand,** sweating and cool on the thirsty tongue.
—Ray Bradbury, *Martian Chronicles*

Here <u>were</u> **soft <u>pillows</u> on large couches and walls . . .**

Falling and turning the roads into sheets of ice <u>was</u> a **sleet.** ∎

Singular Subjects Followed by Plural Words

When the noun headword* of a subject phrase is singular but is followed
by plural modifiers, it still takes a singular verb:

Not **The purpose of student teaching <u>internships</u> appear**
reasonably clear in the minds of most educators.

But **The purpose of student teaching internships <u>appears</u>**
reasonably clear in the minds of most educators.
—academic journal
(*Purpose*, not *internships*, governs the verb.)

* the nucleus, the word that the others modify

In some cases the reverse will happen: plural subjects will be modified by a singular modifier. The verb will then be plural:

The purpose and the funding of the internship appear set.

A subject continues to be singular even when it is followed by a phrase introduced by *along with*, *as well as*, *in addition to*, *together with*, and the like:

Not   There **were** a soft pillow on a large couch, as well as walls filled with books and a rug . . .

But   There **was** a soft **pillow** on a large couch, as well as walls filled with books and a rug . . .

Not   A soft pillow, as well as a large couch and walls filled with books, **were** available.

But   **A soft pillow,** as well as a large couch and walls filled with books, **was** available.

Collective Nouns

Collective nouns (words like *class*, *team*, *band*, *family*, *group*, *committee*, *audience*, *crowd*, and *couple*) are singular when we regard the group as a unit, and plural when we regard it as a collection of individuals or parts:

The couple is quarreling with other customers over where to sit.

The couple are quarreling with each other over where to sit.

The word *number* is a collective noun, meaning that it can be singular or plural, depending on our meaning. When preceded by *a*, it is always plural; when preceded by *the*, singular.

A number of teaching internships are available.

The number of teaching internships is low.

Noun Clauses as Subjects

In formal writing noun clause subjects always take singular verbs, even with plural complements:

What frustrates the workings of intellect is the passions and the emotions: ambition, greed, fear, facesaving, the instinct to

dominate, the needs of the ego, the whole bundle of personal
vanities and anxieties.

—Barbara Tuchman, "An Inquiry into the Persistence of Unwisdom in
Government"

When the subject is plural, though, and the noun clause is the complement, the verb must be plural.

Not Your heart and soul **is** what I aim for. —song lyric

But Your heart and soul **are** what I aim for.

Or What I aim for **is** your heart and soul.

Titles, Words as Words, and Plural-Sounding Words

These are all treated as singular nouns:

Cats, one of the longest-running hits on Broadway, is finally
going out of production.

I kept reading this advice in newspapers and hearing it on the
radio and hearing it during television performances, which is
to say from the media,* much as I hate to say it because
"media" is such an odious word.

—Russell Baker, "Racket and Reality"

Measurements and Figures

Subjects require a singular verb when they name a unit of measurement,
a period of time, or an amount of money:

These days, **$6,000** is not much to pay for a new car, nor is **25
miles** far to drive for such a bargain.

Voice

Voice is the characteristic of a verb that expresses whether the subject
of the verb either is doing something or having something done to it.
There are two voices, *active* and *passive*.

Active Voice

The **active voice,** as the term implies, suggests that the subject is indeed
an "actor" or agent (both from a Latin word meaning "to do"). In an

* plural of *medium*

active voice sentence the "news" is usually about what the subject is doing:

subj   verb   subj   verb

"I <u>discovered</u> early that **crying** <u>makes</u> my nose red, and the

subj   verb

knowledge <u>has helped</u> me through several painful episodes."

—Edith Wharton, *House of Mirth*

■   A falling sleet **turned** the roads into sheets of ice.

Passive Voice

The **passive voice** form of the verb means that the subject is indeed "passive" (from a Latin word meaning "to endure"), that the subject is acted upon instead of being an actor. In passive voice sentences the "news" is about what is happening to the subject:

> Mrs. Wilcox **cannot be accused** of giving Margaret much information about life. —E. M. Forster, *Howards End*

> It **was discovered** early by me that my nose **was made** red by crying, and I **have been helped** through several painful episodes by this knowledge.

■   The roads **were turned into** sheets of ice by the falling sleet.

The active voice is by nature more dynamic and direct (notice that the passive voice even uses extra words). The passive voice is suitable for emphasizing the dependence or helplessness of the subject (and sometimes for understatement, as in the Forster example). Beware, however. The passive voice allows someone to report an action or result without identifying who or what did it ("The roads were turned into sheets of ice"). As a result, it is useful for those who are trying to evade responsibility:

> "Mistakes were made."

> "Our earlier statement has been rendered inoperative."

> (Translation: Because you found out we were lying, we are going to withdraw our earlier statement and pretend we never made it.)

Passives *can easily be revised* into the active voice (We *can easily revise* passives . . .). We simply reverse the process described earlier: we take the subject of the passive sentence and make it the direct object of an active sentence:

Passive   **Mrs. Wilcox** <u>**cannot be accused**</u> **of giving Margaret much information about life.**

*   subj   verb*

Active   **No one** <u>**can accuse**</u> **Mrs. Wilcox of . . .**

*   verb   dir obj*

Uses of the Passive

Writers are frequently cautioned against using the passive voice because it is wordy, indirect, and relatively listless. Nevertheless, it is a tool like any other, and there are certain jobs for which it is well suited. In addition to those cases where from tact (or fear of a libel suit) we might want to avoid open mention of the doer, there are some instances in which the passive voice serves quite well:

▸ when we want to stress the passivity, dependence, or even help-lessness of the subject:

Today's global age of electronics is built on a miniature foundation of microscopic circuits engraved on silicon chips.
—*Scientific American*, Feb. 1990

Sharks, the skillful and storied hunters of the deep, are being threatened by even tougher predators—people.
—*New York Times*, 8 May 1990

▸ when, for the sake (or the appearance) of scholarly objectivity, we wish to represent certain notions as established or "givens," a common practice in scientific writing:

The immune system is commonly likened to an army and its various cells to soldiers. —*Scientific American*, Jan. 1988

The highest tides in the world are found in the Upper Bay of Fundy, which lies between New Brunswick and Nova Scotia.
—*Scientific American*, Nov. 1987

▸ when we want to use the *by* phrase to emphasize the identity of the doer of an action (which will appear in the emphatic final position):

We **were driven** through dark unfamiliar streets **by** one of those London cabbies who seemed to find his way like a night animal, with only the tiny slits of blue showing from the masked headlights that gave no light to drive by, but only warned pedestrians.   —Mary Lee Settle, "London—1944"

"The world **is held together by** the love and compassion of a very few people."   —James Baldwin, interview

■

> The roads **were turned** into sheets of ice **by** the falling sleet.

❿ when the phrase identifying the agent or doer would be too long in an active voice sentence, as some would say is the problem with the following newspaper leads:

Active   **A former engineering professor who says he invented the intermittent windshield wiper now used by every car and truck company in the world** has won a bellweather patent-infringement case against the Ford Motor Company.   —*New York Times*, 31 Jan. 1990

Passive   **A bellweather patent-infringement case against the Ford Motor Company** has been won by a former engineering professor who says he invented the intermittent windshield wiper now used by every car and truck company in the world.

Active   **Early findings from the most comprehensive large study ever undertaken of the relationship between diet and the risk of developing disease** are challenging much of American dietary dogma.
—*New York Times*, 8 May 1990

Passive   **Much of American dietary dogma** is being challenged by early findings from the most comprehensive large study ever undertaken of the relationship between diet and the risk of developing disease.

Other than for such purposes, though, it is usually best to avoid the passive, a form whose very indirectness can easily communicate a sense of uncertainty and evasion.

Mood

The **mood** of a verb indicates how the speaker or writer regards a statement. There are three moods in English: *indicative*, *imperative*, and *subjunctive*.

Indicative Mood

The **indicative** (from a Latin word meaning "to show or indicate") expresses that the statement is either a fact or a question about a fact. Most sentences are in the indicative:

The cheetah, a virtual running machine, **is** a model of aerodynamic engineering.

How **is** one to explain the cheetah's march to extinction?

—*Scientific American*, May 1986

Imperative Mood

The **imperative** (from a Latin word meaning "to command") gives an order, invitation, or plea. We form the imperative with the infinitive and with *you* as a subject, usually understood (or unstated):

Take a test drive today!   —a million commercials

It's not as easy as Chevy makes it look. Just **ask** Ford.
—magazine ad

Make a value judgment. The best car in its class. The longest warranty. Most rear seat leg room. The lowest price. And now an even better value with $500 cash back.   —magazine ad

Subjunctive Mood

The **subjunctive** is usually conjectural, expressing wishes, uncertainties, possibilities, suggestions, or statements contrary to fact:

Every man's work, whether it **be** literature or music or pictures or architecture or anything else, is always a portrait of himself.
—Samuel Butler, *Notebooks*

Note that the form of the subjunctive often differs from that of the indicative. With most verbs the difference is in the third-person singular, present tense:

Indicative	*Subjunctive*
He/she/it falls.	He/she/it fall.
He/she/it skids.	He/she/it skid.
(He falls.)	(Should he fall.)

The *be* verb, however, has subjunctive forms in the present and past tenses:

Present Tense

Indicative		Subjunctive	
I am	we are	(that) I be	we be
you are	you are	(that) you be	you be
he/she/it is	they are	(that) he/she/it be	they be

Past Tense

Indicative		Subjunctive	
I was	we were	(If) I were	we were
you were	you were	(If) you were	you were
he/she/it was	they were	(If) he/she/it were	they were

Uses of the Subjunctive

If the indicative is about "what is," the subjunctive, as well as certain *modals* (*can*, *might*, and the like), enables us to express what can or might be. Although the subjunctive does not occur as frequently as it once did, there are still instances where it is considered appropriate:

▶ in noun clauses expressing wishes, demands, requirements, or recommendations:

The division of labor among the cells of multicellular organisms requires that each cell population **be** able to call on the services of some cell populations and respond to the requirements of others. —*Scientific American*, Oct. 1985

Let the main ideas which are introduced into a child's education **be** few and important, and let them **be** thrown into every combination possible.
—Alfred North Whitehead, "The Aims of Education"

❱ in *if* clauses expressing conditions contrary to fact:

"If Thomas Jefferson **were** alive today, Terry Holland* would not be leaving the University of Virginia!" —sportscaster

❱ in certain idiomatic expressions left over from a time when the subjunctive was much more common:

Long **live** the king!   **Be** that as it may.

Suffice it to say.   **Come** rain or **come** shine.

Verbals

Recall that verbals are principal forms of verbs functioning as other parts of speech—as nouns, adjectives, or adverbs. Verbals, also called *nonfinite verbs,*[†] have all the properties of verbs except one: they can have tense, voice, and mood, and they can form phrases by taking modifiers and complements, but *by themselves*, without helping verbs, they cannot serve as main or predicate verbs. Rhetorically, their principal value is to breathe some of the vitality of verbs into other parts of speech that are otherwise static or inert. There are three verbals: *gerunds, participles*, and *infinitives*, and an important related structure called an *absolute*.

Gerunds

Whether alone or in phrases, **gerunds** are *-ing* forms of the verb serving as subjects, objects, appositives, or anything else a regular noun can be. Because of their *-ing* form, however, with its message of continuing action, gerunds are livelier than nouns, which usually name something already complete, fixed:

subj   prep obj

In many ways **writing** is the act of **saying** *I*, of

prep obj

imposing oneself upon other people, of

prep obj

saying listen to me, see it my way, change your mind.

—Joan Didion, "Why I Write"

---

* Terry Holland resigned as coach of the Virginia basketball team at the end of the 1989–90 season.

† Nonfinite (like *infinite*) means "not limited," that is, by person, number, or tense.

dir obj   dir obj
The telephone kept ringing and Castang kept not answering.
—Nicholas Freeling, *No Part in Your Death*

subj   subj compl
Enjoying living was learning to get your money's worth and

subj compl
knowing when you had it.   —Ernest Hemingway, *The Sun Also Rises*

subj
Having a football coach who works only with kickers is unu-

subj
sual. **Having one who's a woman is unheard of. Carol A. White
of Georgia Tech is both.**   —*Sports Illustrated*, 14 Nov. 1988

Participles

Alone or in phrases, **participles** are forms of the verb ending in *-ing* (present participles) or *-ed* and *-en* (past participles), usually serving as adjectives. Present participles with their perpetual motion *-ing* express an idea of simultaneous action. The **past participle** is less energetic, suggesting passivity or receptivity. (Remember, the past participle is the form we use in the passive voice.)

> We fought four hard rounds, **stabbing, slugging, grunting, spitting, cursing, crying, bleeding.**   —Richard Wright, *Black Boy*

> **Enchanted** or **enthralled,** I stopped her constantly to ask for details.   —*Black Boy*

> It was a genuinely awful speech, **rooted** at the beginning in a lie, **directed** at an imaginary enemy, **sustained** by false argument, **proposing** a policy that already had failed, **playing** to the galleries of prejudice and fear.
> —Lewis H. Lapham, "A Political Opiate," *Harper's*, Dec. 1989

Notice how the participial phrases work in the previous example:

> It was a genuinely awful speech,
>   rooted at the beginning in a lie,
>   directed at an imaginary enemy,
>   sustained by false argument,
>   proposing a policy that already had failed,
>   playing to the galleries of prejudice and fear.

■ *Revision Notes: Participles and Shorter Subjects* ■

Participial phrases offer one solution to overloaded subject phrases. In the following sentence a compound twenty-eight-word subject overpowers the predicate (normally the main carrier of news), making it almost anticlimactic, an afterthought:

> **The upheavals in the Communist countries in Eastern Europe and the Bush Administration's talk of closing bases and withdrawing troops from Greece, Britain, Italy, West Germany and Turkey have stepped up** the political momentum toward greater military spending cuts in Western Europe. *—New York Times*, 31 Jan. 1990

Granted, the sentence is overloaded to begin with and would probably read more gracefully if broken down into two or more shorter ones. A participial phrase opener, however, makes the one-sentence version more readable:

> **Impelled by the upheavals in the Communist countries in Eastern Europe, and by the Bush Administration's talk of closing bases and withdrawing troops from Greece, Britain, Italy, West Germany and Turkey,** political momentum is stepping up for greater military spending cuts in Western Europe.

In effect, the parallel participles illustrate five reasons why the speech was awful. The main clause *tells* and the participial phrases *show*.

Exercise: Finding Right Places

Because of the placement of its lengthy participle, the following sentence has a twenty-eight-word subject phrase. Relocate the participle and make any other changes necessary to make the sentence more readable:

> LONDON, Feb. 27—A long-secret document outlining concessions that the two main Protestant parties in Northern Ireland

are willing to make to break a political impasse in the British province was disclosed today in an Irish newspaper.

—*New York Times*, 28 Feb. 1990

Dangling Participles When a participle opens a sentence, structure dictates that it modify the noun or pronoun that immediately follows it, usually the subject of the main clause. But when meaning clashes with structure, and the participle attributes an action to the subject that it could not logically perform, we have a dangling participle:

subj
Tossing and turning all night, my alarm clock rang as soon as I finally got to sleep.

subj
Leaning against a tree, the warm brownish bark was soft to my touch.

Obviously, an alarm clock does not toss and turn all night, nor does bark merely lean against trees. Revised, the sentences make more sense:

Tossing and turning all night, I had just gotten to sleep when my alarm clock rang.

Leaning against a tree, I felt the soft, warm, brownish bark.

Leaning against a tree, I felt the brownish bark, warm and soft to my touch.

Exercise

Even professional writers occasionally write dangling modifiers. Can you correct the following?

1 Knowing that Mrs. Mallard was afflicted with heart trouble, great care was taken to break to her as gently as possible the news of her husband's death.
   —Kate Chopin, "The Story of an Hour"

2 Looking eastward from the summit of the Pacheco Pass one shining morning, a landscape was displayed that after all my wandering still appears as the most beautiful I have ever beheld. —John Muir, *The Yosemite*

3 Walking across the square to the hotel everything looked new and changed. —Ernest Hemingway, *The Sun Also Rises*

4 Trying to duck away, his left arm and his head became tangled on the wrong side of the top rope.
—Norman Mailer, "The Death of Benny Paret"

5 Driving east, the air through the car windows felt like the outdoor side of a window air conditioner, and you could smell the wet, sticky, East Texas air.
—Allen Weir, "Things About to Disappear"

6 Standing here beside the sleeping bag, out of the moonlight, more stars were visible. —Tony Hillerman, *A Thief of Time*

7 Whizzing down the autostrada, a steady stream of signs tell me how far I am from towns along the way.

- Anthony Lewis, *New York Times*, 2 Feb. 1990

Infinitives

Infinitives are *to* forms of the verb functioning as nouns, adjectives, or adverbs, although the *to* is frequently understood. Lacking the *-ing* form of the participle and gerund, infinitives are relatively static, but being free of any time reference whatsoever, even simultaneity, they do have an open-endedness that allows the writer a unique opportunity to generalize about certain activities, to express ideas of potentiality ("To dream the impossible dream").

Noun Infinitives

subj   compl
To read critically is **to read** with power.
—Andrei Codrescu, *The Disappearance of the Outside*

subj
To shift the structure of a sentence alters the meaning of that sentence, as definitely and inflexibly as the position of a camera alters the meaning of the object photographed.
—Joan Didion, "Why I Write"

subj
It is no less difficult **to write** sentences in a recipe than sentences in *Moby Dick*. —Annie Dillard, *The Writing Life*

appos
To have walked on the moon, that would be nice, but

appos
to be able to dance like Fred Astaire, that would be heaven.
—Tom Shales, "Fred Astaire, The Poet of Motion"

■   *Revision Notes: Infinitives and Gerunds*   ■

Noun infinitives and gerunds are often interchangeable:

Writing is the act of saying *I*.
(*To write* is the act of saying *I*, or, perhaps better, *To write* is to say *I*.)

Enjoying living was learning to get your money's worth.
(*To enjoy* living was *to get* your money's worth.)

Having a football coach who works only with kickers is unusual.
(*To have* a football coach who works only with kickers is unusual.)

To shift the structure of a sentence alters the meaning.
(*Shifting* the structure of a sentence alters the meaning.)

Contrast the variations. Sometimes the difference may seem too subtle to matter; other times the difference may be crucial. Do the following versions seem to work equally well? How do they *sound*?

Infinitive **To have walked on the moon,** that would be nice, but **to be able to dance like Fred Astaire,** that would be heaven.
—Tom Shales, "Fred Astaire, the Poet of Motion"

Gerund **Having walked on the moon,** that would be nice, but **being able to dance like Fred Astaire,** that would be heaven.

Gerund The telephone kept **ringing** and Castang kept **not answering.**   —Nicholas Freeling, *No Part in Your Death*

Infinitive The telephone continued* **to ring** and Castang continued **not to answer.**

* Idiom requires the verb change.

Note: Infinitive noun phrases are sometimes introduced by such words as *how*, *what*, *when*, *where*, *which*, and *whom*:

                prep obj   dir obj
Attention to how to say helps writers decide what to say.
—Constance Weaver, *Grammar for Teachers*

Adjective Infinitives

In early summer there are plenty of things for a child **to eat** and **drink** and **suck** and **chew.** —E. B. White, *Charlotte's Web*

(What kind of things? Things *to eat and drink and . . .*)

And when is there time **to remember, to sift, to weigh, to estimate, to total?** —Tillie Olsen, "I Stand Here Ironing"

Throughout history investigators have strived to build parachutes **to perform from ever greater heights, to decelerate at ever quicker rates, to withstand faster speeds, to provide ever gentler rides** and **to deliver ever heavier payloads.**
—*Scientific American*, May 1990

Adverb Infinitives

To write a column you need the egocentric confidence that your view of the world is important enough **to be read.**
—Ellen Goodman, "On Being a Journalist"

One by one we would be called home **to fetch** water from the hydrant in the back yard, **to go** to the store and **buy** meal for tomorrow, **to split** wood for kindling.
—Richard Wright, *Black Boy*

                    adj

He was eager **to be abroad in it, to know** his people; **to escape** for a little from the cares of building and founding, and **to go** westward from the old isolated Indian missions . . .
—Willa Cather, *Death Comes for the Archbishop*

(How eager? Eager to . . .)

> ■ *I write to make a difference. "It is always a writer's duty," said Samuel Johnson, "to make the world better." I write to give pleasure and promote aesthetic bliss. To honor life and to praise the divine beauty of the natural world. I write for the joy and exultation of writing itself. To tell my story.*
> —Edward Abbey, "A Writer's Credo"

Dangling Infinitives   To open a sentence an adverbial infinitive should modify the subject. When it does not, it is a dangling modifier, as in the following:

To better serve you in the future, please feel free to call ahead with any changes in your reservation.

■   *Revision Notes: Absolutes and Participles*   ■

In some cases absolute phrases may be turned into participial phrases, and vice versa. Consider the following from *Of Mice and Men* by John Steinbeck:

Absolute   A water snake slipped along on the pool, **its head held up like a little periscope.** (original)

Participle   A water snake slipped along on the pool, **holding its head up like a little periscope.**

Participle   Another little water snake swam up the pool, **turning its periscope head from side to side.** (orig.)

Absolute   Another little water snake swam up the pool, **its periscope head turning from side to side.**

Which you use depends on your focus: the simultaneity of an action—one thing happening at the same time as another—or a detail of an action.

To eliminate the confusion we must revise the entire sentence:

To better serve you in the future, we must be notified in advance of any changes in your reservation.

To ensure better service in the future, please call ahead with any changes in your reservation.

Absolutes

Consisting of a verbal and its subject, **absolutes** (sometimes called *nominative absolutes*) are phrases acting as modifiers of clauses or sentences, meaning that they are always set off by commas and that they can appear before, after, or in the middle of the structures they modify. When the verbal is a form of *be*, it may be understood. Appearing often in narrative and descriptive writing, absolutes are sometimes difficult to define, but usually easy to recognize and use. They allow the writer to move from the general to the specific, to go from the general action reported in the main clause to a specific detail of that action:

Pinkie shivered as he waited, **his gloved hand deep in his damp pocket.** —Graham Greene, *Brighton Rock*
(his gloved hand *being* deep/*thrust* deep)

At night the city is full of new sounds, the pulls and stresses of the wind, until you feel it has become a ship, **its old timbers groaning and creaking with every assault of the weather.**
—Lawrence Durrell, *Justine*

He woke in the chair and found himself leaning back, **his arms folded and his face turned upwards like a radar dish.**
—Saul Bellow, *The Dean's December*

Absolutes can also express some notion of cause:

The staircase window having been boarded up, no light came down into the hall.   —Elizabeth Bowen, "The Demon Lover"

The preparations being complete, the two private soldiers stepped aside and each drew away the plank upon which he had been standing.
—Ambrose Bierce, "An Occurrence at Owl Creek Bridge"

Here's one familiar to both supporters and opponents of gun control:

A well-regulated militia,* being necessary to the security of a free State, the right of the people to keep and bear arms, shall not be infringed.   —Second Amendment, U.S. Constitution

Summary

Gerund	A falling sleet began **turning** the roads into sheets of ice.
	A falling sleet caused **the road's turning into sheets of ice.**
Participle	A **falling** sleet turned the roads into sheets of ice.
	A sleet fell, **turning** the roads into sheets of ice.
Infinitive	A falling sleet began **to turn** the roads into sheets of ice.
	A sleet fell **to turn** the roads into sheets of ice.
Absolute	**A sleet falling,** the roads turned into sheets of ice.
	A sleet having fallen, the roads turned into sheets of ice.

* We no longer place a comma between the subject and its participle in an absolute construction.

Exercise

The following are more opening sentences from popular newspapers, magazines, and journals. What kind of interest or momentum do the verbals contribute to the stories they introduce? Given the nature of the opening, how would you expect the rest of the stories to go? Are the writers using any general strategies that might be useful with other material?

1 Asked to choose the most distinctive feature of the human species, many people would cite our massive brain. Others might mention our ability to make and use sophisticated tools. A third feature also sets us apart: our upright mode of locomotion, which is found only in human beings and our immediate ancestors.   —*Scientific American,* Nov. 1988

2 Kayaking the protected waters of south-eastern Alaska is an increasingly popular way to explore the state's wilderness waterways. Paddlers on guided and independent tours explore Glacier Bay and Misty Fiords . . .   —*Sunset,* June 1989

3 Capturing the proud spirit of Spain in northern New Mexico, Fiesta de Santa Fe celebrates its 276th year September 9 through 11.   —*Sunset,* Sept. 1989

4 Strung higgledy-piggledy along a seven-mile confusion of roads, England's Stoke-on-Trent, a city known as the Potteries, has a quarter-million people in six towns, Tunstall, Burslem, Hanley, Stoke-upon-Trent, Longton and Fenton—each with its own town hall.   —*Smithsonian,* Mar. 1989

5 Diving into Lake Malawi's tropical blue waters is like falling into a blizzard of fishes. A rainbow-hued fluorescent blizzard. —*Smithsonian,* Dec. 1989

6 Dipping a paddle, dropping a fishline, dining at dockside, walking grassy headlands, or watching a working waterfront—a hundred delightful involvements can draw you to the waters of San Francisco Bay.   —*Sunset,* Nov. 1988

7 Reintroducing the gray wolf to Yellowstone National Park after more than a 50-year absence would have minimal effect on other wildlife in the park or livestock on surrounding ranches, the National Park Service said in a report today. —*Los Angeles Times,* 17 Apr. 1990

8 To be born and raised in the United States is to be told that, in this land of opportunity, you too may someday grow up to be president. Getting straight A's and eating your broccoli is thought to help.

To be born Armenian and raised in America is to be steeped in another dream. —*Los Angeles Times*, 17 Apr. 1990

9 Chugging along in a narrow-gauge steam train, inching down cool mine shafts, swishing a gold pan in a clear stream, or riding horseback past ramshackle mine camps . . . in Colorado's historic gold country, it's easy to touch the past.

—*Sunset*, June 1989

10 Bowing to pressure from a student strike supported by faculty and alumnae, the trustees of Mills College voted today to rescind their decision to admit men to the 138-year-old women's college. —*New York Times*, 19 May 1990

7

Adverbs

Definition

Adverbs are words like those boldfaced in the following sentences:

> The aim of life is to live, and to live means to be aware, **joyously, drunkenly, serenely, divinely** aware.   —Henry Miller

> I suppose other things may be **more** exciting to others when they are at school but to me **undoubtedly** when I was at school the **really completely** exciting thing was diagramming sentences and that has been to me **ever since** the one thing that has been **completely** exciting and **completely** completing.
> —Gertrude Stein, "Poetry and Grammar"

> I love America **more** than any other country in the world, and, **exactly** for this reason, I insist on the right to criticize her **perpetually.**   —James Baldwin, "Autobiographical Notes"

> **Certainly** instruction in grammar by modern methods does **not** lead to any deeper understanding of **how** to resolve the prob-

lems that arise **incessantly** when we struggle to put thoughts
into words.
—Geoffrey Nunberg, "The Grammar Wars," *The Atlantic*, Dec. 1983

Adverbs, then, are modifiers of verbs, adjectives, other adverbs, or
entire clauses—of anything, in other words, not modified by adjectives.
In describing, qualifying, limiting, intensifying, or otherwise sharpening these words or structures, they usually give details of time, place,
degree, or manner. Like the other major modifier, the adjective, adverbs
are often subjective, interpretive, *telling* words.

Adverbs and Adjectives

Because they are often similar, and because many adverbs derive from
adjectives, adjectives and adverbs are sometimes confused. Although
they may not always be different in form, however, they are always
different in function. Adjectives modify nouns and pronouns; *adverbs
modify everything else.*

Adjectives	*Adverbs*
joyous awareness	**joyously** aware
more excitement	**more** exciting
a **complete** excitement	**completely** exciting
for this **exact** reason	**exactly** for this reason
the right to **perpetual** criticism	the right to criticize **perpetually**

Classes of Adverbs

On the basis of meaning, we can classify adverbs according to whether
they answer the questions *when* (adverbs of time), *where* (place), *how*
(manner), *to what extent* (degree), and *why* (cause).

Time   I had never **before** understood what "despair"
meant, and I am not sure I understand **now,** but I
understood **that year.**
—Joan Didion, "Goodbye to All That"
(*That year* is a noun phrase used adverbially: "I understood *then*.")

He was **once** wounded and left for dead in the
marketplace at Thame, **afterwards** had charge of
King Charles I's person at Carisbrooke Castle, and
later turned Royalist.   —Robert Graves, *Good-Bye to All That*

Place Some horses were looming in the rain, not near yet.
—D. H. Lawrence, *The Rainbow*

There the torches blazed the brightest, **there** the moon shone **out** like the day, and **there,** in tar-and-feathery dignity, sat his Kinsman, Major Molineux.
—Nathaniel Hawthorne, "My Kinsman, Major Molineux"

Manner He ducked, **excitedly, awkwardly,** into his brother's arms and out again, like a boxer from a clinch.
—Lawrence Durrell, *Balthazar*

I shall not argue that the study of grammar will enable students to write **interestingly, effectively, elegantly, eloquently, logically, persuasively,** or even **clearly** and **Intelligently.** —Bergan Evans
(But he will give a lesson on how to use the adverb of manner in a series.)

Degree And I did not really live in that world, **so** narrow and **so** trivial, **so** cruel and **so** unconscious.
—Katherine Anne Porter, "St. Augustine and the Bullfight"

Cause Someone asked me **why** a surgeon should write. **Why,** when the shelves are already too full?
—Richard Selzer, "The Art of Surgery"

Forms of Adverbs

Many adverbs have no distinctive form (*now, then, there, where, almost, very*). In fact, there is even a group of adverbs that have the same form as adjectives: *fast, hard, ill, well, better, best*, and so on. A larger group, though, derive from adjectives by adding -*ly*: *softly, rapidly, noisily, industriously, nervously*, and so on. In addition, there is another group of adverbs that have the same form as prepositions, most of them expressing spatial relationships: *up, in, out, off, over*, and so on. When these words are being adverbs, of course, they take no objects:

Adverb They went **out.**

Preposition They went **out** the window.

Note: Some adverbs have two forms:

bright/brightly	loud/loudly
close/closely	near/nearly
deep/deeply	tight/tightly
high/highly	wrong/wrongly

The Case of Hopefully

The adverb *hopefully* has attracted a host of critics who object to its use as a sentence modifier, as in the following:

Hopefully, this is the last time we will have to replace it.

Their logic is that "hopefully" does not modify any specific word in the sentence (like *is* or *replace*), so it is imprecise and even misleading. Such critics will accept the following use:

We installed the used engine hopefully. (with hope)

The use of *hopefully* as a sentence modifier is informal, a colloquialism meaning something like "it is hoped" or even "with luck," and poses no difficulties for native speakers. Whether or not the term ever becomes acceptable to grammarians, it is overused, which is reason enough to avoid it in our writing.

Sometimes these pairs are interchangeable, sometimes not. Idiom determines which we use.

Not   She came **nearly.**

But   She came **near.**

Not   She **slow** came near.

But   She **slowly** came near.

Not   **Late** she has stayed away.

But   **Lately,** she has stayed away.

Comparison of Adverbs

Like adjectives, many adverbs of manner, time, and place have degrees of comparison. The largest group of adverbs, those ending with *-ly*, express the comparison by using *more* and *most, less* and *least*:

Positive	*Comparative*	*Superlative*
eagerly	more eagerly	most eagerly
boldly	more boldly	most boldly
rapidly	less rapidly	least rapidly
easily	less easily	least easily

One-syllable adverbs form their comparisons like adjectives by adding
-*er* and -*est*:

Positive	*Comparative*	*Superlative*
fast	faster	fastest
hard	harder	hardest
soon	sooner	soonest

Some adverbs have irregular forms in the comparative and superlative
degrees:

Positive	*Comparative*	*Superlative*
badly	worse	worst
little	less	least
much	more	most
well	better	best

Note: All adverbs can use *least* to form the superlative.

In making comparisons the same guidelines apply to adverbs as to
adjectives. In formal writing we use the comparative to express a greater
or lesser degree, or to refer to *two* in a comparison:

Not   Of the two methods, the older one works **best.**

But   Of the two methods, the older one works **better.**

In formal writing we use the superlative to indicate the greatest degree
or to describe *three or more* in a comparison:

Of all the writers we surveyed, Gertrude Stein uses adverbs
most enthusiastically.   (not *more enthusiastically*)

Adverb and Adjective Confusion

Adverbs and adjectives perform different functions. One cannot do the
job of the other, at least not in formal writing. In daily life, though,
we often hear them confused (especially in sports broadcasts):

"We won the series because we played real **good.**"

Good is an adjective and as such can modify a noun but not a verb, as it does in the previous sentence. They play *well* but speak *poorly*. Another favorite:

"I feel **badly** about losing the series."

Badly is an adverb. The team probably lost because it *played* badly. If you are a fan, you feel *bad* ("feel" is a linking verb and takes a predicate adjective: *bad*). If, on the other hand, you cry at jokes, or with your eyes closed cannot distinguish an apple from a pineapple, you are feeling *badly*. (In this structure "feeling" is an intransitive, not a linking, verb, so it is followed by an adverb.) In colloquial speech *badly* is becoming an adjective.

link verb   adj
I feel **bad** [because I am ill].

intrans verb   adv
I feel   **badly** [because I am insensitive].

Double Negatives

In formal writing we do not use double negatives because, logically, one cancels the other. In everyday speech, though, we frequently hear people use double negatives, probably for emphasis:

"I **didn't** say **nothing**."

"He **won't never** shut up."

But in Standard English:

"I didn't say **anything**."   (Or, "I said *nothing*")

"He won't **ever** shut up."   (Or, "He will *never* shut up.")

Adverbs That Connect

In addition to being modifiers, some adverbs also introduce or connect clauses: *relative*, *interrogative*, and *conjunctive* adverbs.

Relative Adverbs

A *relative adverb* functions much like a relative pronoun, introducing a dependent clause while referring back to an antecedent in the main clause. The relative adverb also modifies the verb of the dependent clause:

She strolled around the house to the backyard **where** the blackberry vines clambered over the fence.

—John Steinbeck, *Cannery Row*

(*Where* refers back to *backyard* but modifies *clambered*.)

· The yellow traffic light fell on her temple, **where** I saw a single vein near the surface of the skin, crooking with the slight groove of the bone.   —Saul Bellow, *The Dangling Man*

Some other relative adverbs are *after, before, when,* and *why.*

Interrogative Adverbs

Interrogative adverbs, like interrogative pronouns, are used to introduce questions. We distinguish between the two by their functions *within the clause.* While the pronoun serves as a subject, complement, or object, the adverb modifies a verb, adjective, or adverb:

When is the game?   (adverb: The game is *when*?)

What is the game?   (pronoun: The game is *what*?)

Why are you playing?   (adverb: You are playing *why*?)

Who is playing?   (pronoun subject)

They asked **how** we were doing.   (adverb: doing *how*?)

Do you know **when** the election will be?   (adverb: be *when*?)

Conjunctive Adverbs

We use *conjunctive adverbs* to express a logical transition between independent clauses, entire sentences, or even between paragraphs:

accordingly	however	nonetheless
also	incidentally	otherwise
anyhow	indeed	still
besides	instead	then
consequently	likewise	therefore
finally	meanwhile	thus
furthermore	moreover	
hence	nevertheless	

To the extent that they connect, they are acting like conjunctions, but their principal effect is to provide a logical bridge or rhetorical transition; *hence,* some prefer to call them transitional adverbs.

Punctuation note: When these adverbs connect two independent clauses in a compound sentence, they are punctuated by a semicolon and a comma, as in the previous sentence. Without the semicolon, we have a comma splice.

> I was wearing a heavy coat, but I was absolutely freezing in the cold; **however,** Hemingway, when I asked him, said he wasn't a bit cold.

> I was wearing a heavy coat, but I was absolutely freezing in the cold; Hemingway, when I asked him, **however,** said he wasn't a bit cold.

> I was wearing a heavy coat, but I was absolutely freezing in the cold. **However,** Hemingway, when I asked him, said he wasn't a bit cold.   —Lillian Ross, "First Impression of Hemingway"

> Farming cannot take place except in nature; **therefore,** if nature does not thrive, farming cannot thrive.
> —Wendell Berry, "Nature as Measure"

Many consider such words to be less formal when they do not appear immediately after the semicolon.

> Farming cannot take place except in nature; if nature does not thrive, **therefore,** farming cannot thrive.

Adverbs and Adverbials

Adverbs are single-word modifiers of verbs, adjectives, other adverbs, or clauses. **Adverbials** are phrases and clauses that perform the same function. As a result, adverbials can also be classified according to time, place, manner, degree, and cause.

Time
> prep phrase
> I went up to Diamond Lake **for a few days**
> noun phrase
> that summer . . .   —Margaret Laurence, "The Loons"
> (I went up to Diamond Lake *for a few days then.*)

> prep phrase
> The first sound **in the mornings** was the clumping of the mill-girls' clogs down the cobbled street.
> —George Orwell, *The Road to Wigan Pier*
> (The first sound *then* was . . .)

dep clause

He was lacing up his shoes **when he spied the bluejay feather.** —Truman Capote, *Other Voices, Other Rooms*

(He was lacing up his shoes *then.*)

When the sleet fell, the roads turned into sheets of ice. ■

prep phrase

Place Each weed that grew **out of the gravel** looked like a live green nerve.

—Flannery O'Connor, "The Violent Bear It Away"

(Each weed that grew *there* . . .)

The first sound in the mornings was the clomping of

prep phrase

the mill-girls' clogs **down the cobbled street.**

—Orwell, *The Road to Wigan Pier*

(the clomping of the mill-girls' clogs *there*)

prep phrase

Manner Along the lake girls lay **like cut flowers** in the unnatural heat of a Sunday afternoon in May.

—John LeCarré, *A Small Town in Germany*

(The girls lay *how?*)

dep clause

Cause Grammar is a piano I play by ear, **since I seem to have been out of school the year the rules were mentioned.** —Joan Didion, "Why I Write"

inf phrase

They came down to the plain **to hunt** and

inf phrase

to grow their crops, but there was always a place to go back to. —Willa Cather, *Death Comes for the Archbishop*

Because a sleet was falling, the roads turned into sheets ■ of ice.

Wrong Places: Adverbs

Adverbs and adverbials are more mobile than any other part of speech; nevertheless, we cannot put them just any place, as the following illustrates:

Malone wants to play very badly in the Olympics.
—sports column

Depending on how we read this sentence, it can have two meanings, although the writer probably meant the following:

Malone wants very badly to play in the Olympics.

The original is confusing because "very badly" can modify either "wants" or "to play" (as in, He wants to play poorly). The same would be true if we reworded the modifier:

Malone wants to play very much in the Olympics.

This version means either that he very much wants to play, or that he wants to have a good deal of playing time. When a structure can modify in either direction, we call it a *squinting modifier*, as in the following:

The local American Peace Corps volunteer I was looking for later told me that the children were astonished by the sight of me. —*Washington Post*, 18 Aug. 1991

Did the writer look for the Peace Corps volunteer later, or did the volunteer tell something later? The second turned out to be the case. To avoid confusion, we need to relocate the modifier:

The local American Peace Corps volunteer I was looking for told me later that the children . . .

Later the local American Peace Corps volunteer I was looking for told me . . .

The same remedy works with other kinds of misplaced adverbial modifiers:

I acted as if it didn't bother me on the outside.

The person probably meant to say, "I acted *on the outside* as if it didn't bother me."

8

Prepositions

Definition

Prepositions are words like those boldfaced in the following sentence:

> They had a house **of** crystal pillars **on** the planet Mars **by** the edge **of** an empty sea, and every morning you could see Mrs. K eating the golden fruits that grew **from** the crystal walls, or cleaning the house **with** handfuls **of** magnetic dust which, taking all the dirt **with** it, blew away **on** the hot wind.
> —Ray Bradbury, *Martian Chronicles*

As the example shows, a *preposition* does the following:

▶ forms a modifying phrase *by* linking a noun or noun substitute (its object) *to* some other word *in* the sentence, usually a noun or a verb

▶ links *by* expressing or defining a relationship *between* its object (and its modifiers) and the word modified

In the Bradbury sentence, then, "of crystal pillars" is a phrase inside of a phrase, an adjectival modifier of "house," the direct object of "had": the house is composed of crystal pillars.

     subj   verb   dir obj

They   had   a house **of** crystal pillars

```
         noun        prep phrase (adj)
    a   house    of crystal pillars
```

```
         prep          obj
         of crystal pillars
```

The next two phrases modify *had*:

```
    They had it   on the planet Mars
                  by the edge of an empty sea
```

As this example shows, prepositional phrases can also be part of other prepositional phrases:

```
                  prep obj
    by the edge of an empty sea
```

```
                   prep obj
              of an empty sea
```

Note: On rare occasions prepositional phrases can also function as nouns:

```
             subj
    Outside the Public Library is where we first met.
```
—William Saroyan, *Bicycle Rider in Beverly Hills*

Kinds of Prepositions

In structural terms there are two kinds of prepositions, simple and compound. *Simple prepositions* are one-word prepositions. Many of the same words can act as adverbs. The difference is that adverbs appear alone while prepositions have objects. Here are the most common:

about	before	concerning	like
above	behind	despite	near
across	below	down	of
after	beneath	during	off
against	beside	excepting	on
along	besides	for	onto
amid	between	from	opposite
among	beyond	in	out
around	but	inside	over
as	by	into	past

regarding	throughout	under	upon
save	till	underneath	with
since	to	until	within
through	toward(s)	unto	without

Note: By some estimates, nine prepositions account for about 90 percent of all prepositional use: *of, on, to, at, by, for, from, in*, and *with*.

Compound prepositions are groups of words, often just pairs of prepositions, serving as single prepositions. Here are most of them:

across from	down by	in view of
ahead of	down from	in with
along with	down to	off into
apart from	down upon	off to
as for	due to*	on account of
aside from	except for	on through
as well as	exclusive of	out against
at about	for fear of	out for
away at	for the sake of	out of
away from	in addition to	out through
back in	in behalf of	over by
back of	in back of	over in
back through	in case of	over on
back to	in company with	over to
back toward	in favor of	owing to
back with	in front of	rather than
because of	in place of	pertaining to
belonging to	in regard to	right about
by means of	inside of	right along
by reason of	in spite of	right between
by way of	instead of	right from
contrary to	into	together with

* Be warned that some people object to the use of *due to* to mean "because of": "The A's have learned that relief ace Dennis Eckersley will be out for two weeks *due to* a strained shoulder muscle." Despite its occasional use by some professional writers, *due to* is still risky in formal writing.

up against	with a view	with the exception of
up by	with reference to	within
up on	with regard to	without
up to	with respect to	

> **Because of** a falling sleet, the roads turned into sheets of ice.

Prepositions and Idiom

English forms many idiomatic expressions with prepositions. Hence, we can alter the meaning of many verbs, nouns, and adjectives by combining them with specific prepositions. We are in the habit *of*, not *by* or *with*; we infer *from* and are proficient *in*; on some occasions we agree *to*, and on others we agree *with* or *on*; and so forth. Occasionally tripping up even native speakers, such idioms are among the last details mastered by those learning English as a second language. If you have difficulties with prepositional idioms, you should listen for awkward-sounding structures when reading your papers aloud. If some expression sounds questionable, consult an unabridged dictionary. It will include sample quotations to illustrate idiomatic usage.

Prepositions and Case

Pronouns serving as objects of prepositions are in the *objective case* (*me, him, her, us, them*). This practice does not cause difficulty for most users, except when a preposition has compound objects. We often hear people say, "between you and I," or "like you and I," when technically the form should be "between you and me," and "like you and me." When in doubt, place the first-person pronoun first. Few will like the sound of "between *I* and you" or "like *I* and you."

Prepositions and Subject-Verb Agreement

Sometimes there is confusion when a singular subject is modified by a prepositional phrase with a plural object. The noun or pronoun nearest to the verb is plural, so some yield to the impulse to make the verb plural:

sing   pl
Each of **them** **is** . . .   (each is)

sing   pl

The **source** of the <u>troubles</u> **is** . . .   (the *source* is)

The same rule applies when there is an intervening relative pronoun:

                   sing   pl

Not   A phrase is a **group** of related <u>words</u> that **function** as a single part of speech.   (*words* function)

But   A phrase is a **group** of related <u>words</u> that **functions** as a single part of speech.   (a *group* functions)

Prepositions at the End of Sentences

Even people who cannot tell a preposition from a parsnip "know" that a preposition is something you should not end a sentence *with*. This belief is a distortion of some stylistic advice dating from the seventeenth century. Observing that the final position in a sentence is emphatic, the poet and critic John Dryden recommended that we should *usually* save it for a word heavy in meaning—a noun or adjective or verb— and not for a preposition, which generally has less meaning (being what modern grammarians call a *structure* rather than a *content* word). Dryden did not say that writers should never do it, only that they should not do it too often. His rhetorical opinion was eventually accepted as a "rule," even by professional writers like Aldous Huxley:

> All men are snobs about something. One is almost tempted to add: There is nothing **about which** men cannot feel snobbish.
> —"Selected Snobberies"

To some, "about which" has a formal, even awkward ring to it, but Huxley would have risked the criticism of purists if he had written, "There is nothing which men cannot feel snobbish *about*."

Wrong Places: Prepositional Phrases

Prepositional phrases acting as adjectives almost always go right after the word they modify, but those acting as adverbs are more mobile. This mobility does not mean, however, that we can place them just anywhere:

> As early as 10,000 years ago Paleo-Indians hunted species of bison that are now extinct **on foot and with spears.**
> —"A Paleo-Indian Bison Kill," *Scientific American*, Jan. 1967

"On foot and with spears" is too far away from "hunted," and our first impulse is to attach the phrase to "extinct." The effect would be less awkward if we relocated the phrase:

> As early as 10,000 years ago, **on foot and with spears,** Paleo-Indians hunted species of bison that are now extinct.

Or:

> As early as 10,000 years ago, Paleo-Indians hunted now-extinct species of bison **on foot and with spears.**

Notice that the first revision also changes the focus from how the early Indians hunted to the fact that their prey is now extinct. The "news" of the sentence has changed.

And what of the following lapse by a highly respected novelist? Can you rephrase the sentence to help it read more clearly?

> There was no point in telling Phuong, for that would be to poison the few months we had left **with tears and quarrels.**
> —Graham Greene, *The Quiet American*

For a moment the sentence seems to say that they have this time left with tears and quarrels, and the narrator does not want to poison it. Of course, he actually means that tears and quarrels will poison the time they have left. Because of the misplaced prepositional phrase, meaning and structure conflict, arm-wrestling when they should be working hand in hand.

Here's one more example from an ad in the classifieds:

> For sale, Mazda RX7 driven by prof. woman with great body and low miles, $3400.

Conjunctions

Definition

Conjunctions are words like those boldfaced in the following sentences:

> Steroids can enhance muscle mass. They also can kill you, **if** they do not just decrease sexual capacity, injure your liver **and** heart, **and** do sundry other damages. Some people say: It's the athlete's body, he can mess it up **as** he pleases—besides, sports often involve injury. **But** it is one thing to injure yourself in exertion, another to injure yourself with chemicals in pursuit of the ultimate "edge." **And** it is surely unfair to force your opponent to choose between risking harm **and** competing at a disadvantage.
>
> —George F. Will, *The Morning After: American Successes and Excesses, 1981–1986*

Conjunctions, then, are connectors, words that join words, phrases, or clauses.

Kinds of Conjunctions

Normally, we distinguish three kinds of conjunctions: *coordinating, subordinating,* and *correlative.*

Coordinating Conjunctions

Coordinating conjunctions join equals—words, phrases, or clauses of the same grammatical rank. There are only seven:

and   but   or   nor   for   yet   so

Elements have the same grammatical rank when they serve parallel functions (subjects, objects, modifiers of the same word, independent clauses in a compound sentence, and so on). In other words, coordinating conjunctions announce the arrival of similar or related structures (and information). When the structures are not similar or related, we have faulty parallelism.

That morning he looked rugged **and** burly **and** eager **and** friendly **and** kind.   —Lillian Ross, *Portrait of Hemingway*

compls
That morning he looked   rugged **and**
                          burly **and**
                          eager **and**
                          friendly **and**
                          kind.

The fight raged down the steps **and** into the street **and** across the lot.   —John Steinbeck, *Cannery Row*

prep phrases (modifying *raged*)
The fight raged   down the steps **and**
                   into the street **and**
                   across the lot.

There was a crowd of kids watching the car, **and** the square was hot, **and** the trees were green, **and** the flags hung on their staffs, **and** it was good to get out of the sun **and** under the shade of the arcade that runs all the way around the square.   —Ernest Hemingway, *The Sun Also Rises*

ind clauses
There was a crowd of kids watching the car, **and**
the square was hot, **and**
the trees were green, **and**
the flags hung on their staffs, **and**

prep phrases
it was good to get   out of the sun **and**
                      under the shade of the arcade . . .

If sentence elements are parallel, we can insert conjunctions between them:

He lisped, he writhed, he flopped, he moaned, he howled, he fell back in despair.   —Jack Kerouac, *On the Road*

He lisped, **and** he writhed, **and** he flopped, **and** he moaned, **and** he howled, **and** he fell back in despair.

Coordinators as Openers

To say that coordinating conjunctions link words and structures of equal rank is also to say that they link related or "equal" ideas. It is quite natural, then, for them to appear frequently at the head of a sentence or even a paragraph, announcing its cohesion with the previous one. In other words, conjunctions are like adverbs: they can contribute to the cohesion of an entire essay by working between as well as within paragraphs. The following from George Orwell's "Shooting an Elephant" illustrates:

> To come all that way, rifle in hand, with two thousand people marching at my heels, and then to trail feebly away, having done nothing—no, that was impossible. The crowd would laugh at me. **And** my whole life, every white man's life in the East, was one long struggle not to be laughed at.
> **But** I did not want to shoot the elephant. . . .

A sleet fell **and** turned the roads into sheets of ice.
A sleet fell, **and** the roads turned into sheets of ice.

Subordinating Conjunctions

Subordinating conjunctions join unequals—clauses (and ideas) that are not of equal grammatical rank. More particularly, subordinators transform independent clauses into dependent adverb and noun clauses.

My mother left the room. My father grew angry with me.
My mother left the room **when** my father grew angry with me.   —Lillian Hellman, *An Unfinished Woman: A Memoir*

The "when" turns the second independent clause into an adverbial: "My mother left the room *then*." Here are some more examples:

Impulses are irregular. Habits, in a civilized society, have to be regular.
Impulses are irregular, **whereas** habits, in a civilized society, have to be regular.   —Bertrand Russell, *The Conquest of Happiness*

Marco Polo brought pasta from China to Italy. This idea is congenial to Italians. The hamburger came from Germany. This
idea is congenial to Americans.

The idea **that** Marco Polo brought pasta from China to Italy is
as congenial to Italians **as** the idea **that** the hamburger came
from Germany is to Americans.
—Corby Kummer, "Pasta," *The Atlantic,* July 1986

A sleet was falling. The roads turned into sheets of ice.
Because a sleet was falling, the roads turned into sheets
of ice.
The roads turned into sheets of ice **because** a sleet was
falling.
After the sleet fell, the roads turned into sheets of ice.

Because there are so many ways for ideas to be subordinate or
unequal, subordinating conjunctions far outnumber coordinators. The
following are the most common:

after	inasmuch as	though
although	in case	unless
as	in order that	until
as if	in that	when
as long as	now that	whenever
as though	once	where
because	rather than	whereas
before	since	whether
even though	so long as	while
how	so that	
if	that	

Subordinating conjunctions appear at the beginning of dependent
clauses to show their relationship to the independent clauses to which
they are attached:

When I was five, I had an experience that marked me for life.
—Flannery O'Connor, "Living with a Peacock"

I practiced the yo-yo **because** it pleased me to do so, without
the slightest application of will power.   —Frank Conroy, *Stop-Time*

Like *as a Conjunction*

In formal usage *like* is a preposition, not a conjunction. It should not introduce clauses, although it frequently does so in everyday conversation. We frequently hear *like* used in structures where formal usage calls for *as*:

Informal   Do **like** I say, not **like** I do.   (standard parental advice)

Formal   Do **as** I say, not **as** I do.

A sun was bursting the sky open, **like** Studs Lonigan busted guys in the puss.
—James T. Farrell, *Young Lonigan*
(*the way* Studs Lonigan busted guys in the puss)

Punctuation note: When such dependent clauses open sentences, they are usually set off with commas. When the clauses are brief, however, many writers will omit the punctuation, not feeling a need to reinforce the natural pause between *sentence anticipators* and the core of the sentence. Thus, O'Connor could have written:

When I was five I had an experience that marked me for life.

Such dependent clauses are usually not set off with commas *when they occur later in the sentence*, unless the writer wants to emphasize the qualification:

Such dependent clauses are usually not set off with commas, when they occur later in the sentence.

This second version implies that they usually *are* set off with commas when they occur earlier. Now, compare the following two versions by reading them aloud:

Such dependent clauses are usually not set off with commas unless the writer wants to emphasize the qualification.

Such dependent clauses are usually not set off with commas, unless the writer wants to emphasize the qualification.

A comma marks a pause, an interruption, setting elements apart for separate attention. In the second version the comma does indeed emphasize the qualification.

Correlative Conjunctions

Correlative conjunctions are simply conjunctions that are used in pairs to connect *either* words and phrases of equal grammatical rank *or* dependent and independent clauses. The following are the most common coordinating correlatives:

both . . . and   either . . . or
neither . . . nor   not (only) . . . but (also)

He writes **not** of the heart **but** of the glands.
—William Faulkner, Nobel Prize acceptance speech

He writes   **not** of the heart
             but of the glands.

He **neither** stirred **nor** fell, but every line of his body had altered.   —George Orwell, "Shooting an Elephant"

He   **neither** stirred
      nor fell but
every line of his body had altered.

It is good that large numbers of people should be craftsmen, **not** because there is the smallest prospect of their producing a correspondingly large number of good works of art, **but** because craftsmanship is something which most men and women find psychologically satisfying.
—Aldous Huxley, *Beyond the Mexique Bay*

The following are the most common *subordinating correlatives*:

although . . . yet   though . . . yet
if . . . then   since . . . therefore

If the sleet falls, **then** the roads will turn into sheets of ice.

If, after the ages of building and destroying, **if** after the measuring of light-years and the powers probed at the atom's heart, **if** after the last iron is rust-eaten and the last glass lies shattered in the streets, a man, some savage, some remnant of what once we were, pauses on his way to the tribal drinking place and feels rising from within his soul the inexplicable mist of terror and beauty that is evoked by old ruins—even the ruins of the greatest city in the world—**then,** I say, all will still be well with man.   —Loren Eiseley, "The Illusion of the Two Cultures"

■   *Conditional Propositions*   ■

The *if . . . then* correlatives figure in what logicians call a *conditional proposition*. The *if* clause contains the *antecedent*, a condition that is sufficient to guarantee a given consequence; the *then* clause expresses the *consequent*, that which of necessity follows from the antecedent. The two clauses interrelate, the conditional proposition not being true unless the consequence necessarily follows from the antecedent. To disprove the proposition, one must only demonstrate that the consequent does not always follow. Scientific writers often use such propositions to test theories, as in the following discussion of the idea that a meteor impact caused the extinction of the dinosaurs:

> Catastrophes have an important role to play in evolutionary thinking as well. **If** a chance impact 65 million years ago wiped out half the life on the earth, **then** survival of the fittest is not the only factor that drives evolution. Species must not only be well adapted, they must also be lucky.
> —"An Extraterrestrial Impact," *Scientific American*, Oct. 1990

In many cases, the *then* in a conditional proposition is understood, as in the following:

> **If** we do not redefine manhood, [then] war is inevitable.
> —Paul Fussell

As the preceding and the following illustrate, correlatives (subordinating or coordinating) need not appear in simple pairs:

> The loneliness of the city was brought home to me one early sleepless morning, **not** by men like me tossing in lonely rooms, **not** by poverty and degradation, **not** by old men trying with desperate futility to be out among others in the great roaring hive, **but** by a single one of those same pigeons which I had seen from my hotel window.   —Loren Eiseley, *The Night Country*
> The loneliness of the city was brought home to me . . .
>   **not** by men like me tossing in lonely rooms,
>   **not** by poverty and
>   degradation,

not by old men trying with desperate futility . . .
but by a single one of those same pigeons . . .

Wrong Places: Faulty Parallelism with Correlatives

Coordinating correlatives must join *like things*—parallel ideas placed in parallel structures, something forgotten occasionally *not only* by students *but also* by Nobel Prize winners:

> I feel that this award was **not** made to me as a man, **but** to my work . . .   —William Faulkner, Nobel Prize acceptance speech

> this award was **not** made to me as a man (verb phrase)
> **but** to my work (prep phrase)

Mr. Faulkner, noted for using *not . . . but* structures often and well, is guilty here of a mild case of *faulty parallelism*. He has used correlatives to join unlike things: a verb and its modifying adverb. He could have avoided this inaccuracy by placing *not* after the verb *made*:

> I feel that this award was made **not** to me as a man, **but** to my work . . .

> I feel that this award was made   **not** to me as a man,
>   **but** to my work . . .

Or:

> I feel that this award was **not** made to me as a man, **but** made to my work . . .

> I feel that this award was   **not** made to me as a man,
>   **but** made to my work . . .

Exercise

Can you correct the faulty parallelism of the following professional writers?

1 The romantics did **not** aim at peace and quiet, **but** at vigorous and passionate individual life.
—Bertrand Russell, *A History of Western Philosophy*

2 For the problem of the multiplicity of life **not only** confronts the American woman, **but also** the American man.

—Anne Morrow Lindbergh, *A Gift from the Sea*

3 A direct solution of social problems disturbs too many fixed arrangements. Society **either** does not want such solutions, **or** society is not up to them—it comes to the same thing.

—Paul Goodman, "Utopian Thinking"

The Rhetoric of Grammar

The Rhetoric of Sentences

Subjects: Short and Long

Consider the following two sentences:

> The noise of a late-lingering flock of wild geese going out to its day's feeding in the wheat fields **woke** me the next morning.   —H. L. Davis, *The Winds of Morning*

> We **ate** muskrat that night in a campsite on flat ground beside Big Sandy Creek, in Wilkinson County, innermost Georgia— muskrat with beans, chili powder, onions, tomatoes, and kelp.
> —John McPhee, "Travels in Georgia"

Then consider the next two:

> Alaska's annual grueling 1,200-mile Iditarod sled-dog race from Anchorage to Nome over some of the most remote terrain in the world **begins** Saturday.
> —*New York Times*, 28 Feb. 1990

> I **had** an acquaintance whose father became a very rich man in a very brief time through selling very ugly aluminum awnings.
> —Joseph Epstein, "Confessions of a Low Roller"

These pairs contrast two ways of distributing information in sentences:

For clarity, emphasis, and intelligibility, most readers will prefer the second version in each pair. This preference testifies to the equal importance of phraseology (right words) and location (right places). A basic sentence, we remember, is composed of two interacting phrases— the subject and the predicate. Most sentences begin with the subject phrase, which makes little sense until it is activated by the predicate phrase. The predicate phrase, in turn, does not make sense unless we can recall the subject phrase *in its entirety*. In other words, a sentence hinges on this transaction between the subject and the predicate, which does not begin until the subject is complete. When the subject is cumbersome (the subjects of the first sentence in each pair average over twenty words), the transaction drags. When the subject is brief, as it is in the second sentence in each pair, the transaction flies.

As a rule, then, sentences are clearer and more emphatic when most of the information is saved for the predicate. Clarity depends not so much on the amount of information as on its wording and location. Compare the original with a revision:

> **The noise of a late-lingering flock of wild geese going out to its day's feeding in the wheat fields woke me the next morning.**   (subject/predicate = 20/5)
>
> **I was awakened the next morning by the noise of a late-lingering flock of wild geese going out to its day's feeding in the wheat fields.**   (subject/predicate = 1/26)

Furthermore, the standard subject-predicate structure highlights the material in the predicate. The sentence's news, what the reader must take away from the sentence, is usually in the predicate. In this case the news is not the narrator's awakening but its cause. Nouns and noun phrases are names; verbs are actions. Put another way, subjects are mere static labels until predicates breathe life and motion into them. The story is in the predicate.

Exercise

Revise the following sentences to eliminate the overloaded subjects and the anticlimactic predicates. Attempt to keep as much of the original information as possible by relocating it. In some cases, however, it may be necessary to spread out the information over several sentences. There is more than one "right" answer, but the general solution is to get the verb closer to the beginning of the sentence.

1 The Senate debate on a landmark immigration bill that would make the first major changes in this country's legal immigration policy in 25 years and would set a new limit of 60,000 immigrants admitted annually **began** yesterday.

—*San Francisco Chronicle*, 12 July 1989

2 The congressman who introduced William Lucas at a Senate hearing on Lucas' nomination to the government's chief civil rights enforcer abruptly **took back** his support yesterday.

—Associated Press, 21 July 1989

3 The ratification of the agreement between the U.S. and the Soviet Union to ban all intermediate-range nuclear missiles and the apparent progress in the so-called Strategic Arms Talks (START), which have as their primary aim a 50 percent cut in the number of long-range ballistic missile warheads, **have given** many observers reason to be optimistic about the prospects for further reductions in nuclear arms.

—*Scientific American*, Sept. 1988

4 The mystery of how developing organisms choreograph the activity of their genes so that cells form and function at the right place and at the right time **is now being solved**.

—*Scientific American*, Aug. 1991

5 The testimony of Canadian sprinter Ben Johnson in Toronto last week before Canada's inquiry into the use of drugs and banned practices **produced** no big surprises.

—*Sports Illustrated*, 29 June 1989

6 How the linear information contained in DNA can generate a specific three-dimensional organism in the course of development from the fertilized egg **is** one of the great mysteries of biology. —*Scientific American*, Oct. 1985

7   A controversial Senate measure that would place broad re-
    strictions on the kind of work that can be supported by the
    National Endowment for the Arts **applies** to the National En-
    dowment for the Humanities as well.
    —*Chronicle of Higher Education*, 9 Aug. 1989

Subjects: Concrete and Abstract

Consider the two following sentences:

Decisions regarding the amount of education produced and
consumed **are made** without fully taking into account all of
the costs and benefits.

School boards [or, we] make decisions regarding the amount
of education produced and consumed without fully taking into
account all of the costs and benefits.

And the next two:

An understanding of the nature of knowledge in different
areas of learning **is** essential background for educators to have
in order to "put to work" the valuable resources available to
education.

Educators must understand the nature of knowledge in different areas of learning in order to "put to work" the valuable
resources available to education.

Again, for liveliness most readers would prefer the second version
in each pair. The credit for this preference belongs to the subjects, but
this time because of their content, not their length. The subjects of the
first versions are abstractions: ideas and activities that the reader cannot
visualize. (See the section "Abstract Nouns" in Chapter 3, "Nouns.")
Those of the revisions are human beings, alive, energetic, and responsible: someone identifiable is doing something, is acting. And once the
actor becomes more concrete, the action itself materializes. The improvement is more than cosmetic: just as movie ghosts can float through
walls, abstract subjects and predicates are likely to slip through the
reader's mental grasp.

In cases where we have tried too hard to be "academic" or authoritative, and our writing has become too abstract, we can begin reno-
vation by thinking directly and concretely about our subjects. We can
ask ourselves the simple question, "Who or what is doing something

here?" "School boards" and "educators" have much more presence and energy, and are easier to think about with accuracy and precision, than "decisions regarding the amount of education produced and consumed" or "an understanding of the nature of knowledge in different areas of learning."

Exercise

The following sentences, all of which are from academic journals, have problems with more than abstract subjects. (See discussion of passive voice in Chapter 6, "Verbs"; see also the section "Turning *Be* Words into Action Words" in Chapter 14, "The Rhetoric of Verbs and Verbals.") For the moment, however, concentrate on improving them by substituting good, strong subjects. In some cases you may have to make a guess about the implied actors.

1 The use of practical preparation experiences in teacher education programs has been expanded in recent years to include a formalized series of early field experiences.

2 One of the features of a quality program is the provision of print and non-print materials and learning facilities in quantity and quality consistent with the improvement of teaching.

3 Curricular innovations offering simulated participation in adult society, on adult terms, to exceptional youth only are not sufficient to promote realization of children's unique and varied potentials for social design and civic action.

4 In recent years, education has experienced numerous alterations in the methods espoused in teacher preparation programs because of increased attention to individualized instruction and competency based teacher education.

5 One of the major criticisms directed toward the graduates of initial teacher preparation programs is their inadequate or lack of preparation in subject knowledge.

6 The age-related trend away from a concern about facilities and discipline toward a more intellectualized preoccupation with curriculum and organizational environment, was clearly evidenced by the senior high responses.

7 More effort is being made by teachers to awaken the interest of the child and to allow him to pursue that interest at his own pace and in his own best learning style.

8   The assumption underlying the majority of these reports is
that competition should be relied upon as the motivation to
promote reform.

■ ▬▬▬▬▬▬▬▬▬▬▬▬▬▬▬▬▬▬▬▬▬▬▬▬▬

Sentences as News Carriers

Another way to look at sentences is to see them as carriers of "news"—
an idea or a specific piece of information that the content and structure
serve to highlight. In most basic patterns, as we saw, the news is not
in the subject but in the predicate—in the statement made about the
subject, usually either an identification or quality or action. Hence:

> **Taylor was wrong.**   —Bharati Mukherjee, *Jasmine*

The news here is starkly simple and adequate to the situation: Taylor
believed something and was disproven. All the necessary information
is in the adjective.

In some cases, though, the major news is not in the subject and
verb but in a modifier:

> **I became an American in an apartment on Claremont Avenue
> across the street from a Barnard College dormitory.**   —*Jasmine*

The principal news here is not the character's transformation (becoming
an American), which was announced earlier in the story, but its location, the environment in which it occurred. But look how a change
in word order changes the news:

> **In an apartment on Claremont Avenue across the street from a
> Barnard College dormitory, I became an American.**

Here, the act of becoming an American is the major revelation of the
sentence. The location sets the stage and makes the event climactic.
These two versions underscore the importance of word order, of right
places, in conveying news. A sentence is a sequence of information,
and the sequence determines emphasis.

In other cases repetition can carry the news:

> **She was a pale child with pale eyes and pale hair.**   —*Jasmine*

The news here is not simply the paleness of three separate things about
the child—her complexion, eyes, and hair. The three work together
to carry a message about her thoroughgoing paleness. She is completely, profoundly pale.

Other times several complete statements can work together to carry
the news:

There were scores of policemen swinging heavy nightsticks,
but none of them pounced on me at the bottom of the escala-
tor.   —*Jasmine*

The guilt and anxiety of the character (an illegal alien) tie these two
observations together. The "but," which usually expresses a contrary
idea, here implies the narrator's expectation that the authorities will
recognize and arrest her. The real news is her state of mind.

The idea of "news," then, is a vague but useful one. It means that
sentences (and paragraphs and essays) are unified by a controlling rhetorical purpose, the intention to impart some governing revelation or
to have some specific effect on the reader. All the details and component
parts work to clarify and emphasize this idea. Where sentences are
fused, or where they are run-ons or fragments, or where a paragraph
is rambling and disorganized, the writer has not settled on the news.
Looking for the news, whether explicit or implicit, is a good place to
start when our sentences do not seem to work.

Some Right Places: Modifiers, Anticipators, and Interrupters

Clarity and emphasis depend as much on word location as upon word
choice, especially in the case of *sentence modifiers*, those elements that
stand outside of the basic sentence patterns or main clauses. Sentence
modifiers (also called nonrestrictive or free modifiers) can appear in
three locations: before or after the main clause, or between major elements in the main clause:

▶ trailing modifier:

	subj	pred		mod

The robots   waited,   in yellow hair the color of the sun
and the sand.

	subj	pred		mod

A sleet   fell,   turning the roads into sheets of ice.   ■

▶ sentence anticipator:

	mod		subj	pred

In yellow hair the color of   the robots   waited.
the sun and the sand,

—Ray Bradbury, *Martian Chronicles*

■
                                mod   subj   pred
    Turning the roads into sheets of ice,   a sleet   fell.

▶   sentence interrupter:

        subj   mod   pred
    The robots,   **in yellow hair the color**   waited.
                   of the sun and the sand,

■
        subj   mod   pred
    A sleet,   **turning the roads into sheets of ice,**   fell.

Trailing Modifiers

The most common way to modify a sentence is to begin with the main
clause, a "complete" statement, and then add detail. The effect is usually that of increasing precision, with the main clause making a generalization and the *trailing modifiers* giving specifics. Take the following
example:

> Science gets most of its information by the process of reduc-
> tionism.

This statement is clear enough, but it only *tells*. It makes an assertion
without giving support. The full sentence, though, both tells and
shows:

> Science gets most of its information by the process of reduc-
> tionism, **exploring the details, then the details of the details,**
> **until all the smallest bits of the structure, or the smallest parts**
> **of the mechanism, are laid out for counting and scrutiny.**
> —Lewis Thomas, "The Tucson Zoo"

Or take a broad statement like the following:

> There had been a warm thaw all day.

Again, this sentence tells us something, but it doesn't show us anything.
It generalizes but does not illustrate. In the original, however, the writer
did not stop with the simple sentence pattern:

> There had been a warm thaw all day, **with mushy yards and**
> **little streams of dark water gurgling cheerfully into the streets**
> **out of old snow-banks.**   —Willa Cather, *My Antonia*

The main clause tells and the trailing modifiers show, just as a paragraph might begin with a thesis statement and follow with supporting arguments or illustrations. In fact, Cather could just as easily have put the information in several sentences:

> There had been a warm thaw all day. Yards were mushy and little streams of dark water gurgled cheerfully into the streets out of old snow-banks. . . .

In popularity, this general-to-specifics method easily outpaces others for presenting information in sentences and paragraphs.

Sentence Anticipators

Sometimes the news in the main clause depends on preconditions. These may be reasons, putting cause before effect, or they may set the stage some other way. In any event, the **sentence anticipator** structure signals that the importance of the news in the main clause derives from the prefatory information. Context creates significance. Take the following rather unpromising piece of news:

> He ran to the gardener's shed.

By itself, this action is bare. In the original, though, Dylan Thomas prepared for the event:

> **One morning towards the middle of December, when the wind from the farthest hills was rushing around the house, and the snow of the dark hours had not dissolved from lawns and roofs,** he ran to the gardener's shed.
> —*Adventures in the Skin Trade*

Or take a more complicated main clause:

> Women in bright dresses and men in bright shirts coasted and clustered.

The people could be coasting and clustering anywhere, but the writer is describing a group of friends having "a Renoir picnic on a construction site":

> **Among random piles of lumber and sand and tile, between cement mixer and bench saw and sawhorses,** women in bright dresses and men in bright shirts coasted and clustered.
> —Wallace Stegner, *All the Little Live Things*

And because sentence anticipators or sentence openers often have a built-in pause at the end, they are not always set off with commas:

When I get back home Du and another boy or man are on the living-room sofa talking in earnest Vietnamese.
—Bharati Mukherjee, *Jasmine*

Sentence Interrupters

Another kind of structure, by beginning an action and then suspending it, exploits tension. A sentence moves naturally from subject to predicate. When we read the subject, we expect immediately to see how it will interact with the predicate. Sometimes, though, the writer halts the momentum with intervening information, a **sentence interrupter**, implying that completion of the statement requires such material:

The thin village dogs walked lazily away from us.

The picture is clear if not memorable:

The thin village dogs, **pale in the moonlight, their shadows black below them,** walked lazily away from us.
—V. S. Naipaul, *A Bend in the River*

Notice how the writer pauses to sharpen the picture before presenting the action, which is then more striking. Naipaul mentions the village dogs, then the details that make them noticeable. Or consider this simple statement:

Jim Chee drove now uneasily.

Given the context, this can be significant news. However, it can be even more forceful:

Jim Chee, **who had always considered himself an excellent driver,** drove now uneasily.   —Tony Hillerman, *Listening Woman*

Exercise

A   Read each of the following sentences carefully, trying to appreciate the writer's location of sentence modifiers. What is the relationship of the information in the modifiers to that in the main clause? Then read the main clause without the sentence modifiers. How well does the main clause stand alone? Next, experiment with relocating the sentence modifiers in relationship to the main clause (sometimes this will require changing the form of the modifiers). What effect does this relocation have on the impact of the information in the main clause? Are there any versions in which relocating the modifiers does not work at all?

1 **Full grown without memory, the robots waited.** In green silks the color of forest pools, in silks the color of frog and fern, **they waited.** —Ray Bradbury, *Martian Chronicles*

2 **I see best the eyes,** large and softly brown with what seemed to be some hurt beginning to happen behind them—the deep trapped look of a doe the instant before she breaks for cover.
—Ivan Doig, *This House of Sky*

3 After months of being forbidden to drink, forbidden to smoke, forbidden to eat toffees, after months on a gloomy diet of grapefruit, raw carrots and underdone steak, **the girls were letting down furiously.**
—Nicholas Freeling, *King of the Rainy Country*

4 **Olivares,** who read the newspapers, though they were weeks old when he got them, who liked cigars better than cigarettes, and French wine better than whiskey, **had little in common with his younger brother.** —Willa Cather, *Death Comes for the Archbishop*

5 **The train,** which was black and sleek and elegant, and was called the Fireball, **had pulled more than halfway across the bridge when the engine nosed over toward the lake and then the rest of the train slid after it into the water like a weasel sliding off a rock.** —Marilynne Robinson, *Housekeeping*

6 **Leaphorn had been walking almost three hours,** slowly, cautiously, trying to follow tracks in the gathering darkness, **when he heard the sound.** —Tony Hillerman, *Listening Woman*

7 **She rose formidably and moved across the restaurant,** like a warship going into action, a warship on the right side in a war to end wars, the signal flags proclaiming that every man would do his duty. —Graham Greene, *Brighton Rock*

8 Considered by some in the 1960s to have become outdated, unprofitable, inefficient, messy, unnecessary, and out of style—to be just taking up space where revenue-producing office and apartment towers might stand—**the Pike Place Market might easily have been lost to urban-renewal efforts,** for which $40 million in federal funds had been appropriated and sat waiting.
—Ellen Posner, "A City That Likes Itself," *The Atlantic*, July 1991

B   Read and try to understand a writer's syntactic muscle-flexing as he describes a man harvesting a wheat field (you may have to read it several times):

> **Clyman Teal**—swaying and resting his back against the clean-grain hopper, holding the header wheel of the Caterpillar-drawn John Deere 36 combine, a twenty-nine-year-old brazed and wired-together machine moving along its path around the seven-hundred-acre and perfectly rectangular field of barley with seemingly infinite slowness, traveling no more than two miles an hour, harvest dust rising from the separating fans within the machine and hanging around him as he silently contemplates the acreage being reduced swath by swath, a pale yellow rectangle peeling toward the last narrow and ir-regular cut and the finished center, his eyes flat and gray— **squinted against the sun.** —William Kittredge, "The Van Gogh Field"

What effect do you think the writer is trying to achieve? How might the form and detail of the sentence fit the subject matter? See if you can create a loose imitation, perhaps writing about some action or process that unfolds "with seemingly infinite slowness" (like trying to write a paper).

More Right Places: Parallelism and the Series

Sentences carry meaning two ways: with words and with structures. We do not simply read words to understand their dictionary meaning; we also read to understand their function in the sentence. The reader then, must make a double effort to grasp both kinds of meaning. Take the following abridgment of the opening to *Cannery Row*:

> Cannery Row in Monterey in California is a poem.

We read the sentence by words and functions, like this:

subj   pred

Cannery Row in Monterey in California   is a poem.

We have to know the separate meanings of the first six words, but we must also know that they work together in a phrase to be the subject of the sentence. We then have to know the meaning of the next three words and realize that they work together as a unit, as the predicate making an assertion about the subject. Within the predicate we must then note that there are two subfunctions, the verb function and the complement or predicate noun function.

When sentences become a continuous sequence of both new words and new functions, particularly for extended periods, reading begins to creak and strain. Hence, writers frequently lighten their readers' task by using parallelism or a series—structural repetition. In Steinbeck's original sentence, then, there are twenty-six words, well above average length (about fourteen words by one count), but there are only three functions:

Cannery Row in Monterey in California is a poem, a stink, a grating noise, a quality of light, a tone, a habit, a nostalgia, a dream.   (subject + verb + complements)

The reader must register the individual meaning of words like "poem," "stink," and "grating noise," but the structural meaning remains the same; they all serve as complements, pointing back to the subject, "Cannery Row." In fact, because of the structural repetition, the reader has the luxury of focusing almost entirely on the meaning of the words. But parallelism has one more major effect. It does not merely ease the reading: by placing different words in the same structures, it is able to suggest that they have a related meaning. Their kinship is not only a functional one. In this case "a poem, a stink, a grating noise, a quality of light, a tone, a habit, a nostalgia, a dream" all share some common meaning because they are different names for that elusive place called Cannery Row.

Any structure in a sentence may be multiplied into a series:

How can the poem and the stink and the grating noise—the quality of light, the tone, the habit and the dream—be set down alive?   —Steinbeck, *Cannery Row*

```
                subjs
How can   the poem and
          the stink and
          the grating noise—
          the quality of light,
          the tone,
          the habit and
          the dream—be set down alive?
```

Our attitudes were made, defined, set, or connected; our ideas were discovered, discarded, enlarged, torn apart and accepted.
—Richard Wright, *Black Boy*

main clauses	main verbs
Our attitudes were	made,
	defined,
	set, or
	connected;
our ideas were	discovered,
	discarded,
	enlarged,
	torn apart, and
	accepted.

Parallelism creates such a strong expectation of similarity that writers can even omit certain words, knowing the reader will supply them:

Their steel helmets were square, their faces pale and sad.

—John LeCarré, *A Small Town in Germany*

ind clauses

Their steel helmets were square,
their faces [were] pale and sad.

These boys and girls were will-less, their speech flat, their gestures vague, their personalities devoid of anger, hope, laughter, enthusiasm, passion, or despair.   —Wright, *Black Boy*

ind clauses

	prep objs
These boys and	
girls were will-less,	
their speech [was] flat,	
their gestures [were] vague,	
their personalities [were] devoid of	anger,
	hope,
	laughter,
	enthusiasm,
	passion, or
	despair.

Ellipsis is the term for omitting words that are nevertheless understood to be present.

Writers also frequently reinforce their parallelism by repeating one or more words in each item in a series:

Throughout this period I read nothing, thought nothing, was nothing.   —Lawrence Durrell, *Justine*

Throughout this period I   _{preds} read nothing,
                                   thought nothing,
                                   was nothing.

A great artist transforms our world, removes scales from our eyes, plugs from our ears, gloves from our fingertips, teaches us to perceive reality differently.

—John Edgar Wideman, "Michael Jordan Leaps the Great Divide"

A great artist   _{preds} transforms our world,
                       _{dir objs}
               removes   scales from our eyes,
                              plugs from our ears,
                              gloves from our fingertips,
              teaches us to perceive reality differently.

He told himself he liked her, and repeated this; he liked her around him, liked to look at her, liked her laugh, liked her near him, liked to think of doing things for her, suffering, fighting, playing football, defending her against demons and villains, and anybody.   —James T. Farrell, *Studs Lonigan*

He   _{preds} told himself he liked her, and
       repeated this;
he   liked her around him,
       liked to look at her,
       liked her laugh,
       liked her near him,   _{gers}
       liked to think of   doing things for her,
                            suffering,
                            fighting,
                            playing football,   _{prep objs}
                            defending her against   demons and
                                              villains, and
                                            anybody.

Within a paragraph repetition can also emphasize the parallel function of entire sentences:

An economy that contains few different niches for people's differing skills, interests and imaginations is not efficient. An economy that is unresourceful and unadaptable is not efficient. **An economy that can fill few of the needs of its own people and producers** is not efficient.

—Jane Jacobs, "Cities and the Wealth of Nations," *The Atlantic*, Mar. 1984

In sum, parallelism—both in sentences and in paragraphs—provides not only clarity and emphasis and emotion, but also momentum. By not requiring us to register new structural information, parallelism—especially in a longer series—propels us from item to item. Properly used, it creates energy, symmetry, and focus.

Parallelism: The Rhetoric of Reversal

Parallelism, or at least parallelism of more than three or four items, creates a special effect, one based on repetition. It usually works by placing like words in like places. Sometimes, however, writers will use the very predictability of a parallel series to create startling reversals:

> I am an expert in stucco, a veteran in love, and an outlaw in Peru.   —student admissions letter
>
> an expert in stucco,
> a veteran in love, and
> an outlaw in Peru

The writer has pulled the rug out from under his readers by playing on and then betraying their expectations. His parallel series of balanced phrases conditions us to expect that *in* will be used the same way throughout. "Peru," however, changes the equation. The humorist Jon Carroll achieved a similar effect when he said that the best way to be popular is to "take credit and the first train out of town." Or consider the following:

> Larry Joe Bird emerged from the Boston Celtics' locker room at their practice site, Hellenic College in Brookline, Mass., last Friday afternoon, wearing jeans, an LSU Tigers cap (a gift from a fan) and a resigned expression.   —*Sports Illustrated*, 28 Nov. 1988
>
> wearing   jeans,
>   an LSU Tigers cap and
>   a resigned expression

Again, the last item violates our expectations. We do not wear an expression the same way we wear a hat, although the meanings are related. "A resigned expression" is emphatic for being the last item in the series, but it is even more emphatic because it breaks a principle. Parallelism usually works by placing "like things in like packages."

Here, the last package includes an item that is out of place. Of course the real subject of the story concerned Bird's need for resignation (because of injuries).

Other Places: Inversion

Sentences work because most of the time we can depend on certain structures to be in certain places. This predictability simplifies the reader's task: we often know in advance what kind of structure to expect, even if we can't predict the content. But this very predictability also gives writers another important resource. By departing from the standard word order (subject + verb + complement [+ adverbs]), they can heighten the reader's awareness by placing information in unexpected locations. The result is a degree of emphasis and interest often lacking in more predictable word orders. Take the following sentence from *East of Eden* by John Steinbeck:

> Associates he had, and authority and some admiration, but friends he did not have.

This is a compound sentence with two clauses in the transitive verb pattern (subject + verb + direct object), but with some of the elements reversed:

> direct object   subject   verb   direct object   direct object,   *but*
> direct object   subject   verb

The normal order would read:

> He had associates and authority and some admiration, but he did not have friends.

■

Exercise

A   Inversion is common in descriptive writing, especially where the writer is presenting locations. Read the following carefully, then revise each into the usual order: subjects first, then verbs, then any complements and adverbs. What happens to any sense of emphasis or drama? How does the "news" change? What reasons can you find for using inversion? And finally, what practical conclusions can you draw about the order in which you present information in sentences?

1   In the distance, on the horizon, stood the mountains, fat and placid as cows.   —Lisa Goldstein, *The Red Magician*

2   Southward, on the far side of the river, lies the Moab valley between thousand-foot walls of rock, too small to be seen from here.   —Edward Abbey, *Desert Solitaire*

3   On the side of the box car was the sign of the Great Northern Railroad, a mountain goat gazing through a white beard on a world painted red.   —Norman Maclean, *A River Runs Through It*

4   Emblematic of urban life in Seattle, and of its citizenry's stubborn grip, so far, on the real, is the Pike Place Market, a modest turn-of-the-century farmer's market that sits on a hill overlooking Puget Sound, just at the edge of the downtown business district.

—Ellen Posner, "A City That Likes Itself," *The Atlantic*, July 1991

5   From out the haze came the growl of a small airplane, invisible, and then the growl rose to a shriek as the plane plunged toward the earth.   —Peter Matthiessen, *At Play in the Fields of the Lord*

6   Out of the tangled jungle, among the ceiba* and mahogany trees, sprang Tikal†, with its 3,000 structures, ten reservoirs, and six temple-pyramids.

—David Roberts, "The Decipherment of the Ancient Maya," *The Atlantic*, Sept. 1991

7   On his pickup—which has three spare tires, a gun rack, and a searchlight—is a load of driftwood he has collected from the boat-landing eddy.   —John McPhee, *Coming into the Country*

8   Out of the clutter, looming up from the shaley roadway and backdropped by a yellow shale hillside, stood a high square grayish house, as if it were a giant crate absent-mindedly put down there.   —Ivan Doig, *This House of Sky*

B   Using content taken from your own observations, write imitations of some of the sentences.

In Summary

▶   A sentence is a sequence of phrases or word groups.

▶   A sentence presents a sequence of related information in order to make a single point (its "news").

* tropical silk-cotton tree
† ancient Mayan city

❯ Sentences carry meaning two ways: in words and in structures.

❯ Word location is often as important as word selection.

For Openers: Sentence Types

Basic Patterns

D. Constantine Conte lives in two worlds.

One is filled with the big money and beautiful people of Hollywood, where Mr. Conte, a six-foot, 200-pound man, hobnobs with movie stars and movie makers, such as Nick Nolte and Dino DiLaurentis. In this world, Mr. Conte, known as Dino to his friends, is a successful Hollywood producer, whose credits include "48 Hours" and "Conan the Barbarian." He's the man who co-produced "Another 48 Hours," the just-released sequel starring Eddie Murphy and Nick Nolte. And he's the man who, friends say, is generous and trustworthy, who always has a kind word for a secretary and whose mother lives at his home. . . .

But then there's the other world. In this one, Dino Conte is a convicted felon and onetime confederate of a reputed New York City mobster. . . .

—John R. Emshwiller, "Shadow Life: Hollywood Figure Has Criminal Past, Alleged Links with Mobsters," *Wall Street Journal*, 13 July 1990

Using a basic sentence pattern, one with almost no elaboration, this story begins tersely with a one-sentence paragraph: a simple generalization that turns out to be an understatement. In fact, the idea of "living in two worlds" is a cliche, but one that seldom applies so well as it does to the subject of the newspaper story. We can generalize with basic patterns, delivering concise, authoritative, even dramatic pronouncements ("The world is warming"). Usually, though, such statements require support and development. Hence, as abrupt as this opener is, it demands (and promises) explanation. Such a curt beginning has an energy and a momentum lacking in more leisurely openings, while suggesting the type of development that will follow. In fact, think of how easily we might write an essay about a public figure or a personal acquaintance: "X [my brother/neighbor/cat] lives in two worlds/leads two lives/has two personalities . . ."

Short Sentences

The world is warming. Climatic zones are shifting. Glaciers are melting. Sea level is rising. These are not hypothetical events from a science-fiction movie; these changes and others are already taking place, and we expect them to accelerate over the next years as the amounts of carbon dioxide, methane and other trace gases accumulating in the atmosphere through human activities increase.

—"Global Climatic Change," *Scientific American*, Apr. 1989

This paragraph starts with a rapid-fire sequence of four intransitive pattern sentences, a pattern that stresses action. Furthermore, they are in what we call the present progressive, a tense that reports an action happening right now. The cumulative effect of the repeated patterns is to dramatize the momentum and energy of a process that may be irreversible but that we must confront because it is already well underway. In other words, the authors exploit the properties of one kind of sentence structure to communicate a sense of urgency, to show as well as tell.

Here's another example:

For two weeks, David Ortega pouted. He paced. He stormed. He moped. He despaired.

Ortega, a Cal linebacker, had blown a play, a big one, against Oregon in the Bears' opener. Actually, he made two big blunders— first he took a fake, and then he missed a tackle.

—*San Francisco Chronicle*, 8 Oct. 1989

The sportswriter here also exploits the rapid-fire effect of a series of basic patterns, using but one prepositional phrase to modify the entire paragraph. The series creates a staccato rhythm that conveys the frenzy and unrest of the tormented athlete. The general tactic is to begin with a dramatic, almost violent narrative action, one that needs explaining. Even a mildly curious reader will want to know why Ortega has been carrying on so. Then the second paragraph explains. Even without such lively and imitative sentences, this kind of narrative opener is effective. Novelists have long known how to hook their readers by presenting characters engaged in mysterious behavior. Nonfiction writers have now added the tactic to their repertoires.

Interrogatives

Can a machine think? Can a machine have conscious thoughts in exactly the same sense that you and I have? If by "machine" one means a physical system capable of performing certain functions (and what else can one mean?), then humans are machines of a special biological kind, and humans can think, and so of course machines can think. And, for all we know, it might be possible to produce a thinking machine out of different materials altogether—say, out of silicon chips or vacuum tubes. Maybe it will turn out to be impossible, but we certainly do not know that yet.

In recent decades, however, the question of whether a machine can think has been given a different interpretation entirely. The question that has been posed in its place is, Could a machine think just by virtue of implementing a computer program?

—"Is the Brain's Mind a Computer Program?" *Scientific American*, Jan. 1990

Questions are good attention-getting openers for both readers and writers. For us as readers, they engage us immediately, asking us to respond, to search our own minds for some kind of provisional answer. For us as writers, they suggest a natural way of proceeding, either by giving our own answers immediately, or by postponing them until we summarize conventional thinking on the subject. They also make effective transitions within and between paragraphs, especially in informational and persuasive writing.

Imperatives

Imagine for a moment a doomsday scenario in which all life on the earth is suddenly annihilated. **Imagine** further that all the carbon in this dead organic matter is burned to form carbon dioxide and that the carbon dioxide is released into the atmosphere. The amount of carbon dioxide this scenario generates is less than human beings will have produced by burning fossil fuels within 200 years of the Industrial Revolution.

—"Modeling the Geochemical Carbon Cycle," *Scientific American*, Mar. 1989

The imperative, like the interrogative, is another way of engaging the reader more actively. As openers, both ask the reader to do something immediately, in this case to imagine a scenario. The imperative has an understood *you* as its subject; it is a form of direct address. Hence, it is almost like a wake-up call, or like being called on in class. Whatever our current or intended level of participation, the imperative asks us to step it up. To an extent, it also lessens the degree of formality and shortens the distance between writer and reader (as does the outright use of *you*). Writing works to the extent that the reader is involved, that the reader is participating with the writer in making meaning. The interrogative and the imperative help make this happen.

Fragments

Newspapers. Telephone books. Soiled diapers. Medicine vials encasing brightly colored pills. Brittle ossuaries of chicken bones and T-bones. Sticky green mountains of yard waste. Half-empty cans of paint and turpentine and motor oil and herbicide. Broken furniture and forsaken toys. Americans produce a lot of garbage, some of it very toxic, and our garbage is not always disposed of in a sensible way. . . . —William J. Rathje, "Rubbish!" *The Atlantic*, Dec. 1989

The title of the article and an accompanying picture informed the reader of the subject. Nevertheless, the noun fragments accomplished several purposes. One was to make the subject less abstract by presenting a series of dramatic if all-too-familiar images. Such strong sensory images not only make it easier for us to think about the problem concretely, but also stimulate us emotionally. But the fragments involve us most strongly by creating a structural puzzle: How will they relate to some future sentence? Fragments require inferential leaps, both structural and thematic. Used with restraint, and in such emphatic locations as openings, they can be effective.

"There" Pattern

There are some things that human beings can see only out of the corner of the eye. The niftiest examples of this gift, familiar to children, are small, faint stars. When you look straight at one such star, it vanishes; when you move your eyes to stare into the space nearby, it reappears. If you pick two faint stars, side by side, and focus on one of the pair, it disappears and now you can see the other in the corner of your eye, and you can move your eyes back and forth, turning off the star in the center of your retina and switching the other one on. There is a physiological explanation for the phenomenon: we have more rods, the cells we use for light perception, at the periphery of our retinas, more cones, for perceiving colors, at the center. —Lewis Thomas, "Lines of Inquiry"

Thomas uses the certitude and matter-of-factness of the "there" structure to remind the reader of a familiar phenomenon. He wishes to start with the phenomenon, not prove it, then move on from its existence to explaining its workings. The device is abrupt but efficient. Annie Dillard uses the same technique to open her essay "The Deer at Providencia":

There were four of us North Americans in the jungle, in the Ecuadorian jungle on the banks of the Napo River in the Amazon watershed.

Dillard doesn't want to explain how her party got there. Her interest is in something that happened while they were there. Both writers use the "there" pattern to avoid lengthy introductions. Imagine how quickly you can get into an essay or narrative by beginning, "There are three things I won't tolerate," or, "There were two of us waiting for the light to change."

"There" Pattern Series

There is the 15-year-old whose parents kicked him out of the house because he is gay. **There is** the 14-year-old girl whose mother brought home a man to help with the bills in exchange for sex with the girl. **There is** the 17-year-old boy who held up a store in his tattered neighborhood the day before he was awarded a college scholarship.

The stories are from guidance counselors in New York City public schools. As the problems they confront have grown vastly more serious than those of 20 or even 10 years ago, these counselors remain heavily overloaded.

—Felicia R. Lee, "Trying Times for Guidance Counselors," *New York Times*, 12 Feb. 1990

Here the "there" structures itemize some of the more tragic and sensational cases encountered by New York City guidance counselors. Each "there" emphasizes and individualizes; together, the repeated openers stress a common denominator. Notice also that the last sentence is not introduced by an *and*, which might suggest that the final case is the last of some sequence (the device of **asyndeton** applies to sequences of similarly structured sentences as well as to words and phrases). Instead, the structure suggests incompleteness, that the writer could continue, perhaps indefinitely, citing other equally serious cases.

One more:

There is a secret shrine on a sage-covered hill in the heart of the Zuni reservation where Indians exercise a radically new concept of their property rights every time it rains or snows, every time the sun bears down with the heat of day.

Inside the little red stone building sit 38 rare wooden statues of Zuni war gods, two to three feet high, austere and cylindrical, with rounded heads and stark, sharp faces. All belonged to museums and private collections, some for more than a century, until the Zunis launched a quiet, careful campaign to win them back. . . .

—Robert Suro, "Zuni's Efforts to Regain Idols May Alter Views of Indian Art," *New York Times*, 13 Aug. 1990

The Rhetoric of Nouns

A Tale of Two Openers

Consider the two following narrative openers:

> In the late summer of that year we lived in a house in a village that looked across the river and the plain to the mountains.
> —Ernest Hemingway, *A Farewell to Arms*

> At precisely 10 A.M. on Nov. 9, just 20 days after his team, the Oakland A's, lost the 1988 World Series, Dennis Lee Eckersley banged open the door and strode into the health and fitness facility at the University of Massachusetts Medical Center in Worcester.   —*Sports Illustrated*, 12 Dec. 1988

As starkly unalike as these two openers are, both are controlled by nouns or, more particularly, by the quality of detail carried in the nouns. Through its choice of nouns, each forecasts its own plan of development, makes its own particular demands on the audience, and sets its own distinctive pace. The first sentence relies on the most broadly inclusive type of noun, the common noun: "summer," "year," "house," "village," "river," "plain," and "mountains." The second, in typical *Sports Illustrated* fashion, exploits proper nouns, the specific, particular ones that we capitalize: "Nov. 9," "the Oakland A's," "1988 World Series," "Dennis Lee Eckersley," the "University of Massachusetts," and "Worcester." Though rhetorically opposite in key respects, the two are excellent examples of their kind.

Of course, we might explain some of the differences between the two openers by acknowledging that they represent two different types of writing; the first is "literary" and the second is journalistic. Hemingway, the novelist, was writing a general story for a general audience. By avoiding or postponing precise, circumstantial detail, he was broadening his appeal, striving for an effect of universality: initially, the reader is invited to fill in the "blanks," to supply the images of particular houses and villages. The story could have taken place wherever there was a house, a village, a river, a plain, and some mountains. It could have happened on any continent and in any age. At the same time, he was also encouraging his readers to maintain, or at least to begin with, a degree of detachment and reflection, to keep enough emotional distance to allow room for judgment and understanding. His language invites readers to think about *significance*.

The readers of journalism do not want philosophical generalities; they want accurate, timely information—the kind expressed by highly concrete and particular nouns. The readers of *Sports Illustrated* are especially hungry for precise details. They buy the weekly magazine to learn more about the sporting events they have already watched on television or read about in daily newspapers. They want to be more than casual spectators. They want to go behind the scenes of the action, to have an insider's knowledge, to feel they are right next to athletes as they train or compete (or seek physical therapy). Composing a much more specialized audience than the one Hemingway addressed, they are highly sports literate (they do not have to be told that Eckersley was the star relief pitcher of the Athletics who gave up a game-winning home run to Kirk Gibson of the Los Angeles Dodgers in the first game of the 1988 World Series). They already have a wide store of information, so journalists must strain to satisfy their appetite for fresh, up-to-date detail (for example, most probably didn't know Dennis Eckersley's middle name). Such writing is indeed "news," but it is also the nature of news to become quickly dated.

The difference in types of writing alone, however, does not explain all the contrasts between the Hemingway and *Sports Illustrated* openers. Many novels and short stories begin as specifically as the *Sports Illustrated* article, and many newspaper and magazine stories have begun almost as generally as *A Farewell to Arms* (Hemingway himself served a vigorous apprenticeship as a journalist). The contrasting noun use in the two sentences owes to two quite different but equally legitimate ways of beginning stories, articles, and essays—ways that embody assumptions about audience and forecast the method of development.

Look again at the first sentence:

In the late summer of that year we lived in a house in a village that looked across the river and the plain to the mountains.

This is essentially the same kind of opening as the following:

The status of women has aroused widespread interest among students of population only recently.

—"The Changing Status of Women in Developing Countries," *Scientific American*, Sept. 1974

Any experienced reader knows that the writers will descend from their level of generality and begin to fill in detail; and soon enough, we learn that Hemingway's story takes place in northern Italy during the First World War, and that the "students of population" are economists, sociologists, and political scientists who have begun to shift their study of economic status from men to women. Such *general-to-specifics*, whole-to-parts openers remind us of movies that begin with a panoramic shot of a city before focusing on one block, then one building, then one face.

Generalized openings often assume little previous knowledge on the part of the audience. They begin nonthreateningly, in almost a leisurely fashion, using broadly inclusive terms to establish an overview before getting down to the more demanding detail work. "Telling" precedes "showing"; major points appear before their support and illustration.

By comparison, the *Sports Illustrated* opening is relatively abrupt. In the manner of a *specifics-to-general*, parts-to-whole approach, and assuming an informed audience that will not be overwhelmed by the wealth of detail, it plunges right into a sharply particularized event:

At precisely 10 A.M. on Nov. 9, just 20 days after his team, the Oakland A's, lost the 1988 World Series, Dennis Lee Eckersley banged open the door and strode into the health and fitness facility at the University of Massachusetts Medical Center in Worcester.

This is drama. Action unfolds directly before us, with explanation to follow. For now, we want to see what will happen, then why. The same appeal can work as well in openers to scientific articles:

> On the evening of April 7, peasants clustered on the darkening hillsides surrounding China's Xichang launch site, waiting. Towering more than 43 meters above the launch pad sat China's Long March 3 rocket, ready for lift-off.
>
> —"The New Space Race," *Scientific American*, July 1990

Both articles soon move from the particulars (and proper nouns) to a discussion of broader issues and what the events typify (relying heavily on common nouns for generalization). Of the two, however, the *Sports Illustrated* passage is much more detailed: it uses eight proper-noun structures in one sentence while the other uses only five in two. Proper nouns cry out to be remembered (names, places, dates), and eight in one sentence is a challenge. *Sports Illustrated*, however, is a weekly magazine meant to be read within five or six days of an event, by a highly informed audience whose memories are fresh. So much detail, so much information, creates a sense of immediacy and authenticity, but it also makes demands on the reader. Writers can only afford to be so generous with information when they have an informed audience, when they know what their readers know. The co-authors of the *Scientific American* article also wanted the drama and emotion of a live event, but they could not presuppose readers familiar with the launching of a Chinese communications satellite.

Exercise

A To appreciate the difference in noun use, imagine the *Sports Illustrated* sentence done in the more generalized Hemingway style:

> One fall morning shortly after his team had lost a championship series, an athlete entered a health facility on the East Coast.

The following are some more opening sentences from *Sports Illustrated*. First, examine the detail. How much previous knowledge is assumed on the part of the reader? Then, revise them by making all of the details, especially the nouns, much more general. If you wish, even feel free to imitate Hemingway.

1   The sun was still high above Disneyland's Space Mountain last Friday, tracking steadily across the sky toward Sleeping Beauty's Castle, when Nolan Ryan, about to face the New York Yankees, took a surgeon's scalpel from his locker in Anaheim Stadium and began to whittle away at the fingers on his right hand.   —*Sports Illustrated*, 23 Aug. 1979

2   Cleveland nosetackle Bob Golic was relaxing Saturday night in the lobby of the Westin Hotel in Cincinnati, enjoying the Christmas lights and the overall feeling of peace and goodwill—and pondering a question totally out of sync with the holiday mood: Why is the Browns' defense so crummy?
—*Sports Illustrated*, 22–29 Dec. 1986

3   The chill of Halloween still lingered in the air on Sunday morning as the 18th New York City Marathon flowed across the Verrazano-Narrows Bridge and onto Brooklyn's Fourth Avenue.   —*Sports Illustrated*, 9 Nov. 1987

4   Low, smoky clouds rolled in off the Wasatch Mountains above Provo, Utah, last Saturday night as high jumper Hollis Conway prepared for his second attempt at an American record 7'9¾".
—*Sports Illustrated*, 12 June 1989

5   On the afternoon of Feb. 10, Oklahoma quarterback Charles Thompson hobbled out of the Sooners' football office and headed toward his car, which was double-parked across from Bud Wilkinson House, the athletic dormitory on Jenkins Avenue in Norman.   —*Sports Illustrated*, 27 Feb. 1989

6   When Michael Chang, nothing more than a tender Chinese-American boy playing far away from his Southern California home and subsisting on his mom's noodles cooked in their hotel room, won another extraordinary tennis match Sunday, he did far more than prevail through a grueling 21 hours and 261 games to become the first American man to win the French Open since Tony Trabert did so 34 years ago.
—*Sports Illustrated*, 19 June 1989

B   Compose a series of similar sentences, using people of your acquaintance and writing with similar detail about their actions. The simpler the better—notice how in many of the openers above people are doing everyday things: walking through doors, getting out of cars, dressing. Notice especially how the accumulation of particular details (of *facts*), based heavily on proper nouns, creates a sense (and perhaps an illusion) of significance. For example, do you think some of the detail

Another Use for Generality

Nouns and their modifiers allow us to be as precise or vague as we wish (and it is safe) to be. Examine the level of generality in the following sentences from a daily newspaper column. What explains the writer's choice of detail? And what does the choice of detail suggest about his readers' knowledge?

> Now pay attention: that high-ranking city official's estranged wife has become buddy-buddy with the ex-wife he dumped to marry her—so much so that they've decided to team up and testify against him in a tax case coming up shortly in Fresno.
>
> —Herb Caen, *San Francisco Chronicle*, 9 Aug. 1989
>
> That aging real estater who fancies himself a swinger is a candidate for indictment on charges involving narcotics and underage girls.
>
> —Herb Caen, *San Francisco Chronicle*, 16 Aug. 1989

In sum, we can write for insiders by being either extremely detailed or extremely vague.

is sometimes unnecessary, like middle names? In the second sentence is it really significant that Bob Golic was relaxing in the lobby of the Westin Hotel in Cincinnati?

Nouns and Levels of Generality

As the traditional definition of a noun suggests (the name of a person, place, or thing), it signifies something, calling up an image or idea. The vividness or vagueness of this image or idea is usually our first consideration as writers, and it is the basis for classifying each noun according to its *level of generality*, or for where it fits on a *scale of abstraction*. This scale is a sequence of related words climbing from the most specific to the most general, with each successive word being more inclusive but less precise. Hence, if we were to rank the different nouns that could apply to someone's pet cat, the scale could look like this:

being   ⟶   anything that exists

organism   ⟶   one kind of being

animal   ⟶   one kind of organism

mammal   ⟶   one kind of animal

feline   ⟶   one kind of mammal

tabby   ⟶   one kind of feline

Aslan   ⟶   one particular tabby

Nouns figure importantly in two mental processes, the process of grouping things and qualities into ever broader and higher classes (**abstraction**), and the process of dividing things and qualities into particulars (**concretion**). The two processes are interdependent, the first allowing us to generalize, the second to illustrate. When our nouns are too inclusive and general, the reader is left unmoored and unfocused; when our nouns are too precise and the details too abundant, the reader is dizzied and disoriented. Too much generalization leaves the reader with nothing to visualize, to see; too much detail leaves the reader with too many images, with a cluttered storeroom of odds and ends. Effective writing integrates the two processes, soaring to generalization for an overview and dipping to particulars for support and authenticity. Lively writing also moves back and forth between the levels, the way movies alternate close-ups with longer shots. Stay at one level—any level—for too long, and the reader begins to doze.

The following illustrates how one writer moves from generalities to particulars, from abstractions to concrete illustrations:

. . . [1]The values of our present economy do indeed suggest that it is better to perish with some ostentation of fashion and expense than to survive by modest competence, thrift, and industry.

[2]In saying such things, one must anticipate the accusation that one is simply indulging in nostalgia—sentimentalizing the past, yearning naively for the survival of quaint anachronisms and relics. [3]That might be true if one were dealing only with rare and isolated instances. [4]The fact is, however, that these instances are not rare or isolated. [5]The decline of the Indian agricultures in the Southwest follows exactly the pattern of the decline of local agricultures everywhere else in the country. [6]The economy of extravagance has over-thrown the economies of thrift. [7]Local cultures and agricultures such as those of the Hopi and the Papago do not deserve to survive for their picturesque trappings or their interest as artifacts; they deserve to survive—and to be emulated—because they embody

the principles of thrift and care that are indispensable to the
survival of human beings.

—Wendell Berry, "Three Ways of Farming in the Southwest"

Nouns and Modifiers

Sometimes we cannot find a noun that covers the precise amount of
reality we want to discuss, a noun that enables us, in the words of
Barry Lopez, to "talk clearly about the world." Such a noun may not
even exist, or it might be too technical for our audience (thus, *xenophobia*
is a valuable word, but many do not know that it is an umbrella term
for *racism*). Our solution is to take one that comes reasonably close and
shape it to fit our purposes by using modifiers. Paradoxically, the more
modifiers we add, the less reality we describe.

boy

a blond boy

a pale blond boy

a gangling pale blond boy

a gangling pale blond boy of eighteen

a gangling pale blond boy of eighteen with not too much chin . . .

Articles and Levels of Generality

One identifying trait of nouns is that they can be preceded by articles,
either definite (*the*) or indefinite (*a/an*). Most of the time, *the* definite
article will make a noun more concrete and specific, while *an* indefinite
article will make a concrete noun more abstract and general. For example, in the following sentence E. B. White deliberately repeats indefinite articles to give a sense of generality and timelessness to his
childhood experiences at a lake:

> Approaching **a** dock in **a** strong following breeze, it was diffi-
> cult to slow up sufficiently by the ordinary coasting method,
> and if **a** boy felt he had complete mastery over his motor, he
> was tempted to keep it running beyond its time and then re-
> verse it **a** few feet from the dock.   —"Once More to the Lake"

Compare:

> Approaching **the** dock in **the** strong following breeze . . .

In narratives and descriptions the usual practice is to introduce new detail with the indefinite *a/an*:

One morning in the Alaska autumn, a small sharp-nosed helicopter, on its way to a rendezvous, flew south from Fairbanks with three passengers.

—John McPhee, *Coming into the Country*

Once the narrator establishes that there is *a* helicopter, then it becomes *the* helicopter. *The* implies that, in context, the helicopter is known, that the reader is now familiar with it. *The* is usually a sign that writer and reader have shared knowledge, that the two enjoy a kind of intimacy. Hence, a common device of fiction and feature story writers is to begin their narratives with *the*, creating the illusion that the reader is already an insider, is already close to the subject:

The grandmother didn't want to go to Florida. She wanted to visit some of her connections in east Tennessee and she was seizing at every chance to change Bailey's mind.

—Flannery O'Connor, *A Good Man Is Hard to Find*

The fictional pretense is that the reader already knows the identity of the grandmother and Bailey.

In certain contexts repeated *the*'s, especially before plural nouns, can also identify people and objects as being representative of their class, as something to be considered generically:

I drove on past the gaudy neons and the false fronts behind them, the sleazy hamburger joints that look like palaces under the colors, the circular drive-ins as gay as circuses with the chipper hard-eyed car-hops, the brilliant counters, and the greasy kitchens that would have poisoned a toad.

—Raymond Chandler, *The Little Sister*

Levels of Generality and Invention

Invention was the word ancient rhetoricians used for the process of finding something to say. Knowing what we want to say naturally suggests words to use, but the reverse is also true. The properties of words can also suggest content. General nouns, for example, often invite detail expressed in more concrete terms. Consider the following:

The creek-meadow in season was full of **flowers**.

The wind brought **rubbish of all kinds** around the house every day.

All things around him acquired a miraculous immediacy and intensity.

These three statements vary in their degrees of generality, but they share one thing in common: a vague, fuzzy image. Their authors wanted a clearer picture, however, so they wrote the following versions:

The creek-meadow in season was full of **flowers—wild daisies, lamb-tongues, cat-ears,** big patches of **camas lilies** as blue as the ocean with a cloud shadowing it, and big stands of **wild iris** and **wild lilac** and **buttercups** and **St. John's wort.**
—H. L. Davis, *Honey in the Horn*

The wind brought **rubbish of all kinds** around the house every day: **pieces of old newspaper, dead leaves, feathers, pieces of string, twigs.**   —William Saroyan, *The Bicycle Rider in Beverly Hills*

All things around him—the still **woods** in the blazing afternoon, the separate, quivering **leaves** of the trees, the round, bright **ball** of the sun overhead, the spongy **earth** underfoot, the **sticks** and **stones** and darting **birds**—acquired a miraculous immediacy and intensity.
—Ross Lockridge, Jr., *Raintree County*

All three writers used a popular device for sentence expansion, the *noun appositive* (an appositive renames or redefines an earlier structure and can substitute for it). More accurately, they used an *appositive series*, a string of specific nouns illustrating a general one (another version of the general-to-specifics pattern). Notice that some of the noun appositives have themselves been made more specific by the addition of modifiers (not simply "the woods" but "the still woods in the blazing afternoon," not "camas lilies" but "big patches of camas lilies as blue as the ocean with a cloud shadowing it").

Noun Appositives and Simplicity

Noun appositives can also allow us to keep our main clauses from becoming too cluttered, particularly with overloaded subject phrases, as in the following:

The mountain-island of Gont that lifts its peak a mile above the storm-racked Northeast Sea **is** a land famous for wizards.

People do not become prize-winning novelists by writing many sentences like this one. Instead, they write like this:

The island of Gont, a single mountain that lifts its peak a mile above the storm-racked Northeast Sea, is a land famous for wizards.   —Ursula LeGuin, *A Wizard of Earthsea*

The appositive *sentence interrupter* conveniently subdivides the information for the reader.

Nouns and Sound Effects

Some nouns have the property that ancient Greeks called **onomato-poeia,** the property of sounding like the things they name. Those uncomfortable with the technical term call them "echo words."

Into the silence of the house there fall accentuating sounds, the closing of a door in another room, the **ticking** of drops from a faucet, the **rustling** of steam in the radiator, the **thrum** of a sewing machine upstairs.   —Saul Bellow, *The Dangling Man*

The spruce trees beside the road stood dark against the sun, and the only sound there that day was the faint **clicking** and **ticking** of grasshoppers as they jumped like mechanical toys.
—Margaret Laurence, *The Stone Angel*

Such nouns (or any other onomatopoetic words) are more vivid and evocative because they show as well as tell, carrying some of the properties of the things they name. Their effectiveness reminds us that observant writers do more than simply watch; they listen (and smell and touch).

Nouns as Metaphors

Nouns also frequently serve as **metaphors,** a kind of figurative comparison in which one thing is called another. Look, for example, how an elderly character in a novel expresses his growing cynicism:

I am a tea bag left too long in the cup, and my steepings grow darker and bitterer.   —Wallace Stegner, *All the Little Live Things*

By comparing his "bitterness" to the steepings of "a tea bag left too long in the cup," Stegner is able to give concreteness to an idea he could have stated abstractly: "I am becoming cynical and resentful in my old age." Students of metaphor use the terms *tenor* and *vehicle* to identify the objects of comparison:

Tenor   himself (life)

Vehicle   teabag (tea cup)

The inference, of course, is that he has lived too long.

Or look at how a naturalist explains what we can learn from a study of wood:

> The autobiography of an old board is a kind of literature not yet taught on campuses, but any riverbank is a library where he who hammers or saws may read at will.
>
> —Aldo Leopold, *A Sand County Almanac*

The usual formula for noun metaphors is to say, "A is B," a riverbank is a library. (See the section "Metaphoric Verbs" in Chapter 14, "The Rhetoric of Verbs and Verbals.")

When a comparison is more complex, a metaphor can extend over several sentences:

> She was a wind on the ocean. She moved men, but the helm determined the port.
>
> —Zora Neale Hurston, *Their Eyes Were Watching God*

In other words, she moved men, but they set the course.

Or consider another two-sentence metaphor in which Annie Dillard describes the difficulties of writing:

> You are a Seminole alligator wrestler. Half naked, with your two bare hands, you hold and fight a sentence's head while its tail tries to knock you over.   —*The Writing Life*

In some cases a metaphor can be apt because it is, paradoxically, inappropriate. What are more unlike, for example, than an ocean and a desert? Nevertheless, one writer compares the two to describe the habitat of dolphins:

> [1]The habitat of the spotted dolphin is clear, deep, tropical ocean. [2]Its home waters are warm, lovely to look at, sparse of life—a marine desert. [3]Spotted dolphins roam that country like Bedouins. [4]Their oases are the plumes of upwelling and nutrients in the lee of islands; their ululations are cries rising high above the hearing range of human beings; their dunes are the blue swells. [5]They gather occasionally in herds of a thousand or more—several schools in a temporary federation—but more often they are seen in bands of a few hundred. [6]Like many of the ocean's hosts, they are fewer than they once were.
>
> —Kenneth Brower, "The Destruction of Dolphins," *The Atlantic*, July 1989

Dolphins as Bedouins in a marine desert feeding at oases of upswelling nutrients—most writers would have missed such a comparison.

Among other uses, metaphors help writers deal with *abstractions*, those vague, general nouns that are sometimes difficult to grasp because they do not call up sensory images. Even mature readers can struggle with extended passages of abstract writing, as F. L. Lucas was aware when he made the following complaint:

> As life becomes more complex, sophisticated, and scientific, language is constantly tending to fade from a gallery of pictures to a blackboard of mathematical symbols. —*Style*

Without metaphor Lucas's wording would have illustrated the malady rather than the cure: "Language is becoming more abstract." But *language* is not merely an abstraction to Lucas; it is (or should be) "a gallery of pictures," varied, extensive, and colorful.

Mixed and "Literary" Metaphors

The best metaphors are spontaneous, arising naturally out of the writer's imagination. Some metaphors, though, have become cliches and lost whatever power they once had. As evidence, speakers and writers often use them without "seeing" them. The result is the mixed metaphor:

> This is just the tip of an iceberg and it is going to open up a whole tangled web.

What the person meant, of course, was that something was just the beginning and that it was going to, well, open up a whole can of worms. In revising, we should check metaphors for consistency, watching for mixed or cliched metaphors, intentional or unintentional.

Writers can also invite trouble by trying to force metaphors, to produce them on command or be too clever or "literary." The results of such efforts to show off are often ludicrous, as when one novelist wrote the following:

> From several miles out, the town appeared as no more than a mole on the jaw of the broad, fertile valley . . .

A good metaphor offers a vivid and appropriate image. What is appropriate about calling a town a mole, even if it does disfigure the landscape? (Or is this mole like a beauty spot?)

Metaphors are potent but often unruly. Too often, a metaphor begins as an honored guest and ends as a rude distraction.

Ultimately, this must be said of metaphors and similes both: they are most valuable not as stylistic devices but as ways of thinking. A good metaphor is only secondarily an ornament; it is primarily a new way of seeing our subject, a way of reaching out and comparing it with things that exist in totally different spheres of being (like oceans and deserts). In other words, metaphors are another way of making connections, of understanding.

The Noun Series

The *noun series* or catalog can itself provide special effects, whether or not it acts as an appositive. The series, especially a long one, contains more than additional information. The very length of the structure, even apart from the individual meaning of the items in the series, conveys a message about variety and fullness, about exuberance and vitality. A long noun series often suggests that the world is filled with multiple and diverse experiences, especially for the observant and the receptive. Take the following, which uses accumulated details to dramatize the diversity and energy of Wilkes County, North Carolina:

> It is a long, very gradual climb from Greensboro to Wilkes County. Wilkes County is all hills, ridges, woods and underbrush, full of pine oaks, sweet-gum maples, ash, birch, apple trees, rhododendron, rocks, vines, tin roofs, little clapboard places like the Mount Olive Baptist Church, signs for things like Double Cola, Sherrill's Ice Cream, Eckard's Grocery, Dr. Pepper, Diel's Apples, Google's Place, Suddith's Place and—yes!—cars.
> —Tom Wolfe, "The Last American Hero"

As a writer, you should learn to master series of all kinds but especially the noun series. Depending on their length, their punctuation, and (of course) their content, they can energize any description. Notice, for example, how E. B. White exploits the noun series to convey a child's enthusiasm about a country dump:

> Below the apple orchard, at the end of a path, was the dump where Mr. Zuckerman threw all sorts of trash and stuff that nobody wanted any more. Here, in a small clearing hidden by young alders and wild raspberry bushes, was an astonishing pile of old bottles and empty tin cans and dirty rags and bits of metal and broken bottles and broken hinges and broken springs and dead batteries and last month's magazines and old discarded dishmops and tattered overalls and rusty

■   *Writers' Notebook*   ■

Precise, concrete details carry an aura of authenticity, specific details being more convincing than general ones. (Which sounds more convincing, "The dog ate my homework," or, "Our eighteen-month-old Dalmation was angry about being left alone in the apartment, so she chewed up three of my textbooks and my term paper"?) Good details, especially in lists, do not occur accidentally. Unless gifted with uncommon memory, a writer does not simply think them up or recall them. They are the product of deliberate observation, and of note taking. Learn to look for defining details. Compile your own lists. And do not view the items on your list materialistically. They are not simply objects. They have uses and histories and associations. They reveal the characters and personalities and values of the people who create them or collect them or even discard them. And finally, learn what things are called, especially when writing about a group or subculture that has developed its own language, its own slang or jargon.

spikes and leaky pails and forgotten stoppers and useless junk of all kinds, including a wrong-size crank for a broken ice-cream freezer.   —*Charlotte's Web*

"And useless junk of all kinds," as if most adults would be able to see anything else.

■

Exercise

The following are sentences interesting for their use of nouns. Read each one carefully, observing what nouns contribute to the impact and meaning. Then, write a simplified version, staying as close to the meaning of the original as possible. "Destylize" it. Finally, write an imitation of the sentence, supplying your own subject matter. For example:

He stared very hard at Noah, and Noah stared very hard at him.   —Charles Dickens, *Oliver Twist*

He and Noah stared very hard at one another.

We support our candidate, and our candidate supports us.

(We will support them now, and they will support us later.)

1 An abstract noun neither smiles nor sings nor tells bedtime stories.   —Lewis H. Lapham, "Notebook," *Harper's*, Jan. 1989

2 The car slid along Los Angeles to Fifth, east to San Pedro, south again for block after block, quiet blocks and loud blocks, blocks where silent men sat on shaky front porches and blocks where noisy young toughs of both colors snarled and wisecracked at one another in front of cheap restaurants and drugstores and beer parlors full of slot machines.
—Raymond Chandler, *Pickup on Noon Street*

3 The bombs burst one after another . . . explosion . . . explosion . . . burst of flame.
—Harrison E. Salisbury, *The 900 Days: The Seige of Leningrad*

4 The sound of the approaching grain teams was louder, thud of big hooves on hard ground, drag of brakes and the jingle of trace chains.   —John Steinbeck, *Of Mice and Men*

5 He was far away from himself, and the slap of the waves on the shore, the splash of people in the water, all the noise and shouts of the beach were not in the same world with him.
—James T. Farrell, *Young Lonigan*

6 Only the distant thud of gun-fire disturbed the silence—like someone kicking footballs—a soft bumping, miles away.
—Siegfried Sassoon, *Memoirs of an Infantry Officer*

7 In one farmyard we pass we notice an old Chevy panel truck painted in psychedelic swirls, an April Easter egg nested against a weathered gray barn.   —Richard Rhodes, "Death All Day"

8 I must remember their isolation entirely from health, fun, enthusiasm, gladness, hunger, intelligence, or hope.
—William Saroyan, *Bicycle Rider in Beverly Hills*

9 A green plant is a machine that runs on solar energy. Light powers photo-synthesis, the process by which a plant converts carbon dioxide and water into sugars, starch and oxygen.
—*Scientific American*, Apr. 1988

10 Under this *portale* the adobe wall was hung with bridles, saddles, great boots and spurs, guns and saddle blankets, strings of red peppers, fox skins, and the skins of two great rattlesnakes.   —Willa Cather, *Death Comes for the Archbishop*

11 We need more coyotes, more mountain lions, more wolves and foxes and wildcats, more owls, hawks and eagles.
—Edward Abbey, *Desert Solitaire*

12 A writer has to deal in facts, things, particulars, concrete objects, and specific people, situations, and images.

—Wallace Stegner, "Writing as Graduate Study"

Nouns in Paragraphs

In addition to operating separately as labels, and in sentences as the specifiers of the reality we are talking about, nouns also operate in paragraphs by identifying their basic subject matter. A paragraph, we remember, is a sequence of related sentences developing a single idea. That single idea is a series of statements about a subject or topic. In most paragraphs nouns are the principal identifiers of this topic and by their repetition help ensure unity, coherence, and emphasis. Consider the following:

> [1]Every planet and satellite in the inner solar system is pitted with **craters.** [2]The **craters** on the moon were discovered by Galileo when he turned his telescope on the sky in 1609. [3]The **craters** on the earth have mostly been identified by geologists in recent decades. [4]The **craters** on Mars were discovered by the spacecraft *Mariner 4* in 1965. [5]The **craters** on Mars' two moons, Phobos and Deimos, were photographed by *Mariner 9* in 1971. [6]The **craters** on cloud-shrouded Venus were revealed when the surface of the planet was mapped by radar in 1972. [7]And the **craters** on Mercury abound in pictures sent back by *Mariner 10* in 1974. [8]No planet in the outer solar system has yet been photographed with sufficient resolution to reveal whether or not it is **cratered.**
>
> For students of the solar system the ubiquity* of the craters on the surface of the inner planets and satellites is fortunate. The form and number of the craters provide a wealth of information about both the astronomical and the geological processes that shaped the planets. . . .
>
> —"Cratering in the Solar System," *Scientific American,* Jan. 1977

The structure of this paragraph is simple but effective. It begins with a generalization about cratering on the planets and satellites of the inner solar system, then supports the generalization with a series of illustrations about the discovery of craters on each of the respective bodies.

* the state or ability to be or seem to be everywhere at the same time

In identifying the basic topic of the paragraph and the essay, "craters" appears as the last word of the predicate of the first sentence; then it is the subject of the next six sentences: "the *craters* on . . ." And the last sentence, which makes a qualification (none *yet* found on the outer planets), ends with a related or *cognate* ("born together") words: "cratered."

Most paragraphs will not identify their topics so explicitly in every sentence, relying instead on other devices of cohesion like chains of pronouns and synonyms. More instructive is the writer's willingness to repeat his key content word. He does not seek needless variation by calling them pits or cavities or volcanolike structures. He does not even feel obliged to use pronouns ("*Ones* on Mars . . . *Those* on cloud-shrouded Venus"). Their common name is craters so craters the writer calls them. Furthermore, he is saying that they are everywhere, and so they are, in every sentence.

Paragraphs

Examine noun use for appropriateness and effectiveness in the following paragraphs:

1   What is the apparent function of the writing: To tell a story? To explain a situation? To argue a position?

2   Do the nouns encourage the reader to imagine general or specific scenes? To weigh ideas or to make distinctions? To be detached or involved emotionally?

3   How do the writers vary the level of generality?

4   Do the paragraphs repeat key nouns to maintain thematic continuity?

5   How are the paragraphs punctuated?

No. 1

[1]My mother's suffering grew into a symbol in my mind, gathering to itself all the poverty, the ignorance, the helplessness; the painful, baffling, hunger-ridden days and hours; the restless moving, the futile seeking, the uncertainty, the fear, the dread; the meaningless pain and the endless suffering. [2]Her life set the emotional tone of my life, colored the men and women I was to meet in the future, conditioned my relation to events that had not yet happened, determined my attitude to situations and circumstances I had yet to face.

[3]A somberness of spirit that I was never to lose settled over me during the slow years of my mother's unrelieved suffering, a somberness that was to make me stand apart and look upon excessive joy with suspicion, that was to make me self-conscious, that was to make me keep forever on the move, as though to escape a nameless fate seeking to overtake me.

—Richard Wright, *Black Boy*

No. 2

[1]What is truth? [2]I don't know and I'm sorry I raised the point. [3]I mean to dodge it if I can, for the question leads at once into a bog of epistemological* problems too deep for me—or as I might say otherwise, beyond the scope of this essay. [4]I will state only what I believe, that truth, like honor, generosity, tolerance, decency, is something real, that truly exists, whether we can define it or not. [5]Subjectively, truth is that statement of cases which accords with my own view of the world—insofar as I have one—and which corresponds to the actual shape, color, substance of things and events— insofar as we can share and agree upon such matters. [6]What is reality? [7]For the purposes of daily life, as well as for the composition of stories and essays, I am willing to go by appearances. [8]It appears to me, for example, that torture is wrong, a hideous wrong, and always wrong; that the death penalty—the cold-blooded infliction of death by instruments of the state—is an evil greater than murder; it seems to me, judging by appearances only—that it's wrong to allow children to die of malnutrition and equally wrong—worse than wrong, criminally stupid—to bring children into the world when you are not prepared to feed and care for them; it appears to me that the domination of many by the few, whatever the creed behind it, whatever the means, leads always to injustice and is therefore wrong, always wrong, leading to greater wrongs. [9]I cite these banal, crude, and simple examples only to demonstrate that there is a moral area in which the true can easily be distinguished from the false. [10]I cheerfully agree that there are other areas where the distinction is more difficult to ascertain.

—Edward Abbey, "A Writer's Credo"

No. 3

[1]A fifty-five-gallon steel drum is thirty-four and three-quarters inches high and twenty-three inches in diameter, and is sometimes

---

* the study of the nature and limits of knowledge

called the Alaska State Flower. [2]Hundreds of them lie around wherever people have settled. [3]I once considered them ugly. [4]They seemed disappointing, somehow, and I wished they would go away. [5]There is a change that affects what one sees here. [6]Just as on a wilderness trip a change occurs after a time and you cross a line into another world, a change occurs with these drums. [7]Gradually, they become tolerable, and then more and more attractive. [8]Eventually, they almost bloom. [9]Fifty-five-gallon drums are used as rain barrels, roof jacks, bathtubs, fish smokers, dogpots, doghouses. [10]They are testing basins for outboard motors. [11]They are the honeypots of biffies, the floats on rafts. [12]A threat has been made to use one as a bomb. [13]Dick Cook, who despises aircraft of all types, told a helicopter pilot he would shoot at him if he ever came near his home. [14]The pilot has warned Cook that if he so much as points a rifle at the chopper the pilot will fill a fifty-five gallon drum with water and drop it on the roof of Cook's cabin. [15]Fifty-five-gallon drums make heat stoves, cookstoves, flower planters, bearproof caches, wood boxes, well casings, watering troughs, culverts, runway markers, water tanks, solar showers. [16]They are used as rollers for moving cabins, rollers to smooth snow or dirt. [17]Sliced on the diagonal, they are the bodies of wheelbarrows. [18]Scavenged everywhere, they are looked upon as gold.   —John McPhee, *Coming into the Country*

No. 4

[1]When Foster helped his ex-wife clean out the attic of the house where they had once lived and which she was now selling, they came across dozens of forgotten, broken games. [2]Parcheesi, Monopoly, Lotto; games aping the strategies of the stock market, of crime detection, of real-estate speculation, of international diplomacy and war; games with spinners, dice, lettered tiles, cardboard spacemen, and plastic battleships; games bought in five-and-tens and department stores feverish and musical with Christmas expectations, games enjoyed on the afternoon of a birthday and for a few afternoons thereafter and then allowed, shy of one or two pieces, to drift into closets and toward the attic. [3]Yet, discovered in their bright flat boxes between trunks of out-grown clothes and defunct appliances, the games presented a forceful semblance of value: the springs of their miniature launchers still reacted, the logic of their instructions would still generate suspense, given a chance. [4]"What shall we do with all these games?" Foster shouted, in a kind of agony, to his scattered family as they moved up and down the attic stairs.

"Trash 'em," his younger son, a strapping nineteen, urged.

—John Updike, "Still of Some Use"

No. 5

¹In the hinterlands of some cities, beginning just beyond their suburbs, rural, industrial, and commercial workplaces are all mixed up together. ²Such city regions are unique, having the richest, densest, and most intricate of all economies except for those of cities themselves. . . .

³By no means do all cities generate city regions. ⁴For example, Glasgow has never done so, even though in the latter half of the nineteenth century and the first decade of this century Glasgow was at the forefront of industry and technology, its engineers and engineered products renowned throughout the world, finding export markets far and wide. ⁵Fifty miles to its east lies Edinburgh, cultural and commercial capital of Scotland. ⁶Edinburgh has had its export triumphs too, but has never generated a city region either. ⁷Nor have even the combined economies of the two cities created a dense, rich mixture of city and rural activities in the space that lies between them. ⁸Marseille is the most important French seaport, and it has built up considerable industry in addition to its shipping work. ⁹But Marseille has no city region to speak of, even though it is the metropolis of all southern France. ¹⁰In the sixteenth century, Naples was the largest city in Christendom. ¹¹It enjoyed a vast export trade in dyed and woven silks, linens, laces, ribbons, braids, and sweetmeats. ¹²At the time, smaller cities like Milan, Paris, London, Antwerp, and Amsterdam were shaping and extending true city regions, but not Naples. ¹³Rome has an amazingly small and feeble city region, considering the city's size. ¹⁴Copenhagen has generated a city region, but not Dublin, Belfast, Cardiff, Liverpool, Lisbon, Madrid, Zagreb, or Moscow. ¹⁵Sao Paolo has one, but not Rio de Janeiro, Buenos Aires, or Montevideo. ¹⁶Neither Havana nor Santiago de Cuba has generated one, before or during Castro's regime. ¹⁷San Juan never generated one, under either Spanish or American rule.

—Jane Jacobs, "Cities and the Wealth of Nations," *The Atlantic*, Mar. 1984.

For Openers: Nouns

Noun Series

The suds of a shampoo, the lather of a shaving cream, the head on a glass of beer—each of these commonplace sudsy objects exemplifies a material whose properties are far from common. Each is an aqueous foam, an impermanent form of matter in which a gas, often air, is dispersed in an agglomeration of bubbles that are separated from one another by films of a liquid that is almost but not entirely water. Although aqueous foams have been a subject for scientific investigation since the 17th century, much remains to be learned about the complex chemical and physical phenomena that interact in even a single foamy bubble.

Like any other form of matter, an aqueous foam maintains its configuration only when it cannot readily transform itself into an arrangement embodying less energy. In the case of a foam . . .

—"Aqueous Foams," *Scientific American*, May 1986

Tadpoles, herring, basking sharks, flamingos, mallards and blue whales form an unlikely family. The group ranges from the smallest free-living vertebrates to the largest and includes amphibians, fishes, birds and mammals. These organisms are all suspension feeders: they eat by processing massive volumes of water through their feeding apparatus and filtering out small organisms and other fragments of organic material.

Vertebrate suspension feeders subsist on minute plants and animals too small to be sensed and captured individually. Typically they engulf many food particles during each feeding bout, and they are unselective about what they eat. For example . . .

—"Suspension-Feeding Vertebrates," *Scientific American*, Mar. 1990

Both of these articles begin with lists, the first of familiar things and the second of seemingly incompatible ones. Both lists raise immediate questions: What is there left to know about anything so familiar? and, What is the connection between creatures so unalike? The first opening creates a little more tension and therefore a little more emphasis by putting the list in an anticipatory appositive series (the authors could have gone even further and listed them independently as fragments). (See the section "Sentence Confusions" in Chapter 1, "Sentences.") The second uses the series as compound subjects of the sentence:

Tadpoles, herring, basking sharks, flamingos, mallards and blue whales form an unlikely family.

The series would have been even more emphatic as appositives:

Tadpoles, herring, basking sharks, flamingos, mallards, blue whales—these form an unlikely family.

Both articles use lists successfully to get the reader's attention, then exploit the list's natural momentum to move naturally to definitions and the body of the discussion. Lists, especially longer ones, have a built-in energy and help establish the topicality of one's subject ("Here is all this reality that needs explaining!").

Concrete, Proper Nouns

In the Norwegian fishing town of Tromso, 225 miles above the Arctic Circle, retailers keep their Coca-Cola not in coolers but in "warmers"—to prevent it from freezing. In Spain, a Coke dispenser sits on the deck of the Fortuna, King Juan Carlos's yacht. And across the globe in South Korea, baseball fans in the bleachers have a Coke and a squid.

The sun never sets on Coca-Cola Co.'s empire. The company sells roughly 47% of all the soda pop consumed world-wide, more than twice as much as its nearest competitor, PepsiCo Inc.

—Michael J. McCarthy, "The Real Thing," *Wall Street Journal*, 19 Dec. 1989

The first paragraph is structured around a series of proper nouns, the repeated brand name of Coca-Cola and the place names that illustrate the breadth of its "empire." It is this breadth that is the implicit unifying thesis, although the idea is not introduced explicitly until the second paragraph. Such a degree of concreteness and specificity illustrates and verifies a point that could have been made much more abstractly: "Coca-Cola is sold all over the world." The introduction of so many proper nouns so early in a story is typical of the *specifics-to-general*, parts-to-whole approach. Thesis-statement-first openings have the advantage of directness and clarity, but they can also make the following support seem anticlimactic. In this particular case such a beginning would be risky because it would not seem to carry any "news": most people know that Coca-Cola is sold all over the world. The proposition is not one that needs defending. The brunt of the article, however, is on the marketing strategies that have made Coca-Cola so successful and created the reality most of us take for granted.

General Nouns

Plant adaptations can be remarkably complex. Certain species of orchids, for example, imitate female bees; other plants look and smell like dead animals, and still others have the appearance of stones. These strange adaptations to life represent just a few of the sophisticated means by which plants enhance their chances of survival.

The idea that one species can imitate another in order to deceive an enemy and thus escape predation has fascinated biologists for more than a century. This particular survival strategy was first described in 1862 . . .

—"Mimicry in Plants," *Scientific American*, Sept. 1987

General nouns belong in the opening sentence of a *general-to-specifics* paragraph. The first sentence here immediately addresses the topic, an interesting and almost inexhaustible one. The author hasn't stated the overobvious, only announced his intention to explore a rich subject: how plants survive and propagate by mimicking insects, animals, rocks, and even other plants. The rest follows.

12

The Rhetoric of Pronouns

Pronouns and Coherence

Pronouns do much more than serve as understudies for nouns. They contribute heavily to tone and rhetorical distance (the distance between writer and audience), and they control narrative point of view. Also, because pronouns, more than any other part of speech, take their meaning from other words, especially from those in previous sentences and paragraphs, they have a unique responsibility for paragraph coherence (from the Latin for "sticking together"). Look what the repetition of *it* does to make the following passage "stick together":

> ¹The Carmel is a lovely little river. ²**It** isn't very long but in **its** course **it** has everything a river should have. ³**It** rises in the mountains, and tumbles down a while, runs through shallows, is dammed to make a lake, spills over the dam, crackles round boulders, wanders lazily under sycamores, spills into pools where trout live, drops in against banks where crayfish live. ⁴In the winter **it** becomes a torrent, a mean little fierce river, and in the summer **it** is a place for children to wade in and for fish-

ermen to wander in. [5]Frogs blink from **its** banks and the deep ferns grow beside **it**. [6]Deer and foxes come to drink from **it**, secretly in the morning and evening, and now and then a mountain lion crouched flat laps **its** water. [7]The farms of the rich little valley back up to the river and take **its** water for the orchards and the vegetables. [8]The quail call beside **it** and the wild doves come whistling in at dusk. [9]Raccoons pace **its** edges looking for frogs. [10]**It's** everything a river should be.

—John Steinbeck, *Cannery Row*

Pronouns make excellent coherence devices for several reasons. To begin, they are usually less emphatic than nouns and thus can bear much more frequent repetition. Imagine the above passage without pronouns: "The Carmel is a lovely little river. The Carmel isn't very long but in the Carmel's course the Carmel has everything a river should have. The Carmel rises in the mountains . . ." Such repetition quickly becomes a din.

Pronouns improve coherence for another reason: a noun signifies by itself; a pronoun asks the reader to remember its antecedent. If we were to replace all of the pronouns in the passage with their antecedent, the Carmel, then the paragraph would become a series of staccato, self-contained sentences, each one making relative sense by itself: "Frogs blink from the Carmel's banks and the deep ferns grow beside the Carmel. Deer and foxes come to drink from the Carmel . . ." Gone is the momentum. By repeating the pronoun, though, Steinbeck draws us back each time to the noun that is the subject of the passage. Each successive "it," in other words, reconnects us with the Carmel, pointing back to what has already been said. And, in addition to this connectedness, the repetition also has a cumulative effect. All of the *it* statements add up to the totality of the lovely little river.

There are other devices of coherence besides the pronoun: logical arrangement, repetition of key terms, transition words, demonstrative adjectives, organizing metaphors, and—increasingly in modern prose —fragmented sentences (which usually rely upon surrounding sentences to make sense). Because of its unique properties, though, its reliance on context and the ease with which it can be repeated, the pronoun is the most important single one.

Pronouns and Paragraph Structure

Repeated pronouns can do much more than support paragraph coherence, however. In many cases a change in the dominant pronouns signals a change of direction or focus. In effect, pronoun shifts can reflect or reinforce thematic development. N. Scott Momaday illustrates this in a passage that relies upon pronouns to make its central statement. To observe how he accomplishes this effect, circle the dominant pronouns in the following passage, then put boxes around key pronouns that may appear only once or twice.

> [1]My grandmother was a storyteller; she knew her way around words. [2]She never learned to read and write, but somehow she knew the good of reading and writing; she had learned how to listen and delight. [3]She had learned that in words and in language, and there only, she could have whole and consummate being. [4]She told stories, and she taught me how to listen. [5]I was a child and I listened. [6]She could neither read nor write, you see, but she taught me how to live among her words, how to listen and delight. [7]"Storytelling; to utter and to hear . . ." [8]And the simple act of listening is crucial to the concept of language, and more crucial even than reading and writing, and language in turn is crucial to human society. [9]There is proof of that, I think, in all the histories and prehistories of human experience. [10]When that old Kiowa woman told me stories, I listened with only one ear. [11]I was a child, and I took the words for granted. [12]I did not know what all of them meant, but somehow I held on to them; I remembered them, and I remember them now. [13]The stories were old and dear; they meant a great deal to my grandmother. [14]It was not until she died that I knew how *much* they meant to her. [15]I began to think about it, and then I knew. [16]When she told me those old stories, something strange and good and powerful was going on. [17]I was a child, and that old woman was asking me to come directly into the presence of her mind and spirit; she was taking hold of my imagination, giving me to share in the great fortune of her wonder and delight. [18]She was asking me to go with her to the confrontation of something that was sacred and eternal. [19]It was a timeless, *timeless* thing; nothing of her old age or my childhood came between us.
>
> —N. Scott Momaday, *House Made of Dawn*

Pronouns and Formality

In writing, as in relationships of any kind, distance is all. And in writing, distance—the space between ourselves and our audience—dictates our choice of pronouns. If we wish a formal relationship with our readers, we can hold them off by avoiding first-person and second-person pronouns and by using the indefinite *one* when we wish to refer to people in general. If we want to invite more familiarity by shortening the distance between ourselves and our readers, we can take liberties with *I* and *me* and, especially, with *we* and *you*.

The first-person pronoun is not appropriate for all levels of writing. It usually does not have a place in technical manuals or business reports, which are often understood to issue from organizations rather than from individuals. In such cases the writer is trying to play an impersonal role; individual opinion might even weaken *one's* authority. In other cases, though, *I* can mean that the writer is a witness or even has a personal stake in the issue, a commitment that many readers appreciate. Furthermore, when we use *I*, we are openly announcing that we stand behind our statements, that we are not taking refuge behind an abstract role. Many, though, including some teachers of writing, find the first person sloppy and self-indulgent, especially when a writer seems to be representing a summary of personal opinion as reasoned argumentation. Quite defensibly, they argue that our logic and our data should stand by themselves, that we should not be seeming to ask our readers to accept something on our authority alone. Certainly the personal recommendation is no substitute for strong supporting evidence, but the implied concern of the *I* can strengthen the rational appeal with an additional layer of emotional appeal.

The Formal Rhetoric of One

Formal writing is "serious" writing. It assumes that one is in an earnest, no-nonsense, get-down-to-business mood and addressing an audience in the same mood. Usually, the formal writer (or speaker) is in an abstract and general role, that of political candidate, environmentalist, concerned citizen. As a formal writer one appeals to one's audience logically, remaining aloof from any emotional connection and relying principally upon the authority of one's role and expertise. If the pose seems too impersonal for some, it does broadcast respect, respect for the material and for the audience.

Exercise

The formality and seriousness of James Baldwin's essays, even when he is writing about issues of intense personal interest, are reflected in his choice of pronouns. Observe what *one* contributes to the tone and reliability of the following brief excerpt from *Nobody Knows My Name*.

What relationship does he wish to establish with his readers? How, in other words, is the reader invited to respond? Experiment with changes in the passage by substituting *we* and *you* for *one*. What is the effect of these pronouns? Does a change in pronouns encourage any other changes?

> **Any real change implies the breakup of the world as one has always known it, the loss of all that gave one an identity. And at such a moment, unable to see and not daring to imagine what the future will now bring forth, one clings to what one knew, or thought one knew; to what one possessed or dreamed that one possessed.** —"Faulkner and Desegregation"

The Rhetoric of Informality: I, We, *and* You

As informal writers we appeal to a larger and more general audience. We are writing more personally, attempting to relate to our audience on a more familiar basis. By appealing to our readers not as abstraction to abstractions (candidate to voters, professional to amateurs, lecturer to students) but as person to persons, we are speaking in a more common and comfortable tone. We are appealing to our audience not as people strenuously poised for serious public or professional business (and more likely to be critical), but as reasonably intelligent and inquisitive fellow beings. In a manner of speaking, formal writing presupposes an audience in the mood for a lecture, an audience almost compelled to read, or at least highly motivated.

Informal writing, on the other hand, presupposes only normal curiosity, an audience reading for mental recreation, or at least a writer not willing to impose on the reader. And perhaps even more important, informal writing often implies that we have a personal investment in the issue. For this reason, informal writing usually has an additional layer of emotional content. Often, the formal writer is saying, "This is my professional opinion," whereas the informal writer is saying, "Formalities aside, I think this is interesting."

In informal writing, which often presupposes that we are on a more friendly basis with our audience, we take greater liberties, especially with pronouns. We use the first-person singular and plural, and we use both the indefinite *you* (meaning "everyone in general") and the more specific *you* (speaking directly to the audience). Common in informal writing, too, is the imperative in which the writer addresses the reader with an implied *you*, as in the following:

> Suppose there were no critics to tell **us** how to react to a picture, a play, or a new composition in music. Suppose **we** wandered innocent as the dawn into an art exhibition of unsigned paintings. By what standards, by what values would **we** decide whether they were good or bad, talented or untalented, successes or failures? How can **we** ever know that what **we** think is right?
>
> —Marya Mannes, "How Do You Know It's Good?"

Exercise

Observe how pronouns contribute to the informality of the following passage. What else contributes to the informality? Revise the passage so that it is more formal, substituting pronouns but also making any other changes that seem appropriate.

> I often go to the supermarket for the pure fun of it, and I suspect a lot of other people do too. The supermarket fills some of the same needs the neighborhood saloon used to satisfy. There you can mix with neighbors when you are lonely, or feeling claustrophobic with family, or when you simply feel the urge to get out and be part of the busy, interesting world.
>
> —Russell Baker, "Small Kicks in Superland"

The Persuasive We

In persuasion of any kind, the attempt to gain the consent and cooperation of others, there may be no more important word than *we*. The first-person plural tells our audience that we identify with them, that we have a common stake in the affair at hand. As long as we separate ourselves from our audience, as long as we think about *us* and *them* (or *me* and *you*), we lose the inclination and the incentive to find a common ground. In the planning of a persuasive paper, the *we* can even serve as what classical rhetoricians called a "heuristic" (from the same Greek word "to invent or discover" that gives us *eureka*). We can begin by writing *we* on a blank piece of paper, then listing all the ways that we and our audience are indeed "we." Instead of thinking how we can trick or entice or threaten *them* into submitting to *our* idea, or how we can overpower *their* thinking or revise *their* wrongheadedness, we should ask ourselves, earnestly and honestly, what we have in common with our audience, what interests *we* share. Often, because they share common goals but disagree only on effective means, participants in a debate are not true adversaries. Thinking *we* encourages us to dwell on our much more important similarities, thereby shrinking our differences to their proper dimensions.

Exercise

Examine the communicative strategy of the following passage. In what way is it informed by *we*-thinking and *we*-writing? In what way do the pronouns get our attention and our sympathy, thereby affecting our receptivity to the writer's suggestions?

> [1]Americans are probably the most pain-conscious people on the face of the earth. [2]For years we have had it drummed into us—in print, on radio, over television, in everyday conversation—that any hint of pain is to be banished as though it were the ultimate evil. [3]As a result, we are becoming a nation of pill-grabbers and hypochondriacs, escalating the slightest ache into a searing ordeal.
>
> [4]We know very little about pain and what we don't know makes it hurt all the more. . . .
>
> —Norman Cousins, "Pain Is Not the Ultimate Enemy"

Note that Cousins identifies "we" from the start: Americans. He eventually proposes more education about the nature of pain (much of it is normal and goes away by itself) and about the health-damaging effects of the pain medication we take.

Pronouns and Delayed Revelation

In the normal order, pronouns follow their antecedents, the nouns to which they refer. In such cases the pronouns keep calling us back. In special cases, though, writers sometimes create suspense by using the pronoun first, making the reader wait for the explanatory noun. This tactic can work at the sentence level:

> **That** is what Athenian education aimed at, to produce men who would be able to maintain a self-governed state because

they were themselves self-governed, self-controlled, and self-reliant.   —Edith Hamilton, *The Ever-Present Past*

Journalists often use the same technique, titillating us with curious facts about "them" before we learn who "they" are:

> **They** come from places like Oklahoma and Southern California, refugees from a world that seems spinning out of control. **They** are selling **their** homes and leaving **their** families, searching for sanctuary from the New Age of Apocalypse.
>
> "Something is going to happen," said Sharon Rosenberger, one of hundreds of New Age pilgrims who have moved to Yelm, a farming hamlet south of Seattle, to be close to Ramtha, a 35,000-year-old "channeled entity."
> —*San Francisco Chronicle*, 4 Sept. 1989

So "they," these people behaving so mysteriously, turn out to be "New Age pilgrims."

Some writers pursue this tactic of delayed revelation through an entire paragraph or even a series of paragraphs:

> [1]**They** live up alongside the hills, in hollow after hollow. [2]**They** live in eastern Kentucky and eastern Tennessee and in the western part of North Carolina and the western part of Virginia and in just about the whole state of West Virginia. [3]**They** live close to the land; **they** farm it and some of **them** go down into it to extract its coal. [4]**Their** ancestors, a century or two ago, fought their way westward from the Atlantic seaboard, came up on the mountains, penetrated the valleys, and moved stubbornly up the creeks for room, for privacy, for a view, for a domain of sorts. [5]**They** are Appalachian people, mountain people, hill people.
> —Robert Coles, *Migrants, Sharecroppers, Mountaineers*

Coles could have opened by immediately identifying his subject: *"The Appalachian people* live up alongside the hills, in hollow after hollow." The result would have been a competent expository paragraph, one beginning with a simple statement, then building on it. The reader could stop at any point and have a reasonably complete picture. Coles, however, draws us along to the end of his paragraph, tantalizing us, before he answers the question he has raised: Who are these people? His strategy, a popular one, exploits the nature of the pronoun and the need of the human mind to find meaning, to solve mysteries. A personal pronoun requires a noun somewhere, so we must keep reading to discover the sense.

In some cases the tactic has another advantage: by postponing the identifying name, the writer avoids any stereotypes or preconceived notions the reader may have about the subject. Used in this fashion, the tactic can even allow the writer to reawaken the reader's interest in the familiar, the new news in the old news, as in the following example:

> ¹In full array, **it** looks like a huge, dreamland insect. ²**It** is so well thought out that the Museum of Modern Art in New York has one in its permanent Design collection. ³**It** is carried routinely by astronauts, Everest conquerors and polar explorers. ⁴In 1960, the Russians gleefully displayed **one** among the other "CIA equipment" found in Gary Powers' downed U-2.
>
> More, perhaps, than sheltered bank accounts and fine wristwatches, chocolates and cuckoo clocks, **it** says "Switzerland." **It**, of course, is the Swiss Army Knife.
>
> —"On Everest or in the Office, It's the Tool to Have," *Smithsonian*, Oct. 1989

Exercise

Attempt a revision of the previous paragraph by writing it in the conventional fashion, identifying the subject immediately. How does it compare with the original?

And then there is the following:

> He was an undersized little man, with a head too big for his body—a sickly little man. His nerves were bad. He had skin trouble. It was agony for him to wear anything next to his skin coarser than silk. And he had delusions of grandeur. . . .
>
> —Deems Taylor, "The Monster"

Taylor, a music critic and composer, builds his essay around a contrast: on the one hand, the man's outrageous and repellent personal qualities; on the other, his unparalleled contributions to music. Not until the twelfth paragraph of a fifteen-paragraph essay does he reveal the identity of the "monster": Richard Wagner.

Pronouns and Narrative Distance

By today's standards, many traditional narrators began their stories in almost a leisurely fashion. They would open with broad details of setting and then gradually introduce their characters. The following is typical of such openers:

> It was early on a fine summer's day, near the end of the eighteenth century, when a young man, of genteel appearance, journeying towards the north-east of Scotland, provided himself with a ticket in one of those public carriages which travel between Edinburgh and the Queensferry . . .
>
> —Walter Scott, *The Antiquary* (1816)

The first character we meet is "a young man," a generic type. Then he becomes "the young man" and remains so until the reader finally learns his name (Scott also knew about delayed revelation). The young man is like any other stranger who is simply "a someone" and from whom we are distanced by unfamiliarity. Part of the early complication is, in fact, the young man's very strangeness, which gradually disappears as we learn more and more about him. The story begins, in other words, with the understanding that the reader is an outsider and that the writer is like a considerate host who in due time will make the necessary introductions.

By contrast, modern narrators, whether novelists or journalists, often burst right into an action, using pronouns to establish an assumed (and pretended) familiarity with the reader. Consider the following:

> She had the purse in her hand when she came in. Standing in the middle of the floor, holding her bathrobe around her and trailing a damp towel in one hand, she surveyed the immediate past and remembered everything clearly. Yes, she had opened the flap and spread it out on the bench after she had dried the purse with her handkerchief.
>
> —Katherine Anne Porter, "Theft"

We use personal pronouns freely upon the assumption that the antecedents are known to our audience. But in the above case, who is "she"? Porter is treating us as if we already know, as if—more accurately—we are *in* the know, as if we are insiders. We are soon rewarded with an even greater intimacy; we are allowed to know what "she" is thinking. The explanations will develop gradually as we piece together the details. Porter's effect depends on the rhetoric of pronouns and the convention of familiarity with their antecedents.

Pronouns and the Rhetoric of Vagueness

Writing is a constant process of deciding how much detail is relevant. We can as easily overburden our readers with unnecessary detail as we can leave them underinformed. Sometimes our effect depends on making our subject as specific as an individual fingerprint. Other times, it depends on keeping our subject vague and elusive. We know what it means in a horror movie when someone pronounces, "There is *something* out there!" Not being limited in its nature, "something" is potentially more frightening than an enraged grizzly bear or the Creature from the Black Lagoon or an army of invading aliens. "Something," by its very lack of precision as an indefinite pronoun, takes in all the possibilities— and more, including the neighbor's puppy. In other words, concreteness and specificity may clarify a subject and answer our questions, but they also halt inquiry and stifle the imagination, as the following writer appreciates:

> I was sleeping soundly on a fairly chilly night. The room was black as pitch. . . . I felt **something** on my foot, **something** palpable and heavy, **something** alive, **something** present, **something** breathing, and most seriously of all, **something** on my foot.   —Pat Conroy, *The River Is Wide*

Notice also how the effect is amplified by another trait of indefinite pronouns, the tendency of their modifiers to come afterward ("something *breathing*, something *on my foot*").

■

Exercise

Examine pronoun use in the following sentences. To what extent do pronouns carry the "news," and which specific pronouns accomplish this? What effects are achieved by the writers' use of pronouns? To put it another way, how do the writers succeed by drawing on their intuitive understanding of the properties of pronouns? What happens when you revise the sentences to eliminate devices like repetition or unusual word order?

1 At school they tried to teach me how to write an essay, and how to draw a large brass pot full of zinnias.
—Gilbert Highet, *Explorations*

2 More happened then: she chased him, caught him, threw him down, pounded him.   —Garrison Keillor, *Leaving Home*

3 Yes, surely the American flag is the ultimate male sex symbol. Men flaunt it, wave it, punch noses for it, strut with it, fight for it, kill for it, die for it. —Russell Baker, "The Flag"

4 Throughout this period I read nothing, thought nothing, was nothing. —Lawrence Durrell, *Justine*

5 There was something beyond all that, something beyond energy, beyond history, something I could not fix in my mind. —Joan Didion, "At the Dam"

6 This was what he craved, that someone should care about him, wish him well. —Saul Bellow, *Seize the Day*

7 I think they were very much in love, my mother and father. —Truman Capote, *Grass Harp*

8 Political and religious systems, social customs, loyalties and traditions, they all came tumbling down like so many rotten apples off a tree. —William Golding, "Thinking as a Hobby"

9 In December they began to appear—the sleds of the children, painted bright red or yellow, narrow sleds with runners, sleds for sliding down hills in fur earlaps and a woolen muffler trailing behind, Christmas presents, small sleds, big enough for a boy taking a belly-flopper, or a boy and a girl clutching each other as they raced around icy curves. —Harrison E. Salisbury, *The 900 Days: The Siege of Leningrad*

10 I was a loner and a loser who had pretty much failed at everything: at the novel, at screenwriting, at marriage, and, over and over again, at romance. —Larry McMurtry, *Some Can Whistle*

Pronouns and Point of View

In telling a story, whether it be fact or fiction, our first decision concerns pronoun choice. We must decide from what angle we are going to portray the events. We can use the angle of someone inside the story— a participant or direct witness—and use a first-person *I* narrator— something happening to *me*. Or we can distance ourselves and the reader somewhat by using a third-person narrator (*he*, *she*, *they*)—something happening to others. Or, we might even use a second-person *you* narrator and speak directly to a character—something happening to *you*. Once again, the choice of pronoun dictates the degree of intimacy or distance—between the storyteller and events as well as between the storyteller and the reader.

The following are opening paragraphs to narrations. What conclusions can you draw about the relative advantages and limitations of each point of view? Which treatment invites us to look more exclusively at the events, for example, and which at the personality of the narrator? Which encourages greater reader identification, and which more detachment? Which is more "natural"? And—this is crucial—how many other variables do you see influenced by point of view, like the nature and amount of detail?

First Person

¹That spring, when I had a great deal of potential and no money at all, I took a job as a janitor. ²That was when I was still very young and spent money very freely, and when, almost every night, I drifted off to sleep lulled by sweet anticipation of that time when my potential would suddenly be realized and there would be capsule biographies of my life on dust jackets of many books, all proclaiming: ". . . He knew life on many levels. From shoeshine boy, freelance waiter, 3rd cook, janitor, he rose to . . ." ³I had never been a janitor before and I did not really have to be one and that is why I did it. ⁴But now, much later, I think it might have been because it is possible to be a janitor without really becoming one, and at parties or at mixers when asked what it was I did for a living, it was pretty good to hook my thumbs in my vest pockets and say comfortably: "Why, I am an apprentice janitor." ⁵The hippies would think it degenerate and really dig me and it made me feel good that people in Philosophy and Law and Business would feel uncomfortable trying to make me feel better about my station while wondering how the hell I had managed to crash the party.   —James Alan McPherson, "Gold Coast"

Exercise

Rewrite the McPherson passage by putting it in the third person. What must you change besides the pronouns? In a first-person account the language is that of the character. Hence, word choice is a direct form of characterization: the character talks like this. By contrast, the language of a third-person narration is that of the storyteller, not of the character. The language tells us *about* the character. Furthermore, some kinds of third-person narrators will even reveal the characters' thoughts,

drawing inferences and making value judgments. Other kinds will remain detached, outsiders, mere witnesses.

Second Person

[1]You see yourself as the kind of guy who appreciates a
quiet night at home with a good book. [2]A little Mozart on the
speakers, a cup of cocoa on the arm of the chair, slippers on
the feet. [3]Monday night. [4]It feels like Thursday, at least.
[5]Walking from subway to apartment, you tell yourself that you
are going to suppress this rising dread that comes upon you
when you return home at night. [6]A man's home, after all, is
his castle. [7]Approaching your building on West Twelfth Street,
you observe the architect's dim concept of European for-
tresses: a crenelated tower atop the building is fitted with a
mock portcullis. [8]You let yourself in the front door and gingerly unlock the mailbox. [9]No telling what might be inside.
[10]One of these days there could be a letter from Amanda explaining her desertion, begging forgiveness or asking you to
send the rest of her stuff to a new address.

—Jay McInerny, *Bright Lights, Big City*

This kind of narration is rare, in stories or in movies. The largest
difficulty is that of probability. Characters can easily tell their own
stories and use the first person; a narrator can easily use the third person
and tell a story about someone else. But who but an invisible companion
can be addressing a character throughout a narrative? Or is the character
here talking to himself? Nevertheless, the technique does create a sense
of immediacy and a quality of intimacy lacking in the other points of
view. *You,* after all, could be you, the reader.

Exercise

Try to rewrite the McInerny paragraph in either the first or the third
person. Do you have to add or leave out anything? What changes does
a new point of view require? And how does it affect our sympathy for

the character? And finally, to get a feel for this unusual technique, use the second person to write a brief narrative about yourself.

Third Person

¹The jockey came to the doorway of the dining room, then after a moment stepped to one side and stood motionless, with his back to the wall. ²The room was crowded, as this was the third day of the season and all the hotels in town were full. ³In the dining room bouquets of August roses scattered their petals on the white table linen and from the adjoining bar came a warm, drunken wash of voices. ⁴The jockey waited with his back to the wall and scrutinized the room with pinched, crepy eyes. ⁵He examined the room until at last his eyes reached a table in a corner diagonally across from him, at which three men were sitting. ⁶As he watched, the jockey raised his chin and tilted his head back to one side, his dwarfed body grew rigid, and his hands stiffened so that the fingers curled inward like gray claws. ⁷Tense against the wall of the dining room, he watched and waited in this way.

—Carson McCullers, "The Jockey"

Exercise

A   Try to rewrite the McCullers passage in either the first or second person. Make any changes necessary to render the account believable. Would the jockey, for example, think of describing the bar noise as "a wash of voices"? Would he describe his own eyes as being "crepy" or his hands as "gray claws"? The language of the passage is that of the narrator, not of the character. The detail is also that observed by an onlooker. We are seeing the jockey from the outside. How much of the jockey can you present in the second or third person? Using the first or second person, what information might you have to reveal?

B   To get a sense of just how strongly pronouns control the tone of a narrative, write an account of something that happened to you, but using the third person. If you are then feeling adventurous, try the second person.

Paragraphs

Examine pronoun use in the following paragraphs:

1   How do the pronouns contribute to unity and coherence?

2   What degree of formality or informality do the pronouns encourage?

3   What contribution do the pronouns make to the writer's rhetorical strategy?

4   How do the narrative paragraphs exploit point of view?

5   How are the paragraphs punctuated?

No. 1

[1]The state gets a bad press today. [2]It does too little, it does too much. [3]It serves itself, it serves anyone but you and me. [4]The rich seek to deny it the wealth it needs to run. [5]The poor demand more of it than any organization can deliver. [6]"Special-interest" pressure groups condemn it when it heeds the pleas of others. [7]Individualists decry it as interfering when it tries to play fair with all. [8]Disarmers depict it as warmongering. [9]The defense community warns that it neglects the simple necessities of national security. [10]The law-and-order lobby complains that it is soft on criminals. [11]The civil libertarians allege that it wants to send honest men to jail. [12]Everyone, left, right, center, wants more or less of the state and finds few good words to say about it unless he gets what he wants. [13]Even the Marxists, who put their shirt on the state's back, look forward to the time when it will wither away. [14]The state seems to have no friends at all.

—John Keegan, "Shedding Light on Lebanon," *The Atlantic*, Apr. 1984

No. 2

[1]Insects are legion; some are active only in bright sunlight, some in both sunlight and shade, some only at twilight. [2]Some, such as the common housefly, travel at high speed and make rapid turns. [3]Others, such as the dragonfly, alternately fly straight, maneuver and hover. [4]Still others, such as the praying mantis, remain motionless for hours at a time. [5]All these insects rely for their survival on vision, and all of them perceive the world through many-faceted compound eyes, yet their habits and their visual requirements are quite different. [6]How does the compound eye work as an optical sampling de-

vice? [7]To what extent does it reveal the functions for which the insect uses its eyes? [8]To what extent does the smallness of the facets of the insect eye limit its sensitivity? [9]What is the barrier to the insect eye's working at low light intensities with the small lenses of the facets? [10]How do the compound eyes of insects arrive at a compromise between optical resolution and the sensitivity needed to overcome optical noise?

—"The Compound Eye of Insects," *Scientific American*, July 1977

No. 3

[1]Illiterates cannot read the letters that their children bring home from their teachers. [2]They cannot study school department circulars that tell them of the courses that their children must be taking if they hope to pass the SAT exams. [3]They cannot help with homework. [4]They cannot write a letter to a teacher. [5]They are afraid to visit in the classroom. [6]They do not want to humiliate their child or themselves.

[7]Illiterates cannot read instructions on a bottle of prescription medicine. [8]They cannot find out when a medicine is past the year of safe consumption; nor can they read of allergenic risks, warnings to diabetics, or the potential sedative effect of certain kinds of nonprescription pills. [9]They cannot observe preventive health care admonitions. [10]They cannot read about "the seven warning signs of cancer" or the indications of blood-sugar fluctuations or the risks of eating certain foods that aggravate the likelihood of cardiac arrest.

—Jonathan Kozol, *Illiterate America*

No. 4

[1]I suppose that jazz listening and prizefight watching are my two most passionate avocations, and this is largely so because the origins of my aesthetic urges are in the black working class. [2]At times these avocations are a bit difficult to reconcile: boxers like to train in the early afternoon and jazz musicians like to jam late at night. [3]But I think they are, on the whole, more deeply related than one might suspect. [4]They are such direct expressions, not of emotion, but rather of *emotive power*, and they are such risk-taking endeavors. [5]My most vibrant memories I bear from my childhood are of my uncles crowded around a very small black-and-white television, drinking beer and watching the Gillette Friday Night Fights: my aunts would be in another room listening to old jazz records such as Lionel Hampton's "Flying Home" and Billie Holiday's "Don't Explain." [6]The men would join later to play Charlie Parker records and lots of rhythm and blues

stuff. [7]I liked those Friday nights as much as I have ever liked anything.

—Gerald Early, "The Passing of Jazz's Old Guard: Remembering Charles Mingus, Thelonious Monk, and Sonny Stitt"

For Openers: Pronouns

Eight times within the past million years, **something** in the earth's climatic equation has changed, allowing snow in the mountains and the northern latitudes to remain where it had previously melted away. The snow compacted into ice, and the ice built up into glaciers and ice sheets. Over tens of thousands of years, the ice sheets reached the thicknesses of several kilometers; they planed, scoured and scarred the landscape as far south as central Europe and the midwestern U.S. And then each glacial cycle came to an abrupt end. Within a few thousand years the ice sheets shrank back to their present-day configuration.

Over the past 30 years, evidence has mounted that these glacial cycles are ultimately driven by astronomical factors: slow, cyclic changes in the eccentricity of the earth's orbit and in the tilt and orientation of its spin axis. . . .

—"What Drives Glacial Cycles?" *Scientific American*, Jan. 1990

"Something" is an indefinite pronoun, a word we use to identify a thing we do not know or understand, a mystery. Rhetorically, then, the word perfectly expresses the problem: What is it that causes glacial cycles? "Something" temporarily signifies the cause. The rest of the article, predictably, sets about to explain what the something is, to account for the cause. Such an opening is a popular and effective way to explain a process or some other phenomenon: remind the readers what the puzzle is, refresh their knowledge of its details, then explain it.

Personal Pronouns: Delayed Revelation

He was born in a London slum, **he** lacked a university education and **he** was unemployed except for a six-year stint as a telegraph clerk. Yet by virtue of **his** talent and sheer force of will, Oliver Heaviside became one of the leading Victorian physicists. He clarified and extended the electromagnetic theory of James Clerk Maxwell, discovered the circuit principle that made long-distance telephony possible and foresaw television, over-the-horizon radio and several aspects of Einstein's theory of relativity.

Although Heaviside was greatly esteemed by the scientists of his time, he is now almost forgotten . . .

—"Oliver Heaviside," *Scientific American*, June 1990

Delayed revelation here prepares for a surprise, setting the reader up for the "yet" statement: "he" came from very unpromising circumstances, ones that would never forecast his eventual achievement. This kind of opening is a popular way to establish that there is often "news" in familiar topics (many electrical engineers and physicists, the prime audience for the article, would know of Heaviside's achievements but not know about his personal life). By postponing identification of the subject, the antecedent of "he," the writer also sidesteps any prejudices and other preformed opinions that might interfere with the reader's response or receptivity.

Personal Pronouns: I *and* You

Sometimes a good idea comes to **you** when **you** are not looking for it. Through an improbable combination of coincidences, naivete and lucky mistakes, such a revelation came to **me** one Friday night in April, 1983, as I gripped the steering wheel of **my** car and snaked along a moonlit mountain road into northern California's redwood country. That was how I stumbled across a process that could make unlimited numbers of copies of genes, a process now known as the polymerase chain reaction (PCR).

Beginning with a single molecule of the genetic material DNA, the PCR can generate 100 billion similar molecules in an afternoon. The reaction is easy to execute . . .

—Kary B. Mullis, "The Unusual Origin of the Polymerase Chain Reaction," *Scientific American*, Apr. 1990

Familiarities like the first-person pronoun and the indefinite *you* are generally considered to detract from our authority when we write about serious subjects. In this case, however, the writer chooses to lessen the usual distance between writer and audience that prevails in scientific literature. Scientific writing often takes readers through the steps of an experiment, allowing us to be "observers." Mullis, however, invites an even closer involvement, taking us through a narrative of his intellectual adventures as he makes progressive strides toward solving the problem of gene copying. Instead of a dry explanation of the chemical process, we get a story, one filled with drama and interest, not exclusively for biochemists.

Many articles on many different subjects use this "process" or "intellectual Odyssey" technique. This approach has at least three advantages over most informational writing: the human presence adds emotion; the sequence of discoveries exploits the drama and tension of narratives; and the method of progressive disclosure allows the writer to educate the reader in small, unthreatening stages.

Indefinite Pronoun: One of

One of the world's most spectacular sand beaches runs from New England down the Atlantic coast, winding around Florida to reach along the northern edge of the Gulf of Mexico . . .

—"Beaches and Barrier Islands," *Scientific American*, July 1987

One of the least understood phenomena of animal life is that in every generation the union of an egg cell and a sperm leads to the formation of an embryo endowed with a predictable spatial organization. This is to say that embryonic cells differentiate into distinct cell types, arrange in recognizable and reproducible patterns to form specific tissues and organs. How these spatial patterns are formed is one of the great enigmas of developmental biology . . .

—"Biological Regeneration and Pattern Formation," *Scientific American*, July 1977

One of the most fundamental questions in archaeology is that of how agriculture came into being. How and why was a way of life based on hunting and gathering replaced by one based on plant and animal husbandry? The question is clearly complex . . .

—"Gazelle Killing in Stone Age Syria," *Scientific American*, Aug. 1987

This formula uses the indefinite pronoun *one* to establish the importance or topicality of the writer's subject. *One* refers to the specific object or idea under consideration, and the *of* phrase locates it in a general class, presumably an interesting and important one. The general classes here are the world's most spectacular sand beaches, the least understood phenomena of animal life, and the most fundamental questions in archaeology (notice that each class is introduced by a superlative: "most spectacular," "least understood," "most fundamental"). In other words, the formula announces the intention to deal with a major, even "superlative" issue. This approach gives writers a head start on establishing the significance of their subject (it *tells* the reader of its magnitude), but it also incurs the challenge of all bold claims—that of delivering the promised goods.

13

The Rhetoric of Adjectives

Pity the poor adjective. Adjectives rarely receive good press: writing texts routinely warn against their overuse; teachers urge the cultivation of nouns and verbs; one editor has called them natural enemies of the noun; and even their defenders concede that there is something self-indulgent and syrupy about using very many of them. The noun's the thing, some argue, and the adjective is only catching a ride, like a pilot fish on a shark. However, even Gertrude Stein, no lover of adjectives herself, did point out that nouns are often only the names of the things we are already talking about. Rhetorically, this observation means that the real news in a sentence may not be in the nouns. In fact, almost any part of speech may bear the real news, may be the center of rhetorical focus, and often it is the adjective.

Adjectives can have varying degrees of importance in a sentence, depending on four factors: meaning, location, number, and punctuation.

General and Specific Adjectives

Writers add adjectives to make nouns less general, to tighten them up and make them more precise. With unmodified nouns, for example, the following sentence tells us little:

She had a manner and a voice.

"Manner" and "voice" take in *all* manners and voices. The original, though, uses two complementary adjectives to present a simple but vivid characterization:

She had a **shy** manner and a **gentle** voice.

—W. Somerset Maugham, *Of Human Bondage*

If adjectives make nouns less general, adjectives themselves can have varying degrees of generality or specificity. Consider some of the following pairs:

the cool air	the frosty air
the uneven surface	the coarse surface
the smooth surface	the velvet surface
the unpleasant taste	the bitter taste
the unpleasant sound	the grating sound
the unpleasant odor	the acrid odor
the loud voice	the booming voice
the difficult child	the quarrelsome child
the dirty rag	the greasy rag
the red letter	the scarlet letter

Our first choice should be an apt noun, one that does not need a modifier. Such a noun being unavailable, we should then look for an apt adjective, one neither too general nor too specific. (Would a red letter have been so shocking on Hester Prynne?)

Trite and All-Purpose Adjectives

We should beware of the adjectives that come first to mind. They may be apt, but overuse has made them worn-out and predictable, destroying their *news* value (*fluffy* clouds, *bitter* end, *sad* commentary, *overwhelming* urge). Even worse than cliched adjectives, which are at least paired with specific nouns, are the all-purpose adjectives. The reigning favorites are *positive* and *negative* (which usually mean simply *good* and *bad* or *favorable* and *unfavorable*, but in context can be replaced with much more specific terms):

He experienced negative feelings.
(He was unhappy, angry, disappointed, and so on.)

Your report received a positive reception.   (They liked your report.)

A fee increase could have a negative impact on enrollment.
(A fee increase could hurt enrollment.)

As a general rule, save *positive* and *negative* for writing about electricity.

Denotation and Connotation

The following pair of sentences illustrates the difference between denotative and connotative meaning:

The hills across the valley of the Ebro were long and white.
—Ernest Hemingway, "Hills Like White Elephants"

The hills across the valley of the Ebro were worn and barren.

Although both sentences describe the same place, they differ rhetorically. The first sentence is objective and representational; the second is subjective and expressive. The first is about the hills, the second about the hills and the observer's feelings toward them. Adjectives make the difference: "long" and "white" are **denotative** words—neutral terms that signify without expressing preference. "Worn" and "barren" are **connotative**, not referring simply to objective qualities but suggesting value judgments and carrying emotional overtones. Other parts of speech—nouns, verbs, adverbs—have varying degrees of denotation and connotation, but adjectives are especially prone to emotional coloration. For this reason many teachers and editors caution about using them, at least in writing that strives for objectivity. The more adjectives we use, the more likely we are to lapse into subjectivity.

Adjectives: Representational and Expressive

As the discussion of connotation and denotation suggests, adjectives are crucial in distinguishing two conflicting motives for writing, *representation* and *expression*. **Representational writing** strives, as the label suggests, for faithful and factual representation, usually of some object or person or event or idea external to the writer. Our central consideration in such writing is to present our subject as it exists in its own right, apart from our own approval or disapproval. Setting aside our personal preferences, we "record" or "report" (we *show*) by focusing on the qualities and characteristics observable to any neutral witness. In this kind of writing, the subject is all; the writer exists only as a conduit for information, a clear lens through which the audience wishes only to see without distortion. Take, for example, the following description of a porcupine:

> The **slow-moving** animal bears 30,000 **sharp** quills: **big, loosely attached guard** hairs, **spongy, light** and **stiff** . . . the **long** quills spear whatever passes within a **critical** distance of their **white** shafts and **black** tips. —*Scientific American*, June 1990

The adjectives here record observations; they do not make value judgments. Another writer might find the quills "springy" instead of "spongy," but the idea is the same. The facts here speak for themselves; they need no interpretation to be vivid and even suggestive.

In **expressive writing** the lens is at least as important as the scene. The lens may be telescopic or microscopic, clouded or rosy, uncommonly lucid or peculiarly distorted, but the reader's interest is in the writer's distinctive way of seeing. Rather than existing in its own right, the subject exists in connection with the writer, as a stimulus for feelings and ideas. The expressive writer is not simply a conduit for information but a responder and an interpreter, and it is the response and the interpretation that the reader values, whether it be sensitive and insightful or aggressive and opinionated. If representational writers are our reporters and recorders, our proxy witnesses limited to neutral, nonjudgmental language, then expressive writers are our critics and tasters, people with a license to indulge their personal opinions and use impassioned language. One writer who used this license freely was the Baltimore journalist H. L. Mencken, as illustrated by his description of the coal and steel towns of Westmoreland County, Pennsylvania. (See "Paragraphs," No. 1, later in this chapter.) A more recent example:

> I present this **plain** and **simple** argument not to defend but to define an **old** and **honorable** tradition in American letters, one still **alive** despite **temporary** muffling by this **gross, slimy, gluttonous** slum of a decade, this age of Reaganism and Servility. —Edward Abbey, "A Writer's Credo"

We do not have to agree with such an evaluation. It may only illustrate one kind of response and give us a standard by which to gauge our own. If Abbey's stance seems immoderate, it at least communicates a sense of urgency, the message that the issue matters and that responsible people must choose a position. (As a character in Graham

Greene's *The Quiet American* says, "Sooner or later, one has to take sides—if one is to remain human.") One person's neutrality is another person's indifference.

Although we can easily contrast representation and expression, motives reflected in the choice of adjectives, actual writing often contains elements of both, even scientific writing:

> The rim of the Pacific, the Mediterranean and central Asia experience most of the world's earthquakes, both **spectacular and small**.

> The **harsh, lifeless** surface of the moon may well be the best place in the inner solar system for human beings to study the universe around them.   —*Scientific American*, Mar. 1990

Objective description dominates both of these statements, but an element of subjectivity asserts itself. In the context of the articles, "small" and "lifeless" describe verifiable qualities. "Spectacular" and "harsh," however, reflect human response or evaluation, even if most people would agree. To a certain extent, they are *telling* words. A little of such vocabulary is often acceptable, especially when it is uncontroversial.

Representation	*Expression*
subject-focused	writer-focused
objective	subjective
impersonal	personal
unemotional	emotional
nonpreferential	preferential
showing	telling

Adjectives: Right Places

Adjectives are either *attributive*, usually appearing next to the nouns they modify, or they are *predicate*, connected to their noun subjects by linking verbs:

Attributive	She had a **shy** manner and a **gentle** voice.
Predicate	Her manner was **shy** and her voice was **gentle**.

By the very nature of the linking verb pattern, predicate adjectives are usually more emphatic than attributive ones: the fresh news, the rhetorical focus, falls at the end of the pattern after the relatively colorless verb:

> Her manner was **shy**.

A predicate adjective has the stage all to itself; an attributive adjective is in a supporting role (even if it is sometimes a scene-stealer) and so shares the stage with a noun:

a **shy** manner   a **gentle** voice

Emphatic Adjectives

Because they are the names of the things we are talking about, nouns are primary, and adjectives, because they are merely attributes added to nouns, are secondary. Nevertheless, we are often not concerned with the entirety of a thing, but only with a selected quality or two. The lobster dinner on the menu may be described a hundred ways, but one adjective may override them all: *expensive*. When selected qualities are more relevant than the whole, or when the shared qualities of a series of objects are paramount, writers have a variety of ways to bring to the fore or to highlight adjectives—to put the right adjectives in the right places:

▶ by inversion of the normal sentence pattern:

Hard, shiny, and **brittle** he* was, with a good polish on his back, and legs bent like wire.
—Richard Llewellyn, *How Green Was My Valley*
(The complements precede the subject and verb.)

Masterly and **dry** and **desolate** he looked, his thin shoulder-blades lifting his coat slightly; blowing his nose violently.
—Virginia Woolf, *Mrs. Dalloway*

▶ by locating adjectives outside of a noun phrase:

The forest rose about him, **mysterious** and **alien**.
—Flannery O'Connor, "The Violent Bear It Away"
(*The mysterious and alien forest* rose about him.)

Liquid and **shiny**, a mix of rain and clay, the trail took them higher.   —Tim O'Brien, *Going After Cacciato*

Friendless, dejected, and **hungry,** he threw himself down in the manure and sobbed.   —E. B. White, *Charlotte's Web*

But what was in it now was not water but the richest wine, **red** as red-currant jelly, **smooth** as oil, **strong** as beef, **warming** as tea, **cool** as dew.   —C. S. Lewis, *Prince Caspian*

* an ant

▶ by using adjectives as appositives:

There was a **blurry** moon up, **pale** and **watery**, in the gently moving branches of the tree. —Patrick White, *The Tree of Man*

The trees and earth were **moon-dry**, **silent** and **airless** and **dead**. —John Steinbeck, *East of Eden*

▶ by using adjectives in balanced or contrasting structures:

He had never seen such a sea of **white** faces, **red** bodies, and **earnest** eyes in all his born days.
—Charles Dickens, *The Pickwick Papers*

She looked at the **strong** body of the **weak** man.
—Patrick White, *The Tree of Man*

Wilbur's stomach was **empty** and his mind was **full**.
—E. B. White, *Charlotte's Web*

▶ by using adjectives in patterns of repetition:

Every word that serves no function, **every** long word that could be a short word, **every** adverb which carries the same meaning that is already in the verb, **every** passive construction that leaves the reader unsure of who is doing what—these are the thousand and one adulterants that weaken the strength of a sentence. —William Zinsser, *On Writing Well*

When I called on him I found him in a **small** room in which a **small** fire was burning in a **small** grate in a **small** fireplace.
—William Saroyan, *Bicycle Rider in Beverly Hills*

He could not have landed in a **better** place at a **better** time with a **better** man. —Elting E. Morison, "The Master Builder"

The Adjective Series

We can also highlight adjectives by compounding them in a series, especially a longer series of four or more items. An average, representative series has three items. A longer series not only calls attention to itself by its very length, it also has a cumulative force:

I wanted to be **whole, powerful, indestructible, efficient, effective, able**. —William Saroyan, *Bicycle Rider in Beverly Hills*

He is **selfish** and **quarrelsome** and **mean** and **disobedient**.
—John Steinbeck, *East of Eden*

The news here is that all these qualities concentrate in one individual. When these qualities are related, the message is one of consistency, even strength. Look what happens, though, when the list takes a sudden turn (from a review of Alvin Toffler's *Powershift: Knowledge, Wealth and Violence at the Edge of the 21st Century*):

> Unhappily, [*Powershift*] has all the weaknesses but only half the strengths of its predecessors: It is **pretentious, bombastic, repetitive,** infuriatingly **facile,** shamefully **simplistic** and more or less entirely **right.**
> —Curt Suplee, "Everything New Is Old Again," *Washington Post*, 26 Nov.–2 Dec. 1990, natl. weekly ed.

Punctuating an Adjective Series

As the previous examples suggest, there is also a rhetoric of punctuation, the impact of a series being partially dependent on how its items are connected and separated. Normally, we use commas to punctuate coordinate adjectives, concluding with an *and* before the final item. The Saroyan sentence omits this final *and* to suggest, in this case, that "able" is climactic, that it caps the previous qualities ("I wanted to be whole, powerful, indestructible, efficient, effective, *able*"). The Steinbeck example itemizes the qualities by separating all of them with "and." The repeated conjunction forces us to read more slowly and pay more attention to each adjective (being the verbal equivalent of plus signs in math, the *and*'s do not compete with the adjectives): "He is selfish *and* quarrelsome *and* mean *and* disobedient." Compare with the more standard form: "the selfish, quarrelsome, mean, and disobedient child."

In addition to standard punctuation, asyndeton, and polysyndeton (see the sections "Polysyndeton: Many Conjunctions" and "Asyndeton: Missing Conjunctions" in Chapter 17, "The Rhetoric of Conjunctions"), there is one little used option:

> The **high cold empty gloomy** rooms liberated me and I went from room to room, singing.   —James Joyce, "Araby"

Technically, these are *coordinate adjectives* and would normally be separated by commas. The structural message would be that the rooms are high + cold + empty + gloomy—separable qualities. Joyce is saying, however, that the rooms are these things all at once, and there is no single adjective to express such a combination of qualities. There is also not a single adjective to describe the following kind of student:

She was every school-teacher's nightmare: a **beautiful preco-cious popular bossy over-sexed** rebellious *intelligent* pupil.

—Iris Murdoch, *The Sacred and Profane Love Machine*

Exercise

Examine adjective use in the following sentences. First, study the devices in each that the writer has used to bring the adjectives to the fore. Next, attempt revisions by "destylizing" them. That is, make them as much like standard sentences as you can: restore normal word order, eliminate repeated words, eliminate series when possible by replacing them with more general words. (Example: He is a selfish, quarrelsome, mean, and disobedient child = He is a rotten child.) Finally, drawing on your own experiences, write imitations of some of the sentences.

1 Bad news has good legs.   —Richard Llewellyn, *How Green Was My Valley*

2 "You notice, it's always twilight here, this land, always October, barren, sterile, dead."   —Ray Bradbury, *Martian Chronicles*

3 In the most commonplace, tiresome, ridiculous, malicious, coarse, crude, or even crooked people or events I had to seek out rare things, good things, comic things, and I did so.
—William Saroyan, *Bicycle Rider in Beverly Hills*

4 The mask was rigid and carved and cold and sightless.
—Bradbury, *Martian Chronicles*

5 The full moon shone high in the blue vault, majestic, lonely, benign.   —Willa Cather, *Death Comes for the Archbishop*

6 And when they laughed, there was no warmth or joy in the sound: high, shrill, ugly, and hysterical, their laughter only asked the earth to notice them.
—Thomas Wolfe, *You Can't Go Home Again*

7 I turned a corner past the slobbery hum of a vacuum cleaner, let myself into my dark office and opened the windows.
—Raymond Chandler, *The Little Sister*

8 Sturdy, pink-faced and chubby, he looked a typical optimist.
—Siegfried Sassoon, *Memoirs of an Infantry Officer*

9 The sky was dark and gloomy, the air was damp and raw, the streets were wet and sloppy.   —Charles Dickens, *The Pickwick Papers*

10 What a rare, peculiar bird he was, with those pointed shoulders, that bare head, his loose nails, almost claws, and those brown, soft, deadly, heavy eyes.   —Saul Bellow, *Seize the Day*

11 He was always a stranger to me, always somehow alien and remote.   —Richard Wright, *Black Boy*

12 Bright, lithe, willowy, radiant, Rita Hayworth flitted and floated through films as though suspended on wires.
—Tom Shales, "Rita Hayworth: The Glory of a Goddess"

13 My manners are exquisite, my feelings are delicate, my gestures refined, my moods unpredictable.
—Bharati Mukherjee, "A Wife's Story"

14 That magnificent lakefront, those terrific windy boulevards, that stupendous Sears skyscraper, like a slab of living rock left standing when the rest of a precipice was quarried away— Chicago is a city fit for giants.   —Jan Morris, "A Passion for Cities"

15 It's charming, disarming, wicked, witty, eccentric, electric, brainy, bold. Best of all, it's yours now—before you send a cent.   —magazine ad

Modifiers: Adjectival, Phrasal, and Clausal

Depending on the desired amount of emphasis, we sometimes have a choice of adding modifiers either as simple words or as phrases or clauses:

> There was a woman who was beautiful, who started with all the advantages, yet she had no luck.
> —D. H. Lawrence, "The Rocking Horse Winner"

	expl	verb		subj
Adjectival	There	was	a **beautiful** woman.	
Phrasal	There	was	a woman **of beauty**.	
Clausal	There	was	a woman **who was beautiful**.	

In most cases the single adjective before the noun is less emphatic than the phrase or clause. In our example, the prepositional phrase is more emphatic than the lone adjective because of its rhythm and because it expresses the quality in a concluding noun—"beauty"; the adjective clause is the most emphatic of the three because it has both the force of a verb and the presence of "beautiful" in the predicate position. A preponderance of modification that is clausal, however, burdens and slows us when we write, and read.

■

Revision Exercise

Applying what you have learned about adjectives, work Erasmus variations on the Lawrence sentence, comparing each version with the original. How does the emphasis change with each revision? For example:

There was a woman, beautiful, privileged, but unlucky.

■

Clausal	A sleet was falling **which turned the roads into sheets of ice.**
Phrasal	A sleet fell, **turning the roads into sheets of ice.**
	A sleet fell, turning the roads into sheets **of ice.**
Adjectival	A sleet fell, turning the roads into **icy** sheets.
	A **falling** sleet turned the roads into **icy** sheets.

■

An Adjective Checklist

1   Are all your adjectives necessary? Do they add appropriate detail? Are any redundant? Have any added an unnecessary degree of precision?

2   Are there any unmodified nouns that would function better in the passage if they were made more precise?

3   Are the adjectives suitably general or particular, abstract or concrete?

4   Do any of the adjectives have inappropriate connotations?

5   Did you lapse into any cliched, all-purpose, or otherwise predictable adjectives?

6   Was it appropriate to highlight any of your adjectives?

7   Do your adjectives describe the subject or express your feelings toward it?

Paragraphs

Examine adjective use in each of the following paragraphs:

1 Begin by deleting as many adjectives as possible (predicate adjectives will have to stay). What happens to the content of the paragraph? To the theme? To tone and precision? To coherence?

2 Examine the adjectives for meaning—for connotation and denotation, objectivity and subjectivity. To what extent is the paragraph representational or expressive? Is the paragraph showing or telling or doing some of both?

3 Choose one subjective, expressive paragraph and revise the adjectives to make it as neutral and representational as possible. In other words, use adjective selection to alter the tone and purpose of the passage. In the process of making the paragraph more representational, do you see any other changes that might be in order?

4 How are the paragraphs punctuated?

No. 1

¹On a winter day, not long ago, coming out of Pittsburgh on one of the swift, luxurious expresses of the Pennsylvania Railroad, I rolled eastward for an hour through the coal and steel towns of Westmoreland county. ²It was familiar ground; boy and man, I had been through it often before. ³But somehow I had never quite sensed its appalling desolation. ⁴Here was the very heart of industrial America, the center of its most lucrative and characteristic activity; the boast and pride of the richest and grandest nation ever seen on earth— and here was a scene so dreadfully hideous, so intolerably bleak and forlorn that it reduced the whole aspiration of man to a macabre and depressing joke. ⁵Here was wealth beyond computation, almost beyond imagination—and here were human habitations so abominable that they would have disgraced a race of alley cats. ·

⁶I am not speaking of mere filth. ⁷One expects steel towns to be dirty. ⁸What I allude to is the unbroken and agonizing ugliness, the sheer revolting monstrousness, of every house in sight. ⁹From East Liberty to Greensburg, a distance of twenty-five miles, there was not one in sight from the train that did not insult and lacerate the eye. ¹⁰Some were so bad, and they were among the most pretentious— churches, stores, warehouses, and the like—that they were downright startling: one blinked before them as one blinks before a man with his face shot away. ¹¹A few masterpieces linger in memory,

horrible even here: a crazy little church just west of Jeannette, set like a dormer-window on the side of a bare, leprous hill; the headquarters of the Veterans of Foreign Wars at another forlorn town; a steel stadium like a huge rat-trap somewhere further down the line. [12]But most of all I recall the general effect—of hideousness without break. [13]There was not a single decent house within eye-range from the Pittsburgh suburbs to the Greensburg Yards. [14]There was not one that was not misshapen, and there was not one that was not shabby.

—H. L. Mencken, "Libido for the Ugly"

No. 2

[1]To the human senses, the most obvious patterning of the surface waters is indicated by color. [2]The deep blue water of the open sea far from land is the color of emptiness and barrenness; the green water of the coastal areas, with all its varying hues, is the color of life. [3]The sea is blue because the sunlight is reflected back to our eyes from the water molecules or from very minute particles suspended in the area. [4]In the journey of the light rays into deep water all the red rays have been absorbed, so when the light returns to our eyes it is chiefly the cool blue rays that we see. [5]Where the water is rich with plankton, it loses the glassy transparency that permits this deep penetration of the light rays. [6]The yellow and brown and green hues of the coastal waters are derived from the minute algae and other micro-organisms so abundant there. [7]Seasonal abundance of certain forms containing reddish or brown pigments may cause the "red water" known from ancient times in many parts of the world, and so common in this condition in some enclosed seas that they owe their names to it—the Red Sea and the Vermilion Sea are examples.

—Rachel L. Carson, *The Sea Around Us*

No. 3

[1]Most of the intelligent land animals have prehensile, grasping organs for exploring their environment—hands in man and his anthropoid relatives, the sensitive inquiring trunk in the elephant. [2]One of the surprising things about the porpoise is that his superior brain is unaccompanied by any type of manipulative organ. [3]He has, however, a remarkable range-finding ability involving some sort of echo-sounding. [4]Perhaps this acute sense—far more accurate than any man has been able to devise artificially—brings him greater knowledge of his water surroundings than might at first seem possible. [5]Human beings think of intelligence as geared to things. [6]The hand

and the tool are to us the unconscious symbols of our intellectual achievement. [7]It is difficult for us to visualize another kind of lonely, almost disembodied intelligence floating in the wavering green fairyland of the sea—an intelligence possibly near or comparable to our own but without hands to build, to transmit knowledge by writing, or to alter by one hairsbreadth the planet's surface. [8]Yet at the same time there are indications that this is a warm, friendly and eager intelligence quite capable of coming to the assistance of injured companions and striving to rescue them from drowning. [9]Porpoises left the land when mammalian brains were still small and primitive. [10]Without the stimulus provided by agile exploring fingers, these great sea mammals have yet taken a divergent road toward intelligence of a high order. [11]Hidden in their sleek bodies is an impressively elaborated instrument, the reason for whose appearance is a complete enigma. [12]It is as though both man and porpoise were each part of some great eye which yearned to look both outward on eternity and inward to the sea's heart—that fertile entity so like the mind in its swarming and grotesque life.

—Loren Eiseley, "The Long Loneliness"

No. 4

[1]Mathematics, rightly viewed, possesses not only truth, but supreme beauty—a beauty cold and austere, like that of sculpture, without appeal to any part of our weaker nature, without the gorgeous trappings of painting and music, yet sublimely pure, and capable of a stern perfection such as only the greatest art can show. [2]The true spirit of delight, the exaltation, the sense of being more than man, which is the touchstone of the highest excellence, is to be found in mathematics as surely as in poetry. [3]What is best in mathematics deserves not merely to be learnt as a task, but to be assimilated as a part of daily thought, and brought again and again before the mind with ever-renewed encouragement. [4]Real life is, to most men, a long second-best, a perpetual compromise between the ideal and the possible; but the world of pure reason knows no compromise, no practical limitations, no barrier to the creative activity embodying in splendid edifices the passionate aspiration after the perfect from which all great work springs. [5]Remote from human passions, remote even from the pitiful facts of nature, the generations have gradually created an ordered cosmos, where pure thought can dwell as in its natural home, and where one, at least, of our nobler impulses can escape from the dreary exile of the actual world.   —Bertrand Russell, "The Study of Mathematics"

No. 5

[1]*An Officer and a Gentleman* seems to come out of a time warp. [2]It's a slick, high-pressured, and well-acted variant of the picture that was made fairly regularly in the thirties and forties: the selfish or arrogant fellow with a chip on his shoulder who joins some branch of the military, learns the meaning of comradeship, and comes out purged—straight and tall, a better human being, one of the team. [3]This is not a genre I'm just wild about; the regenerative moral powers of military discipline interest me less, maybe, than practically any other movie subject I can think of. [4]But I have to admit that the director, Taylor Hackford (his only other feature was last year's *The Idolmaker*), has devised snappy and enjoyable variations on this old familiar tune, even though the script, by Douglas Day Stewart, is schematic, in the manner of TV drama, circa 1955. [5](The minor characters have tragedies so that the major characters can learn lessons. [6]And the people who do what they should are rewarded by happiness, on a good income.) [7]If I wanted a corpse revived, I'd call Taylor Hackford *before anybody else*. [8]Is that a compliment? [9]Yes and no. [10]Somebody who is this astute about jazzing up formula romantic melodrama might be tempted to use the same over-charge even on a live project. [11]He works on us—he fingers the soft spots on our infantile skulls. [12]And he never dawdles: he has a headlong style; he gives the picture so much propulsion that it gains a momentum of its own. [13]It's crap, but crap on a motorcycle.

—Pauline Kael, review of *An Officer and a Gentleman*

For Openers: Adjectives

Thematic Adjectives

The universe is rather **lumpy**: stars gather into galaxies, and galaxies in turn form clusters. With time the universe gets **lumpier** as the gravitational pull of galaxy clusters attracts other galaxies from neighboring regions. Modern theories of galaxy formation assume that in the past the universe was much **smoother** than it is today and that all galaxies and clusters have grown out of small incongruities in an otherwise nearly uniform distribution of matter. The implications of these theories have been studied in great detail, but one basic question still looms above the others: What are the initial incongruities, and where did they come from?

Enter cosmic strings, exotic, invisible entities spun by theories of particle physics. Strings are threads remaining from the fabric of the new-born universe. . . .   —"Cosmic Strings," *Scientific American*, Dec. 1987

The use of "lumpy" illustrates a common tactic for describing complex or remote or otherwise quite technical subjects: reduction to familiar terms. The universe is lumpy, and so are old mattresses and pancake batter. The author could have used the technical language of astrophysicists to describe the galactic phenomenon, but such vocabulary would have immediately limited the audience to insiders. "Lumpy" suggests that nonastrophysicists may be able to follow the discussion (*Scientific American* publishes many articles directed at more general readers). The familiar adjective also suggests another possible attitude: that many "technical" subjects can be approached less technically, that overly-specialized, jargon-laden treatments often mystify and complicate their subjects unnecessarily. We can clarify many specialized discussions by asking several questions: How can I put this in everyday language? and, How would I explain this to an audience of nonspecialists? (Or, perhaps better yet, how can I *justify* this to such an audience?)

Here's another example:

Plant adaptations can be remarkably **complex**. Certain species of orchids, for instance, imitate female bees; other plants look and smell like dead animals, and still others have the appearance of stones. These strange adaptations to life represent just a few of the sophisticated means by which plants enhance their chances of survival.   —"Mimicry in Plants," *Scientific American*, Sept. 1987

As in the previous example, the article begins with a thesis statement whose principal news is contained in an adjective. The structure of the paragraph is basic: the first sentence makes a generalization, the second sentence offers supporting illustrations, and the last sentence summarizes. The subject is plant adaptations; the thesis is that they are complex. Two more adjectives in the last sentence, "strange" and "sophisticated," help maintain thematic continuity. Together, "complex," "strange," and "sophisticated" are all abstract, "telling" words that take their life from the illustrations in the second sentence, a relationship that demonstrates the interdependence of abstract and concrete terms. The formula is a familiar one: "Y is complex [or some other attribute]"; then follows the support.

Let's look at one more:

Valdez, Alaska, is a **small** town with two **big** claims to fame. The first is that on Good Friday 1964 this community of some 4,000 souls was rocked by the most powerful earthquake ever recorded in North America, a catastrophe that killed 33 residents. The second is that Valdez (pronounced val-DEEZ in the local tongue) is the northernmost ice-free port on the continent and has thus become home to the southern terminus of the Trans-Alaska pipeline.

If the water is free of ice year-round, however, the land that surrounds it is anything but . . .

—"Looking for New Challenges, Hard-core Climbers Turn to Ice," *Smithsonian*, Jan. 1988

This article uses contrasting adjectives to begin an indirect approach to its real subject, ice-climbing: Valdez is a "small" town with two "big" claims to fame. The tactic is familiar in popular journalism: "Such-and such is best known for this, *but* . . ." Then we learn another reason why the place is worth our attention. One way to find new topics or to revive old ones is to look for little-known sides to familiar subjects. In other words, one way to introduce new news is to relate it to old news.

14

The Rhetoric of Verbs and Verbals

> ■ *Verbs act. Verbs move. Verbs do. Verbs strike, soothe, grin, cry, exasperate, decline, fly, hurt, and heal. Verbs make writing go, and they matter more to our language than any other part of speech.*
> —Donald Hall, *Writing Well*

In form, function, and meaning, verbs are the most complex part of speech. With all their variations in tense and voice and mood, with the ability of their nonfinite forms (gerunds, participles, infinitives) to function as other parts of speech, with their nuances of meaning (verbs may be not only abstract or concrete, static or dynamic, literal or figurative, but also descriptive, onomatopoetic, and so on), they offer the writer more expressive possibilities, more opportunities for control, than any other part of speech.

The Rhetoric of Meaning

Even as they have a rhetoric of form, verbs have a rhetoric of meaning, one apart from the messages signaled by tense and mood and voice. Like nouns, verbs can be abstract or concrete, can be literal or figurative, can even echo or imitate the action they depict. In one important respect, however, verb meaning differs from noun meaning: verbs can be either static or dynamic; nouns are generally static, the names of things already formed.

Static and Dynamic Verbs

When we call verbs "action words," we are thinking of transitive and intransitive verbs, the verbs that enable subjects to scream or laugh or sing, to raise voices or hurl shouts. These **dynamic verbs** move and energize our sentences:

> The solar system as a whole, like a merry-go-round unhinged, **spins, bobs,** and **blinks** at the speed of 43,200 miles an hour along a course set east of Hercules.*
> —Annie Dillard, *Pilgrim at Tinker Creek*

Not all significant news is narrative action, however. For the sake of description and definition we need the relatively colorless (and also less distracting) linking verbs, or **static verbs,** especially *be.* But if forms of *be* seem bland and uneventful next to verbs like *spin* or *bob* or *blink,* they have the advantage of certitude. Often functioning almost like the grammatical equivalent of an equals sign, *be* signals that the subject and its complement are synonymous, no questions asked ("This is that way, period!"). Because of its very certitude, the fact that it does indeed express *a fact,* the *be* verb is well suited for expository details, especially for descriptions and definitions:

> The average half-life of caffeine in the body, meaning the time it takes the body to get rid of half the caffeine consumed, **is** three to six hours.
> —Corby Kummer, "Is Coffee Harmful?" *The Atlantic,* July 1990

---

* a constellation

Their generic name notwithstanding, the rare earths **are** neither rare nor earths (metal oxides). They **are** metallic elements,
and all but one **are** more abundant in the *earth* than gold, silver, mercury, or tungsten.
—*Scientific American*, Jan. 1988

Turning Be Words into Action Words: Nominal Versus Verbal Styles

Overreliance on forms of *be* can deaden even expository and persuasive
writing, especially by expressing as a definition an idea that might better
be expressed as an action. Consider the following:

The essentiality of practice in the acquisition of teaching skills
is an unexamined assumption in teacher education.
—academic journal

The sentence makes an abstract statement about an abstract subject.
In fact, the subject itself is actually a compound of four abstractions:
essentiality, practice, acquisition, and teaching skills. But instead of
expressing a static equivalence between entities we cannot visualize,
why not look for some action? To have an action, though, we need to
have an actor. Conveniently, the idea of an assumption implies an as-
sumer, a living body or group in action. The context will usually suggest which one.

Teacher trainers have always assumed that practice is essential
for student teachers.

Or, even better:

We have always assumed that student teachers need practice.

As a general rule, living human agents make better subjects than do
abstractions.

Overuse of the *be* verb also typifies a **nominal style**, a style that
relies on nouns rather than verbs to carry the principal meaning. The
nominal (from a word meaning "noun") style consistently relies on the
more static noun to carry the news, a practice that requires more words
and, worse, often creates a sense of impersonality, distancing the actor
from the action. The **verbal style** uses verbs to carry the heaviest part
of the news, a practice that is more economical and energetic, and that
also encourages the writer to find a more human or at least a less abstract
subject.

Nominal	*Verbal*
We make the **assumption** that . . .	We **assume** that . . .
We had a **discussion** of the problem.	We **discussed** the problem.
The halfback **made penetration** into the line.	The halfback **penetrated** the line.
This unit **has the capability** . . .	This unit **can** . . .

Exercise

Attempt to enliven the following sentences by replacing the *be* verb (or other linking verbs) with more active verbs, and by converting nominal structures to verbal ones. In attempting to make the sentences more readable, feel free to make any other changes, including word substitutions and elimination of the passive voice.

You may wish to fine-tune the sentences even further, considering different audiences for your revisions, from informal to formal, from personal acquaintances to members of a professional society.

1   The purpose of the student teaching internship appears reasonably clear in the minds of most educators.

2   Collaborative research between university faculty members and teachers has been tried on both sides of the Atlantic.

3   The assumption underlying the majority of these reports is that competition should be relied upon as the motivation to promote reform.

4   Competitive motivation is likely to be important in the performance of each of these roles.

5   The traditional classroom with a large group, programs with continual teacher guidance or review, emphasis on the basics and discipline, and the use of some multi-media and concrete materials has been the way a vast majority of our schools have been conducted.

6   Another force that caused a greater emphasis to be placed on the practical in teacher education was this country's attempt to provide an equal education for all children.

7 The benefits to teachers of doing research in their classrooms include [are?] increased colleagueship and enhanced opportunity for reflection about practice.

Abstract and General Versus Concrete and Descriptive Verbs

Consider the following sentence:

The train stopped.

This statement presents an abstract narrative detail: a train went from being in motion to being stationary. Anything moving can do the same—a car, a watch, a baseball game—and each in its own peculiar way. How the train stopped is left to the imagination (and may not even matter for certain narrative purposes). One writer, however, wanted to be more specific:

The train **slowed, shuddered** to a halt.

—Angela Carter, "The Bloody Chamber"

The reader can see and almost hear a train that slows and then shudders to a halt. "Shuddered" is a visual image, presenting the shaking and swaying of a train, perhaps even invoking the accompanying noise, the rattle and banging of cars. By being more sensory, the action is more precise and even more emotional (in part because *shuddering* is something living creatures do, usually from a motive like fear or disgust). Or compare the following:

The plane slowly took off.

The plane **lurched** forward, **lifted** over the low trees, **gained** height. —Louise Erdrich, *The Beet Queen*

The first sentence presents a generic action, using the most commonplace verb to relate a plane's departure. In the second sentence, however, Erdrich uses a series of concrete, descriptive verbs to turn a familiar experience into a vivid, one-time event. The plane is not simply and routinely lifting off; it is laboring up into the air. Erdrich's sentence does not simply recount the event; it re-creates it.

Descriptive Verbs: Imitation

Descriptive verbs can go beyond simple concreteness. By sound and rhythm they can suggest the very actions they depict. Recall that when the sounds of verbs imitate their meanings, we say that they are *onomatopoetic*:

> The legs of his canvas trousers **whispered** against one another.
> —Truman Capote, *The Grass Harp*

> As the boat **bounced** from the top of each wave the wind tore through the hair of the hatless men. And as the craft **plopped** her stern down again the spray **slashed** past them.
> —Stephen Crane, "The Open Boat"

> The westbound lane **boiled** and **boomed** with vehicles which were rushing German reserves to the front.
> —Kurt Vonnegut, Jr., *Slaughterhouse-Five*

By repetition and punctuation, a writer can also make a verb series "imitate" an event, as the following illustrate:

> It rang three times, stopped, rang again and stopped, rang a few more times and stopped.   —Gay Talese, *Honor Thy Father*

> The lightning waved and darted round him its silent flames, the water of the deluge fell, ran, leaped, drove—noiseless like the drift of mist.   —Joseph Conrad, *Under Western Eyes*

> They dove, splashed, floated, splashed, swam, snorted. They were like happy seals.   —James T. Farrell, *Young Lonigan*

The three previous sentences illustrate some of the power and energy of the *verb series*, especially sequences of action verbs—in these cases, intransitives.

In the following sentence William Saroyan uses an abstract verb phrase to introduce an action, then illustrates it with a series of concrete verbs that are punctuated to re-create the rhythm of the action:

> But best of all was when the wind had great power, when it was erratic and **did swift and sudden things,** <u>stopped</u> suddenly, <u>picked up</u> suddenly, <u>ran</u> in a circle, <u>sprinted</u> straight ahead, <u>stopped, turned, came back.</u>   —*Bicycle Rider in Beverly Hills*

The concrete verbs, in effect, form an appositive series, with the introductory "did swift and sudden things" *telling*, and the series *showing*. The abrupt punctuation, omitting the usual *and* that appears before the final item (*asyndeton*), reinforces the action.

By contrast, a writer can also create an opposite effect with a verb series, an effect of slow, deliberate progression, by using **polysyndeton,** placing a conjunction between each item:

He flipped the steaks and pressed them down with his spatula and gathered up the wilting onions and forced them down into the meat. —John Steinbeck, *In Dubious Battle*

This is the picture of a man making his meal precisely, carefully. Compare this with what happens when we use conventional punctuation:

He flipped the steaks, pressed them down with his spatula, gathered up the wilting onions, and forced them down into the meat.

Metaphoric Verbs

A *metaphor* is an implied comparison, usually illustrated in noun structures. (See the section "Nouns as Metaphors" in Chapter 11, "The Rhetoric of Nouns.")

The sun was a pink hedge-rose above the frozen lake.
—Janet Beeler Shaw, "No Place to Be on Christmas"

Stocking-footed, she looked girlish. She was a cat stepping into a barn where there were mice to be caught.
—"No Place to Be on Christmas"

In actual practice, however, metaphors occur at least as frequently in verbs and verbals, where they can possess a subtlety and grace they often lack in their starker noun forms:

My mind **stampedes.**
—Amy Hempl, "In the Cemetery Where Al Jolson Is Buried"

Spring **jitterbugs** inside me. —Gretel Ehrlich, "Snow"

Across the median, steady traffic **turtled** north, family heirlooms strapped to roof carriers.
—Bob Schacochis, "Written in the Big Wind," *Harper's*, Sept. 1991

Literally, of course, only a herd of frightened cattle or horses can stampede, only dancers can jitterbug, and the traffic was of automobiles (the roof carriers are a clue). Only figuratively can our thoughts stampede, a season dance inside of someone, or cars be turtles. Even given the license of figurative language, how can we use these images in a noun construction without sounding excessively or self-consciously "literary"?

Mixed Metaphors

Because verbal metaphors are more subtle than noun ones, it is easier to fall into the error of "mixing" them, of using inconsistent imagery:

> Last year they **planted the seeds** and this year they **ballooned.** —sportscaster
>
> You can't **go to the well** too often or you will **get burned.** —sportscaster

These **mixed metaphors** were uttered in the heat of broadcasting live sporting events. Successful broadcasters and commentators are expected to be "colorful," a demand encouraging use of **cliches** or prefabricated expressions. In the spontaneity of live commentary, with little time for deliberation, broadcasters can easily mismatch their images. Writers, however, have the luxury of weighing their words and revising. If they read their material aloud and listen and visualize, they should catch such blunders.

Alert listeners and readers notice mixed metaphors, so some people intentionally create them. Commenting on budget cuts threatened by a massive budgetary deficit, one legislator quipped that "Everyone's sacred cows are coming home to roost." In a satiric novel Tom Wolfe used the same image to express his besieged hero's predicament at a fashionable party:

> All at once he was alone in this noisy hive with no place to roost. —*The Bonfire of the Vanities*

Birds, not bees, roost, but at least both fly.

> My thoughts are a herd of stampeding cattle.
>
> Spring was a dancer doing the jitterbug inside me.
>
> Across the median, the cars were a line of turtles heading north . . .

A form of metaphor is **personification,** a figurative device in which a writer attributes to something inanimate the powers of the living. Personification generally relies upon verbs:

> Over in a corner a round oak table **brooded** on its heavy pedestal. —Cynthia Ozick, "Rosa"

Objectively speaking, of course, a table does not have emotions; it cannot brood, sulk, pout, or fret. Subjectively, though, to a writer or to a character in a story, a table can seem to brood. Indirectly, the idea of brooding reveals at least as much about the narrator or character as about the table. (See the section "Adjectives: Representational and Expressive" in Chapter 13, "The Rhetoric of Adjectives.")

Exercise

A   To understand and appreciate the function of verbal metaphors in the following sentences, begin by being literal-minded: try to visualize the images literally instead of figuratively. Then replace the metaphoric verbs or verbals with nonmetaphoric equivalents. What happens to the quality of the description? What do the metaphors allow the writer to express? Then try turning the verbal metaphors into noun constructions. Finally, using your own observations, select two or three sentences and write imitations of them.

1 From her feet the ground sloped sharply into view, and violets ran in rivulets and streams and cataracts, irrigating the hillside with blue, eddying round the tree stems, collecting into pools in the hollows, covering the grass with spots of azure foam.
—E. M. Forster, *A Room with a View*

2 The nine islands of the Azorean archipelago knuckle up out of the Atlantic eight hundred miles west of Portugal, each one a terraced garden lifting corn, bananas, figs, and oranges to the sky.   —*Esquire*, Feb. 1990

3 A fine-edged light, aluminum foil, tented the buildings and the power plant.   —Janet Beeler Shaw, "No Place to Be on Christmas"

4 People at the table laughed and shook their heads as they shovelled up their eggs.   —Raymond Carver, "Where I'm Calling From"

5 But extending a grimy hand and beaming his most killing D'Artagnan smile, Beargrease is already waving like a returning hero to the faces buoying beneath those windshields.
—Bruce Duffy, "Catching a Westbound Freight"

6 The late-summer moon, like a veined marble bowl, spills out an abundance of light.
—Melissa Brown Pritchard, "A Private Landscape"

7 The wind was brawling out of the north when they told her she had to move.   —Helen Norris, "The Love Child"

8 The air is windpressed into a lens, magnifying and sharpening and silencing—everything is silenced in the uproar of the wind that comes ransacking down out of the North.

—Walker Percy, *The Moviegoer*

9 The wind veers around to the north and blows away the storm until the moon swims high, moored like a kite and darting against the fleeing shreds and ragtags of cloud.

—*The Moviegoer*

10 With the canoe beaked over us, we slid down the driveway, turned left and picked up speed, then turned left again and cruised.   —James Dickey, *Deliverance*

B   Examine verb use in the following sentences. How does each sentence use the verb to create special effects, to convey the "news"? What other elements besides verbs contribute to the effect? Finally, to what degree does each sentence report an event as opposed to expressing the writer's feelings toward it? What is the balance, in other words, between objective presentation and subjective interpretation?

1 The plane jounced and wobbled to the end of the runway, where it roared a moment, shaking like a leaf; then it spun around and came back down the strip, bounding the ruts and depressions like some huge ancient bird seeking to get aloft.

—Peter Matthiessen, *At Play in the Fields of the Lord*

2 The mists swarmed past the window and the cabin darkened; lights, flickering off and on, bounced and shuddered with the plane itself, which roared confusedly in its descent through the updrafts of the rain forest.   —*At Play in the Fields of the Lord*

3 The plane dipped, rolled, buzzed, glided above us and I was no more impressed than if it had been some sort of insect.

—Louise Erdrich, *The Beet Queen*

4 The train gave a lurch, moved forward, faltered, stopped again, and a low concerted groan went through the car.

—William Styron, *Sophie's Choice*

5 The craft pranced and reared and plunged like an animal.

—Stephen Crane, "The Open Boat"

6 The rain slackens and tires hiss on the wet asphalt.

—Walker Percy, *The Moviegoer*

7 I pulled out the broom and tore out a batch of straws and tossed them into the fire and watched them smoke, turn black, blaze, and finally become white wisps of ghosts that vanished. —Richard Wright, *Black Boy*

8 Sunday afternoon sunlight streamed dustily through the heavy lace curtains of the window, squirmed in the red roses of the carpet, filled the cluttered parlor with specks and splinters of light. —John Dos Passos, *Manhattan Transfer*

9 The frozen twigs of the huge tulip poplar next to the hill clack in the cold like tinsnips. —Annie Dillard, *Pilgrim at Tinker Creek*

10 A whirling air in his swim bladder balances the goldfish's weight in the water; his scales overlap, his feathery gills pump and filter; his eyes work, his heart beats, his liver absorbs, his muscles contract in a wave of extending ripples.
—*Pilgrim at Tinker Creek*

11 She blushed, gulped, swallowed, looked shocked and horror-stricken. —James T. Farrell, *Young Lonigan*

12 He could read, he could even work complicated sums in his head, but he could not write a complete sentence.
—Mavis Gallant, "In a War"

13 It took a great deal of goading to persuade the turtle to seize the broomstick at all—it plainly would have preferred the hand that held it—but it finally took it, held it, and crushed and pulped it. —Franklin Burroughs, "A Snapping Turtle in June"

14 Beyond it, in every field and wood, the alert ears of rabbits rose from their holes, the sleepy heads of birds came out from under wings, owls hooted, vixens barked, hedgehogs grunted, the trees stirred. —C. S. Lewis, *Prince Caspian*

15 Wind drove rain in at him when he opened the street-door, drove it into his face as he walked a block back to the garage on the corner. —Dashiell Hammett, *The Glass Key*

Verb Tense and Narration: Past Tense

Narration tells a story, a connected series of events, but there can be no story without a teller and a time. The first is a matter of pronouns (see the section "Pronouns and Point of View" in Chapter 12, "The Rhetoric of Pronouns"), the second of verbs.

Most stories, whether fact or fiction, are told in the past tense, which reports one-time events that have already occurred. An event reported in the past tense has a sense of actuality, of completion. It is settled; it happened that way. Furthermore, the distance also implies time for evaluation, time to separate relevant from irrelevant detail. And although the past tense presupposes a narrator looking back, in control, and presumably a survivor of the events, it can nevertheless achieve effects of excitement and suspense, even when supplemented with interpretation, as illustrated in the following account of white-water canoeing:

> [1]For a second I couldn't see anything at all, and rode like I was standing still with aerated water filling my mouth and little fluttering bumps coming up through the canoe shell. [2]With nothing to see go past, motion died. [3]It was like being in a strange room in a cold building or a shaking cave filled with cold steam. [4]I was wet clear through before I could think: the sun was killed on my shoulders in an instant. [5]I lanced out again to the right with the paddle, mainly because that was the last place I had taken a stroke, and if it was right then it might be right now. [6]I was sure that we had to turn, keep turning left if we could; the right felt like death, and if I couldn't keep it away from us we would spin broadside and the whole river and all the mountains it came from would fall on us, would pour into the canoe ton after ton, neverending. [7]I dug again, but couldn't tell what I had made us do. [8]Something snatched at the paddle and I pulled it out and dug again, and again. [9]The river showed in front in a blinking leap, and we came shooting forward as though launched to take off into the air. [10]We were going faster than I had ever been in anything without an engine. [11]The force of water around the paddle blade was stupendous; I felt as though I had dipped into some supernatural source of primal energy.
>
> —James Dickey, *Deliverance*

Present-Tense Narration

Present-tense narrations can be of two types, depending on the use of detail. On the one hand, writers often use the present tense to narrate a "process," an abstract or generalized or habitual action. Compare the following two versions:

> She got up at seven and turned the radio on.
>
> She gets up at seven and turns the radio on.

The first sentence narrates a particular event. Even though she may have risen many times at seven and turned on the radio, the form refers to one specific occasion. By contrast, the second sentence narrates a routine, something she does almost every day. Under certain circumstances, the present tense suggests, the same predictable things will occur. Hence, John Cheever uses the present tense to dramatize the monotonous domestic routine of his fictional characters in "The Season of Divorce":

> ¹She gets up at seven and turns the radio on. ²After she is dressed, she rouses the children and cooks the breakfast. ³Our son has to be walked to the school bus at eight o'clock. ⁴When Ethel returns from this trip, Carol's hair has to be braided. ⁵I leave the house at eight-thirty, but I know that every move that Ethel makes for the rest of the day will be determined by the housework, the cooking, the shopping, and the demands of the children. ⁶I know that on Tuesdays and Thursdays she will be in the A & P between eleven and noon, that on every clear afternoon she will be on a certain bench in a playground from three until five, that she cleans the house on Mondays, Wednesdays, and Fridays, and polishes the silver when it rains. ⁷When I return at six, she is usually cleaning the vegetables or making some other preparation for dinner. ⁸Then when the children have been fed and bathed, when the dinner is ready, when the table in the living room is set with food and china, she stands in the middle of the room as if she had lost or forgotten something, and this moment of reflection is so deep that she will not hear me if I speak to her, or the children if they call. ⁹Then it is over. ¹⁰She lights the four white candles in their silver sticks, and we sit down to a supper of corned-beef hash or some other modest fare.

Since the present tense can report recurrent or general events (what some individual or group does repeatedly), it is ideal for certain kinds of academic assignments, those calling for accounts of governmental, scientific, or other processes—the impeachment of a public official or the filling of a seat on the Supreme Court, photosynthesis or the behavior of star clusters:

> Deep in space, a star cluster performs a cosmic dance to the tune of gravity. During a human lifetime the stars barely move; over a longer span, in which years are equivalent to seconds, they trace out a tangled figure of orbits. Occasionally a

single star encounters a neighbor in a pas de deux* that hurls
it out into space. If such escapes are more than occasional, the
cluster gradually shrinks and the core begins to collapse.

—"Computer Recreations," *Scientific American*, Feb. 1985

A second type of present-tense narration, one enjoying a growing
popularity with fiction writers and journalists, exploits the immediacy
of an event unfolding before the reader's eyes. Past-tense action, by
definition, is over, completed. This sense of completion means that
both writer and reader are distanced by time from the events. The
reader may not know the outcome, may even be in suspense about what
happened (a response mystery writers understand well), but everything
has been decided. It is only our knowledge of the outcome that is
actually in doubt. By contrast, a present-tense event is *coming out*;
where, we will see. The following is a familiar use of the present tense
in modern journalism:

> EMPORIA, Va.—A high-school student pushes through the mob
> in front of the eight giant pillars of the Greensville County
> Court House and thrusts a scrap of paper at the gubernatorial
> candidate. It says: "This is to certify that Edwin Taylor was
> present at Doug Wilder's speech."
>
> Edwin Taylor, the 17-year-old student, is black, and so is
> Doug Wilder, the Democratic nominee for governor in Vir-
> ginia. They both stand only yards from the monument to Con-
> federate war dead who fought "in defense of rights they
> believed sacred" at the center of this tiny town near the North
> Carolina border. And then, in the autumnal sunshine, the stu-
> dent brandishes the paper signed by Mr. Wilder. "It's special to
> me that we might have a black governor," he says. "If we do
> have a black governor, we all have hope."
>
> —David Shribman, "Now Vastly Changed, Virginia May Choose a Black
> Governor," *Wall Street Journal*, 11 Oct. 1989

The event, by its very particularity, is specific and nonrepeatable, the
amount and nature of the detail preventing the usual generalizing effect
of process narration. On the contrary, the immediacy, reinforced by
the liberal use of quotations, is the closest a narrated event can come
to actual dramatization, to something happening before us now instead
of in someone's remembered past.

Journalists and storytellers also use the *present progressive* to catch
the immediacy of actions taking place *now*:

* in ballet, a dance or figure for two dancers

¹At 1:30 in the afternoon on a muggy spring Monday in Boston, the Oakland Athletics are working on their data base. ²Tony La Russa, the Oakland manager, and three of his aides are working in the small, spartan office used by the visiting team's manager, just off the larger but still cramped room where the team dresses. ³There will be a game tonight at Fenway, and the pulse of the ballpark is quickening. ⁴For the men in La Russa's office the atmosphere is like that inside a cramped bunker during a day of desultory shelling at Verdun. ⁵The booming cannons echoing in the concrete cubicle at Fenway are actually beer kegs being unloaded, none too gently, from trucks and onto the concrete floor on the other side of the cubicle's wall. ⁶The only soft sounds in the office are the splats of tobacco juice into paper cups.

—George F. Will, *Men at Work: The Craft of Baseball*

Exercise

A   Revise the two previous paragraphs from *The Wall Street Journal* and *Men at Work* into the more conventional past tense. What happens? How does the impact of the events change? Does it seem appropriate to alter any of the other details?

B   Revise the James Dickey white-water canoeing episode into the present tense. Concentrate on reporting the concrete details of the action. Minimize the presence of the narrator, excluding any imaginative interpretation of the events. If you think it is necessary, invent details. What effects are gained? Lost?

Uses of the Participle

Participles are dynamic adjectives or, more precisely, words halfway between adjectives (qualities) and verbs (actions). Because they generally modify nouns, we think of them functionally as adjectives, but participles have much of the rhetorical force of verbs. The past participle is closer to a standard adjective, but sometimes its connotations of passivity are part of the news:

Carved by six million years of stream erosion, Waimea Canyon cuts a crimson slice in Kauai's western side.   —*Sunset*, Feb. 1990

Actions are either sequential or simultaneous. We usually express sequence by using consecutive verbs and verb phrases, sometimes reinforced by *and*'s ("I cut a slice and ate it"). Simultaneity we express with the present participle, its *-ing* form carrying the idea of uninterruptedness ("Lifting the knife quietly and looking furtively over my shoulder, I cut myself a slice"). In the following, for example, we see three separate and simultaneous physical actions preparing for the action in the main clause:

> **Standing in the middle of the floor, holding her bath robe around her and trailing a damp towel in one hand,** she surveyed the immediate past and remembered everything clearly.   —Katherine Anne Porter, "Theft"

Sometimes this stage-setting is extensive:

> **Crumpled into a wad of wrinkles,** like the fossilized brain of a dryad*; **looking weathered; seeming slow and rough enough to be a product of natural evolution;** its brownness the low-key brown of potato skin and peanut shell—dirty but pure; its kinship to tree (to knot and nest) **unobscured by the cruel crush of industry; absorbing the elements like any other organic entity; blending with rock and vegetation as if it were a burrowing owl's doormat or a jack rabbit's underwear,** a No. 8 Kraft paper bag lay discarded in the hills of Dakota—and appeared to live where it lay.
> —Tom Robbins, *Even Cowgirls Get the Blues*

Most often, participial phrases appear after main clauses, themselves presenting a generalized action that the participials make more detailed and precise:

> In the cockpit I push gently on the throttle, **easing it forward, rousing the motor, feeding it, soothing it.**
> —Beryl Markham, *West with the Night*

Exploiting the grace and fluidity of the present participle, supplemented by the effect of parallelism, a writer can add them almost indefinitely:

> For centuries, ever since the first inhabitants, fleeing enemy tribes, settled in the bogs where no one cared to bother them, <u>the Dutch struggled against water and learned how to live with it:</u> **building on mounds, constructing and reconstructing**

---

* in myth, a nymph living in a tree

seawalls of clay mixed with straw, carrying mud in an endless
train of baskets, laying willow mattresses weighted with
stones, repairing each spring the winter's damage, draining
marshes, channeling streams, building ramps to their attics to
save the cattle in times of flood, gaining dike-enclosed land
from the waves in one place and losing as much to the re-
vengeful ocean somewhere else, progressively developing
methods to cope with their eternal antagonist.
—Barbara Tuchman, "Mankind's Better Moments"

Writing a sentence over a hundred words long but still perfectly clear,
Tuchman uses eleven participial phrases to describe how the Dutch
learned to thrive in almost impossible circumstances. And the series is
not simply a mechanical listing; it is climactic, the last phrase telling
what the first ten have shown: how the Dutch *progressively* developed
methods "to cope with their eternal antagonist."

Exercise

Examine the narrative and descriptive functions of participles and *absolutes* in the following sentences. Try revisions in which you reduce
the number of such structures, turning some of them into main verbs
or even into separate sentences. Experiment with relocating them. What
happens to the news?

1   Antelope, moving in small, graceful bands, travel at 60 miles
an hour, their mouths open as if drinking in the space.
—Gretel Ehrlich, "The Solace of Open Spaces"

2   Cloud and water mixed into each other, dripping with colors,
merging, overlapping, liquefying, with steeples and balconies
floating in space, like the fragments of some stained-glass window seen through a dozen veils of rice-paper.
—Lawrence Durrell, *Bitter Lemons*

3   Uninvited and uninsultable, his skin thicker than bear hide,
he moves in on them one by one.
—Mordecai Richler, "Notes on an Endangered Species"

4   The blue boat rides up and down the bayou, opening the
black water like a knife.   —Walker Percy, *The Moviegoer*

5   Witt had from the first found it necessary to lead Corde step
by step, rehearsing him, instructing him, making certain that

he would interpret budgetary, educational, institutional policies appropriately.   —Saul Bellow, *The Dean's December*

6   I had seen her jump rope, inexhaustibly, with lots of tricks,
on one foot, or with a quick two-step, or skipping through
the snapping arcs, hip-hopping through a double rope, the
left and the right coming from opposite directions, and do it
faster and longer than anyone else.
—E. L. Doctorow, *Billy Bathgate*

7   Spade's thick fingers made a cigarette with deliberate care,
sifting a measured quantity of tan flakes down into curved
paper, spreading the flakes so that they lay equal at the ends
with a slight depression in the middle, thumbs rolling the
paper's inner edge down and up under the outer edge as
forefingers pressed it over, thumbs and fingers sliding to the
paper cylinder's ends to hold it even while tongue licked the
flap, left forefinger and thumb pinching their end while right
forefinger and thumb smoothed the damp seam, right forefinger and thumb twisting their end and lifting the other to
Spade's mouth.   —Dashiell Hammett, *The Maltese Falcon*

Participles and the Clumsy As Clause: Phrasal and Clausal Modification

Look what happens when we revise the Tuchman paragraph by turning
each participial phrase into an *as* clause:

. . . the Dutch struggled against water and learned how to live
with it, **as** they built on mounds, **as** they constructed and re-
constructed seawalls of clay mixed with straw, **as** they carried
mud in an endless train of baskets . . .

With this pattern the train of clauses becomes endless, and awkward.
As tells that an action is simultaneous; furthermore, it introduces a
clause, not a phrase, with all the weight of a finite verb. As a rule,
clausal modification is heavier (but also more emphatic) because it contains
a full verb. But a little emphasis goes a long way. *Phrasal modification* is
more graceful and less obtrusive. If we think of a sentence as a drive,
a dependent *as* clause is a sharp turn, and a participial phrase a gentle
curve. Nevertheless, less skilled writers often overrely on the *as* structure to present simultaneous action:

> She seemed to commune silently with spirits only she knew
> were there **as she watched the tall grass rustle softly in the**
> **breeze,** and felt the warmth of the sun shine down on her
> wheat-colored hair, **as she began to sing softly.**
> —popular romance novel

Of course this sentence has other problems besides its overreliance on the *as* clause. It lacks any rhetorical focus. What is its main point, its news? And which details are the most important? And what about the natural sequence of the events?

> She seemed to commune silently with spirits . . . and
> felt the warmth of the sun shine down on her . . .

These are hardly equal actions. Furthermore, the point of view changes, going from how she seemed (how she looked to someone else), to what she was feeling. Participial phrases would reduce some of the confusion:

> **Watching the tall grass rustle softly in the breeze,** and **feeling**
> **the warmth of the sun shine down on her wheat-colored hair,**
> she seemed to commune silently with spirits only she knew
> were there, then she began to sing softly.

Exercise

The following are more narrative sentences, from a best-selling romance novel, encumbered with *as* clauses. Try to make them more graceful by replacing the clausal with phrasal modifiers. To revise the sentences successfully, you will have to decide about the principal "news" of each.

1 Her eyes were the color of the summer sky, her limbs long and graceful as she suddenly began to run, pressing the damp grass beneath her feet as she headed toward the river.

2 He set down his drink and threw open the door to the terrace as a cool breeze swept in and he followed her down the stairs to the sand, as she began to run, feeling the wind on her face and in her hair, and for the first time in a long time she was happy.

3 From the distance she looked every bit a woman as she stood holding her long pale blond hair on top of her head with one hand, as the curves of her exquisite body were swallowed slowly by the icy water.

4   Crystal stood alone in her room for a moment, humming to herself as she peeled off her nightgown, and tossed it easily into a damp heap in the corner, as she glanced up at the dress she would be wearing to Becky's wedding.

5   "I hate him, Mama! I hate him!" She was referring to her brother as her long brown hair hung damply down her back, and tears stung her eyes as she looked angrily at her mother and sister, berating Jared.

6   The ice cream was dripping messily as she fought not to lose what was left, and looked like a child herself, leaning into the street as it dripped on the cowboy boots and she grinned at the little girl watching her.

Paragraphs

Examine the various uses to which successful writers put verbs and verbals in each of the following paragraphs, allowing for the type of writing (narrative, descriptive, and so on):

1   What kind of verbs prevail, "action" or linking?

2   What is the governing tense?

3   To what extent are the verbs abstract or concrete, dynamic or static, neutral or descriptive, literal or figurative?

4   Do the writers create any effects with sound, rhythm, or repetition?

5   To what extent do the writers extend verb force to other parts of speech by using gerunds, infinitives, and participles?

6   Do the verbals have any of the qualities mentioned in questions 3 and 4?

7   If the paragraph is a narrative, experiment with different tenses. What happens to the effect of the narrative? Does a different tense suggest any other changes?

8   How are the paragraphs punctuated?

No. 1

On a new minicomputer:

¹The most important characteristic of the 32-bit mini was its system of storage. ²Storage in a computer resembles a telephone sys-

tem, in the sense that every piece of information in storage is assigned a unique number, so that it can be readily found. [3]If the standard length of a phone number is seven digits, then enough unique numbers can be generated to serve the needs of New York CIty; but if a three-digit area code is added, every telephone customer in America can have a unique number. [4]The 32-bit supermini was a computer with an area code. [5]Since the advent of Data General, most minis had been "16-bit" machines. [6]The standard length of the numbers that such a machine assigns to items in its storage is 16 bits, 16 binary digits. [7]A 16-bit machine can directly generate only about 65,000 unique numbers in its storage system. [8]A 32-bit machine, however, can directly generate some 4.3 *billion* different numbers.   —Tracy Kidder, *The Soul of a New Machine*

No. 2

On snapping turtles:

[1]The shell and skin are a muddy gray; the eye, too, is of a murky mud color. [2]The pupil is black and shaped like a star or a spoked wheel. [3]Within the eye there is a strange yellowish glint, as though you were looking down into turbid water and seeing, in the depths of the water, light from a smoldering fire. [4]It is one of Nature's more nightmarish eyes. [5]The eyes of dragonflies are also nightmarish, but in a different way—they look inhuman, like something out of science fiction. [6]The same is true of the eyes of sharks. [7]The snapper's eye is dull, like a pig's, but inside it there is a savage malevolence, something suggesting not only an evil intention toward the world, but the torment of an inner affliction. [8]Had Milton seen one, he would have associated it with the baleful eye of Satan, an eye reflecting some internal hell of liquid fire—whether in Paradise or here on a soft June day, with the bobolinks fluttering aloft and singing in the fields. [9]Snapping turtles did in fact once inhabit Europe, but they died out by the end of the Pleistocene, and so were unknown to what we think of as European history. [10]But they look, nevertheless, like something that Europeans had half imagined or dimly remembered even before they came to the New World and saw them for the first time: a snapper would do for a gargoyle, or a grotesque parody of a knight on his horse, a thing of armored evil.

—Franklin Burroughs, "A Snapping Turtle in June"

No. 3

[1]The cheetah, a virtual running machine, is a model of aerodynamic engineering. [2]Its skull is small and lightweight and its limbs

are long and slender, not unlike a greyhound's. [3]Its heart, vascular system, lungs and adrenil glands are all enlarged, enhancing the animal's ability to accelerate and navigate during a high-speed chase. [4]In addition, the cheetah's claws are semi-retractile: they are always extended like cleats, in contrast to the claws of other species in the cat family (*Felidae*), which are normally withdrawn and covered with a protective sheath. [5]These various adaptations have made the cheetah a particularly effective hunter on the flat, open savannas of central and southern Africa, where it has a higher rate of successful kills than even the lion. [6]After stalking its prey the cheetah launches a high-speed chase (often clocked at up to 70 miles per hour), pushes over or trips its winded victim and swiftly kills the prey by strangulation in its strong feline jaws.

—"The Cheetah in Genetic Peril," *Scientific American*, May 1986

Compare paragraphs 2 and 3. Both are descriptive accounts of two fierce beings. To what extent do they use "objective" and "subjective" detail? How do you account for the difference in tone and treatment? What assumptions does each make about its audience? (Remember the two big questions about audience: What do they know? What do they want?)

No. 4

[1]Recently, on a flight to West Palm Beach, as a south wind carried wave after wave of rain against the windows, I felt it again, the deep boom of Provincetown Bay slapping at foundations, sucking its breath in, holding it, then heaving it out. [2]We were threading our way between storm systems in an eerie yellow-green light, the wake of a passing tornado. [3]Bouldery clouds, stacked precariously on one another, trembled, stretching, towering higher and higher above the plane, then suddenly toppled, the plane falling with them as if through a trap door. [4]I had entered the realm of process, where skying was all that mattered. [5]To the left, racing us, was a thick black cloud, flat as a mattress, a flying carpet with three dark threads tentacling down. [6]As we banked, cloud after cloud tumbled toward us, breakers, whitecapped, foaming, spewing spray—and then it was the ocean, all its teeth bared.

—Susan Mitchell, "Dreaming in Public: A Provincetown Memoir"

No. 5

[1]On the night of last August 24, a small, angular contraption hurtled over the cloud tops of Neptune. [2]It swooped barely 3,000 miles above the great blue planet's north pole, plunged down the

night side, scooted past the large moon Triton at a distance of 24,000 miles and vanished into the void. [3]During that brief encounter the visitor meticulously snapped thousands of images and radioed them to the earth. [4]Scientists waiting at the Jet Propulsion Laboratory in Pasadena, Calif., cheered and uncorked champagne as the pictures— humankind's first close-up look at the eighth planet—came into focus on their screens.

[5]*Voyager 2* had taken 12 years to reach Neptune, the fourth and final destination of a planetary pilgrimage that included Jupiter and Saturn (both were also visited by the probe's twin, *Voyager 1*), as well as Uranus. [6]Of all the planets on the itinerary, Neptune was the least known. [7]Overhauling the on-board computer programs and gingerly firing the thruster rockets, the Voyager team steered the aging ship to a flawless encounter. [8]From signals that reached the earth with a strength of less than a ten-quadrillionth of a watt, the team gleaned images of breath-taking clarity . . .

—June Kinoshita, "Neptune," *Scientific American: Exploring Space* (special issue), 1990

What properties of verbs and verbals does the writer exploit to re-create the visit of *Voyager 2*? How much of the detail is neutral reporting and how much interpretation? And what is the effect of delaying identification of the visitor?

No. 6

[1]A loudspeaker honks and burbles. [2]Incredibly, and for the next hour, we have take-off and landing limits. [3]Our plane is getting through; and sure enough, presently it bumbles out of the fog from the runway. [4]I go with our group to Gate Nine, shudder into a freezing night with a dull grey roof. [5]The jet crawls towards us, howling and whistling with rage, perhaps at the fog or perhaps at the human bondage which keeps it only just under control. [6]For a moment or two, it faces us—no, is end-on to us; for here there is no touch of human, or animal, or insect, no face—only four holes that scream like nothing else in creation. [7]Then it huddles round and is still. [8]Doors open and two streams of passengers ooze out. [9]Their faces are haggard. [10]They ignore the night that has caught up with them. [11]They stagger, or walk with the stiff gait of stage sleep-walkers. [12]One or two look stunned, as if they know it is midnight more or less but cannot remember if it is today or tomorrow night and why or what. [13]Strange vehicles flashing all over with red lights come out of the darkness, not for the passengers, but to tend the jet. [14]They crouch under the wings and the front end, attach themselves by tubes while all their lights flash, and lights on the jet flash, and the

engines sink from a wail to a moan—a note, one might think, of resignation, as if the machine now recognizes that it is caught and will have to do the whole thing over again. [15]But for half an hour they feed it well, while it sucks or they blow, and we stand, imprisoned by the freezing cold and our own need to be somewhere else. [16]Jet travel is a great convenience.   —William Golding, "Body and Soul"

What happens when you put the previous account into the conventional past tense?

For Openers: Verbs and Verbals

Be-*Word Sentences: Definition*

A glaze is the glassy coating that seals and adorns the surface of a ceramic body. Modern industrial glazes are usually colorless and transparent, as on a porcelain dish, or colored and opaque, as on a bathroom tile. But a visit to any art museum reveals that ceramic glazes encompass an immensely more diverse repertoire of visual effects. Blue faience glazes on ancient Egyptian amulets glow with intensity undiminished since the day they emerged from the kiln. Scenes rendered in red and black slip glazes spring to life on the sides of Grecian vases. Bright tricolor lead glazes, luminous celadons and dazzling porcelains speak to the taste and power of the Chinese imperial court.

Long before there were synthetic dyes and plastics, ceramic glazes offered artisans an unparalleled range of permanent colors and textures, which could be manipulated to satisfy a diversity of cultural demands. In most cultures . . .

—"Ancient Glazes," *Scientific American*, April 1990

Opening with a definition enables writers to identify their subjects immediately ("A glaze is the glassy coating . . ."). In some cases the definition also serves as a reminder, refreshing the reader's knowledge of the subject. Definitions typically use the static *be* verb. In the example here the writer's rhetorical strategy is to exploit this static beginning by contrasting it with a dynamic conclusion. The first two sentences are relatively inert defining and describing statements: "A glaze *is* . . . Modern industrial glazes *are* . . ." In the third sentence, however, the writer shifts into the more energetic narrative mode: "But a visit to any art museum *reveals* . . ." Then the subject, glazes, begins to act: they "*glow*," "*spring* to life," and "*speak* to . . . taste and power." The structural message is that glazes are a much more lively and interesting subject than the reader would at first think.

Present Tense: Generalized Narrative

In June immense schools of small, silvery fish called capelin **enter** the hundreds of bays that dot the eastern coast of Newfoundland to perform a fascinating ceremony. The males and females separately **approach** the gravel beaches and **are borne** ashore in waves so laden with their bodies as to be virtual walls of fish. There, on the gravel, the females **lay** their eggs and the males **fertilize** them; then most of the fish **die**. . . .   —"The Spawning of the Capelin," *Scientific American*, May 1990

After this account of the annual ritual of the capelin, the article goes on to discuss the fish's life cycle and the ecology in which they survive, including their role in feeding seals, cod, whales, and seabirds. The more intricate, unusual, and even fragile a ritual, the more questions it raises about why it should continually repeat itself. Opening with a generalized narrative raises immediate questions: What happens after most of the spawning fish die? What did the spawning fish do before they hit the beach? Such a beginning, with all of its mystery, propels both writer and reader into the explanation, which will include a more precise detailing of the event and an account of the larger network of which it is a part.

Present Tense: Narrative Opener

With engines on full afterburners, an F-111 jet dives toward the floor of the Nevada desert. After descending from an altitude of nine kilometers to only 100 meters, the jet levels off. It is traveling slightly faster than the speed of sound (Mach 1.2). The F-111 tears through the air, generating shock waves that kick up clouds of sand. . . .

—"High Performance Parachutes," *Scientific American*, May 1990

A narrative opening creates immediate drama. Something is happening, and our natural instinct is to follow its outcome. We can postpone an explanation even while our curiosity grows (not until the sixth sentence does the writer reveal what the plane is doing). As it turns out, the jet releases a test capsule containing a newly developed parachute designed to slow automobile-sized objects from supersonic speeds to 70 kilometers an hour within the first 50 meters. The writer uses the narrative opening as a concrete and energetic way of introducing his topic, an explanation of the events and technology that led to the development of such a parachute. Narrative openings enliven *expository writing*, writing that explains and informs. Being active and concrete, they seize the

the reader's imagination where abstract generalizations often fail. By comparison, look how quiet a more conventional beginning seems:

Over a three-year period at Sandia National Laboratories in Albuquerque, N.M., working in cooperation with the Departments of Energy and Defense, my colleagues and I succeeded in developing a parachute that can be used at supersonic speeds.

Past Tense: Narrative Opener

Perched on the gunwale of a skiff here, Juarez Christiano Gomes chuckled to himself as he watched a trail of small bubbles rising to the surface of Tucurui Lake.

Suddenly, a cedar log shot out of the water like a wooden Polaris missile.

"The underwater power saw!" Mr. Gomes cried gleefully as one ton of wood crashed back into the roiled waters of this normally placid lake in eastern Amazonia.

While a canoist corralled the floating log, Mr. Gomes, a spry 58-year-old backwoods inventor, spun his vision of a new growth business for the Amazon: underwater logging.

Brazil's growing charcoal, furniture and home construction industries are placing mounting demands on the Brazilian logging industry. And there is a lot of wood under the water brought by three hydroelectric power dams that flooded 2,000 square miles of Amazon forest in the 1980's. . . .

—James Brooks, "In an Amazon Lake, Underwater Logging Blooms," *New York Times*, 14 Aug. 1990

This story could have been told much more abstractly and impersonally, reporting that Brazilians had mastered underwater logging, and then moving on to discuss both the contributing events and the economic consequences. Instead, the writer uses a narrative opener to make his subject concrete and immediate and personal. Rather than a generality (the Brazilian logging industry), we get Juarez Christiano Gomes perched on the side of his skiff as a cedar log comes shooting to the surface "like a wooden Polaris missile." Such an opening reaches beyond the abstract technological and economic issues to capture the emotions of the people involved, the joy and exuberance of the resourceful Gomes as he exults at his accomplishments. The approach works because we are usually more interested in stories than in reports and explanations, especially when the stories are about humans successfully overcoming challenges (like that of salvaging a submerged forest).

The story also uses the narrative opener as a variation on the *specifics-to-general* method of organization. It begins with concrete action, then gradually introduces explanatory detail ("this normally placid lake in eastern Amazonia"). Not until the fourth paragraph does the writer make the transition from narrative to exposition. Narrative openers work not only because they can make abstractions concrete and dramatic, but also because they arouse the reader's curiosity: What is this guy doing out in a lake with log missiles erupting all around him?

Exercise

Rewrite the opener to the logging story by using a general, nonnarrative beginning. Make it as interesting as you can. Then try revising the story into the present tense. Is there an appreciable difference between the two versions?

Subjunctive: Hypothetical Opener

If one **were** looking for a place where it would be easy to hunt for fossils, one's first choice would probably not be southeastern Asia. The latitudes are tropical, monsoons dominate the climate and lush vegetation covers most of the land. Yet early investigators who visited southeastern Asia did make some discoveries. . . .

—"The Mesozoic Vertebrates of Thailand," *Scientific American*, Aug. 1985

The hypothetical subjunctive establishes what investigators would probably do, if they *were* to accept conventional wisdom. Then the article goes on to discuss the valuable fossil record found in northeastern Thailand, one covering 100 million years. This use of the subjunctive is one variation of a generic approach: the citation of commonly held beliefs, then a correction of them. The tactic creates an immediate tension, one between the old (and outdated) news and the new news. Many studies, especially academic ones, use this method, which has an additional advantage: it provides a background or context that gives significance to the upcoming discussion.

Infinitive Phrase Opener

To distribute their seeds far and wide, plants often enlist the help of animals. Some produce seeds that temporarily attach themselves to the hairs of mammals or the feathers of birds. Commercial orchard trees and some other plants have seeds that fruit-eating animals ingest and that germinate when excreted or regurgitated. Vertebrates are not the only animals that disperse seeds, however—ants, too, are important.

Biologists are just beginning to recognize the specialized mechanisms that make ants a major force in the spread of plants around the world. . . .   —"Seed Dispersal by Ants," *Scientific American*, Aug. 1990

Let us suppose the writer had started with the subject: "Plants often enlist the help of animals to distribute their seeds far and wide." This reverses the natural order of cause and effect or of motive and action: first there is purpose, then there is action. The authors use inversion, moving the adverb structure to the head of the sentence, to put the cause or motive first. At the same time, they create tension and stimulate curiosity. Because of the natural link between purpose and action, the immediate statement of purpose will hook an inquisitive reader. This kind of opener is also dynamic, but the action is the action of ideas.

In addition to the causal opener, the paragraph uses a popular strategy, one that exploits a climactic structure. It begins by reminding the reader of common knowledge about the subject (old news), then concludes with the new news, the fresh information. (As is often the case, the old news gives significance to the new.) The authors further reinforce the climax with punctuation, using a dash to set off the revelation about ants.

15

The Rhetoric of Adverbs

The Mobile Adverb

Adverbs can perform some of the same rhetorical functions as other parts of speech. Like conjunctions, they can be transition and sequence markers; like pronouns, they can strengthen paragraph coherence; like prepositional phrases (which often function as adverbs), they can establish details of time and location. In one respect, however, adverbs are unparalleled: their mobility. In a writer's search for the right place, no other part of speech offers so many choices. Take the following:

> She continued her path, **inevitably**.   —D. H. Lawrence, *The Rainbow*

Lawrence had a variety of possibilities, depending on what he wished to emphasize:

> Inevitably, she continued her path.
> Inevitably she continued her path.
> She inevitably continued her path.
> She continued, inevitably, her path.

And even:

> She continued her path inevitably.

The writer's focus determines which version works best. Lawrence obviously wanted to stress not her continuation but its inevitability, so he saved "inevitably" for the final and usually emphatic position, and then strengthened the word even more by setting it off with a comma. *Location, reinforced by punctuation, equals emphasis.*

Exercise

To develop a feel for the mobility of adverbs and adverbial elements, work variations on the following:

He was certainly not expecting trouble.
—James Jones, *From Here to Eternity*

At the St. Cloud bridge I come to a full stop.
—Henry Miller, *Black Spring*

Adverbs as Sentence Openers

A *sentence opener*, recall, is anything that opens a sentence other than a subject. In many kinds of writing, adverbs and adverbials make appropriate and effective sentence openers. In narration and description, for example, sentences often begin logically with details of time or location. After all, something cannot exist or happen unless it does so somewhere or some time. Before an event can occur, it must be five o'clock (or 5:04), or in the morning, or a week later. Before we see something, we must first locate it, farther away, on the right, *there*:

Now and then he stops at the window to see how the weather looks. —Henry Miller, *Black Book*

Last night I was walking again through the Fourteenth Ward.
—*Black Book*

At the summit of one of the curved Japanese bridges I stand for a moment. —*Black Book*

When I reach my father's home, I find him standing at the window shaving, or rather not shaving, but stropping his razor. —*Black Book*

Certain qualifiers of actions can also fit naturally at the openings of sentences: *suddenly, abruptly, gradually, slowly.*

Suddenly, a shot rang out!

Countermessages

One way to look at sentences is to say that each one carries an explicit piece of news as opposed to an implied contrary. It says *this* instead of *that*. For example:

Suddenly, a shot rang out.
(as opposed to something else happening very quickly)

A shot rang out suddenly. (as opposed to happening another way)

What is the use of telling the reader afterwards that something has happened suddenly? To say a shot rang out *suddenly* is to report the quality of an action as well as to sound redundant (can a shot ring out gradually?). *Suddenly* at the beginning prepares the reader for an action (and a surprise). To put it another way, "Suddenly, a shot rang out!" is narration; "A shot rang out suddenly" is exposition.

In expository and persuasive writing, some adverbs operate logically as sentence openers, words like *first, second, next, then, also, hence, moreover,* and *therefore.* Technically, such adverbs at the head of sentences are sentence modifiers, relating the entire statement to a sequence of reasoning or information. In other words, adverbs operate within paragraphs as well as within sentences, as in the following:

> Our criminal procedures are based on the premise that it is better that many of the guilty should escape than that one innocent be punished. **Hence**, the guilty have the benefit of rules designed to protect the innocent . . .
> —Charles Rembar, "How Much Due Process Is Due a President?"

> French Polynesia is everyone's dream come true. . . . **Administratively** it is an overseas territory of France. **Geographically** it is a collection of hundreds of islands in the South Pacific.
>
> —*The Atlantic*, Sept. 1988

Exercise

Examine adverb use in the following sentences. To what extent do adverbs carry or contribute to the "news"? When appropriate, test the effects of relocating some of the adverbs or adverbials. Eliminate any cases of repetition. Try to revise each sentence by excluding as many

adverbial details as possible. Then, if possible, try changing adverbs
to adverbial phrases or clauses.

1 Injustice **anywhere** is a threat to justice **everywhere.** . . .
Whatever affects one **directly** affects all **indirectly.**

—Martin Luther King, "Letter from Birmingham Jail"

2 Works of art confront us the way few people dare to: **completely, openly, at once.**

—William Gass, "The Artist and Society"

3 The research was **intelligently** designed, **expertly** executed,
and **cautiously** interpreted.

—James Moffett, *Teaching the Universe of Discourse*

4 **Here** was his home and **here** was his heart.

—Harrison E. Salisbury, *The 900 Days: The Siege of Leningrad*

5 **Somewhere** in the darkness a woman sang in a high wild voice
and the tune had no start and no finish and was made up of
only three notes which went **on** and **on** and **on.**

—Carson McCullers, *Ballad of the Sad Cafe*

6 They sprawled and fought, scrambled, clutched, rose and fell
shouting, as **aimlessly, noisily, monotonously** as two puppies.

—Katherine Anne Porter, *Noon Wine*

7 **Finally,** and most important, climactic narrative **never, never,
never** tells us **how** the characters feel. It **doesn't** describe the
emotion, it evokes it.   —Jon Franklin, *Writing for Story*

8 Very few people in any walk of life speak and write **precisely**
and **correctly,** and I don't myself.   —E. B. White, *Letters*

9 Young men and women beginning to write are **generally**
given the plausible but **utterly** impracticable advice to write
what they have to write as **shortly** as possible, as **clearly** as
possible, and without any other thought in their minds except
to say **exactly** what is in them.

—Virginia Woolf, "The Patron and the Crocus"

10 There are tens of millions of people in North America who
were **physically** born here but who are not actually living here
intellectually, imaginatively, or **morally.**

—Gary Snyder, *The Practice of the Wild*

11 Our direct intuitions of Nature tell us that the world is **bot-
tomlessly** strange: alien, **even** when it is kind and beautiful;
having innumerable modes of being that are **not** our modes;
always mysteriously not personal, **not** conscious, **not** moral;

often hostile and sinister; **sometimes even unimaginably,** because **inhumanly,** evil.   —Aldous Huxley, "Wordsworth in the Tropics"

12 I take a dim view of dams; I find it hard to learn to love cement; I am **poorly** impressed by concrete aggregates and statistics in cubic tons. But in this weakness I am **not** alone, for I belong to that **ever**-growing number of Americans, **probably** a good majority **now,** who have become aware that a **fully** industrialized, **thoroughly** urbanized, **elegantly** computerized social system is **not** suitable for human habitation.
—Edward Abbey, *Beyond the Wall*

Adverbs as "Telling" Words

At their best, adverbs are words of precision, intensification, and connection. They enhance our "showing," even in persuasive writing. At their worst, they are empty and misleading qualifiers, attributing unsupported values that the reader is asked to accept on the writer's authority. Hence, in works of persuasion we frequently encounter words like *certainly, clearly, absolutely, apparently, obviously, absolutely, definitely,* and *undoubtedly.* Such words do not reflect on the truth of the propositions they qualify, only on the writer's personal certitude. If I say that something is *certainly* true, I have established the certitude not of my assertion, but of my conviction. I have proven nothing, only asserted my personal belief, trying to substitute insistence for objective demonstration. I have, in effect, found another way of *telling* instead of *showing.* A critical audience, however, will not accept personal fervor as a substitute for reason and evidence. Adverbs make the following statements only *sound* convincing:

> The habit of looking after our own needs **obviously** had something to do with the assertiveness that characterized the American family familiar to readers of American literature.
> —William F. Buckley, Jr.

> Full nuclear exchange would **probably** generate the same kind of dust cloud and darkening that may have wiped out the dinosaurs.   —Steven Jay Gould

> As terrorists know, the president has virtually no means of hitting them, save indiscriminate air strikes, which **probably** would be counterproductive.   —Tom Wicker

The superior individual, whether in politics, business, industry, science, literature, or religion, **undoubtedly** plays a major role in the shaping of a nation.   —Eric Hoffer, *The True Believer*

Clearly the same types of people which now swelled the ranks of migratory workers and tramps had **probably** in former times made up the bulk of the pioneers.   —*The True Believer*

If these statements convince, and in some cases they do, it is because they conclude a previous line of reasoning. *Certainly*, *obviously*, and *probably*—supported by terms of universal generalization like *always*, *ever*, and *never*—"tell" us that we are supposed to accept the writer's conclusions, and to accept them on faith. Such terms are most justifiable in opinion pieces, where the writer has an understanding with the audience. Columnists like Russell Baker, Ellen Goodman, Pauline Kael, and George Will have developed a following of readers who care about what they think. Most of the rest of us are not so lucky.

Lazy Narrative Adverbs

Adverbs can provide narrative as well as persuasive shortcuts, qualifying general, abstract verbs when the writer has been too lazy to find concrete, descriptive ones. Hence, characters *come quietly* into a room when they might *slip* into it, or *walk heavily* instead of *plodding* or *lumbering*, or *run quickly* instead of *rushing* or *dashing* (or even *scurrying* or *scampering* or *sprinting*). We use qualifiers when we cannot find a single word that says exactly what we want. English is rich with verbs, however, so we usually have the luxury of expressing actions economically and concretely, with a single word instead of a word plus the baggage of a modifier.

Exercise

The following are general or abstract verbs, plus their modifiers. See how many you can replace with concrete, descriptive verbs. (See the Appendix.)

pack tightly	push down
hold firmly	get away
stop up	look steadily
find out	walk about idly

tell about   move quickly

go down   read rapidly

lay open

Adverbs in Dialogue

In presenting dialogue, either in fiction or in reporting, we are often tempted to make it easier on ourselves by relying on adverbs to *tell* exactly how each statement is delivered. In many cases the qualifiers are unnecessary, as the following examples from James Jones's *From Here to Eternity* show:

> "I'll see you then," he growled **harshly**.   (He growled gently?)
>
> "Okay," Maggio said **briefly**.
> (How much time do we usually spend saying okay?)
>
> "If you really think I could do it," Holmes said **modestly**.
> (He said boastfully?)
>
> He looked at her closely. "It **completely** exhausts me nervously."   (*Exhaust* means to expend or use up completely.)

In the same novel characters say things *wearily, stiffly, doubtfully, indignantly, soothingly, enthusiastically, indifferently, irritably, argumentatively, suspiciously, helplessly, hopefully,* and *brutally,* as well as *chokingly, dignifiedly, dislikeably, hollowly, stonily,* and even *militarily.* In most cases the situation or the verbs themselves should suggest how things are said. If they do not, then we should revise until they do.

Exercise

There was once a popular series of books for young readers about a hero named Tom Swift. The author was notorious for qualifying Tom's statements with adverbs. This practice later inspired a series of adverbial puns called "Swifties":

> "I am going to have a baby," she said expectantly.
>
> "We will never be able to find a maid," he said helplessly.
>
> "But I like pit bulls," she said doggedly.

■ **Revision Notes** ■

Single adverbs, in dialogue or elsewhere, can often be turned into prepositional phrases. We can act *cautiously* or *with caution, carelessly* or *with care, exuberantly* or *with exuberance, confidently* or *with confidence.* The prepositional form is more emphatic but also more conspicuous, even ponderous. Which do we use in a particular instance? We should be guided by idiom, by our ears, and by our sense of rhetorical purpose. Consider the following pairs:

The rain fell heavily, drearily.
The rain fell with heaviness, with dreariness.

She rose and walked swiftly, diagonally across the field.
She rose and walked with swiftness, on a diagonal across the field.

"I don't have any of their names," he said listlessly.
"Mush!" she said huskily.

Can you think of some others? Such a poor form of punning has little place in most writing, but any wordplay can sharpen our language consciousness.

■

Paragraphs

Examine adverb use in the following paragraphs, beginning with single adverbs but progressing to adverbials (phrases and clauses acting like adverbs):

1 How do they work within sentences to focus, qualify, intensify, and otherwise provide essential content?

2 How do they work within paragraphs both to advance the flow of ideas or information and to provide coherence? What other structures or parts of speech also contribute to paragraph coherence?

3 What effect do adverbs have on the tone of some passages (to make them seem more conversational or formal)?

4   Revise some of the paragraphs, removing adverbs, relocating them, changing them into other structures like prepositional phrases. What happens?

5   How are the paragraphs punctuated?

No. 1

[1]The news report was **fairly** straight-forward. [2]In the middle of the United States—**specifically**, in Maine Township, Illinois—sat a high school that had been closed since 1981. [3]This **wasn't** some ancient, crumbling structure. [4]Maine North High School had **first** opened its doors in 1970. [5]The anticipation **then** was that it would serve a **rapidly** expanding population of youngsters. [6]Within eleven years, **though**, falling enrollment made it apparent that the school was **not** needed. [7]Other high schools in the area had sufficient classroom space. [8]**So** Maine North was shut down.

—Bob Greene, *Esquire*, Jan. 1989

No. 2

[1]The train bore me away, through the monstrous scenery of slagheaps, chimneys, piled scrap-iron, foul canals, paths of cindery mud criss-crossed by the prints of clogs.* [2]This was March, but the weather had been horribly cold and everywhere there were mounds of blackened snow. [3]As we moved slowly through the outskirts of the town we passed row after row of little grey slum houses running at right angles to the embankment. [4]At the back of one of the houses a young woman was kneeling on the stones, poking a stick up the leaden waste-pipe which ran from the sink inside and which I suppose was blocked. [5]I had time to see everything about her—her sacking apron, her clumsy clogs, her arms reddened by the cold. [6]She looked up as the train passed, and I was almost near enough to catch her eye. [7]She had a round pale face, the usual exhausted face of the slum girl who is twenty-five and looks forty, thanks to miscarriages and drudgery; and it wore, for the second in which I saw it, the most desolate, hopeless expression I have ever seen. [8]It struck me then that we are mistaken when we say that "It isn't the same for them as it would be for us," and that people bred in slums can imagine nothing but the slums. [9]For what I saw in her face was not the ignorant suffering of an animal. [10]She knew well enough what was happening to her—understood as well as I did how dreadful a des-

* shoes with wooden soles

tiny it was to be kneeling there in the bitter cold, on the slimy stones
of a slum backyard, poking a stick up a foul drain-pipe.

—George Orwell, *The Road to Wigan Pier*

No. 3

[1]Of all great composers, the most difficult to take seriously is
Wagner—largely because he took himself so seriously. [2]His seven
mature operas— *Tristan und Isolde, Die Meistersinger,* the tetrology
Der Ring des Nibelungen, and *Parsifal*—are enormously long, elab-
orately pretentious, filled with seemingly unmusical declamation,
and relatively short on dramatic action. [3]In addition, most of them
are musically and dramatically flawed. [4]Even if one disregards the Nazi
connection, which still puts many people off, there is quite enough
in Wagner to put anyone off. [5]Yet all these seven operas are great
works, central to our understanding of nineteenth-century culture
and, hence, of ourselves, and learning to take them seriously is an
important part of anyone's musical education.

—William H. Youngren, "How to Hear Wagner," *The Atlantic,* Nov. 1982

No. 4

Note that while the following paragraph is about one particular adverb,
"back," it freely uses many other adverbs both for coherence (pointing
back) and for momentum. The rhetorical point depends both on defining what "back" means and on using adverbs to emphasize, connect,
sequence, and even to establish tone (notice the effect of "well" as a
sentence opener). Then notice the other devices for sentence continuity:
repeated words, pronouns, demonstrative adjectives, and conjunctions.
Finally, note how the editors of the *New Yorker* punctuate the passage.

[1]Richard Nixon is "back." [2]So we learn from *Newsweek,* on whose
recent cover we find a picture of him, smiling broadly. [3]To be "back,"
of course, you must have first been somewhere, then gone somewhere else, and then returned. [4]The most notable spot that Nixon
once occupied and then departed from, we recall, was the Presidency
of the United States. [5]But he hasn't returned *there.* [6]In that sense,
he's not back. [7]To what is he "back," then? [8]Well, he's written an
article for *Foreign Affairs, Newsweek* tells us by way of partial explanation. [9]Also, when he stopped in at a Burger King not long ago
a lot of people asked him for his autograph. [10]In other words, there
are signs that he's acceptable again to the public in some way or
other, and hence to the media—including, above all, *Newsweek,*
which puts him on its cover with the caption "He's Back." [11]The

statement in this context makes itself true: if *Newsweek* says he's back, he is. [12]That still leaves the question of where he was until he came back. [13]*Newsweek* says that since "Watergate" he has been in "exile." [14]This exile, however, is evidently different from what we ordinarily mean by exile. [15]When Napolean was in exile, he was confined to a small island in the Atlantic. [16]Today, Solzhenitsyn is barred from returning to his beloved Russia. [17]But Nixon has been right here in the United States—in California, in New York City, and, lately, in Saddle River, New Jersey—free to come and go as he pleased. [18](*Newsweek* refers to him as the Sage of Saddle River.) [19]"Exile" in the *Newsweek* story seems to mean something like exile from the mass media, from celebrity—a thoroughly modern definition, and one that makes an exile of almost everyone. [20]Implicit in the use of the terms "back" and "exile" is a sort of story—a version of what "Watergate" was. [21]In this version, there is a man called Richard Nixon who was once a great celebrity. [22]Then "Watergate" occurred, and, like a television performer whom the public no longer cares to look at, he disappeared from view. [23]But now "Watergate" has faded from people's minds, and his days in the shadows—in "exile" from public acclaim—are over, and he is again a great celebrity, appearing on the cover of *Newsweek*. [24]He's back.

—"Notes and Comments: Richard Nixon Is Back," *The New Yorker*, 26 May 1986

For Openers: Adverbs

Always *Generalizations*

Human beings have **always** been migratory. Sometime between 100,000 and 400,000 years ago, man's predecessor *Homo erectus* had spread from China and Java to Britain and southern Africa. Later, Neanderthal types spanned Europe, North Africa and the Near East; modern *Homo Sapiens*, originating probably in Africa, reached Sarawak at least 40,000 years ago, Australia some 30,000 years ago and North and South America more than 20,000 years ago. Excluding Antarctica, Paleolithic man made his way to every major part of the globe. Except for species dependent on him, he achieved a wider distribution than any other terrestrial animal.

Since this propensity to migrate has persisted in every epoch, its explanation requires a theory independent of any particular epoch. My own view is that the abiding cause is the same trait that explains man's uniqueness in many other ways: his sociocultural mode of adaptation. . . .

—"The Migrations of Human Populations," *Scientific American*, Sept. 1974

We use words like *always* to make the broadest generalizations. Thus, it is appropriate in the opening sentence of a paragraph that follows a *general-to-specifics* organization (although the article as a whole follows an effects-to-cause structure). The first sentence makes a generalization; the remainder of the paragraph supports it: even the earliest beings identified as humans were in constant migration. The rest of the article focuses on modern migrations, ones caused by economic and technological inequality, and far larger than any in the past. Generalization-first openings have the advantage of clarity. They immediately orient the reader, giving an overview before descending to specifics. The "news" here, though, is not in the generalization itself; for many readers it is old information. The real news is, however, implicit in the generalization: Why is it true? Why *have* humans always behaved this way? There is often a new story in an old story, in a situation we have taken for granted.

Adverbial Although *Clauses*

Although it was midafternoon on July 14, 1989, the bicentennial of the French Revolution, engineers and scientists crowded into a control room at the European laboratories for particle physics (CERN) in Prevessin, France, just across the border from Geneva, Switzerland. Word had got out that the laboratory's Large Electron-Positron (LEP) Collider was ready to take its first beam, and people had flocked there to witness the historic event. CERN's director-general, Carlo Rubbia, and his predecessor, Herwig F. Schopper, who had actively supported the LEP through its early phase, were among the anxious onlookers.

At five minutes to four, the first cluster of positrons completed its maiden circuit around the giant, ring-shaped accelerator. Every one of the hundreds of thousands of components along the 26.7-kilometer circumference of the machine was working flawlessly.

—"The LEP Collider," *Scientific American*, July 1990

Although February 18 of this year marked the 60th anniversary of the discovery of Pluto, the ninth planet in the solar system has guarded its secrets well. This frigid world is so small and distant that it appears as a featureless blob even through the largest earth-based telescopes. It is also the only planet that has not yet been visited by a scientific spacecraft.

—"Pluto," *Scientific American*, June 1990

The first sentence of an article or essay does not have to begin with a main clause. But, because as readers we usually expect that one will start this way, a *sentence anticipator* creates an immediate tension, and tension is energy. The very structure of a sentence opener, if it is a phrase or clause, announces that its news must come first in order for the main clause to make its point. This structural message is amplified further by the meaning of *although*: "in spite of" or "in spite of the fact that." As an opener, then, an *although* clause* signals an immediate conflict: something is happening contrary to expectation or logic. Such conflicts need resolution, and resolutions gratify the reader. *Although* clauses are one more way for an essay to hit the ground running. Furthermore, looking for an *although* angle is not a bad way to brainstorm a topic.

Adverbial When *Clauses*

When the tall man in expensive cowboy boots threads his way through rows of chairs to the front, the classroom falls quiet.

William C. Dear, private investigator, is about to share the secrets of his highly publicized 28-year career. How did he get a body exhumed five years after burial? How did he find that missing kid we saw him escorting home on the evening news? How did he get on TV's "Real Stories," driving a dead man's bullet-holed Bronco?

For 14 would-be private eyes, getting the answers is worth the $1,500 tuition for seven weeks of instruction at the new William C. Dear Academy, the only state-accredited private-investigation school in Texas. . . .

—Christi Harlan, "At This Institution Students Pay $1,500 and Study Garbage," *Wall Street Journal*, 18 Dec. 1989

HOLMDEL, N.J.—**When the skeptics resume their chorus, as they surely will**, Alan Huang will draw consolation from a simple image: seven fresh eggs, all balanced on end.

Mr. Huang, a researcher at AT&T Bell Laboratories here, is trying to develop an optical computer. Instead of electrons doing the calculating, it would use photons of light. An optical computer could run thousands of times faster than its quickest electronic forebear. . . .

—Laurance Hooper and Jacob M. Schlessinger, "Is Optical Computing the Next Frontier or a Nutty Idea?" *Wall Street Journal*, 30 Jan. 1990

(Many believed that developing an optical computer was impossible, like standing an egg on its end. Mr. Huang and his research team did in fact learn to balance eggs,

* and ones beginning with related words: *despite, in spite of, contrary to, even though,* and the like

then went on to develop a prototypal optical computer. The story does not get to the eggs until the tenth paragraph.)

In both cases the writers use narrative *when* clauses to plunge right into the middle of their stories. In each case the action is particular, concrete, and unexplained. The *when* clause identifies a situation or occasion as a cue for a certain kind of response, or as a setting for a certain kind of action, which the main clause then presents. The rest of the story explains what led up to that moment. This use of the adverbial *when* clause is one variation on the *specifics-to-general* pattern of organizing an article or essay. Without the generalities the specific episode is meaningless; without the specific episodes the generalities remain abstract, lifeless, unsubstantiated.

16

The Rhetoric of Prepositions

Prepositions: Doing Without

The best way to appreciate prepositions (or anything else) is to try to do without them. Take this sentence from Ray Bradbury's *Martian Chronicles*:

> They had a house of crystal pillars on the planet Mars by the edge of an empty sea, and every morning you could see Mrs. K eating the golden fruits that grew from the crystal walls, or cleaning the house with handfuls of magnetic dust which, taking all the dirt with it, blew away on the hot wind.
>
> (fifty-eight words)

Imagine the sentence without its prepositional phrases:

> They had a house, and every morning you could see Mrs. K eating the golden fruits that grew, or cleaning the house.
>
> (twenty-two words)

Without the prepositions Bradbury and the reader are earth-bound. Gone are the crystal pillars and Mars and the empty sea and the magnetic dust. Now as barren and lifeless as Bradbury's empty sea, the denuded version starkly dramatizes how much we depend upon the power and flexibility of prepositional phrases to fill out and landscape our sentences. By the simple act of turning nouns into modifiers of nouns, verbs, and other parts of speech, prepositions enable us to achieve innumerable levels of precision and concreteness. Because of this versatility, writers, especially modern writers, depend more heavily on them than on any other method of modification.

Prepositions and Movement

When we want to express movement in narrative writing, we naturally think of verbs and adverbs, but prepositional phrases can also help, especially by expressing a kind of momentum. Look what parallel sequences of such phrases, acting as adverbs, accomplish in the following:

> We were lead **out of** the elevator **through** a rococo hall **into** an anteroom and told to get into our fighting togs.
> —Richard Wright, *Black Boy*

> We were led out of the elevator
> through a rococo hall
> into an anteroom and
> told to get into our fighting togs.

> His gaze drifts **down into** the vale, **across** the swamp, **up over** the solid dusk bank of pines, and rests, bewildered like, on the courthouse tower. —Jean Toomer, *Cane*

> His gaze drifts down into the vale,
> across the swamp,
> up over the solid dusk bank of pines, and
> rests . . . on the courthouse tower.

These sequential phrases are particularly suited for presenting narrative/descriptive accounts with a moving point of view. One writer illustrates with the following richly detailed itinerary:

> With a long slow stride, limping a little from his blistered feet, Bud walked **down** Broadway, **past** empty lots where tin cans glittered among grass and sumach bushes and ragweed, **between** ranks of billboards and Bull Durham signs, **past** shanties and abandoned squatters' shacks, **past** gulches heaped with wheelscarred rubbishpiles where dumpcarts were dumping ashes and clinkers, **past** knobs of gray outcrop where steamdrills continually tapped and nibbled, **past** excavations out of which wagons full of rock and clay toiled up plank roads to

the street, until he was walking on new sidewalks along a row of yellow brick apartment houses, looking in the windows of grocery stores, Chinese laundries, lunchrooms, flower and vegetable shops, tailors', delicatessens.

—John Dos Passos, *Manhattan Transfer*

> With a long slow stride,
>   limping a little from his blistered feet,
> Bud walked   down Broadway,
>   past empty lots . . . ,
>   between ranks of billboards . . . ,
>   past shanties . . . ,
>   past gulches . . . ,
>   past knobs of gray outcrop . . . ,
>   past excavations . . . ,
>   until he was walking on new sidewalks,
>   looking in the windows of   grocery stores,
>   Chinese laundries,
>   lunchrooms,
>   flower and vegetable shops,
>   tailors',
>   delicatessens.

Notice, too, how the sequential phrases allow the writer to integrate descriptive detail into a narrative, an effective and economical tactic whenever possible. Straight description is static, an inert listing of details. The longer the description, the more tiresome it becomes (and the more likely the reader is to skim over it).

Exercise

Revise the Dos Passos sentence so that it is purely descriptive. This change will require you to present the stretch of Broadway without Bud (a mobile human viewer) and the prepositions of movement. Then write a descriptive/narrative passage of your own using a moving point of view and sequential prepositional phrases. How the viewer moves is not important—on foot, by bike, car, or plane—but the scene must be real and the details must have thematic consistency.

Strong and Weak Prepositions

Depending on where they appear, prepositions can be conspicuous or inconspicuous, strong or weak. In other words, their value as content (as opposed to structure) words can vary. Read the following sentences aloud and notice which prepositions you find yourself emphasizing:

> He also wore opals on his fingers and in his cuff links.
> —Vladimir Nabokov, *Speak Memory*

> Where once you could have been utterly alone half a mile off the road, in the bog or up the mountain, you could not now be sure of privacy anywhere.
> —Sean O'Faolain, "The Man Who Invented Sin"

> The hero of the regiment is rarely a hero to the regiment.
> —Frank O'Connor, *The Lonely Voice*

> A house should be of the hill, not on the hill.
> —Frank Lloyd Wright

> On the last day of January 1915, under the sign of the Water Bearer, in a year of a great war, and down in the shadow of some French mountains on the borders of Spain, I came into the world.   —Thomas Merton, *The Seven Storey Mountain*

Notice the last sentence in particular. Most readers will stress the opening preposition of each punctuated phrase and de-emphasize the rest. Sequences of parallel phrases, especially when separated by commas, invite such emphasis.

> On the last day of January 1915,
> under the sign of the Water Bearer,
> in the year of a great war, and
> down in the shadow of some French mountains on the
>   borders of Spain,
> I came into the world.

Exercise

Write an imitation of the Merton sentence, but about your own birth or some other significant event in your life.

If prepositions in parallel series are usually strong ("government *of* the people, *by* the people, *for* the people"), then repeated initial prepositions are even stronger:

> The color came streaming from the paned windows above her. It lit **on** the dark wood of the pew, **on** the stone, worn aisle, **on** the pillar behind her cousin, and **on** her cousin's hands, as they lay on his knees. —D. H. Lawrence, *The Rainbow*

> He walked on in the rain, sweating **with** pain, **with** the horror of being old, **with** the agony of having to relinquish what was life to him. —*The Rainbow*

Look how much emphasis and emotion are lost by not repeating the prepositions:

> He walked on in the rain, sweating with pain, the horror of being old, the agony of having to relinquish what was life to him.

Early rhetoricians had a useful term for this repetition of the same word (or words) at the beginning of each item in a series: **anaphora**.

Prepositions and Comparisons

We can describe something three basic ways: by giving details, by isolating qualities, or by comparing it to something else. When we say that one thing is *like* another, we are using analogy or **simile** (from the Latin *similis*, "similar"). The two most common ways to express a simile are to use the conjunction *as* and the preposition *like*.

Comparisons may be simple or complex, literal or figurative, objective or subjective. The least obvious comparisons are usually the most interesting. Take the following descriptions of something most of us have seen many times:

> A flight of sparrows dropped into the dust and scrabbled for bits of food and then flew off **like a gray scarf twisting in the light**. —John Steinbeck, *East of Eden*

> The wind blows, unrelenting, and flights of little gray birds whirl up and away **like handfuls of confetti tossed in the air**.
> —Edward Abbey, *Desert Solitaire*

However, effective similes, like effective metaphors, do not push a comparison too far. A good simile is like a supporting player; it does

■   *Revision Notes*   ■

Adjectives   Many adjectival details can be expressed either as simple adjectives or in prepositional phrases:

a house of crystal pillars = a crystal-pillared house

crystal pillars = pillars of crystal

the edge of an empty sea = an empty sea's edge

a stand of cottonwoods = a cottonwood stand

wet pits of clay = wet clay pits

■ sheets of ice = icy sheets

The right structure—adjective or prepositional phrase—depends on rhythm, variety, and emphasis (usually, because the phrase ends with a noun, it is more emphatic than the adjective). When in doubt, read the two versions aloud and trust your ear.

Adverbs   Prepositional phrases serving as adverbs can sometimes be revised into single adverbs ("he spoke *with impatience*" becomes "he spoke *impatiently*"). More useful to the writer, though, is the property they share with many other adverbs, mobility; they can appear several different places in a clause:

They had a house of crystal pillars **on the planet Mars.**
(They had a house of crystal pillars *there*.)

On the planet Mars they had a house of crystal pillars.

They had **on the planet Mars** a house of crystal pillars.

Again, where we place the phrase depends on rhythm, variety, and emphasis. Writing is a matter of placing information in effective sequences, in the right places. The three versions have identical information, yet each sequence creates different emphases.

not upstage or steal the limelight. A clever writer, though, can sometimes find a way to put a garish comparison back in its place:

To know rapture is to have one's whole life poisoned. If you like a ridiculous analogy, a tincture of rapture is like a red bandana in the laundry that runs and turns all the white wash pink.   —Phillip Lopate, "Against Joie de Vivre"

Originality in Writing

The descriptions of the flocks of birds illustrate an important truth about originality in writing: true originality is not the product of the writer's "material," but of the writer's vision and treatment. A good cook can scare up a tasty meal out of the meagerest fixings, while a poor cook can ruin the most lavish ingredients. Good writers do not need exotic subject matter, nor do they need unnecessarily exotic language. (See the section "Trying Too Hard" in the Introduction.)

Hard-Boiled Similes

The ingenious simile was the professional hallmark of Raymond Chandler, whose Philip Marlowe stories helped popularize the hard-boiled detective hero. His similes are often far-fetched and self-consciously clever, intended as much to display the user's wit as the subject described, but as the following examples from *The Little Sister* demonstrate, no writer need settle for obvious or cliched comparisons ("smooth as silk," "smooth as glass," "white as a sheet," "hard as a rock"):

> She had a low lingering voice with a sort of moist caress in it like a damp bath towel.

> His mouth was open and his face was shining with sweat and he breathed like an old Ford with a leaky head gasket.

> "Yes," I said in a voice that sounded like Orson Welles with his mouth full of crackers.

Exercise

To find out if you have the stuff to be a writer of hard-boiled detective stories, complete the following comparisons, then turn to the Appendix to see if you do, indeed, compare with Raymond Chandler.

1 His coat was cut from a rather loud piece of horse robe with shoulders so wide that his neck stuck up out of it like . . .
(The coat makes his neck look very thin.)

2 He wore a blue uniform coat that fitted him the way . . .
(not well)

3 She smelled the way . . .   (wonderful)

4 My brain felt like . . .   (sluggish)

5 He had a jaw like . . .   (something large)

6 The belt broke like . . .   (easily)

7 My voice sounded like . . .   (unpleasant)

8 A few locks of dry white hair clung to his scalp, like . . .

9 I lit a cigarette. It tasted like . . .   (not good)

10 Even on Central Avenue, not the quietest dressed street in the world, he looked about as inconspicuous as . . .
(He really stood out.)

Exercise

Study the following sentences for their use of prepositional phrases. Notice how the writers have used prepositional phrases to introduce additional and refining information, and sometimes even to achieve special effects. Experiment with rewriting the sentences—by eliminating the prepositional phrases altogether, or changing the word order, or eliminating repeated prepositions, or in some cases by substituting other structures. Then, drawing on your own observations and experiences, write imitations of some of them.

1 Hong Kong Island has terrific street life—from the never-sleep jumble of Causeway Bay, through the financial chasms of the Central district, to the bustling street markets surrounding the Macao ferry terminal.   —*Sunset*, Jan. 1989

2 One takes up fundamental science out of a sense of pure excitement, out of joy at enhancing human culture, out of awe at the heritage handed down by generations of masters and out of a need to publish first and become famous.
—Leon M. Lederman, "The Value of Fundamental Science," *Scientific American*, Nov. 1984

3 Her children slept on starched sheets under layers of quilts, and in the morning her curtains filled with light the way* sails fill with wind.   —Marilynne Robinson, *Housekeeping*

4 Bareheaded and barefooted, my brother and I, along with nameless and countless other black children, used to stand

---

* Grammarians generally regard this as a shortened prepositional phrase: *in the way that* sails . . .

and watch the men crawl in, out, over, and under the huge black metal engines.   —Richard Wright, *Black Boy*

5 We fly southeast from Heart Mountain across the Big Horn River, over the long red wall where Butch Cassidy trailed stolen horses, across the high plains to Laramie.

—Gretel Ehrlich, "Snow"

6 She followed the track, swaying through the quiet bare fields, through the little strings of trees silver in their dead leaves, past cabins silver from weather, with the doors and windows boarded shut, all like old women under a spell sitting there.

—Eudora Welty, "A Worn Path"

7 A fat brown goose lay at one end of the table and at the other end, on a bed of creased paper strewn with sprigs of parsley, lay a great ham, stripped of its outer skin and peppered over with crust crumbs, a neat paper frill round its shin and beside this was a round of spiced beef.

—James Joyce, "The Dead"

8 The street lamp bent over the curb like a woman who cannot turn homeward until she has found the ring or the coin she dropped in the ice and gutter silt.   —Saul Bellow, *Dangling Man*

9 During the whole of a dull, dark, and soundless day in the autumn of the year, when the clouds hung oppressively low in the heavens, I had been passing alone, on horseback, through a singularly dreary tract of country, and at length found myself, as the shades of the evening drew on, within view of the melancholy house of Usher.

—Edgar Allan Poe, "The Fall of the House of Usher"

10 When adult hatchery trout are suddenly thrust into a stream where wild trout have already established a stable social order, "they run around like a motorcycle gang, making trouble wherever they go," says Dr. Robert A. Bachman, a behavioral ecologist who directs Maryland's freshwater fisheries division.   —*New York Times*, 23 July 1991

11 Ahead of me lies a land that is unknown to the rest of the world and only vaguely known to the African—a strange mixture of grasslands, scrub, desert sand like long waves of southern ocean.   —Beryl Markham, *West with the Night*

12 Six o'clock is the time of day in New Orleans when the light cools down, coming in at angles around the tombs in the cemeteries, between the branches of the live oak trees along

the avenues, casting shadows across the yards, penetrating the glass of a million windows. —Ellen Gilchrist, "Rhoda"

Paragraphs

Examine the power and variety of prepositional phrases in the following paragraphs, focusing on the authors' choice and location of prepositionals:

1 How do the nature and location of prepositional phrases contribute to the unity, coherence, and emphasis of each paragraph?

2 Rewrite one of the paragraphs without its prepositional phrases. What is the effect?

3 To test your own sense of the right words in the right places, experiment with rearranging and revising some of the prepositional phrases (turning them into other structures like single adverbs and adjectives). How does each change affect theme or emphasis?

4 How is each paragraph punctuated?

No. 1

[1]On my right hand there were lines of fishing stakes resembling a mysterious system of half-submerged bamboo fences, incomprehensible in its division of the domain of tropical fishes, and crazy of aspect as if abandoned forever by some nomad tribe of fishermen now gone to the other end of the ocean; for there was no sign of human habitation as far as the eye could reach. [2]To the left a group of barren islets, suggesting ruins of stone walls, towers, and blockhouses, had its foundations set in a blue sea that itself looked solid, so still and stable did it lie below my feet; even the track of light from the westering sun shone smoothly, without that animated glitter which tells of an imperceptible ripple. [3]And when I turned my head to take a parting glance at the tug which had just left us anchored outside the bar, I saw the straight line of the flat shore joined to the stable sea, edge to edge, with a perfect and unmarked closeness, in one levelled floor half brown, half blue under the enormous dome of the sky. [4]Corresponding in their significance to the islets of the sea, two small clumps of trees, one on each side of the only fault in the impeccable joint, marked the mouth of the river Meinam we

had just left on the first preparatory stage of our homeward journey; and, far back on the inland level, a larger and loftier mass, the grove surrounding the great Paknam pagoda, was the only thing on which the eye could rest from the vain task of exploring the monotonous sweep of the horizon. ⁵Here and there gleams as of a few scattered pieces of silver marked the windings of the great river; and on the nearest of them, just within the bar, the tug steaming right into the land became lost to my sight, hull and funnel and masts, as though the impassive earth had swallowed her up without an effort, without a tremor. ⁶My eye followed the light cloud of her smoke, now here, now there, above the plain, according to the devious curves of the stream, but always fainter and farther away, till I lost it at last behind the mitre-shaped hill of the great pagoda. ⁷And then I was left alone with my ship, anchored at the head of the Gulf of Siam.

—Joseph Conrad, *The Secret Sharer*

   Delete all the prepositional phrases from the Conrad paragraph. What percentage of the total is contained in the phrases? What happens to the theme or the rhetorical focus without the prepositional phrases? The paragraph begins with "On my right hand" and ends with "at the head of the Gulf of Siam." What kind of movement occurs between these two phrases? Can you write a close imitation of the paragraph, supplying your own subject matter but using Conrad's sentence structure?

No. 2

   ¹It was a beautiful college. ²The buildings were old and covered with vines and the roads gracefully winding, lined with hedges and wild roses that dazzled the eyes in the summer sun. ³Honeysuckle and purple wisteria hung heavy from the trees and white magnolias mixed with their scents in the bee-humming air. ⁴I've recalled it often, here in my hole: How the grass turned green in the springtime and how the mocking birds fluttered their tails and sang, how the moon shone down on the buildings, how the bell in the chapel tower rang out the precious short-lived hours; how the girls in bright summer dresses promenaded the grassy lawn. ⁵Many times, here at night, I've closed my eyes and walked along the forbidden road that winds past the girls' dormitories, past the hall with the clock in the tower, its windows warmly aglow, on down past the small white Home Economics practice cottage, whiter still in the moonlight, and on down the road with its sloping and turning, paralleling the black powerhouse with its engines droning earth-shaking rhythms in the

dark, its windows red from the glow of the furnace, on to where the road became a bridge over a dry riverbed, tangled with brush and clinging vines; the bridge of rustic logs, made for trysting, but virginal and untested by lovers; on up the road, past the buildings, with the southern verandas half-a-city-block long, to the sudden forking, barren of buildings, birds, or grass, where the road turned off to the insane asylum.

—Ralph Ellison, *The Invisible Man*

Drawing on your own memories, write a loose imitation of the Ellison paragraph. Close your eyes and imagine some pleasantly recollected place from your past, preferably one you later came to question and reappraise, as Ellison did.

No. 3

[1]I had not written anything for fun since medical school and a couple of years thereafter, except for occasional light verse and once in a while a serious but not very clear or very good poem. [2]Good bad verse was what I was pretty good at. [3]The only other writing I'd done was scientific papers, around two hundred of them, composed in the relentlessly flat style required for absolute unambiguity in every word, hideous language as I read it today. [4]The chance to break free of that kind of prose, and to try the essay form, raised my spirits, but at the same time worried me. [5]I tried outlining some ideas for essays, making lists of items I'd like to cover in each piece, organizing my thoughts in orderly sequences, and wrote several dreadful essays which I could not bring myself to reread, and decided to give up being orderly. [6]I changed the method to no method at all, picked out some suitable times late at night, usually on the weekend two days after I'd already passed the deadline, and wrote without outline or planning in advance, as fast as I could. [7]This worked better, or at least was more fun, and I was able to get started. [8]I finished an essay called "The Lives of a Cell," then one about the precautions against moon germs at the time of the first moon landing, then several about the phenomenon of symbiosis, and after six months I'd had six essays published and thought that was enough. [9]I wrote a letter to Ingelfinger,* suggesting that now it was probably time to stop—six essays seemed more of a series than I'd planned, and perhaps the *Journal* would do well to drop the venture and start something new with someone else doing the writing. [10]I got a letter back saying no, I had to keep it up, they were getting letters from

* Franz Ingelfinger, editor of the *New England Journal of Medicine*, who had asked Thomas to write a series of articles

readers expressing interest, and in case I had any doubts myself, I should know that even Lowell had telephoned Ingelfinger and said that the Thomas essays were not bad. [11]Lowell was Dr. Francis Cabot Lowell, an intellectually austere Boston classmate of Ingelfinger's and a severe critic. [12]If Lowell approved of the pieces I should surely keep them going. —Lewis Thomas, "How I Began Writing"

No. 4

[1]As the witch kept talking of the glory and the riches and the great power over men that a sorcerer could gain, he set himself to learn more useful lore. [2]He was very quick at it. [3]The witch praised him and the children of the village began to fear him, and he himself was sure that very soon he would become great among men. [4]So he went on from word to word and from spell to spell with the witch till he was twelve years old and had learned from her a great part of what she knew: not much, but enough for the witchwife of a small village, and more than enough for a boy of twelve. [5]She had taught him all her lore in herbals and healing, and all she knew of the crafts of finding, binding, mending, unsealing and revealing. [6]What she knew of chanters' tales and the great Deeds she had sung him, and all the words of the True Speech that she had learned from the sorcerer that taught her, she taught again to Duny. [7]And from weatherworkers and wandering jugglers who went from town to town of the Northward Vale and the East Forest he had learned various tricks and pleasantries, spells of Illusion. [8]It was with one of these light spells that he first proved the great power that was in him. —Ursula K. LeGuin, *A Wizard of Earthsea*

For Openers: Prepositional Phrases

Repetition

Boopie Dumars* finally comes home this weekend. **After** the victory parade in front of 125,000 screaming fans through the streets of Detroit, **after** the Rose Garden ceremony with the President at the White House, **after** the presentation of a Jeep in New York City

* Joe Dumars is a professional basketball player who led his team, the Detroit Pistons, to the 1989 National Basketball Association championship.

for being named MVP of the NBA's championship series and **after** a lot of fuss he could have lived without, Joe (Boopie) Dumars III will finally return to Natchitoches, La. (pop. 16,000), where a two-day celebration in his honor is planned.   —*Sports Illustrated*, 26 June 1989

The repeated prepositional phrases serve to illustrate and emphasize "finally" in the first sentence, a word suggesting a long-awaited and climactic event. "Finally" *tells*, the prepositional phrases *show*. The pattern is an effective one: "After A, after B, and after C, X is finally happening." Prepositional phrases help set the stage, providing the background and establishing the significance of the crowning celebration. Even the *periodic* structure of the sentence (one postponing the main clause) re-creates the experience of waiting.

Historical Anecdote

On the morning of December 29, 1696, a Dutch captain and his crew were searching for the survivors of a ship that had gone down not far off the coast of Western Australia. Although no survivors were ever found, what the crew did find washed up on the shore of a nearby island—amid rats as big as house cats—was a remarkable fish. The fish, unlike any the sailors had ever seen, was described as being "about two feet long, with a round head and a sort of arms and legs and even something like hands." There is no doubt in our minds (although its specific identity will never be known) that this strange fish—sketchily described so long ago—was a frogfish.

Aptly named, these unusual fishes do bear a surprising resemblance to frogs: their bodies (which range in length from one to 16 inches) are globose and equipped with well-developed leglike fins that enable them to clamber across rocks . . .

—"Frogfishes," *Scientific American*, June 1990

In 1848 Louis Pasteur, examining a certain salt of tartaric acid under a microscope, noticed that it formed two types of crystals, each one a mirror image of the other. He separated the two, dissolved each in water to form two solutions and shined a light beam through each. To his great surprise, one solution rotated polarized light clockwise, the other counterclockwise.

This beautiful discovery, which he made at the age of 25, led Pasteur to develop a theory of molecular structure. Little was known then about the structure of matter on such a small scale . . .

—"The Handedness of the Universe," *Scientific American*, Jan. 1990

The first article is a general treatment of frogfishes (or anglerfish), the kind of broad topic often assigned to students. It describes the creatures, then discusses their variations, their distribution, their natural camouflage, their peculiar eating habits (they dangle a lure to attract prey and can swallow something almost as large as themselves), and their evolutionary relationship to other species of bony fish. The second article deals with the phenomenon of "chirality," or left- and right-handedness as it is found throughout the universe. Narrative openings exploit the universal attraction of a story, the built-in desire to know what happens next, and postpones the clinical and abstract treatment that we usually expect of such subjects. But a story can do more than simply pep up a dry subject; it can also establish a context that makes it more relevant, explaining how it first came to someone's attention or attracted someone's curiosity (and is thus worthy of our own).

Narrative openers add drama and concreteness to even the most abstract discussions. By contrast, imagine the Pasteur article with a more conventional beginning.

Most objects in nature are not identical with their mirror images and therefore are said to possess chirality, or handedness. To distinguish the two forms, they are often designated right-handed or left-handed. In the case of some familiar chiral entities . . .

Gone is the emotional content of the original, the suggestion of Pasteur's excitement and curiosity as he set out to explain the phenomenon. Such abstract beginnings often succeed in frightening off all but the most hard-core readers.

Exercise

The following paragraph begins conventionally with a static generalization. Revise the passage to begin with a prepositional phrase detail (you have at least two possibilities: one of time and one of place).

Hambledon Hill is a landmark of striking proportions that sits astride the valley carved by the Stour River through the chalklands of southwestern England. A Neolithic herdsman who looked up to the hilltop in about 3400 B.C. would have seen an impressive sight. Crowning Hambledon Hill was a huge defensive enclosure with three concentric ramparts. The inner rampart, the most formidable of the three, was supported by

10,000 oak beams as thick as telephone poles. In the ditch around the rampart human skulls placed at intervals added an eerie note to the appearance of the fortifications.

The Neolithic complex at Hambledon Hill had not always been intended for defense. . . .

—"A Neolithic Fortress and Funeral Center," *Scientific American*, Mar. 1985

17

The Rhetoric of Conjunctions

Connections: Explicit and Implicit

Writing, like life, is largely a matter of making connections, of finding and establishing relationships. These relationships may be physical ones that we can observe and experience, like a row of books on a shelf or a series of events, or they may be abstract ones that we must grasp intellectually, like relations of cause and effect. Conjunctions help us to express such relationships, to relate items and ideas to one another, to indicate how one piece of information connects with an earlier (continuity) or leads to another (momentum). By their nature and frequency, and in their role as separators as well as connectors, they can sustain and control either the pace of events or the flow of ideas. And by their presence or absence, they can define the quality of the reader's involvement, either as follower of the writer's explicit connections, or as active participant drawing inferences from the writer's implicit ones:

He is anxious; he is threatened from every side.

—Walker Percy, *The Moviegoer*

(By implication, the threats cause his anxiety.)

He is anxious **because** he is threatened from every side.

(*Because* explicitly identifies the reason for his anxiety.)

A sleet fell; the roads turned into sheets of ice.

(By implication, the sleet turned the roads into sheets of ice.)

By placing clauses side-by-side without a connector and suggesting their logical connection, Percy used a device called **parataxis** (placed beside). Had he inserted a connector like *because*, he would have used **hypotaxis** ("placed beneath"—that is, subordinate). Parataxis requires that the reader be alert and play an even more active role than usual in following the text. Generally speaking, the more familiar we are with our audience (the more we know what they know), the more connections we can expect and allow them to make. The device is popular with modern writers.

Polysyndeton: Many Conjunctions

We normally connect and punctuate a series in the following way:

Tom, Dick, and Harry   (or, Tom, Dick and Harry)

Words alone do not speak; structures also have a voice. This standard way of punctuating suggests that the series is probably an average sampling. The "and" implies a note of finality, telling us that *Harry* is the last name on the list. But consider the following:

Bob and Carol and Ted and Alice   (movie title)

Rhetoricians call this method of linking *polysyndeton* (meaning "many connectors"), a device discussed in earlier chapters. The conjunctions here both link *and* separate, holding the names together in a list but also keeping their identities discrete. The repeated *and*'s serve to itemize, saying that this is a sequence of individuals. The device works because *and* has little dictionary meaning, being the verbal equivalent of a plus sign. In our example "and" is at once a connector and a separator and a pause, allowing the reader's mind to dwell slightly longer on the previous item while waiting for the next.

Repeating conjunctions between each item in a series can either speed up or slow down the list, though usually the latter. If someone asks us how we feel about a person we particularly dislike, we answer deliberately: "He is lazy and dishonest and unreliable and self-serving." Each bad trait enjoys its own moment in the spotlight. If someone asks us after a hard day what we have done with ourselves, we may instinctively respond, "I got up early and fixed breakfast and drove to school and attended four classes and ran several errands and drove back home and fixed dinner and tried to fill out my income tax forms and . . ." The methodical and laborious *and*'s drag out the list, re-creating some of the effort of our day.

When separating verbs and clauses, especially in narratives, repeated *and*'s will usually stress sequentiality, meaning *and then*: "this happened and then this happened and then this happened." Sometimes, though, they will also add a sense of momentum to a narrative, with one action seeming to unroll naturally and inevitably from the previous one.

> Old Bayard flung the match into the grate **and** put the cigar in his pocket **and** closed his desk **and** took his black felt hat from the top of it **and** followed the other from the room.
> —William Faulkner, *Sartoris*

Polysyndeton is an emphatic device, and what and how it emphasizes depends on content and situation.

Exercise

Study the use of conjunctions in the following sentences. Note especially the use of polysyndeton and the variety of its effects, depending on the elements connected. Revise away the polysyndeton and notice how the sentences read. Then, compose imitations, supplying appropriate subject matter from your own experiences.

1   He shoveled the bacon out on a plate and broke the eggs in the hot grease and they jumped and fluttered their edges to brown lace and made clucking sounds.
    —John Steinbeck, *East of Eden*

2   Methodically he primed his brain with half a tumbler of whiskey and then he crossed his hands behind his head and crossed his ankles and then he brought out his thoughts and impressions and perceptions and instincts and began matching them.   —*East of Eden*

3   Rhoda had a closet full of clothes. She had thousands of dollars' worth of skirts and jackets and blouses and dresses and shoes and scarves and handbags.   —Ellen Gilchrist, "Rhoda"

4   A year later Mavis married Alden Cates and went to live on the farm, and in the years that followed she bore him three youngsters and she raised Rhode Island Reds and took prizes at the local poultry shows and grew plump as a pullet herself, so thank goodness fate deals a few decent cards sometimes.   —Margaret Laurence, *The Stone Angel*

5　Templeton poked his head up through the straw. "Struggle if you must," said he, "but kindly remember that I am hiding down here in this crate and I don't want to be stepped on, or kicked in the face, or pummeled, or crushed in any way, or squashed, or buffeted about, or bruised or lacerated, or scarred, or biffed."　—E. B. White, *Charlotte's Web*

6　Most years, it is September or October before the Santa Ana winds start blowing down through the passes, and the relative humidity drops to figures like seven or six or three per cent, and the bougainvillea starts rattling in the driveway, and people start watching the horizon for smoke and tuning in to another of those extreme local possibilities—in this instance, that of imminent devastation.

—Joan Didion, "Letter from Los Angeles," *The New Yorker*, 4 Sept. 1989

7　Now they all watched the tall convict as he bit the end from the cigar neatly and with complete deliberation and spat it out and licked the bite smooth and damp and took a match from his pocket and examined the match for a moment as though to be sure it was a good one, worthy of the cigar perhaps, and raked it up his thigh with the same deliberation—a motion almost too slow to set fire to it, it would seem—and held it until the flame burned clear and free of sulphur.　—William Faulkner, *The Wild Palms*

8　The readers who read between the lines are the readers worth winning. But if the writer forgets them, if his mood in writing is mean or peevish or petty or vain or false, no cleverness and no technique are likely, in the end, to save him.

—F. L. Lucas, *Style*

Asyndeton: Missing Conjunctions

The usual punctuation of a series, remember, is *A*, *B*, *and C* (though many drop the last comma). We usually place a conjunction before the last item, saying, "Tom, Dick, and Harry," with our voices dropping to announce the end of the list. Sometimes, though, writers will omit even this final connector, a device called *asyndeton* ("no connector"). The effects are several. For one, our voice is rising after the concluding item, suggesting that another is coming:

He was cold, hungry, embarrassed, incompetent.

—Kurt Vonnegut, Jr., *Slaughterhouse-Five*

The punctuation implies that the list may be incomplete; he is all these things and probably more. Sometimes, as in this example, the last item will also sound climactic. "Cold," "hungry," and "embarrassed" culminate in "incompetent."

If polysyndeton usually slows down a sequence of actions and makes it more deliberate, asyndeton will often speed it up. In some cases the actions will seem frantic or staccato or even random:

> They dove, splashed, floated, splashed, swam, snorted.
>
> —James T. Farrell, *Young Lonigan*

> And the talk would weave, roll, surge, spurt, veer, swell, having no specific aim or direction, touching vast areas of life, expressing the tentative impulses of childhood.
>
> —Richard Wright, *Black Boy*

In other cases, omitting the usual linking word between two verbs will create a sense of abruptness to the point of simultaneity:

> Derby raised his head, called Campbell a snake.
>
> —Vonnegut, *Slaughterhouse-Five*

Exercise

Study the following uses of asyndeton. What is the effect in each specific case? How do the examples vary? Then experiment with other ways of separating the items. Compare the results. Finally, write imitations of some of the sentences, describing a familiar scene or some action you have observed.

1 But best of all was when the wind had great power, when it was erratic and did swift and sudden things, stopped suddenly, picked up suddenly, ran in a circle, sprinted straight ahead, stopped, turned, came back.
   —William Saroyan, *Bicycle Rider in Beverly Hills*

2 He was fond of saying that he could plow a furrow, cut sorghum, shuck corn, handle a team, build a corn crib, as well as any man.   —Katherine Anne Porter, *Noon Wine*

3 He was a bag of bones, a floppy doll, a broken stick, a maniac.
   —Jack Kerouac, *On the Road*

4 They passed through the dappled shadows beneath the light, went on into darkness again.   —William Faulkner, *Sartoris*

5 Their commander was a middle-aged corporal—red-eyed, scrawny, tough as dried beef, sick of war.
—Kurt Vonnegut, Jr., *Slaughterhouse-Five*

6 Their lives spun off the tilting world like thread off a spindle, breakfast time, suppertime, lilac time, apple time.
—Marilynne Robinson, *Housekeeping*

7 April saw the line of her profile in the shadow of the hat, saw how dry and cool her skin was, saw the composure of her smile.   —Tobias Wolff, "Sanity"

8 We fought four hard rounds, stabbing, slugging, grunting, spitting, cursing, crying, bleeding.   —Richard Wright, *Black Boy*

9 He sang, he danced, he was funny, he was dramatic.
—Tom Shales, "Danny Kaye, The Timeless Jester"

10 One of the few things I know about writing is this: spend it all, shoot it, play it, lose it, all, right away, every time. Do not hoard what seems good for a later place in the book, or for another book; give it, give it all, give it now.
—Annie Dillard, *The Writing Life*

Paragraphs

The following paragraphs illustrate some of the uses of conjunctions in different types of writing:

1 Observe what the conjunctions contribute to paragraph structure. How do they add continuity? Momentum? When do they connect? Separate?

2 Choose one of the paragraphs with an unusually large number of conjunctions and delete as many as possible. What happens?

3 How is each paragraph punctuated, especially to enhance the use of conjunctions?

No. 1

[1]The man always brought back things in his cart. [2]He brought a scratched table and chairs, with mahogany lumps in the proper places. [3]He brought an iron bed, big and noisy, of which the bars had been bent a bit by kids shoving their heads between. [4]And he

brought all those necessities, like flour, and a bottle of pain killer, and pickled meat, and kerosene, and seed potatoes, and a packet of needles, and oaten chaff for the shaggy horse, and the tea and sugar that trickled from their bags, so that you crunched across them, almost always, on the hardened floor.   —Patrick White, *The Tree of Man*

No. 2

[1]When it was suggested to Walt Whitman that one of his works should be bound in vellum,* he was outraged—"Pshaw!" he snorted, "hangings, curtains, finger bowls, chinaware, Matthew Arnold!" [2]And he might have been equally irritated by talk of style; for he boasted of "my barbaric yawp!"—he would *not* be literary; his readers should touch not a book but a man. [3]Yet Whitman took the pains to rewrite *Leaves of Grass* four times, and his style is unmistakable. [4]Samuel Butler maintained that writers who bothered about their style became unreadable but he bothered about his own. [5]"Style" has got a bad name by growing associated with precious and superior persons who, like Oscar Wilde, spend a morning putting in a comma, and the afternoon (so he said) taking it out again. [6]But such abuse of "style" is a misuse of English. [7]For the word means merely "a way of expressing oneself, in language, manner, or appearance"; or, secondly, "a *good* way of expressing oneself"—as when one says, "Her behavior never lacked style."

—F. L. Lucas, "On the Fascination of Style"

No. 3

[1]If we are to spare the countryside, if we are to protect the style of the small town and of the exclusive suburb, keep the organic center of the metropolis and the old neighborhoods, maintain those few remaining streets where the tradition of the nineteenth century and the muse of the eighteenth century still linger on the mood in the summer cool of an evening, if we are to avoid a megalopolis five hundred miles long, a city without shape or exit, a nightmare of ranch houses, highways, suburbs and industrial sludge, if we are to save the dramatic edge of a city—that precise moment when we leave the outskirts and race into the country, the open country—if we are to have a keen acute sense of concentration and a breath of release, then there is only one solution: the cities must climb, they must not spread, they must build up, not by increments, but by leaps, up and up, up to the heavens.   —Norman Mailer, *Cannibals and Christians*

* lamb or calfskin

No. 4

[1]Narcissa resumed her seat, and Simon appeared again, with Isom in procession now, and for the next few minutes they moved steadily between kitchen and dining-room with a roast turkey and a smoked ham and a dish of quail and another of squirrels, and a baked 'possom in a bed of sweet potatoes and squash and pickled beets, and sweet potatoes and Irish potatoes, and rice and hominy, and hot biscuit and beaten biscuit and delicate long sticks of cornbread, and strawberry and pear preserves, and quince and apple jelly, and stewed cranberries and pickled peaches. —William Faulkner, *Sartoris*

For Openers: Conjunctions

But, Yet, *and Reversals*

When Paramount Pictures Corp.'s "Ghost" opened two weekends ago, the odds of success seemed slim at best. The romantic thriller was entering a field glutted with big movies ranging from "Total Recall" and "Die Hard II" to "Another 48 Hours" and "Days of Thunder."

But while many of those pricey, megastar movies are dropping off precipitously, "Ghost" is turning out to be one of the summer's surprise hits. After opening to an impressive $12.2 million on about 1,100 screens, the movie added 300 more screens and sold $12.5 million of tickets last weekend. It continued to gain momentum this week, with ticket sales at about $38 million as of yesterday.

—Lauro Landro, "Late Summer Movies Steal Thunder from Glut of Big-Budget Action Films," *Wall Street Journal*, 27 July 1990

The power of subliminal messages is taken as an article of faith by many people. Critics of advertising often take for granted the power of "hidden persuaders." Many parents stand convinced that messages buried in rock music are poisoning their children's minds. And for vendors of audio tapes, the power of the imperceptible exhortation to strengthen memory and to take off pounds is more than an article of faith—it is a profit center.

But scientists studying the mind's ability to register information outside awareness are locked in debate about the power of messages directed to the unconscious mind. Some, most of whom are cognitive psychologists, say there is no credible scientific evidence that hidden messages can persuade or cure. . . .

—Daniel Goleman, "Research Probes What the Mind Senses Unaware," *New York Times*, 14 Aug. 1990

This formula is popular for essays and articles: "People believe this *but* . . ." Such an opening begins by presenting conventional thinking or expectations, then makes a transition to the *but* or *yet* idea: how such thinking has been challenged or overturned or at least revised. This tactic not only exploits the drama inherent in any reversal, it also provides the background or context that helps give the news its significance (new news has value because of its effect on old news). Imagine the first story with a more direct opener: "Paramount Pictures' 'Ghost' has been a surprise box-office hit." This opener tells of the surprise; the other shows it. One way to explore any subject is to search for a *but* or a *yet* angle:

Nations are political and military entities. **But** it doesn't necessarily follow from this that nations are also the salient entities of economic life or that they are particularly useful for probing the mysteries of economic structure, the reasons for the rise and decline of wealth. Indeed, the failures of national governments to force economic life to do their bidding suggest that nations are essentially irrelevant to promoting economic success. It also affronts common sense, if nothing else, to think of entities as disparate as, say, Singapore and the United States, or Ecuador and the Soviet Union, or the Netherlands and Canada, as economic analogues. All they really have in common is the political fact of sovereignty.

Once we remove the blinders that mislead us into assuming that nations are economic units and try looking at the economic world as it is rather than as a dependent artifact of politics, we see that most regions are grab bags of very different economies, of rich regions and poor ones.

We see, too, that among all the various types of economies, those of cities are unique in their power to shape the economies of other settlements, including ones far removed geographically. . . .

—Jane Jacobs, "Cities and the Wealth of Nations," *The Atlantic*, Mar. 1984

Here the writer opens with a truism, a definition no one would contest. Then she immediately challenges a belief that many would say followed from the first, that political and military unity equals economic unity. The "but" immediately announces her intention to challenge conventional thinking, and challenge it she does, very convincingly. (See the "For Openers" section in Chapter 15, "The Rhetoric of Adverbs," for a discussion of subordinating conjunctions as openers.)

Correlatives: If . . . Then

If human beings live on this planet as the guests of green plants, **then** plants and animals can be said to survive—or fail to survive— as the guests of insects. Since the first cockroach appeared on Earth some 300 million years ago, insects have evolved into an estimated 30 million different species, of which one million have been discovered. Insects account for roughly 85 percent of all animal life, and it has been calculated that the combined weight of Earth's insects is 12 times greater than that of its human population.

In Africa the termites and ants alone outweigh all mammals put together. Between the mosquito and the tsetse fly, insects have dictated the lifestyle and distribution of human population all across the continent. . . .

—"Africa's Drive to Win the Battle Against Insects," *Smithsonian*, Aug. 1988

The article uses a pair of conjunctions to start logically with a conditional proposition, "If . . . then." The antecedent, that human life is dependent on green plants, is obviously true; therefore, the less well known consequent must also be true, or at least its truth will be evident by the time the writer has finished. This approach to a topic is one way of moving from the known to unknown, from a given truth to one implicit or latent in it.

Correlatives: Not . . . But

In David Em's world, paint is **not** a pigment **but** the glow of electronic light on a video screen, and a brush is **not** something with bristles **but** a computer program simulating brush features such as size, shape and the color it is "dipped" in. What the artist holds is a metal-tipped stylus, and to paint with it he draws it lightly across a "digitalizing pad," a sort of magic slate that transmits the corresponding lines to the screen.

Em, 36, went from a traditional art school background to working with industrial plastics for sculpture, and then to the control of light and color on video monitors, before encountering computers. . . .

—"An Impressionist with a Computer," *Smithsonian*, Mar. 1988

In this case the writer uses the "not . . . but" correlatives to show how the subject, David Em, is not a typical painter. He lives in a world of paints and brushes, but not of the standard variety. By using these correlatives, the writer plays on the reader's conventional expectations in order to treat an unconventional topic, positing a familiar landscape (paints, brushes, the stereotypic environment of painters), then substituting some of the key props. The tactic is to begin with what the reader already knows, then to modify it.

Punctuation

End Punctuation: Periods, Question Marks, and Exclamation Marks

Consider the following three sentences:

He is eating the whole thing.

He is eating the whole thing?

He is eating the whole thing!

The first, punctuated with a period, is a simple, matter-of-fact statement, suggesting little of the speaker's attitude. The second, punctuated with a question mark, suggests puzzlement, even surprise. The third, punctuated with an exclamation mark, expresses strong feeling, even shock. Together, the three versions illustrate the power of end punctuation to determine the nature and tone of a sentence.

Periods

We use periods for the following:

Related issues:

After Sentences That Make Statements or Requests, Give Mild Commands, or Ask Indirect Questions

In simplest terms, we use periods at the end of any sentence that is not a direct question or an exclamation.

Statement	You may take a seat.
Request	Please take a seat.
Mild Command	Take a seat.
Indirect Question	You don't have to ask if you can take a seat.

After Deliberate Fragments

In modern prose we frequently run across intentional fragments, usually structures that could be repunctuated to fit into surrounding sentences. Such units still begin with capital letters and end with periods:

Pat Porter, lean and hungry, sat in a restaurant in Raleigh, N.C., and stared at his Thanksgiving dinner. Lasagna. Again.
—*Sports Illustrated*, 5 Dec. 1988

With Some Abbreviations

Periods occur in most abbreviations:

B.C.   Mr.   M.D.
Dr.   Ph.D.   N.Y.

When an abbreviation ends a sentence, its final period also serves as the sentence period:

In front of the church was a sign reading, "Founded on Calvary in 33 A.D." —Samuel Pickering, Jr., "Pictures"

Certain abbreviations, however, are so familiar that the periods are usually dropped:

AP CBS CEO CNN IRA IRS MIT NAACP NCAA TV VIP

Using Abbreviations   If you are not sure whether to drop the periods, consult a dictionary. Your concern, though, may be less whether to use periods than whether to use the abbreviations at all. You should use them only when you are confident your audience will understand. To a group of AP (Associated Press) reporters, the IRA will probably mean the Irish Republican Army; to a group of investment counselors, it will likely mean Individual Retirement Account. If you are addressing your city council, you can throw around expressions like EIR. Elsewhere, the audience may need to be told that an EIR is an Environmental Impact Report. Context and timeliness determine whether you use the abbreviations or the full names. At one time, for example, most Americans would have recognized TVA (Tennessee Valley Authority); now, many would not. When we see a document with numerous and varied abbreviations, we know that it is directed at an audience of insiders.

Using Acronyms   **Acronyms** are artificial words formed from the first letters of organization names. Being words, they do not require punctuation:

MADD—Mothers Against Drunk Driving

NATO—North Atlantic Treaty Organization

NASA—National Aeronautics and Space Administration

OPEC—Organization of Petroleum Exporting Countries

PAC—Political Action Committee

There is a simple difference between acronyms and other capital-letter abbreviations (*CIA, NBC*): acronyms are pronounced as words; the others are spelled letter by letter.

Marking Divisions in Dramatic and Poetic References

When quoting from plays, we use periods to separate acts, scenes, and lines:

> Neither a borrower, nor a lender be;
> For loan oft loses both itself and friend . . .
> —William Shakespeare, *Hamlet* (3.1.75–6)

When quoting from poems divided into books, we use periods to separate book from line number:

> Oh pleasant exercise of hope and joy!
> For mighty were the Auxiliars which then stood
> Upon our side, we who were strong in Love!
> Bliss was it in that dawn to be alive,
> But to be young was very Heaven!
> —William Wordsworth, *The Prelude* (11.105–9)

Before Decimals and Between Dollars and Cents

3.1416 $6,838.20 $5.69

Periods and Other Punctuation

A period is never combined with another punctuation mark at the end of a sentence; for example, when a concluding quotation has its own punctuation.

> *Not*   He wondered aloud, "What will I do?".
>
> *But*   He wondered aloud, "What will I do?"

When a quotation ends a sentence, we usually place the period inside the quotation marks.

Note: When typing, leave *two spaces* after a period before beginning the next sentence.

Question Marks

We use question marks for the following:

Related issue:

After Direct Questions

We use question marks after direct (not indirect) questions. A **direct question** is an actual question; an *indirect question* is a statement about a question.

Direct   Can a 36-question multiple choice test help pick star pro basketball players of the future or select teams of engineers to build industrial automation systems?
The Phoenix Suns and Honeywell Inc. think it can.
—*Wall Street Journal*, 7 Jan. 1990

Indirect   A *Wall Street Journal* article asks if a 36-question multiple choice test can help pick prospective basketball stars or compatible teams of design engineers.

Direct   Can antibodies be made to serve as enzymes? These two classes of proteins seem to have evolved for different tasks.   —*Scientific American*, Mar. 1988

Indirect   A 1988 article in *Scientific American* tries to answer whether one class of proteins (antibodies) can be made to serve the task of another (enzymes).

Use question marks for a series of short questions, even when they are not complete sentences:

She stopped crying and gazed at me. "You'd really tear it apart? Just for my gerbils? The wall?"
—Scott Russell Sanders, "The Inheritance of Tools"

What would I like to shoot? A crocodile? A sloth bear? A panther? Sadly, there were no tigers in his lands anymore, but anything else was possible for the right price.
—Geoffrey C. Ward, "Tiger in the Road!"

Also use a question mark at the end of questions inside of a sentence, at least in dialogue:

"It's not like proposing marriage or anything. What will it cost you?" their mother says scornfully. "Two dollars each?"
—Alice Munro, "Oh, What Avails"

But, the question mark is optional when the question is not in dialogue:

What will it cost me? I wondered.
What will it cost me, I wondered.

However, if the question follows an introductory remark, begin the question with a capital letter and punctuate it with a question mark:

I have just this one question: What will it cost me?

A question mark can even turn a normal statement into a question:

That car gets forty-seven miles to the gallon.
That car gets forty-seven miles to the gallon?

After Doubtful Information

We use question marks inside of parentheses to suggest doubt about our information: a date, a name, a word:

Geoffrey Chaucer (1340?–1400)

Misusing Question Marks

Do not use question marks within parentheses to suggest humor or sarcasm, if only because the practice is too heavy-handed, too *telling*. There are more subtle and effective ways to communicate such feelings.

Exclamation Marks

We use exclamation marks for the following:

▶ after an exclamatory phrase or clause   357
▶ after an emphatic interjection   358
▶ after a strong command   358

Related issue:

▶ misusing exclamation marks   359

Exclaim comes from a Latin word meaning "to cry out." Exclamation marks, then, show strong emotion. In "crying out" your emotion, though, remember the story about the boy who cried wolf; the more often he cried out, the less anyone listened. Exclamation marks should be used sparingly.

After an Exclamatory Phrase or Clause

An exclamation mark after a phrase or clause signals that it has been uttered dramatically and abruptly. We find them most often in dialogue:

"The ant? It might have bitten me. I mean, what difference does it make?"
"It might have bitten you! Ha! How ridiculous! Now it's going to lay eggs in my car!" —Lorrie Moore, "You're Ugly, Too"

Hunters believe that wild animals exist only to satisfy their wish to kill them. And it's so easy to kill them! The weaponry available is staggering, and the equipment and gear limitless.
—Joy Williams, "The Killing Game"

Occasionally a writer will insert an exclamation mark in the middle of a sentence to emphasize an idea:

Only petty minds and trivial souls yearn for supernatural events, incapable of perceiving that everything—everything!— within and around them is pure miracle.
—Edward Abbey, "Cape Solitude"

Exclamation marks frequently appear after expressions beginning with such questioning words as *how*, *what*, and *who*:

How I envy the novelist! —Sylvia Plath, "A Comparison"

The lovely dawn: the lovely pure, wide morning in the mid-sea, so golden-aired and delighted, with the sealike sequins shaking, and the sky, far, far, far above, unfathomably clear. How glad to be on a ship! What a golden hour for the heart of man! —D. H. Lawrence, *Sea and Sardinia*

Exclamation marks in ordinary prose are like those *telling* dialogue guides: "She said sarcastically . . ."

After an Emphatic Interjection

An **interjection** is simply a word that expresses emotion (*ow, oh, wow*). We use exclamation marks to identify the stronger ones:

"It might have bitten you! Ha!"

After a Strong Command

We use periods to identify milder commands, those bordering on requests, and exclamation marks to identify strong ones:

"Junior!" Mrs. Holmes shrilled. "Stop that! Get back in the car!" —James Jones, *From Here to Eternity*

"Sergeant Warden!"
"Yes, Sir!" Warden bellowed, jumping to the window.

"What's the matter with this outfit? This place needs policing. Look there. And there. And over by the garbage rack. Is this a barracks or a pigpen? I want it policed up! Immediately!"

"Yes, Sir!" bellowed Warden, "Maggio!"

—*From Here to Eternity*

Misusing Exclamation Marks

Do not use exclamation marks to suggest humor or sarcasm:

They said the check was in the mail (!).

Also, like question marks, exclamation marks should not be combined with other punctuation.

Commas

We use the comma for the following:

Related issues:

❯   punctuating sentence openers   362

❯   misusing commas   370

Sentences, we remember, are not so much sequences of words as sequences of phrases—word groups acting as units. The major function of commas, then, is to clarify sentences by helping the reader keep such groups both intact and separate: intact so they can perform their united functions, and separate so they do not infringe on other groups. By signaling the mild pauses we take in speech, commas perform these functions by doing two things: separating and enclosing.

Setting Off Independent Clauses

The normal practice is to use a comma before a coordinating conjunction (*and, but, for, nor, or, so, yet*) when it links two independent clauses in a compound or compound-complex sentence:

> Children have never been very good at listening to their elders, but they have never failed to imitate them.
> —James Baldwin, "Fifth Avenue, Uptown: A Letter from Harlem"

> He had been an ape once, but a hairdresser and a surgeon had fixed that.   —Graham Greene, *Brighton Rock*

When two ideas or actions are closely related, the comma is sometimes omitted:

> Clouds started blowing in from the south and the breeze filled the sky with dry pine needles raining down.
> —Gary Snyder, *The Practice of the Wild*

Many teachers and editors still reject the punctuation of independent clauses with commas alone, except when they are in a series of three or more:

> Life has crept upward from the waters, it crawls in the fields, it penetrates the air, it is not unknown even in the frozen wastes of the Antarctic.   —Loren Eiseley, *The Immense Journey*

> Molly changed beds, Sylvie peeled the vegetables, Helen washed the dishes.   —Marilynne Robinson, *Housekeeping*

> The water surged, the quick water bugs skated up and down inspecting brown clumps of algae along the banks, underwater weeds waved like slim snakes whose tails had been staked to the mud.   —Rick DeMarinis, "Weeds"

Note: In the previous examples the similarity of subjects and of clause structure helps reinforce sentence unity. However, when a pair of independent clauses are linked only by a comma, many identify it as a *comma splice*.

Setting Off Items in a Series

We use commas to separate coordinate items in a series of three or more, whether individual words, phrases, or clauses:

> **The lawyer specializing in mergers and acquisitions, the professor with his own bioengineering firm, the celebrity commentator**—these mingle now with heads of companies, even heads of state. —Barbara Ehrenreich, *Fear of Falling*
> (noun phrases/appositives)

> The inside of the shack was even more miserable, **damp and dirty, leftover groceries and magazines torn to shreds by rats and mice, the floor muddy, the windows impenetrable.**
> —Jack Kerouac, "Alone on a Mountain Top"
> (absolutes)

> We fought four hard rounds, **stabbing, slugging, grunting, spitting, cursing, crying, bleeding.** —Richard Wright, *Black Boy*
> (participles)

> The lights **went out, flashed on again, went out for good.**
> —Angela Stuart, "The Fourteenth of April"
> (predicates)

> I walked down the dark street alone, **past houses set back off the street, through the darkness, past privet hedges, under elm trees, through air rich and ripe with promise.**
> —Jean Shepherd, "The Endless Streetcar Ride into the Night, and the Tinfoil Noose"
> (prepositional phrases)

Commas Before the Last Item in a Series   Writers often omit the comma before the last item in a series when it is joined by an *and*. This practice, however, sometimes creates confusion or even prevents us from making certain distinctions, as in the famous line from Robert Frost's "Stopping by Woods on a Snowy Evening":

> The woods are **lovely, dark** and **deep.**

This line means either that the woods are lovely *and* dark *and* deep, or that the woods are lovely *because* they are dark and deep ("dark" and "deep" acting like appositives to "lovely"). If we usually place the comma before the *and*, then we can express the latter idea by leaving it out. Otherwise, the statement is in doubt.

Setting Off Long Introductory Phrases and Clauses

Introductory elements (or sentence anticipators) are clauses, phrases, or words that precede the subject of a sentence:

> **On a train coming in from a grand weekend in Wiltshire,** I met an unattractive, shy young refugee from Germany who had been conscripted into the Pioneer Corps.
> —Mary Lee Settle, "London—1944"
> (prepositional phrase)

> **To make it look easy and natural,** Astaire spent weeks in rehearsal on his dance numbers, and he insisted that directors shoot him so his whole body could be seen in the frame.
> —Tom Shales, "Fred Astaire, the Poet of Motion"
> (infinitive phrase)

> **When students complete a first draft,** they consider the job of writing done—and their teachers too often agree. **When professional writers complete a first draft,** they usually feel that they are at the start of the writing process. **When a draft is completed,** the job of writing can begin.
> —Donald Murray, "The Maker's Eye: Revising Your Own Manuscripts"
> (adverbial clauses)

Punctuating Sentence Openers   Contemporary writers are using commas less frequently to separate openers than did earlier writers. They are probably listening to their own sentences and recognizing the strong natural pause that comes between the subject of a main clause and an introductory element:

> **When people ask me where I'm from** I still say southeastern Oregon, expecting them to understand my obvious pride.
> —William Kittredge, "Home"

> **When I first came to Memphis** it was late summer, and the fields lying eastward from the river were green.
> —Samuel Hynes, "The Feeling of Flying"

> **In view of the fact that there may be as many as 800,000 species of plants on the earth** it is remarkable how few of them have been directly exploited by man.
> —*Scientific American*, May 1977

Setting Off Some Final Adverb Clauses

Final adverb clauses are usually not separated with commas, except when introduced by *although* and *even though*, and by *as*, *since*, or *while* when they express cause or condition rather than time:

> A variety of popular explanations for the Western [techni-cal/economic] miracle have been proposed. Some attribute it to imperialism, **even though** many of the most economically successful countries grew prosperous before resorting to imperialism and such highly affluent countries as Norway and Switzerland never adopted imperialist policies at all.
> —"Science, Technology and the Western Miracle," *Scientific American*, Nov. 1990

Setting Off Nonrestrictive Modifiers

We use commas to set off nonrestrictive or nonessential modifiers, most often noun appositives and adjective clauses:

> Now it surged up again and I hungered for books, **new ways of looking and seeing**. —Richard Wright, *Black Boy*
> (appositive)

> The corona, **the tenuous outer atmosphere of the sun**, has been familiar to observers for centuries as the faint silvery glow surrounding the black disk of the moon during a total eclipse. —*Scientific American*, Mar. 1977
> (appositive)

> The muskrats were out: they can feed under the ice, **where the silver trail of bubbles from their fur catches and freezes in streaming, glittering globes**. —Annie Dillard, *Pilgrim at Tinker Creek*
> (relative clause)

> I left him to his thoughts, **which were probably as small, ugly and frightened as the man himself**.
> —Raymond Chandler, *The Little Sister*
> (relative clause)

Compare the punctuation of these clauses to the following:

> Seldon was in the state of impassioned self-absorption **that the first surrender to love produces**. —Edith Wharton, *The House of Mirth*

> For the next few days I hung about the Exchange Hotel in a state of mind **which need not be described**.
> —Siegfried Sassoon, *Memoirs of an Infantry Officer*

Or even:

> I left him to thoughts **that were probably as small, ugly and frightened as the man himself**.

Can you see why in the following sentence one of the relative *which* clauses needs a comma and the other does not? Read the sentence aloud:

> One thing **which struck him at once** was that every mesa was duplicated by a cloud mesa, like a reflection, **which lay motionless above it or moved slowly up from behind it**.
> —Willa Cather, *Death Comes for the Archbishop*

In terms of meaning, as one rhetorician explained it, **restrictive** (no comma) **modifiers** *define*, while **nonrestrictive** (commas) **modifiers** *comment*. In terms of structure restrictive modifiers form a phrase with the word or phrases they modify; the nonrestrictive modifiers do not:

> I left him to **thoughts that were probably as small, ugly and frightened as the man himself**.

> I left him to his thoughts, **which were probably as small, ugly and frightened as the man himself**.

Setting Off Conjunctive Adverbs and Other Transitional Expressions

We use commas to set off conjunctive adverbs (*however, moreover, nevertheless, therefore*, and the like), as well as other transitional expressions (*as a result, to sum up, for example*, and the like):

> Farming cannot take place except in nature; **therefore**, if nature does not thrive, farming cannot thrive.
> —Wendell Berry, "Nature as Measure"

> **Furthermore**, subsidy programs are not necessarily always compassionate. Empires and large nations plagued with active or latent separatist movements use subsidies to contain restiveness and discontent.   —Jane Jacobs, "The Dynamics of Decline"

Or:

> Subsidy programs, **furthermore**, are not necessarily always compassionate.

> **To begin with**, a flashback is the most potentially disorienting technique in all of the writing craft.
> —Jon Franklin, *Writing for Story*

Setting Off Absolutes

We use commas to set off absolutes, structures consisting of a noun and its modifiers. Unlike noun appositives, which they sometimes resemble, absolutes cannot substitute for any other word and are always set off by commas. Their usual function is to present a detail of an action presented in the main clause:

> The big, lumbering ferryboat was approaching, **its prow slapping the corrugated waves.**
> —Sean O'Faolain, "Lovers of the Lake"

> The women are in the kitchen, **my mother cleaning redfish and Sharon sitting at a window with a lapful of snap beans.**
> —Walker Percy, *The Moviegoer*

Setting Off Contrasted Elements

We use a comma to set off an element that we wish to contrast strongly with an earlier one:

> The romantics did not aim at peace and quiet, but at vigorous and passionate individual life.
> —Bertrand Russell, *A History of Western Philosophy*

> They treated me gently, but unwisely.
> —Mary Lee Settle, "London—1944"

> Whatever else happiness may be, it is neither in having nor in being, but in becoming. —John Ciardi, "Is Everybody Happy?"

We also use commas in certain comparative and contrastive expressions of this type:

> The longer I . . . , the more I . . .
> The more I . . . , the less I . . .
> The older . . . , the more . . .

> I've learned the hard way that **the simpler** an outline is, **the more** it focuses your thoughts on the important relationships in your story. —Jon Franklin, *Writing for Story*

Setting Off Parenthetical Elements

We use commas to set off remarks that either comment upon or add information to the material in the main clause. In this category, too, we can place other interrupters that halt the flow of a sentence to qualify or direct (*too, also, indeed, perhaps,* and the like):

A garden, **of course,** is not always as comfortable as Kroger's [a supermarket chain]: If you grow a garden you are going to shed some sweat, and you are going to spend some time bent over; you will experience some aches and pains.
—Wendell Berry, *The Gift of Good Land*

Abner Doubleday, **as we shall soon see,** most emphatically did not invent baseball at Cooperstown in 1839 as the official tale proclaims; in fact, no one invented baseball at any moment in time.   —Stephen Jay Gould, "The Creation of Myths at Cooperstown"

We take, **it seems to me,** a naively self-righteous view when we argue as if the right of our opponents to speak were something that we protect because we are magnanimous, noble, and unselfish.
—Walter Lippmann, "The Indispensable Opposition"

Normal life, **I know now,** is life that can be explained in one sentence.   —Richard Ford, "Accommodations"

Compare:

I know now that normal life is life that can be explained in one sentence.

In the first version "I know now" has the rhetorical force of a confirming remark, a qualifying but not essential addition. In the second, "I know now" is the main subject and verb, and all the rest is the direct object (a noun clause). The first statement is about life, the second about what the "I" knows.

Setting Off the Source of a Direct Quotation

Most of the time, we use commas to set off the source of a direct quotation (or *dialogue guide*). We do not use the comma, however, when the statement precedes the dialogue guide and takes a question or exclamation mark:

"Was the tape O.K.?" I asked.
"Fine," he said, "but there was one aspect of the thing you neglected to describe and I think it's rather important."
"What's that?"
"The odor."
"I didn't think of it," I said.   —Siri Hustvedt, "Mr. Morning"
(But, "Fine!" he snapped.)

Preventing Misreadings

In its function as a separator, a comma can sometimes mark boundaries between phrases, preventing one from running into another. Without a comma, for example, the following momentarily confuses us:

Before the dog could attack the mailman stepped back.

For a brief moment "the mailman" seems to be the object of "attack"; then we see it is the subject of "stepped back." A comma eliminates the confusion:

Before the dog could attack, the mailman stepped back.

The following also needs a clarifying comma:

When they were free to leave the man's brother picked them up in his old truck and brought them to his apartment in Santa Clara.

Without a comma after "leave," the sentence at first seems to say that it is the man's brother they are leaving:

When they were free to leave, the man's brother picked them up in his old truck . . .

Indicating Omissions

We often use a comma to indicate that a word, usually a verb, has been omitted:

One day dawns clear; the next, cloudy.   —Paul Gruchow, "Bones"
(the next *dawns* cloudy)

The storyteller's world revolves around memory; the novelist's, around imagination.
—Anton Shammas, "Amerka, Amerka: A Palestinian Abroad in the Land of the Free"

The agricultural age was based on plows and the animals that pulled them; the industrial age, on engines and the fuels that fed them. The information age we are now creating will be based on computers and the networks that interconnect them.
—"Communications, Computers and Networks," *Scientific American*, Sept. 1991

Creating Emphasis

In some cases we use commas to set off and emphasize items that, for strict grammatical purposes, do not require separation:

> If they couldn't turn him into bronze or stone, they could transform him into a salable product, which, **in a commercial society,** is the next best thing to immortality.
>
> —Lewis H. Lapham, *Harper's*, Jan. 1989

> Art teaches nothing, **except the significance of life.**
>
> —Henry Miller, "Reflections on Writing"

> How do we reconcile our burgeoning demand for energy with the need to maintain a viable global ecosystem? There is no solution, **as yet.**
>
> —"Energy for Planet Earth," *Scientific American*, Sept. 1990

Then consider the special case of the following:

> On a cold spring day, just before Easter, Jemmy Todd, the postman, walked into the Hardings' kitchen, laid the morning's mail on their breakfast table, and told them that Mr. Sawcombe, their neighbor, had died, early that morning, of a heart attack.   —Rosamunde Pilcher, "Toby"

As opposed to "had died early that morning of a heart attack"—the commas re-create how the postman, carrying gossip as well as mail, dribbles out the information, piece by piece. And, finally, compare the following:

> He works very hard in the morning.

> He works very hard, in the morning.

The comma changes the message, adding an implication missing in the first. Without the comma the sentence might lead to another statement: "He works very hard in the morning, then he takes the afternoon off." The second implies something quite different: "He works very hard, in the morning (but he isn't worth much in the afternoon)." The comma adds a telling and suggestive emphasis to the concluding phrase.

Between Names and Titles or Degrees

The common practice is to separate names from titles or degrees. The one exception is *Jr.*, *Sr.*, or *III*, where the comma is optional:

Sammy Davis Jr.   Kurt Vonnegut, Jr.

Samuel Johnson, L.L.D.   Rex Morgan, M.D.

In Dates, Addresses, Geographical Names, Long Numbers, Direct Address, Salutations, and Closings

Dates In dates, when the day comes after the month, we use a comma between the day and year:

July 4, 1776

When the day precedes the month, no comma is used:

30 June 1954

When a date is used in a sentence, the year is enclosed by commas (perhaps because it is serving like a *nonrestrictive* appositive):

On the morning of December 29, 1696, a Dutch captain and his crew were searching for the survivors of a ship that had gone down not far off the coast of Western Australia.
—"Frogfishes," *Scientific American*, June 1990

When the day of the month is omitted, the comma is not necessary:

December 1696

Note: B.C. and A.D. are not set off by commas:

As early as 400,000 B.C., fire was kindled in the caves of Peking Man. —"Energy for Planet Earth," *Scientific American*, Sept. 1990

The comma here sets off the entire opener: "As early as 400,000 B.C." Because of the natural pause after the opener, the comma is optional.

Addresses and Geographical Names In addresses and geographical names we place a comma between a city and its state, province, or country:

Moscow, Idaho   Calgary, Alberta   San Juan, Puerto Rico

When a city is mentioned in a sentence, its state, province, or country is enclosed by commas (again, because it serves as a *nonrestrictive* appositive):

Charleston, South Carolina, is a long way from earthquake country.
—"Earthquakes in Stable Continental Crust," *Scientific American*, Mar. 1990

Long Numbers We simplify the reading of long numbers by using commas to mark them off in groups of three digits, counting from the right:

$22,643,221   8,000,000,000

Direct Address   We use commas to set off the name of someone directly addressed:

"Everybody hates you, **Dixon**, and my God I can see why."
—Kingsley Amis, *Lucky Jim*

The same practice holds on those occasions when the writer addresses the reader:

An outline, **you see**, has nothing to do with Roman Numerals.
—Jon Franklin, *Writing for Story*

Salutations and Closings   In informal correspondence we use commas after salutations (following the logic of direct address), and in closings:

Dear Santa,	Sincerely,
Dear Mr. Rogers,	Your humble and obedient servant,

In business correspondence the salutation is followed by a colon:

Dear Mr. Rogers:
Regarding the dozen sweaters you ordered . . .

Misusing Commas

Do not use commas to separate major sentence elements, like subjects and verbs, or verbs and direct objects, even when some of these are phrases or clauses:

Not   We were later told,   that our flight had been canceled.
<small>verb · dir obj</small>

But   We were later told   that our flight had been canceled.

Few would place a comma after the verb if the direct object were a single word: We were told *this*. So there should not be a comma when the direct object is a clause:

We were later told **that our flight had been canceled**.

Semicolons

We use semicolons for the following:

▶ to link independent clauses not joined by a coordinating conjunction   371

▶ to link independent clauses joined by conjunctive adverbs and by certain transitional expressions   373

The semicolon falls somewhere between the comma and the period, with more decisiveness than the first and less finality than the second.

Linking Independent Clauses Not Joined by a Coordinating Conjunction

Normally, we use semicolons to link independent (or main) clauses when they are not connected by coordinating conjunctions (*and*, *but*, *for*, *or*, and the like). The semicolon enables a writer to join two or more related ideas into a single "thought" (a sentence is about "one thing," but the thing may have several major parts). Usually, we relate such ideas with a comma and a coordinating conjunction that identifies the nature of the relationship. The semicolon is more compact, taking the place of the comma and coordinator, and suggesting a close relationship between the clauses, which may be parallel in structure, clearly contrasted in meaning, or linked by implicit logic:

> **People today don't talk about their consciences and how to appease them; they talk about guilt-trips and how to avoid them.** —Ellen Goodman, "Mother Teresa and Her Endless Night"

■

Exercise

It is difficult to master punctuation by memorizing abstract, mechanical rules. The best way to master it is by studying and experimenting with actual examples in order to see how punctuation serves rhetorical and stylistic purposes. Good punctuation is not simply "correct"; it is a way of relating and juxtaposing ideas. To test this notion, study the exercise sentences and do the following:

A Notice the kinds of relationships implied by the semicolons; look for the "one idea." Try to express this idea in a single sentence. What was the effect of originally stating the idea in parts?

B   Replace the semicolons with periods. How do the sentences read with the ideas separated?

C   Replace the semicolons with commas and an appropriate conjunction (in some cases, a subordinate conjunction may even fit: *while, as, since*, and the like). What happens when a linking word *tells* the reader about the nature of the relationship? What is the effect of simply having an extra word between the ideas?

D   Look again at the original. What is the effect of connecting the statements so abruptly? What impact does the use of the semicolon have?

E   Look for examples of semicolon use in your reading. Collect some examples of sentences that seem to work particularly well because of the way the writer used semicolons.

1   The grammar of the sentence creates clarity; the rhetoric of the sentence creates emphasis.
—James M. Mellard and James C. Wilcox, *The Authentic Writer*

2   He is anxious; he is threatened on every side.
—Walker Percy, *The Moviegoer*

3   Few people will admit to being superstitious; it implies naivete or ignorance.
—Robertson Davies, "A Few Kind Words for Superstition"

4   A passionate bohemianism was what the University of Chicago student body aspired to; a grim scruffiness was what it often achieved.   —Joseph Epstein, "They Said You Was High Class"

5   The people here had many skills; they could get by on their own.   —V. S. Naipaul, *A Bend in the River*

6   She knew of life's seamy side as a theory; she could not grasp it as a fact.   —E. M. Forster, *Howards End*

7   We are the children of our landscape; it dictates behavior and even thought in the measure to which we are responsive to it.   —Lawrence Durrell, *Justine*

8   Pensacola was peaceful-looking in the winter sunshine; everything was bright with sun, the white-painted buildings, the sandy earth, the palm trees, the quiet waters of the bay.
—Samuel Hynes, "The Feeling of Flying"

9   That day the apartment seemed more chaotic than on my first visit; the desk in particular was a mass of disturbed papers and boxes.   —Siri Hustvedt, "Mr. Morning"

Note: If we substitute a comma for a semicolon in any of the exercise sentences, we usually create a *comma splice*:

The grammar of the sentence creates clarity, the rhetoric of the sentence creates emphasis.

Linking Independent Clauses Joined by Conjunctive Adverbs and by Certain Transitional Expressions

Semicolons are also necessary when independent clauses are connected by conjunctive adverbs (words like *consequently, furthermore, hence, however, nevertheless*, and *therefore*), and by transitional expressions like *for example, for instance, in fact*, and *on the other hand*:

We need our real problems named and explained; **otherwise,** we have no chance to overcome them.
—Shelby Steele, *The Content of Our Character*

Her skin was soft and flushed, and her eyes blurred, and she was not steady on her feet; **nevertheless,** she was looking him straight in the face. —Peter Matthiessen, *At Play in the Fields of the Lord*

I have been acquainted with this passage since the age of twelve; **however,** I only came to understand it fully a year ago, at the age of twenty-two.

Compare the last sentence with this version:

I have been acquainted with this passage since the age of twelve, but I only came to understand it fully a year ago, at the age of twenty-two.

The first version is more deliberately and "tellingly" rational as the writer strives to emphasize his mental breakthrough; the second, more informal. Ultimately, let your context—subject, audience, and occasion—decide the appropriate degree of formality and emphasis.

Separating Independent Clauses Containing Internal Punctuation

Next morning, the wind had dropped; the sky reflected on everything its mild brightness; trees, houses and pavements glistened like washed glass.
—Elizabeth Bowen, "Ivy Gripped the Steps"

The richness of human life is that we have many lives; we live the events that do not happen (and some that cannot) as viv-

idly as those that do; and if thereby we die a thousand deaths,
that is the price we pay for living a thousand lives.

—Jacob Bronowski, "The Reach of Imagination"

She seemed vast and dishevelled, like a huge ill-packed parcel
that had been battered and broken open in the post; every
crevice seemed to have burst open, every undergarment
seemed to have poked its way to the surface.

—Angus Wilson, *Anglo-Saxon Attitudes*

Notice what else the semicolon contributes to the last example. The
sentence contains three independent clauses, but they are punctuated
unevenly; a semicolon appears only once, separating the first statement
from the other two. This punctuation suggests that the statements are
qualitatively different, even though together they constitute one idea.
The first makes a generalization, a judgment; the second and third (after
the semicolon) illustrate the generalization on a lower level of concreteness. The first clause *tells;* the second two *show.* Punctuation reinforces
the message sent by the author's arrangement of ideas; the semicolon
proclaims that the first statement belongs to a class of ideas separate
from the second two.

Separating Items in a Series
Containing Internal Punctuation

Use semicolons to separate units in a sentence when they contain commas (these units may be phrases or clauses). The semicolons preserve
the clarity of the series by helping mark the major and minor divisions:

I lived along the banks of a river—where beaver built their
dams; where mud turtles sunned on half-submerged logs;
where bullheads and northern pike, saugers and buffalo fish
swam the murky waters; where white-tailed deer came down
to drink; where the tracks of mink mingled in the shoreline
mud with the remains of the clams that raccoons had fished
from the shallows.   —Paul Gruchow, "Bones"

Politicians of both parties meet with sustained applause when
they demand longer jail sentences and harsher laws as well as
the right to invade almost everybody's privacy; to search, without a warrant, almost anybody's automobile or boat; to bend
the rules of evidence, hire police spies, and attach, again without a warrant, the wires of electronic surveillance.

—Lewis H. Lapham, "Democracy in America"

```
they demand   longer jail sentences and
              harsher laws as well as
   the right  to invade almost everybody's privacy;
              to search, without a warrant . . . ;
              to bend the rules of evidence,
              hire police spies, and
              attach . . .
```

Misusing Semicolons

Semicolons are used to connect coordinate (or parallel) elements, like independent clauses or items in a series with internal punctuation. They should never be used to separate dissimilar or noncoordinate elements (like phrases and clauses).

Not   He was like that even as a boy; gracious to everyone, but known to very few.   —Willa Cather, *Death Comes for the Archbishop*

But   He was like that even as a boy, gracious to everyone but known to very few.   (clause and adjective phrases)

Not   The Bishop stood holding the candle and watching her face while she spoke her few words; a dark brown peon face, worn thin and sharp by life and sorrow.
—*Death Comes for the Archbishop*

But   The Bishop stood holding the candle and watching her face while she spoke her few words, a dark brown peon face, worn thin and sharp by life and sorrow.
(clause and appositive)

Note: Willa Cather's *Death Comes for the Archbishop* was published in 1927. Her sentences illustrate how much the conventions of punctuation can evolve in half a century. As a rule, it is safer to use more contemporary examples for punctuation models.

Semicolons should also never appear between subjects and their verbs or between verbs and their complements:

Not   An administrator who dreaded high school Spanish when young; cannot believe that a little Eskimo girl can easily be bilingual.

But   An administrator who dreaded high school Spanish when young cannot believe that a little Eskimo girl can easily be bilingual.   —Gary Snyder, *The Practice of the Wild*

And finally, semicolons should never be used to introduce a series. (See the sections "Colons" and "Dashes" in this chapter.)

Colons

We use colons for the following:

The colon is a mark of anticipation: it emphasizes a promise–fulfillment relationship between the items it connects. It is an introducer: it alerts the reader to material that will supplement what has gone before, usually by explaining or amplifying or illustrating.

Introducing a Series

When a colon introduces a series, an independent clause (a complete statement in itself) will precede the colon, and the series will usually function like an appositive, a catalogue of items at a lower level of generality than a word or phrase in the main clause:

They grow the **things that can be preserved easily:** corn and chilies and alfalfa.   —N. Scott Momaday, *House Made of Dawn*

I was a loner and a loser who had pretty much failed **at everything:** at the novel, at screenwriting, at marriage, and, over and over again, at romance.   —Larry McMurtry, *Some Can Whistle*

Investigators who want to study the surface of a metal for wear, cracks or other defects can call on **a wide variety of techniques:** optical microscopy, electron microscopy, scanning electron microscopy and autoradiography among others.
—*Scientific American*, Jan. 1977

It's spring but I was still cataloguing the **different kinds of**

> **snow:** snow that falls dry but is rained on; snow that melts
> down into hard crusts; wind-driven snow that looks blue; pow-
> der snow on hardpack on powder—a Linzertorte of snow.
> —Gretel Ehrlich, "Snow"

Note: Relatively simple series like the preceding may be introduced with a colon or with an introductory word or phrase, but not both:

> They grow the things that can be preserved easily, **such as** corn and chilies and alfalfa.

Longer, more complicated series may often require not only an introductory colon but also semicolons to separate the individual items when even one of these has its own internal punctuation. In the progression from colon to semicolon to comma, the content should remain clear, as in the following:

> The wide windows look out on Harlem's invincible and indes-
> cribable squalor: the Park Avenue railroad tracks, around
> which, about forty years ago, the present dark community
> began; the unrehabilitated houses, bowed down, it would
> seem, under the great weight of frustration and bitterness
> they contain; the dark, ominous schoolhouses from which the
> child may emerge maimed, blinded, hooked, or enraged for
> life; and the churches, churches, block upon block of churches,
> niched in the walls like cannon in the walls of a fortress.
> —James Baldwin, "Fifth Avenue, Uptown: A Letter from Harlem"

> The best player on each of the three teams was having a re-
> markable year: Joe DiMaggio of the Yankees, although hob-
> bled by painful leg and foot injuries, was in his last great
> statistical year, and was in the process of driving in 155 runs;
> Ted Williams of Boston ended up hitting .369 with 127 runs
> batted in; and Lou Boudreau of the Indians led Williams for
> part of the summer and ended up hitting .355, 60 points
> above his career average.   —David Halberstam, *Summer of '49*

Again, notice the relationship between the statements before and after the colon. The introductory or thematic statement before the colon *tells*; the statements after the colon *show*.

Introducing an Explanation or Conclusion

A colon is an emphatic device that calls even more attention to whatever it introduces, acting almost as a fanfare:

And this is the rule of life: Most improvements make matters worse.

—George F. Will, "The Electoral College's Campus Radical," *Washington Post*, 11–17 June 1990, natl. weekly ed.

In the end, this must be said: Any war that isn't worth a woman's life isn't worth a man's life.

—Ellen Goodman, "The Equal Rights to Fight and Die"

In the following, notice how Ellen Goodman uses a colon to supplement the effect of her periodic sentence structure (one that postpones the principal statement to the end):

Like virtually every woman in America who has spent time beside a man behind a wheel, like every woman in America who has ever been a lost passenger outward bound with a male driver, I know that there is one way in which the male sex is innately different from the female: Men are by their very nature congenitally unable to ask directions.

—"In the Male Direction"

Capitalization   A statement introduced by a colon may or may not be capitalized. The capital letter creates a little more emphasis. In typing, leave one space without the capital, two with.

Introducing an Appositive

Other punctuation marks, most often commas, can also introduce appositives, but the colon does so deliberately and precisely, especially at the end of a sentence. In such cases the colon announces the arrival of a careful definition or renaming of what went before. Such deliberate explanation is often necessary when we wish our readers to know in what precise sense we are using certain terms:

Like so many writers, I have only this one "**subject**," this one "**area**": the act of writing.   —Joan Didion, "Why I Write"

The heart is **a pump**: a muscular organ that contracts in rhythm, impelling the blood first to the lungs for oxygenation and then out into the vascular system to supply oxygen and nutrients to every cell in the body.   —*Scientific American*, Feb. 1976

In some cases the appositive will be an entire statement:

Some of the columnists write well, some of them atrociously, but they all try to obey **the first law of the essayist**: Be interested and you will be interesting.   —Gilbert Highet, *Explorations*

The secret of happiness is **this:** <u>let your interests be as wide as</u> <u>possible, and let your reactions to the things and persons that</u> <u>interest you be as far as possible friendly rather than hostile.</u>
—Bertrand Russell, "Happiness"

A colon may also be used before appositives introduced by words like *namely* and *that is*. One writer used the following method:

Bilingual programs didn't exist then, so Eduardo learned his English by the method now formally known as "immersion." **That is,** he had to teach himself. —Tracy Kidder, *Among Schoolchildren*

However, it would have been equally suitable to have used a colon to join the two statements:

Bilingual programs didn't exist then, so Eduardo learned his English by the method now formally known as "immersion": **that is,** he had to teach himself.

Introducing a Statement or Question or Quotation

A comma may also introduce a statement or question, but the colon is more formal and emphatic.

The question is this: What are educators to do when they must serve in a culture inundated by information?
—Neil Postman, "Learning by Story," *The Atlantic*, Dec. 1989

The Yankee pitchers had a phrase for it: "Your turn in the barrel," for it was like being the target in an arcade.
—David Halberstam, *Summer of '49*

In 1961 a copy writer named Shirley Polykoff was working for the Foote, Cone & Belding advertising agency on the Clairol hair-dye account when she came up with the line: "If I've got only one life, let me live it as a blonde!"
—Tom Wolfe, "Only One Life"

Connecting Two Independent Clauses When the Second Amplifies or Explains the First

Colons, like semicolons, can join completed thoughts when they are related (assuming that a sentence or independent clause is a "complete thought"). The colon marks one kind of relationship: that in which the first statement is prefatory to the second. In such cases the colon highlights or emphasizes the clause that comes after the colon. *The two clauses are structural but not rhetorical equals*:

Everything written with vitality expresses that vitality: there are no dull subjects, only dull minds.
—Raymond Chandler, "The Simple Art of Murder"

Clear thinking becomes clear writing: one can't exist without the other.   —William Zinsser, *On Writing Well*

It is a terrible, an inexorable, law that one cannot deny the humanity of another without diminishing one's own: in the face of one's victim, one sees oneself.
—James Baldwin, "Fifth Avenue, Uptown: A Letter from Harlem"

Jabula is a word with more than one meaning in colloquial Zulu: it is used for happiness and for beer.
—James McClure, *The Gooseberry Fool*

It occurred to him (not for the first time) that the world was divided sharply down the middle: Some lived careful lives and some lived careless lives, and everything that happened could be explained by the difference between them.
—Anne Tyler, *The Accidental Tourist*

Applying the preceding rule, can you see how the following statement from Jean Shepherd could have been even more emphatic?

At fourteen you are made of cellophane. You curl easily and everyone can see through you.
—"The Endless Street-car Ride into the Night, and the Tinfoil Noose"

Other Uses

▶ after formal salutations in letters:

Dear Mr. Trump: Dear Ms. Helmsley:

▶ between hours and minutes:

5:04 P.M.

▶ between minutes and seconds in presenting times for athletic events:

3:47.2   (three minutes, forty-seven and two-tenths seconds)

▶ between titles and subtitles in books and articles:

James Baldwin, "Fifth Avenue, Uptown: A Letter from Harlem"
Loren Eiseley, *All the Strange Hours: The Excavation of a Life*

▶ between Bible chapters and verses

Of making many books there is no end, and much study is a weariness of the flesh. —*Ecclesiastes* 12:12

▶ between the city and publisher in bibliographies (MLA format):

Belmont: Wadsworth   New York: Penguin Books

▶ between year and pages in bibliographies (MLA format):

Jacobs, Jane, "Cities and the Wealth of Nations: A New Theory of Economic Life." *The Atlantic,* **Mar. 1984: 41–66.**

Misusing Colons

The colon should not be used between verbs or prepositions and their objects, even when the latter are multiple:

Not   From his mother he had gotten: sensitive feelings, a soft heart, a brooding nature, a tendency to be confused under pressure.

But   From his mother he had gotten sensitive feelings, a soft heart, a brooding nature, a tendency to be confused under pressure.   —Saul Bellow, *Seize the Day*

Not   A writer has to deal in: facts, things, particulars, concrete objects, and specific people, situations, and images.

But   A writer has to deal in facts, things, particulars, concrete objects, and specific people, situations, and images.
—Wallace Stegner, "Writing as Graduate Study"

Also, a colon should not appear after such expressions as *namely, that is,* and *such as:*

Not   As a French philosopher remarked: "It is imperative to send children to bed at eight, so that adults may devote themselves in quiet to serious occupations, such as: bridge, cocktails, dancing and flirting."
—Jacques Barzun, *Teacher in America*

But   As a French philosopher remarked: "It is imperative to send children to bed at eight, so that adults may devote themselves in quiet to serious occupations, such as bridge, cocktails, dancing and flirting."

Notice, however, that in cases of misuse like those illustrated here, writers simply follow the instinct to use a colon before a series.

Dashes

Dashes are typed as two hyphens without a space before or after. We use the dash for the following:

▸   to introduce a series   382
▸   to set off interruptive material   383
▸   to set off some concluding appositives   384
▸   to set off dramatic conclusions   385
▸   to separate independent clauses   385

Related issues:

▸   misusing dashes   386
▸   the colon and the dash   386

The dash is a dramatic or emphatic device that works by creating a meaningful delay between the elements it separates. In some cases it can overlap the function of other punctuation marks: it can enclose like the comma and the parenthesis, introduce a series like the colon, and even separate independent clauses like the semicolon. Nevertheless, it has its own distinctive personality, one making it the best tool for some jobs but one also requiring restraint.

Introducing a Series

Appositive series (renamers or definers of other words) usually follow some larger umbrella term, and in such cases they are usually introduced by a colon:

> They grow **the things that can be preserved easily:** corn and chilies and alfalfa.   —N. Scott Momaday, *House Made of Dawn*

In some cases, however, the series precedes the more general term. Then the appropriate punctuation is the dash:

> They grow corn and chilies and alfalfa—the things that can be preserved easily.

> Choosing, defining, creating harmony, bringing that clarity and shape that is rest and light out of disorder and confusion—the work that I do at my desk is not unlike arranging flowers.
> —May Sarton, "The Act of Writing"

> Tolerance, good temper and sympathy—they are what matter really, and if the human race is not to collapse they must come to the front before long.   —E. M. Forster, "What I Believe"

All his affection and half his attention—it was what he
granted her throughout their happy married life.
—E. M. Forster, *Howard's End*

The following example uses a comma to set off the same kind of series.
Notice how much emphasis is lost.

Patience, alertness, intelligence, and a human good will and
fearlessness, *that* is what you want in a time of change.
—D. H. Lawrence, "The State of Funk"

Compare:

Patience, alertness, intelligence, and a human good will and
fearlessness—*that* is what you want in a time of change.

Lawrence's version presents a series of units piling up before the main
statement. The comma separates both individual members of the series
and the entire series itself. The second version, with the dash, gives us
one unit composed of subunits. Commas separate the members, and
the dash separates the series.

Setting Off Interruptive Material

Dashes can be used to set off certain kinds of interruptive material—
words, phrases, or even complete statements that break with the structure of the main clause ("Her short-cut hair—it was nearly black—lay
. . ."). Sometimes this interruption will be an outright break in thought,
but it has more weight than one set off with parentheses (which suggests
that it is almost an aside). When the interrupter is a full statement, it
must be set off with either a dash or parentheses. When the interrupter
is not a full statement and we have a choice between the three principal
separators, we use the dash when we want the most drama, emphasis,
or emotion:

The pleasures of reading itself—who doesn't remember?—
were like those of a Christmas cake, a sweet devouring.
—Eudora Welty, "A Sweet Devouring"

The prince—I think it best not to give his name, in the light of
what happened later—picked me up in his Jeep the following
morning.   —Geoffrey C. Ward, "Tiger in the Road!"

Her short-cut hair—it was nearly black—lay smooth and shiny
as enamel on her round head.   —Dashiell Hammett, *The Glass Key*

The prisons—at least the prisons I have encountered—are infi-
nitely more hellish than our Hollywood dream makers relate.   —Kenneth A. McClane, "Walls: A Journey to Auburn"

From any catastrophe some good can come. It is not a bad thing to be reminded—the world relentlessly sees to this—of the fragility of all social arrangements.
—George F. Will, "What Earthquakes Teach"

Interrupting appositives *must* be set off with dashes when they contain commas. Any appositive series, of course, will have internal commas:

Verna bent over the old-fashioned bathtub—the kind with legs, and the white enamel worn thin in places—to turn the faucet and start the hot water running.
—Cyrus Colter, "A Man in the House"

Living space for the four of us—my mother, my brother, my father, and me—was a kitchen and a bedroom.
—Richard Wright, *Black Boy*

I began reading the writers—Herodotus, Euripides, Coleridge, Descartes, Rousseau, Thoreau, Raymond Chandler—for whom a conscientious and narrow academic career had left no time.
—David Quammen, "Strawberries Under Ice"

From millions of sources all over the globe, through every possible channel and medium—light waves, airwaves, ticker tapes, computer banks, telephone wires, television cables, printing presses—information pours in.
—Neil Postman, "Learning by Story," *The Atlantic*, Dec. 1987

If we substitute commas for the dashes, the sentences become confusing and unfocused. In each case the only job of the commas is to separate the members of the series, while the dashes clearly mark out the boundaries of the entire appositive series itself, preserving a clear sense of rank between the different elements of the sentence.

Setting Off Some Concluding Appositives

Dashes may sometimes serve to introduce appositives at the ends of sentences. The colon is the usual punctuation mark for such structures, but its effect is considered to be more formal than that of the dash:

I lay there for a long time awake, listening to the soft night-sounds of Brooklyn—a far-off howling dog, a passing car, a burst of gentle laughter from a woman and a man at the edge of the park.   —William Styron, *Sophie's Choice*

One by one I began to hear them—those innumerable, inexplicable sounds that are to be heard at night in a house when

all the casual day sounds are still: timbers that stretch and contract, little insects that make a great creaking noise.
—Sean O'Faolain, "Midsummer Night Madness"

The silence became full of sound: noises you couldn't put a
name to—a crack, a rustle, something like a cough, and a
whisper.   —Graham Greene, *The Quiet American*

Note: Observe how Greene uses punctuation marks to create a
hierarchy or ranking of details in his sentence, from colon to dash to
commas. "Noises" is in apposition to (or renames) "sound," and "a
crack, a rustle, something like a cough, and a whisper" is in apposition
to "noise":

colon

The silence became full of sound:

dash

    noises you couldn't put a name to—

      commas

      a crack,
      a rustle,
      something like a cough, and
      a whisper.

Setting Off Dramatic Conclusions

Some sentences end with a sudden shift in thought or tone, perhaps
an ironic addition or qualifier. The dramatic pause of the dash makes
the concluding remark all the more pointed and emphatic:

Athens was not only the first democracy in the world, it was
also at its height an almost perfect democracy—that is, for
men.   —Edith Hamilton, "The Lessons of the Past"

Separating Independent Clauses

The dash is an acceptable if uncommon way to link two independent
clauses, a task usually performed by a semicolon or by a comma and
a coordinating conjunction, and sometimes even by a colon. When a
dash links independent clauses, it is intruding most closely on the territory of the colon:

The exercise was simple—anyone could do it.
—Samuel Hynes, "The Feeling of Flying"

There was a gust of wind from outside, and the papers on the
desk were whipped into the air—hundreds of white pages

flapped noisily against the bookshelves and walls, blew over the chairs and stacks of newspapers, sliding across the wood floor. —Siri Hustvedt, "Mr. Morning"

Italian brands of dried pasta, whatever they cost, taste better, I think, than most American ones—they have a clean, slightly nutty flavor and above all a texture that stays firm until you finish eating. —Corby Kummer, "Pasta," *The Atlantic*, July 1986

Misusing Dashes

Misuse of the dash consists usually of overuse. There are many dash abusers, or dash-dependent writers. The dependency begins innocently enough, probably while taking in-class notes, where one must jot down things as quickly as possible. The lecture or the discussion goes so rapidly that there is hardly time to catch anything more than phrases and abbreviations, much less have the luxury of writing complete sentences and remembering all the little rules of etiquette governing commas, colons, semicolons, and parentheses. The temptation is to use one mark for everything. Besides, even the word *dash* suggests speed, inviting the note-taker to use it. After that, the rest is easy. Before the user knows it, the dash has become an indispensable all-purpose punctuation mark. Don't let this happen to you. Learn to say no to dashes.

The Colon and the Dash

In some cases we have a choice between the colon and the dash:

As everybody knows, meaning does not come from single words but from words put together in groups—phrases, clauses, sentences.
—Jacques Barzun and Henry F. Graff, *The Modern Researcher*

As everybody knows, meaning does not come from single words but from words put together in groups: phrases, clauses, sentences.

The principal difference is that the dash is usually considered to be less formal than the colon. In an example like the preceding, many readers will not appreciate the difference.

Parentheses

We use parentheses for the following:

Related issue:

▶ definitions and explanations   388

Parentheses are marks of enclosure, always in pairs, used to include additional or casual information that breaks away from the main structure of a sentence or paragraph (dashes and commas can enclose, too, but also appear singly). In the middle of a sentence a parenthesis announces a kind of suspension, a momentary interruption of the thematic flow and perhaps even of the tone. At the end of a sentence a parenthetical addition may be a single word, a phrase, or even one or more complete statements, but it is usually only indirectly relevant to the subject at hand (as opposed to the more directly relevant material usually enclosed by commas).

The grammatical equivalent of poetic license, the parenthesis is a device we use to escape the usual demands of structure. A good sentence should be about "one thing," should have some kind of rhetorical focus, but parenthetical remarks allow the writer to take a few liberties, to stray a little off the main path for a moment. Of course usage varies, but as a rule the fewer the parenthetical remarks, the more effective they are likely to be. Used too frequently, parentheses can make a piece of writing seem disjointed and incoherent. Thus, in more formal writing, parentheses are used sparingly and only for documentation or for brief definitions. In less formal writing, however, where the writer's voice and personality have freer play, parenthetical material may be more common.

Setting Off "Nonessential" Material

Parenthetical material is incidental (but not irrelevant) to the topic under discussion. It may expand, illustrate, clarify, provide helpful background information, or allow the writer to comment or editorialize. Authorial asides are the least formal occasion for parentheses:

> Let us discuss the condition of my desk. It is messy, mildly messy. The messiness is both physical (coffee cups, cigarette ash) and spiritual (unpaid bills, unwritten novels).
> —Donald Barthelme, "Not-Knowing"

> On three or four occasions in my life, I have been strongly drawn to strangers, probably because they seem to me projections of the self I would like to be. Marcos (I never learned his last name) is one of this number.
> —James McConkey, "Heroes Among the Barbarians"

Then there was Oliver H. P. Garrett, my father's surviving
younger brother. (Another brother had been a mountain-
climber and a professional guide who vanished in a blizzard.)
—George Garrett, "My Two One-Eyed Coaches"

The path to truth is rarely straight, marked by a gate of entry
that sorts applicants by such relatively simple criteria as age
and height. (When I was a kid, you could get into Yankee
Stadium for half price if your head didn't reach a line promi-
nently drawn on the entrance gate about four and a half feet
above the ground. You could scrunch down, but they checked.
One nasty, ugly day, I started to pay full price, and that was
that.)   —Stephen Jay Gould, "Nasty Little Facts"

The Gould example, by providing an anecdotal illustration several sentences long, takes risks with its length. Normally, we should be cautious
about both the number and size of parenthetical remarks. Longer parentheses (longer departures from the main point) may strain the reader's memory (and patience).

Definitions and Explanations   "Nonessential" information may be essential—or at least useful—for some readers. Hence, even in more
formal writing, it is standard practice to use parentheses to enclose
information like dates, scientific names, documentation, translations of
foreign words, statistical information, and so on:

Dum pudeo pereo (as I blush, I die) says an old love song.
—Anne Carson, "Kinds of Water"

A hundred years ago the American chestnut (*Castanea dentata*) could have been called the all-American tree.
—*Scientific American,* July 1990

The Greeks are often described as pure thinkers, disdaining
gritty reality for the loftier realm of intellect. That was certainly true of Plato (429–347 B.C.) and, perhaps to a lesser extent, of his younger contemporary Aristotle (384–32 B.C.). But
it was not true of a much earlier giant, Pythagoras.
—"Pythagoras's Bells, *Scientific American,* July 1990

If society could exploit only a small portion of the solar radia-
tion that strikes the earth's surface every year, which is equivalent to 178,000 terawatt-years (or about 15,000 times the
world's present energy supply), our energy problems would be
solved.   —"Energy for Planet Earth," *Scientific American,* Sept. 1990

Parentheses are also useful in presenting definitions, as in the following paragraph about a manuscript entitled *The Surfin'ary: A Dictionary of Surfing Terms and Phrases*, by Trevor Cralle:

> The Surfin'ary is designed to preserve and document a rich subculture, Mr. Cralle says. But it may also have great appeal for surfing wannabes or poser hodads or nons (non-surfers) who want to sound like surfers while avoiding sunburn and salt water and who have never tried to toe up on a stick (to surf). Even people who don't know the difference between a goofy foot (their left) and a natural (their right) can talk like thrashers (surfing showoffs).
> —Jim Herron Zamora, "Why Valley Girls and Mutant Turtles Sound Like Surfers," *Wall Street Journal*, 27 Sept. 1990

Note: To call even more attention to the slang, the writer might also have placed quotation marks around it:

> But it may also have great appeal for surfing wannabes or "poser hodads" or "nons" (non-surfers) who want to sound like surfers while avoiding sunburn and salt water and who have never tried "to toe up on a stick" (to surf). Even people who don't know the difference between a "goofy foot" (their left) and a "natural" (their right) can talk like "thrashers" (surfing showoffs).

Setting Off Enumerations Within a Sentence

We also use parentheses to enclose numbers and letters marking the items in a list:

> A true counterculture requires at least **three things:** **(1)** a distinctive mode of dress, which can include anything from recycled velvet to torn T-shirts, so long as no part of it can be purchased at Benetton; **(2)** some attempt at artistic or literary creativity, even if the only product is an occasional mimeographed disquisition on love, death, and other current issues; and **(3)** (this is indispensable) an absolute contempt for the bourgeoisie, which can be defined flexibly as the ruling class, any class that lets itself be ruled by it, or one's parents.
> —Barbara Ehrenreich, "Hope I Die Before I Get Rich"

Exercise

Using the previous quotation as a model, revise the following passage into a single sentence containing enumerations:

> There are good reasons why fossil fuels are so popular. First, they are accessible in one form or another in all regions of the world. Second, humankind has learned to exploit them efficiently and relatively cleanly to produce the energy services it needs, the relatively simple technology of controlled combustion providing energy for applications at nearly every scale. Third, they make excellent fuels for transportation—because they are portable and store a great deal of chemical energy and because the oxygen required for combustion is ubiquitous in the air. Finally, one form can readily be converted to another, say, from solid to liquid or gas, and the fuels are excellent feedstocks for chemicals and plastics.
> —"Energy from Fossil Fuels," *Smithsonian*, Sept. 1990

Brackets

We use brackets for the following:

▶   to enclose editorial remarks within quotations   390
▶   to include directions to the reader   391
▶   to serve as parentheses inside of parentheses   392
▶   to mark an error with the word *sic*   392

Related issues:

▶   misusing *sic*   393
▶   brackets and parentheses   393

Enclosing Editorial Remarks Within Quotations

Whereas we use parentheses to make comments in our own text, we use brackets to insert our own clarifying remarks, details, or comments (interpolations) into quoted material. As the following examples show, brackets are especially useful when quoting sentences that rely on previous sentences for some of their meaning:

Crossed by colors, lights, and moving shadows, sparkling in the sun, mysterious in the twilight, its [the ocean's] aspects and its moods vary hour by hour.   —Rachel Carson, *The Sea Around Us*

These encouraging developments [the trend toward more efficient use of electrical energy] reflect rapid progress on four separate but related fronts: advanced technologies for using electricity more productively; new ways to finance and deliver those technologies to customers; expanded and reformulated roles for electric utilities; and innovative regulation that rewards efficiency.
—"Efficient Use of Electricity," *Scientific American*, Sept. 1990

"Civilization, if it means anything and if it is ever to exist [wrote Edward Abbey], must mean a form of human society in which the primary values are openness, diversity, tolerance, personal liberty, reason."   —*One Life at a Time, Please*

Or, take the following quote, exactly as it appeared in *Smithsonian*:

In the first century A.D. the Greek geographer Strabo wrote: "Commagene is a rather small country; and it has a city fortified by nature, Samosata, where the royal residency used to be; but it has now become a [Roman] province; and the city is surrounded by an exceedingly fertile, though small territory."
—"In Anatolia, a Massive Dam Project Drowns Traces of an Ancient Past," Aug. 1990

If we wished to use the quote, however, and Commagene had not yet been identified, we could do this:

In the first century A.D. the Greek geographer Strabo wrote: "Commagene [a minor kingdom in what is now southeastern Turkey] is a rather small country; and it has a city fortified by nature, Saomsata, where the royal residency used to be . . ."

Including Directions to the Reader

We sometimes need to direct our readers to material either elsewhere in our text or in other sources:

About 90 percent of the wind power potential of the U.S. is in 12 contiguous states [see illustration at left], where large-scale ranching and grain-production are major industries.
—"Energy from the Sun," *Scientific American*, Sept. 1990

> We had been interested for some time in the development of
> *Xenopus laevis** [see "Gene Transplantation and the Analysis
> of Development," by Eddy M. De Robertis and J. B. Gordon;
> SCIENTIFIC AMERICAN, December, 1979].
>
> —"Homeobox Genes and the Vertebrate Body Plan," *Scientific American*,
> July 1990

The authors could have identified *Xenopus laevis* like this:

> We had been interested for some time in the development of
> *Xenopus laevis* (a South African tree frog) [see . . .].

But someone quoting the passage and wishing to omit the long biblio-
graphical reference would have identified it like this:

> "We had been interested for some time in the development of
> *Xenopus laevis* [a South African tree frog]."

Parentheses Inside of Parentheses

In rare cases, as when one parenthetical remark falls inside of another,
we must place a parenthesis within another parenthesis:

> The authors confessed to a long-standing concern ("We had
> been interested for some time in the development of *Xenopus
> laevis*" [a South African tree frog]).

In general, this practice is awkward and distracting, and therefore to
be avoided.

Marking an Error with the Word Sic

When we must quote material that contains a misspelling, a grammatical error, an inaccurate piece of information, or something otherwise questionable, we identify the problem with the Latin word *sic*
("thus," meaning roughly "this is the way it appeared in the text"). In
other words, a writer uses *sic* to say, "Blame the source, not me." In
the following a biographer quotes from a letter, and a social commentator from a published study:

> "Mrs. Cohn and I, as well as many of our friends, have been
> inexpressably† [*sic*] shocked at the attack which you made
> upon the good name of our son, Roy, in the Senate Chamber
> yesterday . . ."   —Nicholas von Hoffman, *Citizen Cohn*

* a South African tree frog

† inexpressibly

As Stanley Aronowitz reported from the mammoth GM plant at Lordstown, Ohio, "Long hair, marijuana, and rock music is [*sic*] shared by nearly all young workers in the plant."
—Barbara Ehrenreich, *Fear of Falling*

Misusing Sic   Sic is sometimes used deliberately to call attention to someone's mistakes and, by implication, ignorance or even incompetence. As a result, use of the term can seem ill-willed, revealing more about the attitude of the writer than about the accuracy of the quoted material. If we must include the quote, we can often find a way to cite the flawed part, either by paraphrase or by another use of brackets:

As Stanley Aronowitz reported from the mammoth GM plant at Lordstown, Ohio, "Long hair, marijuana, and rock music [are] shared by nearly all young workers in the plant."

Brackets and Parentheses

In sum, we use parentheses to make comments in our own text and brackets to make comments in someone else's.

Ellipses

We use ellipses for the following:

▶ to indicate omissions in quoted material   394
▶ to suggest a hesitation or pause   396

Related issue:

▶ truth in quoting   395

Ellipses (or ellipsis marks, dots, or points) are formed by three spaced periods, with a space before and after. Their function is to indicate that material has been left out of a quotation. Ellipses, then, pair with brackets: both allow the writer to alter quoted material, brackets allowing us to insert, and ellipses to omit. If brackets allow us to introduce clarifying details and observations, ellipses allow us to exclude those which might distract or mislead or otherwise be irrelevant. Rarely does someone say exactly what will slide neatly into the structure of our own sentences and paragraphs, so brackets and ellipses allow us to customize our citations.

Indicating Omissions in Quoted Material

The following is the standard form for using ellipses:

> You can say "I believe . . . ," or you can say "You will under-
> stand . . . ," or you can say "The facts demonstrate . . ." By
> such choices you create your voice.
>
> —Walker Gibson, *Tough, Sweet and Stuffy*

The comma after the ellipses is to punctuate the series: "You can say this, or you can say this, or you can . . ."

In quoting the words of others, form varies according to where the omissions occur. Suppose we wish to quote from the following paragraph:

> The first and most important point about writing is that
> there is no such thing as material by itself, apart from the way
> in which a person sees it, feels toward it, and is able to give it
> organized form and expression in words. For a writer, form is a
> part of content, affecting it, realizing it. A man may go
> through the most dramatic and horrible experiences in war,
> but actually draw out of them less "material" for writing than
> shy Emily Dickinson in the second-floor room of an Amherst
> house, lowering notes in baskets out the window and thinking
> gently of death—or even (biographers speculate) of a man she
> knew but little, whom she might never see again.
>
> —Paul Engle, "Salt Crystals, Spider Webs, and Words"

If we wish to omit the first part of a quote, we do not need ellipsis marks:

> According to Paul Engle, "there is no such thing as material by
> itself, apart from the way in which a person sees it, feels to-
> ward it, and is able to give it organized form and expression in
> words."

If we wish to omit words in the middle of a quote, we use ellipses like this, with spaces before and after the dots:

> According to Paul Engle, "there is no such thing as material by
> itself, apart from the way in which a person . . . is able to give
> it organized form and expression in words."

If we wish to omit words at the end of a quoted sentence, we use ellipses and include the period or other end punctuation:

According to Paul Engle, "there is no such thing as material by itself, apart from the way in which a person sees it, feels toward it, and is able to give it organized form and expression. . . ."

If we wish to omit one or more sentences from a quoted passage, we use the end punctuation plus the ellipses:

According to Paul Engle, "there is no such thing as material by itself, apart from the way in which a person sees it, feels toward it, and is able to give it organized form and expression in words. . . . A man may go through the most dramatic and horrible experiences in war, but actually draw out of them less 'material' for writing than shy Emily Dickinson in the second-floor room of an Amherst house. . . ."

If we wish to omit one or more paragraphs, we place three or four spaced periods centered on their own line.

We mossbacks are fed up with isms. (If you enjoy shouting, one of your most shoutable slogans is, "Down with ism!")

. . . .

It is ever so with isms. The suffix "ism" embodies everything that has made our century bleak: Communism, Marxism, Leninism, Stalinism, Nazism, Hitlerism, Fascism, elitism, populism, fundamentalism, creationism, symbolism, despotism, liberalism, sensationalism, exhibitionism, McCarthyism, nationalism, existentialism, abstract expressionism, sadism, masochism, feminism, modernism, post-modernism and schism, not to mention *machismo*, which is nothing more than another ism gussied up with a terminal "o."   —Russell Baker, "A Good Word for Moss"

If we wish to omit one or more lines of verse, we use an entire row of spaced dots:

I knew a woman, lovely in her bones,
When small birds sighed, she would sigh back at them;
. . . .
Of her choice virtues only gods should speak,
Or English poets who grew up on Greek
(I'd have them sing in chorus, cheek to cheek).
—Theodore Roethke, "I Knew a Woman"

Truth in Quoting   There is one major consideration that should guide our use of ellipses. Our unspoken agreement with our readers is that we will quote honestly and accurately, that we will cite material in a manner consistent with the spirit of the source. We omit words to avoid irrelevancies, not to misrepresent the sentiments of the writer. Ellipsis marks, after all, allow us to take something out of context. With selective quotations we can totally reverse a writer's opinions. Take Wendell Berry's praise of good farming:

> **Good farming is lumped in with bad farming as a low form of drudgery, not esteemed as the high accomplishment that it necessarily must be.**   —*The Gift of Good Land*

With some dishonest editing, we can make Berry say the following:

> **According to the agricultural writer Wendell Berry, even good farming is "a low form of drudgery, not . . . [a] high accomplishment . . ."**

Sometimes we suspect that something like this has happened in those minireviews we find in newspaper movie ads. "The best movie I've seen this year" may originally have been "Not exactly the best movie I've seen this year, or even this week. A turkey. Save your money."

Suggesting a Hesitation or Pause

Sometimes, as when quoting someone, we wish to indicate a hesitation or pause in the person's speech:

> **"It's just that . . . ," she said. The girl was mastering the art of the unfinished sentence.**   —Anne Bernays, *Professor Romeo*

> **Asked if she had any mementoes of the young genius [Robert Louis Stevenson], she would admit to possessing a single lock of hair she had cut from Louis's head some forty years earlier. She was naturally unwilling to part with it, but, well, perhaps . . .**   —Julian Barnes, "The Follies of Writer Worship"

> **A well-known writer got collared by a university student who asked, "Do you think I could be a writer?"**
> **"Well," the writer said, "I don't know. . . . Do you like sentences?"**   —Annie Dillard, *The Writing Life*

Quotation Marks

We use quotation marks for the following:

Enclosing Direct Quotations

Quotation marks identify certain material as an accurate word-for-word reproduction of someone else's speech or writing:

> Gordon Henderson, the hottest new designer on Fashion Avenue, bickers with his backer.
> "One hundred thousand dollars just isn't enough," pouts Mr. Henderson, who wants to hire yet another $2,000-an-hour model and thinks he needs a more lavish stage for his October showing.
> But he will have to settle for a modest auditorium stage at Parsons School of Design and 15 young women to parade his new creations.
> "Gordon, I'm not prepared to be flexible on this," says Ricky Sasaki, the money man. "We're not in show business. We're in the business of selling clothes."
> —Teri Agins, "In Fashion, the Talent and His Money Man Make Promising Team," *Wall Street Journal*, 18 Sept. 1990

> Christopher Finch, in his semiofficial pictorial history of Disney's work, comments: "The Mickey Mouse who hit the movie houses in the late twenties was not quite the well-behaved character most of us are familiar with today. He was mischievous, to say the least, and even displayed a streak of cruelty." But Mickey soon cleaned up his act, leaving to gossip and speculation only his unresolved relationship with Minnie and the status of Morty and Ferdie. Finch continues: "Mickey . . . had become virtually a national symbol, and as such he was expected to behave properly at all times. If he occasionally stepped out of line, any number of letters would arrive at the Studio from citizens and organizations who felt that the na-

tion's moral well-being was in their hands. . . . Eventually he would be pressured into the role of straight man."
—Stephen Jay Gould, "A Biological Homage to Mickey Mouse"

The direct quotation may also be of individual words and phrases. In the following passage the writer uses quotation marks to question the terminology of hunting advocates:

> Hunters like categories they can tailor to their needs. There are the "good" animals—deer, elk, bear, moose—which are allowed to exist for the hunter's pleasure. Then there are the "bad" animals, the vermin, varmints, and "nuisance" animals, the rabbits and raccoons and coyotes and beavers and badgers, who are discouraged to exist. The hunter can have fun killing them, but the pleasure is diminished because the animals aren't "magnificent." —Joy Williams, "The Killing Game"

Direct Quotations, Indirect Quotations, and Paraphrase

We have three ways to report someone else's words. Direct quotation, identified by quotation marks, is an exact transcription of what someone else has said or written. But when we are not exactly sure of the original wording, or when we need only to express the gist of what someone has said, we use indirect quotation (without any quotation marks): a reasonably close representation that is true to the spirit of the original but not to the precise wording. When we want something even shorter and simpler, perhaps because the original is too technical or wordy, we can use **paraphrase**, a summary in our own language.

Direct Quotation   In the opinion of Paul Engle, "Anything is suitable for fiction, which is not a record of incidents happening *to* men and women, but of the response they make within themselves to the incidents. This is because fiction deals with character, which determines action, and thus actions illustrate character. The conduct of a man in a ring fighting an enraged bull or the soft wave of a woman's hand are equally moving and suitable."
—"Salt Crystals, Spider Webs, and Words"

Indirect Quotation   According to Paul Engle, fiction can treat almost any subject because its real business is not incident but people's response to

incident. The fiction writer is concerned
with action only because it illustrates
character. Thus, the performance of a
matador is no better a subject than the way
someone might wave goodbye.

Paraphrase   In the opinion of Paul Engle, the best fiction
deals not with action but with character,
not with external incidents but with the
characters' internal response to such
incidents.

Plagiarism   If we use any of the preceding—the intentional direct or
indirect quotation or paraphrase of someone else's words or ideas—
without acknowledging the source, we are guilty of **plagiarism**. In an
academic or journalistic environment, plagiarism is a capital offense,
resulting in punishments like failure or dismissal. To avoid accidental
plagiarism, be careful about the notes you take when researching. Some
writers put brackets or boxes around any of their own ideas that they
insert in their reading notes.

Enclosing Some Titles

We use quotation marks around the titles of works that are not published
separately but that appear within larger works: articles, essays, short
stories, short poems, book chapters, and episodes of radio and television
programs. We also use quotation marks for songs, lectures, and
speeches. (See the section "Italics/Underlining" in this chapter.)

"Maya Art for the Record"   (article in *Scientific American*)

"In an Amazon Lake, Underwater Logging Blooms"
(article in *The New York Times*)

"A Writer's Credo"   (chapter in Edward Abbey's *One Life at a Time, Please*)

"Crazy, Crazy, Now Showing Everywhere"
(chapter in Ellen Gilchrist's *Victory over Japan*)

Identifying Words Used in a Special Sense

We use quotation marks to alert the reader to our use of words in a
"special" sense: those whose meaning is out of the ordinary, given unusual weight. Quotation marks ask the reader to pay particular attention
to the precise use of a word or phrase.

To begin with, we must keep in mind that things do not have "real" names, although many people believe that they do. A garbage man is not "really" a "garbage man" any more than he is a "sanitary engineer" —Neil Postman, *Crazy Talk, Stupid Talk*

A composition is a bundle of parts. When you compose, you "get it together," but the "it" is not a matter of things or "words": what you get together in composing is relationships, meanings. —Ann E. Berthoff, *Forming, Thinking, Writing*

In the Berthoff quote the quotation marks identify a familiar expression that deserves closer attention. Or consider:

Exhibits [of a gold mine and smelter] explain the industrial alchemy that pulled ore from the mountains, then turned it to pure gold with "grizzlies" (sorters), "jaw crushers" (ore grinders), feeders, and amalgam plates. —*Sunset*, Aug. 1988

The quotation marks here identify local slang, the nicknames miners had for some of their machinery. Note also the use of parentheses.

Setting Off Dialogue

In presenting dialogue, whether real or fictional, we begin a new paragraph for each new speaker, enclosing the quoted words in quotation marks and placing narrative or descriptive material in the same paragraph as the speaker's words:

"Hello," he said. "You are welcome."
"There are clouds in the east," I said. I could not look at him.
"I feel it, rain tonight maybe, tomorrow for sure, cats and dogs."
The breeze had picked up so that the willows on the irrigation ditch were gesturing in our direction.
"I see you wear shoes now. What's the meaning of this?" I pointed to a pair of rubber boots. His pants were tucked inside them.
"Rattlesnakes. For protection. This time of year they don't always warn you."
"They don't hear you," I said. "You're so quiet you take them by surprise." —James Welch, *Winter in the Blood*

Observe that with only two speakers, it is not always necessary to use dialogue guides (*I/he/she said*). Observe, too, that the writer does not rely on "telling" adverbs to describe the tone of the speakers' voices. Instead, he allows the words and the situation to indicate such things. (See Chapter 15, "The Rhetoric of Adverbs.")

Note: When a single speaker goes on for several paragraphs, place quotation marks at the beginning of each new paragraph but at the end of only the last one, the same practice we follow when quoting several paragraphs of written material.

> "Grown-ups tell us, 'Just say no'. That's easy for them to say.
> "Maybe they forgot what it's like.
> "At parties, at school, kids are saying to try this and do that, and they're my friends. I mean how many times can I hear I'm a loser.
> "Sure, I'm scared of drugs. It's just there's so much pressure. You want to say no. But you can take a lot of heat for it."
> —child in an antidrug ad

Quoting Thoughts   In fiction or other imaginative writing it is sometimes necessary to quote a character's thoughts. Practice varies, but usually writers present the thoughts either without quotation marks or with italics:

> I am a woman meeting her husband at a train, she thought, and it made her feel important, glamorous, like someone in a forties movie.   —Joan Wickersham, "Commuter Marriage"
> She allowed him to lead her inside, to close the door. *This is not important,* she thought clearly, *he doesn't mean it, he doesn't love me, nothing will come of it.*
> —Joyce Carol Oates, "The Lady with the Pet Dog"

Using Quotation Marks with Other Punctuation   Quotes inside of quotes use *single* quotation marks:

> As Ann E. Berthoff has observed, "When you compose, you 'get it together', but the 'it' is not a matter of things or 'words': what you get together in composing is relationships, meanings" (*Forming, Thinking, Writing* 47).
> "Grown-ups tell us, 'Just say no'. That's easy for them to say."
> —child in an antidrug ad

Notice that double quotation marks go outside of commas and periods, while single marks go inside.

Misusing Quotation Marks

Writers sometimes use quotation marks to indicate that a term is being used with irony or sarcasm:

> There was the senior who was "desperate" for a job in television and the senior who "had" to go to medical school, and the senior whose life depended on getting a job in publishing, or architecture, or government.
>
> —Ellen Goodman, "Anxiety Is the Class Uniform"

Since it is so easy to do, this practice can quickly get out of control. Because of the following she has developed and the license she enjoys as a syndicated columnist, a professional like Ellen Goodman can indulge in this usage occasionally. For the rest of us, it seems sarcastic and ill-willed and therefore should be used infrequently. Some writers also use quotation marks to emphasize specific attitudes or stereotypic beliefs, even though they are not quoting particular sources:

> The basic problem in the control and the elimination of war in our modern years is the fact that "old minds are predominant in our society," as well as in the policy making areas of society.
>
> —academic journal

This practice is not a conventionally acceptable use of quotation marks. It is an attempt to suggest authority where none exists.

Apostrophes

We use apostrophes for the following:

▶ to form contractions   402
▶ to form the possessive   403
▶ to form certain plurals   404

Related issue:

▶ forming possessives of personal pronouns   404

Forming Contractions

We use the apostrophe to indicate omitted letters or numbers. Apostrophes appear most often in these contractions:

▶ a verb plus *not*:

aren't (are not)	couldn't (could not)
haven't (have not)	shouldn't (should not)
isn't (is not)	wouldn't (would not)

Note: The apostrophe always goes where the letters are missing, not at the juncture between the words (*haven't*, not *have'nt*).

▶ a pronoun and a verb:

I'm (I am)	you're (you are)
I've (I have)	you've (you have)
I'd (I had)	you'd (you had)
I'll (I will)	you'll (you will)
I'd (I would)	you'd (you would)

▶ a subject and a verb:

Jack's here.   (Jack is here.)
You've a better idea?   (You have a better idea?)
Liz'd better leave early.   (Liz had better leave early.)
Someone'll do it.   (Someone will do it.)
I'd rather do it myself.   (I would rather do it myself).

▶ in place of the first two figures of a year (when the context makes clear the century:

'03   the class of '96   a '56 Ford

Note: Such contractions are usually not considered appropriate in formal writing.

Forming the Possessive

We use an apostrophe to form the possessive case (to show ownership, loosely defined) of nouns and indefinite pronouns, according to these rules:

▶ Singular nouns and indefinite pronouns form the possessive with *'s*:

Kari's new job	the car's generator
Chris's excuse	someone's excuse
The Handmaid's Tale	

The same rule applies to acronyms and some abbreviations:

OPEC's NATO's CBS's

Note: Official place names often omit the apostrophe, even when the idea of possession is clearly intended:

Scotts Valley Lakes Basin

▶ Plural nouns ending in *-s* or *-es* take only the apostrophe:

the three cars' insurance
the actresses' guild
the Williams' vacation

▶ Compound words and expressions take the *'s* only after the last word:

the sister-in-law's departure
someone else's departure
the man in the blue coat's departure

▶ To show individual ownership, add *'s* to each "owner":

Tom's and Jerry's careers
Rover's and Fido's papers

▶ To show joint ownership, add *'s* only to the last "owner":

Pam and Susan's office
Bill and Ted's Excellent Adventure

Possessives of Personal Pronouns Never use the *'s* to form the possessives of personal pronouns (*you, it, they,* and so on):

yours (not *your's*)
its (not *it's**)
theirs (not *their's*)

Forming Certain Plurals

We use an apostrophe and an *-s* to form the plurals of letters, figures, signs, and words as words:

Mind your p's and q's.

---

* *It's,* of course, means *it is.* Remember: *his, hers, its.*

A pair of 30.06's
I got three A's and two B's.

With dates, however, practice is divided. Either of the following is commonplace:

1800's/1800s   1950's/1950s

Italics/Underlining

We use italics/underlining for the following:

▶ to identify the titles of books, long poems, magazines, newspapers, plays and musicals, films, works of art, radio and television programs, and generally any works published separately   405
▶ to identify the names of ships, trains, planes, and spacecraft   406
▶ to identify foreign words and phrases not yet adopted into mainstream English usage   406
▶ to identify words used as words   407
▶ to identify certain directions to the reader   408
▶ to identify the scientific names of genera and species   408
▶ to call special attention to certain words and quotations   408

Related issue:

▶ using foreign expressions   407

In printed sources italic typeface slants upward and to the right (for example, *Right Words, Right Places*). In handwriting, typing, and with many word processing programs, we indicate italics with underlining (Right Words, Right Places).

Identifying Titles of Books, Long Poems, Magazines, Newspapers, Plays and Musicals, Films, Works of Art, Radio and Television Programs, and Any Works Published Separately

Books	*Charlotte's Web*, A Wizard of Earthsea
Long Poems	*Paradise Lost*, The Waste Land
Magazines	*Harper's*, Scientific American
Newspapers	*New York Times*, Wall Street Journal
Plays/Musicals	*A Man for All Seasons*, Evita

Films	High Noon, My Left Foot
Works of Art	Woman Brushing Her Hair, The Dying Gaul
Radio/TV Programs	The Jack Benny Show, Mister Rogers

Note: In underlining titles of more than one word, we have the choice of either underlining each word separately or underlining the entire title. (See the section "Quotation Marks: Enclosing Some Titles" in this chapter.)

Identifying the Names of Ships, Trains, Planes, and Spacecraft

We italicize the specific name, not the type (Boeing 747).

the *Rainbow Warrior*	*Voyager 2*
the *Wabash Cannonball*	the *Titanic*
the *Spruce Goose*	USS *Constitution*

Identifying Foreign Words and Phrases Not Yet Adopted into English

Some foreign expressions have been used so frequently that they have become part of the English language:

ad hoc	debris
ad infinitum	dilettante
a la carte	ex officio
a priori	habeas corpus
blasé	hors d'oeuvre
carte blanche	macho
cliche	per diem
coup d'état	tour de force

There are many other expressions, though, which retain their foreign identity and thus are italicized:

al fresco   (Italian: in the open air, outdoors)

bon vivant   (French: a person enjoying good food, drink, and other luxuries)

carpe diem   (Latin: "Seize the day"—to make the most of the present)

gemütlich   (German: agreeable, cheerful)

joie de vivre   (French: delight in being alive)

machismo   (Spanish: strong, aggressive masculinity)

de facto   (Latin: in actual fact, if not legally constituted; compare *de jure*—legally established)

Using Foreign Expressions   Each language has its own store of highly expressive idioms that do not translate exactly into other languages. Sometimes these expressions have such force and aptness that writers and speakers, in their search for the right words, prefer them to the equivalent in their own language. Some expressions are so well known that they are familiar even to those not otherwise acquainted with the language. Using such terms, however, presupposes an audience familiar with the meaning; otherwise, the user will seem snobbish. Once again, the writer must have some notion of what the readers know.

In the following Annie Dillard describes the skill of a stunt pilot by using a French expression that has become a part of the English language and a German expression that has not:

Every performance was a tour de force and a show of will, a **Machtspruch.*** —*The Writing Life*

Identifying Words Used as Words

We italicize to identify words or numbers used as words:

The term *yuppie* disappeared from the media almost as swiftly as it had appeared. In 1986 the editor of a major monthly magazine told me she found the term "tiresome" and never wanted to hear it again.   —Barbara Ehrenreich, *Fear of Falling*

Conversation, especially the speech of senior engineers, contained words and phrases such as these: a *canard* was anything false, usually a wrongheaded notion entertained by some other engineering group or other company; things could be done in ways that created *no muss, no fuss*, that were *quick and dirty*, that were *clean*. *Fundamentals* were the source of all right thinking, and weighty sentences often began with the adverb *fundamentally*, while *realistically* prefaced many flights of fancy. There was talk of *wars, shootouts, hired guns*, and people who *shot from the hip. The win* was the object of all this sport, and *the big win* was something that could be achieved by *maximizing* the lesser one.
—Tracy Kidder, *The Soul of a New Machine*

* an authoritative statement

Note: Outside of academic writing, writers often use quotation marks to indicate words used as words:

The word "relationship" appears for the first time in the 1743 edition of *The Dunciad.*
—Leonard Michaels, "I'm Having Trouble with My Relationship"

In contemporary culture, no idea is so appealing, no word is put to more frequent and more varied use than "creativity."
—Jacques Barzun, "The Paradoxes of Creativity"

On her back door, there was a warning sign forbidding entrance to anyone who used the word "hopefully" incorrectly.   —Howard Moss, "Jean: Some Fragments"

If we want to indicate the plural of words used as words, though, we can see the advantage of italics or underlining:

On the first page, the editor found five *hopefully*'s.
(not "hopefully" 's or "hopefully's")

Identifying Directions to the Reader

To distinguish certain directions from our text itself, we italicize words and phrases like *Continued, To be continued,* and *To be concluded.*

Identifying Scientific Names of Genera and Species

We use italics to identify the binomial or scientific names of plants and animals:

A hundred years ago the American chestnut (*Castanea dentata*) could have been called the all-American tree.
—"Chestnut Blight," *Scientific American,* July 1990

Calling Special Attention to Certain Words and Quotations

Sometimes we wish to emphasize one particular word in a statement:

Brian said (admiringly, I thought), "Did you *write* that story?" I started to answer, when he continued, "Or did you type it?"
—Annie Dillard, *The Writing Life*

America's blue-collar workers *were* in revolt in the late sixties, but not along the right-wing, traditionalist lines sketched by the media.   —Barbara Ehrenreich, *Fear of Falling*

One consequence of affluence was that children, and particularly teenagers, had money to spend. They were *consumers.*
—*Fear of Falling*

We usually represent quotations with quotation marks. Sometimes, however, we want to call even more attention to someone's wording or sentiments:

> Hunters like to call large animals cute names—such as "big guy." Hunters believe that wild animals exist only to satisfy their wish to kill them. And it's so easy to kill them! The weaponry available is staggering, and the equipment and gear limitless. *The demand for big boomers has never been greater than right now. Outdoor Life crows, and the makers of rifles and cartridges are responding to the craze with a variety of light artillery that is virtually unprecedented in the history of sporting arms. . . .* Hunters use grossly overpowered shotguns and rifles and compound bows. They rely on four-wheel-drive vehicles and three-wheel ATVs and airplanes. . . . *He was interesting, the only moving, living creature on that limitless white expanse. I slipped a cartridge into the barrel of my rifle and threw the safety off. . . .* —Joy Williams, "The Killing Game"

In this case notice that the writer does not always identify the source; sometimes it is only implied, as it is elsewhere in the article. The effect here is pronounced, ominous, emotional. The suggestion is that the speakers damn themselves with their own words ("They actually *said* this!"). Here is an example of another kind of use from a short story:

> She taught "The Revolution and Beyond" to freshmen and sophomores, and every third semester she had the senior seminar for majors, and although her student evaluations had been slipping in the last year and a half—*Professor Hendricks is often late for class and usually arrives with a cup of hot chocolate, which she offers the class sips of*—generally the department of nine men was pleased to have her.
> —Lorrie Moore, "You're Ugly, Too"

Slashes

The slash, or virgule, is a slanted line (/) we use for the following:

▶ to indicate alternative words 410
▶ to separate lines of poetry in a prose text 410

▶ to indicate a break between pages in quotes 410
▶ to type fractions and dates expressed in digits 411

Indicating Alternative Words

In some cases we wish to indicate that either of two different wordings may be applicable, as in *he/she* or *and/or*:

> They argued about everything, from what kind of paper towels to buy to what to do about [their child]. **Large/small, concrete/abstract, trivial/momentous**—the number and variety of the things about which they differed, sometimes with a shrug, often on the edge of violence, astonished him.
>
> —Anne Bernays, *Professor Romeo*

> Then, of course, there are growing numbers of so-called senior citizens who are living together with more Social Security and less legality. Two widowed **and/or** retired singles find the cost of marriage very dear in terms of lost pensions or reduced Social Security, and so many don't marry.
>
> —Ellen Goodman, "The Wrong Side of the Generation Gap"

> We have defied censorship **and/or** found ways around it.
>
> —Nadine Gordimer (interview)

In other cases the slash identifies symmetrical relationships or oppositions (*employer/employee* conflicts). Exploiting an intentional fragment, Stanley Elkin uses the slash to express one such contrast:

> The **upstairs/downstairs, city mouse/country mouse, cattleman/farmer** liaisons—all the **slicker/rube** relationships.
>
> —"At the Academy Awards"

Separating Lines of Poetry in a Prose Text

When we wish to quote several lines of poetry within our own text, we use the slash to indicate the line breaks, with a space before and after:

> Many quote but few probably understand Keats' famous statement: "Beauty is truth, truth beauty,—that is all / Ye know on earth and all ye need to know."

Indicating a Break Between Pages in Quotes

For the sake of accuracy, we use the slash to indicate the page breaks in quotations, with no space before and after the slash:

Richard Marius has a useful tip for apprentice writers: "You must find your own writing process. Mine is all wrapped up in notebooks and I urge it on you. A notebook is portable. It is durable and/efficient since you are unlikely to lose pages that are bound together" (*A Writer's Companion* 37–8).

Typing Fractions and Dates Expressed in Digits

To show fractions and dates expressed in digits, we use slashes:

2/3   9/10   7/4/76

Hyphens

We use hyphens for the following:

Hyphens are marks used between the parts of some compound words, some sequences of words used as a single idea or modifier, and the syllables of words divided at the end of a line.

Punctuating Some Compound Nouns

Many nouns in English are compounds, words made of several words. Some of these are written as one word (*statehouse*), some as two (*town house*), and some are hyphenated (*city-state*). Of the three, the first two are the most common. Unfortunately, there is no formula or "rule" to tell how any particular compound should be written. We can tell only by looking in a dictionary, preferably a recent one:

sister-in-law   walk-on
jack-of-all-trades walk-through
cross-reference   walk-up

Linking Two or More Words Serving as a Single Modifier

Sometimes we use hyphens to form compound adjectives of two or more words *before* a noun. In most cases the modifier consists of only a few words: *soft-spoken, well-known, first-class, hard-hitting, house-to-house, up-to-date, slash-and-burn, twelve-year-old.* (See the section "Hyphenated Adjectives" in Chapter 5, "Adjectives.")

> The inspiration for the demolition derby came to Lawrence Mendelsohn one night in 1950 when he was nothing but a **spare-ribbed, twenty-eight-year-old, stock-car** driver halfway through his 10th lap around the Islip, L.I., Speedway and taking a curve too wide. —Tom Wolfe, "Clean Fun at Riverhead"
>
> (But, "Mendelsohn, twenty-eight and spare ribbed, drove stock cars." *Twenty-eight* is hyphenated because it is a compound number.)

We do not hyphenate, however, when the first word of the compound modifier is an adverb ending in *-ly.*

> She has a **highly developed** sense of humor.
>
> We made **sorely needed** repairs.

Sometimes two or more compound modifiers share the same second element. In such cases we do the following:

> The **pine-** and **fir-clad** mountainscape was polished by ice-age glaciation.

In extreme cases we can use hyphens to turn an entire clause into a single modifier:

> She shot my father one of her **how-could-you-have-let-this-happen-to-me?** looks. —John Irving, *The World According to Garp*
>
> Lou Gossett [in *An Officer and a Gentleman*] is playing every **I'm-rough-on-you-for-your-own-good** sergeant you've ever seen. —Pauline Kael, *Taking It All In*

Spelling note: Every compound noun formed with *self-* is hyphenated. The *Webster's New World Dictionary* (Third College Edition, 1988) lists well over a hundred such words, from *self-abasement* and *self-absorption* to *self-winding* and *self-worth.*

Joining a Prefix to a Capitalized Word

We also use hyphens to attach prefixes to proper nouns (the kind we capitalize). In such cases the prefix is not capitalized:

anti-American	post-Civil War
neo-Impressionist	pre-Stalinist
non-European	pro-American

When such prefixes occur before common nouns, they generally do not require a hyphen: *antisocial, intercollegiate, nonessential, semiannual.*

Clarifying the Spelling of Some Words

There are a number of instances in which we use hyphens to avoid awkwardness or confusion. For example, except in the case of a few well-known words (*cooperation, reelection*), we use hyphens to avoid the confusion caused by double vowels or consonants:

anti-imperialist

co-op   (cooperative enterprise versus *coop*, a chicken's condo)

semi-independent

bell-like

We also use hyphens to avoid confusion between certain words that have the same spelling but quite different meanings:

re-form (form again)   reform (improve)

re-lease (rent again)   release (let go)

re-creation (create again)   recreation (relaxation)

Spelling Compound Numbers and Fractions

We use hyphens to spell out numbers from twenty-one through ninety-nine:

thirty-three	sixty-four
one hundred thirty-three	one hundred sixty-four thousand

We hyphenate fractions used as adjectives:

one-fifth   two-thirds   nine-tenths

He claims to be three-fourths vegetarian.

But   Three fourths of our dinner guests will be vegetarians.

Note: Usage suggests that there is disagreement on this practice, and many users hyphenate fractions whether they are nouns or adjectives.

We also use a hyphen to compound a number with another word:

fifteen-minute intermission/15-minute intermission
twelve-inch ruler/12-inch ruler
thirty-four-yard field goal/34-yard field goal
(Television broadcasts usually get this one wrong.)

Dividing Words at the End of a Line

We divide words at the end of lines so that our margins will be reasonably even. A few basic guidelines cover most of the cases, but when in doubt about where to break a word, consult a dictionary.

▶   Do not divide one-syllable words:

Not   ho-
        pe

But   hope

Not   rac-
        ed

But   raced

▶   Divide only between syllables:

syl-la-bles   ex-emp-tion   fla-grant-ly
dif-fer-en-ti-a-tion   in-hi-bi-tion   pro-fus-ion

▶   Divide between double consonants:

hal-lu-ci-nate   im-mor-tal   oc-ca-sion

▶   Do not divide a word that is already hyphenated:

Not   self-pro-   two-tim-
        tecting   ing

But   self-   two-
        protecting   timing

▶   Do not divide a word so that a single letter stands alone:

Not   o-
        pinion

But   opin-
        ion

Some dictionaries indicate this division with a slash: *o/pin-ion*

▶ Do not divide proper names. Even multisyllable names should remain undivided:

Not   Eliza-
       beth

But   Elizabeth

In Ages

We hyphenate ages when they form a compound name or modifier:

the twenty-eight-year-old   the ten-year-old
a twenty-eight-year-old driver   the ten-year-old truck

But:

The stock-car driver is twenty-eight years old.
The truck is ten years old.

Exercise

A The following are a pair of sentences, the first of 130 words, with the punctuation removed. Insert your own punctuation, then compare your decisions with those of the writer by checking the original version in the appendix. A clue: you will be able to use some dashes and parentheses. The goal is not to agree exactly with the writer; it is to punctuate the sentences so they are clear and emphatic.

The cycle of a vigorous city one that maintains its vitality generation after generation seems to run like this first comes a period in which it generates diverse exports in the process earning an increasing diversity and volume of imports second as export generating dies down a significant explosion of import replacing provided a critical mass of replaceable imports has piled up otherwise there is merely a decline third a period in which potential new exports often incorporating innovations are generated in the citys now greatly enlarged and diversified internal economy fourth a period of vigorous export generating and of earning wide ranges and great volumes of new replaceable imports in other words a return to the first phase of the cycle and a preparation for repeating the second phase.

In some cities at some times the phases follow each other very rapidly in others the changes occur slowly but rapid or slow this is the cycle that keeps their economies going.

B The following paragraphs appeared in the August 1988 issue of *Sunset* magazine, a West Coast publication devoted to travel, cooking, and home improvement. The internal punctuation has been removed, including apostrophes and hyphens that contract or combine words. Insert what you consider to be the necessary and clarifying punctuation, then check the appendix to see if you agree with the judgment of the *Sunset* editors. (At the end of each paragraph is the number of internal marks that have been removed—count each pair of marks as two.)

¹To the uninitiated its hard to pin down just where Lakes Basin* is. ²You attempt to triangulate its position using better known locales. ³It lies 2 hours northeast of Nevada City an hour northwest of Lake Tahoe and an hour south of the Feather River Gorge. ⁴Still even these calculations may leave the basins location hazy. (6)

⁵But thats the pleasure of this corner of California. ⁶Finding it is as happily surprising as finding a forgotten $20 bill in your back pocket. (1)

⁷Lakes Basin straddles the crest of the Sierra Nevada in Plumas and Sierra counties. ⁸The Middle Fork of the Feather River runs to the north the North Fork of the Yuba to the south. ⁹Elevations range from 4,000 to 8,000 feet. ¹⁰The pine and fir clad mountainscape was polished by ice age glaciation which is evident also in the chain of granite set lakes that give the region its name. (6)

¹¹Another geological phenomenon first lured settlers here gold. ¹²A couple of years after the strikes at Sutters Mill† argonauts began panning basin streams like Jamison Creek then turned their attentions to hard rock mining of nearby mountains like 7,447 foot Eureka Peak. (6)

¹³By the 1870s the Sierra Buttes Mining Company had dug some 65 miles of tunnels into the peak. ¹⁴Gravity powered trams hauled ore down to the Mohawk Mills 60 stamps each weighing 600 to 950 pounds. ¹⁵Some 400 miners lived down in the company town of Johnsville. (4)

¹⁶Today that hard won wealth is recalled at Plumas Eureka

* Lakes Basin is a place name spelled without an apostrophe.
† This place name is spelled with the usual possessive.

State Park.* [17]Exhibits explain the industrial alchemy that
pulled ore from the mountain then turned it to pure gold with
grizzlies sorters jaw crushers† ore grinders feeders and amalgam plates. [18]Theres a working model of a stamp mill a blacksmith shop a stable and dwarfing them all the Mohawk Mill a
150 foot tall behemoth of sugar pine that looms almost as
large and steeply sloped as the gold rich mountain behind it.
[19]Its being restored. (26)

■

For Openers

Quotation: Brief

"Colors," said Leigh Hunt, a 19th-century poet, "are the smiles
of Nature." Just how does an observer distinguish one smile from
another? To a great extent the answer lies in the three classes of
cone-shaped, color-sensing cells in the retina of the eye. Each class
responds differently to light reflected from a colored object, depending on whether the cells have within them red, green or blue pigments: light-absorbing proteins particularly sensitive to wave-
lengths in either the long-wave (red), intermediate-wave (green) or
short-wave (blue) region of the visible spectrum. The relative
amounts of light absorbed by each class of cones are translated into
electrical signals by retinal nerves and then transmitted to the brain,
where the overall pattern evokes the sensation of a specific hue.

The role of the pigments in color discrimination has been known
for decades, and yet their structures were not elucidated until recently. . . .   —"The Genes for Color Vision," *Scientific American*, Feb. 1989

Hunt's metaphor of rainbow as nature's smile lends itself to an easy
transition. The writer (a molecular biologist) asks a simple question
that even a nonspecialist might raise—how do we distinguish these
"smiles"?—then launches into an explanation of how the eye perceives
color. This account, to remind specialists and inform the rest of us,
prefaces a discussion of the most recent genetic discoveries concerning
the evolution of color vision, the purpose of the article. Using the quote

* "Plumas and Eureka" is a compound indicating a joint identity.
† "Grizzly" was a nickname for a sorter and "jaw crusher" a nickname for ore grinders.

418 Part 3 Punctuation
418 *Part 3 Punctuation*

from poetry is not only a thematic boost; it is a friendlier way to open, a suggestion that the subject may be of interest to a broader audience than that of molecular biologists and geneticists.

Quotation: Extended

On May 15, 1898, the intrepid Arctic explorer Frederick A. Cook made the following notation in his journal: "The winter and the darkness have slowly but steadily settled over us. . . . It is not difficult to read on the faces of my companions their thoughts and their moody dispositions. . . . The curtain of blackness which has fallen over the outer world of icy desolation has also descended on the inner world of our souls. Around the tables . . . men are sitting about sad and dejected, lost in dreams of melancholy from which, now and then, one arouses with an empty attempt at enthusiasm. For brief moments some try to break the spell by jokes, told perhaps for the fiftieth time. Others grind out a cheerful philosophy; but all efforts to infuse bright hopes fail."

We now know that the members of the Cook expedition were suffering from classic symptoms of winter depression, a condition related to a recently described psychiatric disease known as seasonal affective disorder, or SAD. As the journal entry makes clear, recognition of the association between depression and the onset of winter is not new. But in recent years there has been growing interest in SAD and in two behavior disorders, carbohydrate-craving obesity (CCO) and premenstrual syndrome (PMS), that share some of the symptoms. . . .

—"Carbohydrates and Depression," *Scientific American*, Jan. 1989

The extended quotation serves at least two purposes: it presents "the classic symptoms" of winter depression, and it helps establish the scope of the problem, its historical and geographical distribution. In other words, the quote establishes the magnitude and importance of the subject—not a bad way to get the interest of the audience (many of whom will have experienced at least a few of the same symptoms). Lengthy quotes are risky even in midtext, and so the users often excuse them (*It is worth reprinting at length* . . .). In an opener, long quotes may also postpone identification of the subject, a tactic that can stimulate either the reader's curiosity or impatience, depending (of course) on the quote. In any event, such a lengthy opening quote would be suitable only in a longer paper.

Quotation: Paraphrase

Thomas Jefferson described revolution as the extraordinary event necessary to enable all the ordinary events to continue. The extraordinary events of 1989 in Eastern Europe, like Chinese economic reforms a decade ago and Soviet *perestroika*, were born of necessity to improve material well-being in the socialist countries. Yet the stark images of energy-related smog and soot that have emerged with the new openness warn that these economies cannot improve themselves at the expense of the environment. As in the market economies, an energy revolution is needed.

A revealing statistic points toward a solution. . . .

—"Energy for the Soviet Union, Eastern Europe and China," *Scientific American*, Sept. 1990

In this case, the pertinent quote need not be reproduced word-for-word. For their purposes the authors needed only the sentiment, the contrast between extraordinary and ordinary events. But they do more than simply paraphrase a catchy quote. The quote states the theme of the article, the idea that an energy revolution is needed "to enable all the ordinary events to continue" (and, of course, the image is appropriate because of Russia's image of itself as a revolutionary society). Some quotes address our immediate subject, helping to establish its urgency and importance. Other quotes, like this one, state a more general idea that we can adapt for our own purposes. Paraphrase makes a quote more flexible.

Note: In formal academic writing it is necessary to cite the precise origin of every quotation, even those that are paraphrased.

MLA Documentation

Both honesty and credibility require us to acknowledge ideas and information borrowed from others. On the one hand, it is only fair that we admit our indebtedness; on the other, the identification of sources both increases our authority and announces our accountability. By using sources, we establish that we have done our homework, that we are informed on the subject and entitled to an audience. At the same time, by identifying these sources, we also invite readers to verify our credentials. Anyone is free to check our citations and see if we have been accurate and honest in using borrowed material.

> **Documentation—1.a.** The act or an instance of the supplying of documents or supporting references or records. **b.** The documents or references so supplied. [from Latin *documentum*, example, proof, from *docere*, to teach.]
> —*The American Heritage Dictionary of the English Language*, 3rd ed., 1992.

Papers written in the humanities use the documentation format of the Modern Language Association. This system has abandoned the traditional numbered foot- or endnotes for a simpler two-step method:

▶ abbreviated parenthetical references within the text itself

▶ a list of "Works Cited" at the end of the text

Parenthetical References Within the Text

Parenthetical documentation uses abbreviated in-text allusions to material identified more fully in the list of Works Cited. Typically, when we have not identified an author in our text, the parenthetical citation includes the last name of the author and a page number:

According to one critic, much writing instruction

suffers from a joyless concern with mere

practicality. The remedy lies in a rediscovery of

wordplay, of "a self-conscious pleasure in words"

(Lanham 18).

In typing parenthetical references according to MLA style, the following rules are observed:

- no comma or period at the end of the quotation itself
- one space between quotation marks and the beginning parenthesis
  mark
- the author's last name
- title or shortened title *only* when citing one of two or more works
  by the same author, otherwise the title is omitted (use a comma
  between author and title)*
- the page number from the text (one space but *no punctuation* between
  name and page number or between title and page number)
- a period at the end of the sentence after the closing parenthesis

Entry in Works Cited

Lanham, Richard. Style: An Anti-Textbook. New

Haven: Yale UP, 1974.

Note: The title page lists New Haven and London as the places of
publication. When there is more than one location listed, give the first.

If we mention the author's name in the text in a **signal phrase**
("According to Richard Lanham . . ."), then the parenthetical citation
includes the page number only (18). If we use more than one work by
an author, and we have identified his or her name in the text, our
parenthetical citation must include a short title of the work cited and
a page number (*Style* 18). If we do not require a direct quotation, but
wish to use only a paraphrase or summary, we use the same format:

According to one critic, American colleges should

abandon their cold-blooded preoccupation with

practical writing and encourage students to develop

a sense of wordplay (Lanham 18).

* Lanham, *Style* 18

Finally, if we need to use a longer quotation of more than four typed lines, or even give special emphasis to a shorter quotation, we set it off ten spaces from the left margin, double-spacing it without quotation marks. Then the parenthetical citation appears *outside* the final punctuation:

> Not clarity but attention must come
>
> first. Only such a therapy will
>
> compensate for the literary tradition
>
> that even literate Americans do not
>
> possess. Only such an emphasis will
>
> aerate the vacuum of stylelessness into
>
> which prose-style teaching evaporates,
>
> will provide the reinforcement that
>
> society fails to offer. (Lanham 19)

Works by More Than One Author

If we wish to cite works with two authors, we must give their names in the order in which they appear on the title page, linking them with an *and*:

Experienced writers have expanded their repertoires
to include topic-sentence-last paragraphs: "The
inductive, details-followed-by-generalization
approach is useful in persuasive writing, where
it's sometimes wise to support an opinion before
expressing it, and in narration and description,
where suspense is always a good thing" (Weathers and
Winchester 158).

Entry in Works Cited

Weathers, Winston, and Otis Winchester. The New
    Strategy of Style. 2nd ed. New York: McGraw,
    1978.

If a work has three authors, we list them in the order given, not in alphabetical order, and set off the last with a comma and an *and*.

(Jewell, Harbison, and Scherer 86-88)

Entry in Works Cited

Jewell, Jack L., James P. Harbison, and Axel

    Scherer. "Microlasers." Scientific American

    Nov. 1991: 86-95.

If a work has more than three authors, we list the first author followed by *et al.* (Latin for "and others"), but not underlined or in italics:

(Lienhard et al. 87)

Entry in Works Cited

Lienhard, Gustav E., et al. "How Cells Absorb

    Glucose." Scientific American Jan. 1992:

    86-91.

Note: MLA documentation requires *one space* after every colon.

Multivolume Works

When citing from a work of more than one volume, we give the volume (in arabic numerals), colon, space, and page number:

"Honor often seems a highly artificial convention,"
Rebecca West once observed, "but life in any level
of society where it has been abandoned astonishes
by its tortuousness" (1: 18).

Entry in Works Cited

West, Rebecca. Black Lamb and Grey Falcon: A

    Journey Through Yugoslavia. 2 vols. New York:

    Viking, 1941.

(For citations from only one volume of multivolume works, see item 10 in the section "List of Works Cited" later in Part 4.)

Anonymous Author

For works that appear without the author's name, give the title—either complete or in shortened form, depending on length—putting quotation marks around titles of articles and underlining those of books:

Unfortunately, the American public has become

hardened to stories of ecological disaster, like

that of San Diego's recent sewage spill. The

catastrophe left some 180 million gallons a day of

partially treated effluent spewing into the shallow

ocean waters just off the beaches of California's

second largest city ("Sewage" 1A).

Entry in Works Cited

"Sewage Spill Closes San Diego Coastline." San

Jose Mercury News 6 Feb. 1992: 1A+.

Note: The "1A+" means that the story begins on the first page of section A and then continues on later pages.

Indirect Source

Ideally, we want to take our material directly from an original source. Sometimes, though, we cannot find a source but do encounter material from it cited somewhere else. In other words, we sometimes need to use one source's citation from another source. If we quote or paraphrase the borrowing, we introduce it with *qtd. in* ("quoted in"). For example, suppose we cannot find a copy of Herbert Read's *English Prose Style* but want to use a quote appearing in Richard Lanham's *Style: An Anti-Textbook*:

If poetry exists for its own sake, prose does not—

at least according to some influential voices. As

affirmed by Herbert Read, "Poetry is creative

expression: prose is constructive expression" (qtd. in Lanham 94).

Entry in Works Cited

Lanham, Richard. Style: An Anti-Textbook. New

    Haven: Yale UP, 1974.

Note: In drawing from borrowed material, we risk a number of complications. For one, we are taking a statement out of its original context and may be misrepresenting its spirit. To make sure that a quote does, in fact, say what it seems to be saying, we should look to the original. Besides, we don't want to seem lazy.

More Than One Work in a Parenthetical Reference

On some occasions it may be necessary to cite several authorities on the same subject. In such cases use the standard form but separate the entries with semicolons. Suppose, for example, we want to cite Herbert Read's *English Prose Style* and J. Middleton Murray's *The Problem of Style.* Depending on the amount of information given in introducing the citations, the entries could look like this:

▶ if there is only one listing each for Read and Murray in the list of Works Cited:

(Read ix; Murray 60)

▶ if more than one work is listed for both Read and Murray:

(Read, Prose Style ix; Murray, Problem 60)

▶ if more than one work is listed for Read but only one for Murray:

(Read, Prose Style ix; Murray 60)

Entry in Works Cited

Murray, J. Middleton. The Problem of Style.

    1922. London: Oxford UP, 1960.

Read, Herbert. English Prose Style. 1952.

    Boston: Beacon, 1955.

Citing Literary Works

Classic works of prose frequently exist in more than one edition. Thus, to help someone find a passage in an edition other than the one we are using, our citation should include not just the page number but a chapter and a book number (if there is one), in *arabic* numerals. The page number comes first, then a semicolon, then the other information. Suppose we are using the Norton Critical Edition of Nathaniel Hawthorne's *The House of the Seven Gables*:

(71; ch. 5)

Entry in Works Cited

Hawthorne, Nathaniel. The House of the Seven

    Gables. Ed. Seymour L. Gross. New York:

    Norton, 1967.

If a work is divided into books as well as chapters, we cite page, book, and chapter. Thus, a quotation from page 287 in the Modern Library Edition of Dostoyevsky's *The Brothers Karamazov* would be cited like this:

(287; bk. 5, ch. 4)

Entry in Works Cited

Dostoyevsky, Fyodor. The Brothers Karamazov.

    Trans. Constance Garnett. New York:

    Modern Library, 1950.

When citing from classic poetry or plays, we omit page numbers and give the division (canto, book, part, act, scene) and line, with periods but *no spaces* separating the various numbers. Thus, if we want to quote Lady Macbeth—"That which hath made them drunk / Hath made me bold" from act two, scene two:

(2.2.65–66)

If we use the quotation without identifying the source in our text:

(Macbeth 2.2.65–66)

List of Works Cited

At the end of the paper appears the list of Works Cited. This listing should include all the material directly consulted in the writing of the text. Practice varies on whether to include everything that we have read or only those works which we have actually cited. As the title suggests, however, it is usually the latter. In any event, when additional works are included, they should have a close relationship to the topic of the paper. When writing a formal term paper in a course, ask the instructor whether additional works should be included.

■ *Table of Types of Works to Be Included in Works Cited*

Books

1 book by one author
2 two or more works by the same author
3 book by two or three authors
4 book by more than three authors
5 book with corporate author
6 anonymous author
7 edited book (citing author; citing editor)
8 book with editor and author
9 translated book (citing author; citing translator)
10 book in more than one volume
11 republished book
12 book in a series
13 book with a publisher's imprint (division of a press)
14 book with multiple publishers
15 book published before 1900
16 book with incomplete publication information
17 book with a title in its title

18 book in a language other than English

Parts of Books

19 introduction, preface, foreword, or afterword
20 essay, short story, poem, or other work in an anthology

Periodicals

21 article in a journal paginated by volume
22 article in a journal paginated by issue
23 article in a monthly or bimonthly publication
24 article in a weekly or biweekly magazine
25 article in a newspaper
26 editorial in a newspaper
27 unsigned article
28 letter to the editor
29 book review
30 special issue of a journal

Other Sources

31 dissertations: published/unpublished

32 encyclopedia articles: signed/unsigned

33 government publication

34 pamphlet

35 information service

36 published proceedings of conference

37 letters: published/unpublished

38 interviews: published/unpublished

39 lecture

40 work of art

41 recording

42 film or videotape

43 live performance

44 radio or television program

45 computer software

46 map or chart

47 cartoon

■ Books

The entry includes three major units separated by a period and two spaces:

❱ author, with last name first (as given on title page)

❱ title (including any subtitle) underlined, with the first word of the title, any subtitle, and all major words capitalized (regardless of their form in the original)

❱ publication information—place, followed by a colon, publisher (use shortened name), followed by a comma and date of publication

Entries are double spaced, and any lines after the first are indented five spaces.

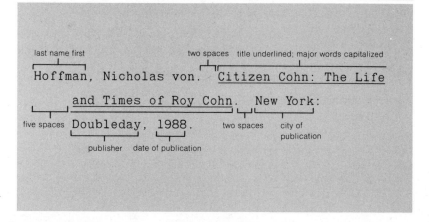

■   *Model Book Entry for Works Cited List*   ■

last name first   two spaces   title underlined; major words capitalized

Hoffman, Nicholas von. Citizen Cohn: The Life

   and Times of Roy Cohn. New York:

five spaces Doubleday, 1988.   two spaces   city of publication

   publisher   date of publication

1 *Book by One Author*

Allen, Paula Gunn. The Sacred Hoop: Recovering the
  Feminine in American Indian Traditions.
  Boston: Beacon, 1986.

Barth, John. The Last Voyage of Somebody the
  Sailor. Boston: Little, 1991.

2 *Two or More Works by the Same Author*

List alphabetically by title. Give the name(s) only for the first entry,
then use *three hyphens and a period*. Where the writer is serving as editor,
use three hyphens and a comma.

Edel, Leon. "The Architecture of James's 'New York
  Edition.' " New England Quarterly 24 (1951):
  169–78.

———. Henry James: A Life. New York: Harper, 1985.

———, ed. Literary Criticism: French Writers, Other
  European Writers, the Prefaces to the New York
  Edition. New York: Library of America, 1984.

———. The Master: 1901–1916. New York: Lippincott,
  1972. Vol. 5 of The Life of Henry James. 5
  vols.

If the author had also appeared as a co-author of another text, however,
do not use hyphens but list the author's full name and the text title,
after the single-author works.

3 *Book by Two or Three Authors*

List by giving the last name of the first author, then list the other
name(s) in regular order, separated with commas and an *and* before the
last name:

Forsyth, Adrian, and Kenneth Miyata. Tropical
  Nature: Life and Death in the Rain Forests of

Central and South America. New York:

Scribner's, 1984.

Merton, Robert K., Marjorie Fiske, and Patricia

Kendall. The Focused Interview: A Manual of

Problems and Procedures. 2nd ed. New York:

Free, 1990.

4   *Book by More Than Three Authors*

When there are more than three authors, we list only the first and add *et al.* ("and others"). When there are multiple editors or translators instead of authors, we place a comma after the last name and add the appropriate abbreviation (*eds.*, *trans.*, or *comps.*—compilers):

Abercrombie, M., et al. The New Penguin Dictionary

of Biology. 8th ed. New York: Penguin, 1990.

Winkler, A. J., et al. General Viticulture.

Berkeley: U of California P, 1974.

5   *Book with Corporate Author*

List the book by the corporate author, then title and publication information:

Poynter Institute for Media Studies. Best

Newspaper Writing 1988. St. Petersburg:

Poynter Inst. for Media Studies, 1988.

World Resources Institute. The 1992 Information

Please Almanac. Boston: Houghton, 1992.

6   *Anonymous Author*

If there is no author's name on the title page, list the work alphabetically by title, beginning with the first major word after any article (*a, an, the*):

Gould's Penal Code Handbook of California. 1990

ed. Altamonte Springs, FL: Gould, 1990.

7 *Edited Book (Citing Author; Citing Editor)*

List an editor as you would an author, but follow the name with a comma and *ed.* (or *eds.* with multiple editors):

```
Chaucer, Geoffrey. The Riverside Chaucer. Ed.

    Larry D. Benson et al. 3rd ed. Boston:

    Houghton, 1987.

Love, Glen A., and Michael Payne, eds.

    Contemporary Essays on Style: Rhetoric,

    Linguistics, and Criticism. Glenview, IL:

    Scott, 1969.

Sims, Norman, ed. The Literary Journalists. New

    York: Ballantine, 1984.
```

8 *Book with Editor and Author*

When a work has both an author and an editor, we list by author if we have cited from the text. For example, if we have quoted from the Penguin edition of *The Taming of the Shrew*, our citation would be as follows. Note that in this case *Ed.* stands for "edited by." Use *Ed.* not *Eds.* for more than one editor.

```
Shakespeare, William. The Taming of the

    Shrew. Ed. Richard Hosley. Baltimore:

    Penguin, 1964.
```

However, if we cite the work of the editor, the order is the following: name of editor(s), comma, *ed.* (or *eds.*), the title, the author introduced with the word *By*, and publishing information:

```
Hosley, Richard, ed. The Taming of the Shrew. By

    William Shakespeare. Baltimore: Penguin,

    1964.
```

When the editor's work is in a preface, introduction, or afterword, we list the editor, the capitalized title of the item (but with no underlines or quotation marks), and the rest of the information about work and author, and then conclude with the page numbers of the item (set off by two spaces):

```
Hosley, Richard.  Introduction.  The Taming of the
     Shrew.  By William Shakespeare.  Baltimore:
     Penguin, 1964.  15-27.
```

And if we cite both the text and the work of the editor, we list the work twice, by author and by editor.

9   *Translated Book (Citing Author; Citing Translator)*

We begin with the author's name and the title, then introduce the translator with *Trans.*:

```
Bourdieu, Pierre.  Outline of a Theory of
     Practice.  Trans. Richard Nice.  Cambridge:
     Cambridge UP, 1977.
Eco, Umberto.  The Name of the Rose.  Trans.
     William Weaver.  New York: Warner, 1984.
Marquez, Gabriel Garcia.  One Hundred Years of
     Solitude.  Trans. Gregory Rabassa.  New York:
     Avon, 1971.
```

When we wish to cite the translator's comments, we begin with the translator's name, followed by a comma and *trans.*, then *By* after the title, and the author's name in normal order:

```
Arrowsmith, William, trans.  The Satyricon.  By
     Petronius.  New York: Mentor-NAL, 1960.
```

Some texts have both translators and editors:

```
Proust, Marcel.  Pleasures and Days and Other
     Writings.  Trans. Loise Varese, Gerard
```

Hopkins, and Barbara Dupee. Ed. F. W.

Dupee. Garden City: Doubleday, 1957.

10 *Book in More Than One Volume*

If you have used all the volumes, cite the total number in arabic numerals after the title:

West, Rebecca. Black Lamb and Grey Falcon: A

Journey Through Yugoslavia. 2 vols. New York:

Viking, 1941.

If you have used only one of the volumes, cite it after the title and then give the total number after the date:

Johnson, Edgar. Charles Dickens: His Tragedy and

Triumph. Vol. 2. New York: Simon, 1952.

2 vols.

When the volumes have been published over a number of years, give the inclusive dates:

Conrad, Joseph. The Collected Letters of Joseph

Conrad. Ed. Frederick R. Karl and Laurence

Davies. 4 vols. Cambridge: Cambridge UP,

1983–90.

11 *Republished Book*

When citing from a later edition of a work, we give the original publication date, with a period, after the title and before the current publication information:

Van Ghent, Dorothy. The English Novel: Form and

Function. 1953. New York: Harper, 1967.

Wallace, Alfred Russel. The Malay Archipelago.

1869. New York: Dover, 1962.

12 *Book in a Series*

When a series name appears on the title page or the preceding page, we include the series name, without underlining or quotation marks, and any series number, followed by a period, before the publication information:

Traversi, Derek. Shakespeare: The Early Comedies.

Writers and Their Work 129. London: Longmans,

1964.

Van Ghent, Dorothy. Willa Cather. U of Minnesota

Pamphlets on American Writers 36.

Minneapolis: U of Minnesota P, 1964.

13 *Book with Publisher's Imprint (Division of a Press)*

When a book is published under an imprint or by a division of a publisher, we include both names, joined with a hyphen and in the order given on the title page. For example, take Peter Matthiessen's *At Play in the Fields of the Lord*, first published in 1965, then republished in paperback by the New American Library in 1967:

Matthiessen, Peter. At Play in the Fields of the

Lord. 1965. New York: Signet-NAL, 1967.

14 *Book with Multiple Publishers*

When the title page lists two publishers, give both in the order of appearance, separated by a semicolon:

Lodge, David. The Language of Fiction. New York:

Columbia UP; London: Routledge, 1966.

15 *Book Published Before 1900*

It is not necessary to cite the name of the publisher for books printed before 1900 (presumably because they are probably no longer available from the original source). For example, take the second edition of Walter Scott's *Rob Roy*, which was published in three volumes in 1818:

Scott, Walter. Rob Roy. 2nd ed. 3 vols.

Edinburgh, 1818.

16 *Book with Incomplete Publication Information*

Some books, especially those published before 1900, appear without the place or date of publication. If we can acquire such information from another source, we include it *in brackets* to indicate that it did not come from the original work. In cases where we can take an educated guess at a date, we can include it in brackets with a *c.* for "circa" (Latin for "around"). We use the following abbreviations to identify missing data:

n.p.   no place of publication (before colon)

n.p.   no publisher (after colon)

n.d.   no date

n. pag. no pagination (after publication information)

Huizinga, Johan. The Waning of the Middle Ages.

    1919. New York: Anchor–Doubleday, n.d.

Consider an undated edition of Tobias Smollett's eighteenth-century novel, *Roderick Random*:

Smollett, Tobias. The Adventures of Roderick

    Random. 1748. London: Hutchinson, n.d.

However, bibliographers have identified the publication date as 1904:

Smollett, Tobias. The Adventures of Roderick

    Random. 1748. London: Hutchinson, [1904].

Had there been no place of publication listed:

Smollett, Tobias. The Adventures of Roderick

    Random. 1748. N.p.: Hutchinson, [1904].

(*n.p.* capitalized because it begins a section)

Had there been no publisher listed:

Smollett, Tobias. The Adventures of Roderick

    Random. 1748. London: n.p., [1904].

Had there also been no pagination, we would need to do the following to explain why we could give no page numbers in our citation:

Smollett, Tobias. The Adventures of Roderick

    Random. 1748. London: Hutchinson, [1904].

    N. pag.

17 *Book with a Title in Its Title*

When the included title is a work published independently and thus usually underlined (like a novel or play), we do not underline it:

Clein, Wendy. Concepts of Chivalry in Sir Gawain

    and the Green Knight. Norman: Pilgrim, 1987.

Gellens, Jay, ed. Twentieth Century

    Interpretations of A Farewell to

    Arms. Englewood Cliffs: Prentice, 1970.

Kittredge, G[eorge] L[yman]. A Study of Sir Gawain

    and the Green Knight. Cambridge: Harvard UP,

    1916.

    (The brackets indicate that Kittredge sometimes published as G. L. and sometimes as George Lyman.)

When the included title is a work usually not published separately and thus enclosed by quotation marks (like a short story or poem), we keep the quotation marks and underline the entire title:

Martin, Jay, ed. Twentieth Century

    Interpretations: A Collection of Critical

    Essays on "The Waste Land." Englewood:

    Prentice, 1968.

18 *Book in a Language Other Than English*

Give all the information as it appears on the title or copyright page. If the title or city of publication seem to need clarification, then provide translations in brackets:

Boll, Heinrich. Das Brot der frühen Jahre

Erzählung. München [Munich]: Deutscher

Taschenbuch, 1978.

Flori, Jean. L'essor de la chevalerie, XI–XII

siècles. Geneva: Droz, 1986.

Froissart, Jean. Les chroniques. Ed. J. A. C.

Buchon. 3 vols. Paris, 1838–40.

(no publisher because published before 1900)

Nardi, Bruno. Il Canto XV del Purgatorio. Roma:

Dante, 1953.

Roy, Jules. La bataille de Dien Bien Phu. Paris:

Julliard, 1963.

Sand, George. Mauprat. 1837. Paris: Garnier,

1969.

Note: The rules of capitalization vary from one language to another. In French capitalize the first word of titles and subtitles and all proper nouns. In German capitalize the first words of titles and subtitles and all others words that would normally be capitalized (such as nouns). In Italian and Spanish also capitalize the first names of titles and subtitles as well as all other words that would normally be capitalized.

■ *Parts of Books*

19 *Introduction, Preface, Foreword, or Afterword*

Begin with the author, then the capitalized name of the part being cited, then the title of the work. If the author of the part is the same as that of the entire work, introduce only his or her last name with a *By*. If the author of the work is different, cite the entire name in normal order. Then conclude with the publication information and the pagination of the part (set off by two spaces):

French, Marilyn. Introduction. The House of

Mirth. By Edith Wharton. New York: Berkley,

1981. v–xxxv.

Larson, Charles R.   Introduction.   <u>Mister</u>

   <u>Johnson</u>.   By Joyce Cary.   New York: Harper,

   1969.   v–xi.

Tolkien, J. R. R.   Foreword.   <u>The Fellowship of the</u>

   <u>Ring</u>.   By Tolkien.   New York: Ballantine,

   1965.   viii–xiii.

20   *Essay, Short Story, Poem, or Other Work in an Anthology*

An anthology is a collection or compilation of works by different authors. Give the author, the title of the work, the title of the collection in which it appears, the editor(s), the publication information, and the pagination (set off by two spaces):

Brewer, D. S.   "Courtesy and the <u>Gawain</u>–Poet."

   <u>Patterns of Love and Courtesy: Essays in</u>

   <u>Memory of C. S. Lewis</u>.   Ed. John Lawlor.

   London: Arnold, 1966.   54–85.

Hornbeak, Katherine G.   "New Light on Mrs.

   Montagu."   <u>The Age of Johnson: Essays</u>

   <u>Presented to Chauncey Brewster Tinker</u>.   Ed.

   Frederick W. Hilles.   New Haven: Yale UP,

   1949.   349–61.

If you find it necessary to use several articles from the same collection, list the collection separately, then use individual entries by citing cross references to the main entry:

Balderston, Katherine C.   "Johnson's Vile

   Melancholy."   Hilles 3–14.

Hilles, Frederick W., ed.   <u>The Age of Johnson:</u>

   <u>Essays Presented to Chauncey Brewster</u>

   <u>Tinker</u>.   New Haven: Yale UP, 1949.

Hornbeak, Katherine G. "New Light on Mrs.

Montagu." Hilles 349–61.

When a collection reprints previously published works, give the data for the original publication and then add *Rpt. in* ("Reprinted in"), the title of the collection, and its publication information:

Lopez, Barry. "The Stone Horse." Antaeus 57

(1986): 220–29. Rpt. in The Best American

Essays 1987. Ed. Gay Talese. New York:

Ticknor, 1987. 151–61.

Walker, Alice. "Her Sweet Jerome." In Love and

Trouble. New York: Harcourt, 1970. Rpt. in

The Signet Classic Book of Contemporary

American Short Stories. Ed. Burton

Raffel. New York: Signet–NAL, 1986.

Walker, I. M. "The 'Legitimate' Sources of Terror

in 'The Fall of the House of Usher.' " Modern

Language Review 61 (1966): 585–92. Rpt. in

Twentieth Century Interpretations of Poe's

Tales. Ed. William L. Howarth. Englewood

Cliffs: Prentice, 1971. 47–54.

In some cases we may be using the original but want to call the reader's attention to its accessibility in a collection. Then we enclose the reprint information in parentheses:

Ribner, Irving. "The Political Problem in

Shakespeare's Lancastrian Trilogy." Studies

in Philology 49 (1952): 171–84. (Rpt. in

Twentieth Century Interpretations of Richard

II. Ed. Paul M. Cubeta. Englewood Cliffs:

Prentice, 1971. 29–40.)

Model Entry for Journal with
Continuous Pagination

last name first   two spaces   title in quotation marks

Davidson, Donald.   "Grammar and Rhetoric: The

— two spaces

Teacher's Problem."   Quarterly Journal of

five spaces   Speech 39 (1953): 425–36.   name of journal underlined

volume   year colon pages

■ *Periodicals*

Entries for journal articles, like those of books, are divided into three main parts separated by two spaces: author's name, title, and publication information.

21   *Article in a Journal Paginated by Volume*

Some publications number their pages continuously throughout an entire volume, as *National Geographic* did until recently. Thus, the May 1988 issue (Volume 173, No. 5) ended on page 694, and the June issue (Volume 173, No. 6) picked up on page 695. In such cases an entry should begin with the author's name, then the title of the article, the name of the journal, the volume number, the year of publication (in parentheses), a colon, and the page numbers (set off by one space):

Friedman, Albert B.   "Morgan le Fay in Sir Gawain

and the Green Knight."   Speculum 35 (1960):

260–74.

Gore, Rick.   "The Eternal Etruscans."   National

Geographic 173 (1988): 696–743.

Noting Inclusive Pagination

When citing the pages of an article, give the second number in full for numbers through 99. For numbers above 99, give the last two digits, unless more are required. Use lowercase roman numerals only when the pages of a book (like a preface or introduction) are so numbered.

2–7	8–19	73–92	98–115
101–07	534–41	946–1012	x–xv

Harris, R. Allen. "Rhetoric of Science." College
   English 53 (1991): 282–307.

Laib, Nevin. "Conciseness and Amplification."
   College Composition and Communication 41
   (1990): 443–59.

Malarkey, Stoddard, and J. Barre Toelken. "Gawain
   and the Green Girdle." Journal of English and
   Germanic Philology 63 (1964): 14–20.

22   Article in a Journal Paginated by Issue

For journals that begin each issue on page 1, give author, title, journal, volume, issue number (if there is one), year of publication (in parentheses), and so on:

Silko, Leslie Marmon. "Landscape, History, and
   the Pueblo Imagination." Antaeus 57 (1986):
   83–94.

If the journal uses only issue numbers, list them as though they were volume numbers.

23   *Article in a Monthly or Bimonthly Publication*

For journals published every one or two months, give the month and year, colon, and page numbers:

Boland, Eavan. "Outside History." American Poetry

   Review Mar.-Apr. 1990: 32-38.

Lohmann, Kenneth J. "How Sea Turtles Navigate."

   Scientific American *Jan. 1992: 100-06.

Mann, Charles C., and Mark L. Plummer. "The

   Butterfly Problem." The Atlantic Jan. 1992:

   47-70.

24   *Article in a Weekly or Biweekly Publication*

For journals published every one or two weeks, give the complete date (day, month—abbreviated except for May, June, or July—and year), colon, and page numbers:

Greenfield, Meg. "A New Year's Resolution."

   Newsweek 6 Jan. 1992: 56.

Phalon, Richard. "Health Junkies." Forbes 3 Feb.

   1992: 60-62.

25   *Article in a Newspaper*

Give the writer's name if there is a byline, the title, the name of the newspaper as it appears on the masthead, but omitting any introductory article: *Spokesman-Review* (not *The Spokesman-Review*). When the city of publication is not identified in the name of the newspaper, add it in square brackets, not underlined, after the name: *Spokesman-Review* [Spokane, WA]. Then give the day, month (abbreviated except for May, June, July), and year, then the section number (if there is one) and page. Some newspapers have multiple editions, so the edition should be specified after the date, set off by a comma:

"How Students Rank the World Over." San Francisco

   Chronicle 6 Feb. 1992: A2.

Yardley, Jonathan. "Thinking the Unthinkable: Too

Many Universities." <u>Washington Post</u> 10–16

Feb. 1992, natl. weekly ed.: 27.

When a story begins on one page and continues on a later one, give the first page number and a plus sign (+):

Wilford, John Noble. "Nubian Treasures Reflect

Black Influence on Egypt." <u>New York Times</u> 11

Feb. 1992, natl. ed.: B5+.

26 *Editorial in a Newspaper*
If the editorial is signed, begin with the author's name. Otherwise, begin with the title, then add *Editorial* (with two spaces on either side), period, and the standard publishing information:

"Mideast Momentum for Peace." Editorial. <u>New York

Times</u> 23 July 1991, natl. ed.: A10.

27 *Unsigned Article*
Simply begin with the title and list alphabetically:

"Can You Live Longer?" <u>Consumer Reports</u> 57 (1992):

7–15.

28 *Letter to the Editor*
A letter to the editor, whether to a newspaper or other periodical, is identified by author, *Letter* instead of title, and then the publishing information:

Parel, Miriam. Letter. <u>New York Times</u> 4 Feb. 1992,

natl. ed.: A14.

Sanders, Scott Russell. Letter. <u>Harper's</u> Mar.

1990: 5.

29 *Book Review*

Start with the reviewer's name, then give the title if there is one, *Rev. of*, the title of the work reviewed, a comma, *by*, and the name of the author. When reviewing an edited or translated work, use *ed.* or *trans.* instead of *by*:

```
Carlson, Ron.  "King Lear in Zebulon County."  Rev.

    of A Thousand Acres, by Jane Smiley.  New York

    Times Book Review 3 Nov. 1991: 12.

Sanders, E. P.  Rev. of The World of Biblical

    Literature, by Robert Alter.  New York Times

    Book Review 9 Feb. 1992: 14.

Schwartz, John.  Rev. of Rising Sun, by Michael

    Crichton.  Newsweek 17 Feb. 1992: 64.

Wolfe, Alan.  Rev. of A People's Charter: The

    Pursuit of Rights in America, by James

    MacGregor Burns and Stewart Burns.  Washington

    Post 3-9 Feb. 1992, natl. weekly ed.: 36.
```

30 *Special Issue of a Journal*

Begin with the editor if there is one, then the underlined title of the special issue, followed by a period, two spaces, and *Spec. issue of* and the name of the journal:

```
The Changing Culture of the University.  Spec.

    issue of Partisan Review 58 (1992).

Energy for Planet Earth.  Spec. issue of Scientific

    American Sept. 1990
```

■ *Other Sources*

31 *Dissertations: Published/Unpublished*

Doctoral dissertations are listed in *Dissertation Abstracts International* (*DAI*). Before volume 30 (1969), the source was called *Dissertation Ab-*

stracts. *DAI* now publishes in three series: A for humanities and social sciences, B for sciences, and C for European dissertations. When citing a dissertation listed in *DAI*, use the following form:

Johnson, Sandra Humble. "Literary Epiphany in

the Work of Annie Dillard." DAI 50 (1990):

3589-A. Bowling Green U.

When you are working directly with an unpublished dissertation, omit the references to *DAI* and identify with *Diss.* and the institution:

Novak, James Ballaz. "Magic as Theme in Sir Gawain

and the Green Knight." Diss. Syracuse U,

1979.

When a dissertation has been published, treat it like a book (underlining the title), give the publication information (Diss. Syracuse U, 1979), and then give the order number if the work has been published by University Microfilms International (UMI).

32 *Encyclopedia Articles: Signed/Unsigned*

Give the author if there is one, the title of the entry, the name of the encyclopedia, the edition if it is identified, and the year. Page and volume numbers are usually unnecessary because such works are arranged alphabetically.

Barron, Oswald. "Heraldry." Encyclopedia

Britannica. 11th ed. 1910-11.

"Savoy." The New Encyclopedia Britannica:

Macropaedia. 1989 ed.

Taylor, Hal R. "Rice." Collier's Encyclopedia.

1990 ed.

33 *Government Publication*

Except where an author is given, begin with the name of the government and the name of the issuing agency:

United States. Dept. of Health, Education, and

   Welfare. Office of Child Development. Infant

   Care. Washington: GPO, 1973.

United States. Internal Revenue Service. 1981

   Statistics of Income: Corporation Income Tax

   Returns. Washington: GPO, 1984.

Note: "GPO" stands for "Government Printing Office."

34 *Pamphlet*
Treat pamphlets like books: list author, title, and publication information.

35 *Information Service*
When citing material from information services—like ERIC (Educational Resources Information Center) or NTIS (National Technical Information Service)—treat it like any other printed material, but identify the source at the end. When the material has been published previously, give the original information, then the name and identification number of the service from which it is available:

Bello, Rafael A., and George M. Pigott. "Dried

   Fish Patties: Storage Stability and Economic

   Considerations." Journal of Food Processing

   and Preservation 4 (1980): 247-60. NTIS PB81-

   223661.

Evans, Judith T. Characteristics of Open

   Education: Results from a Classroom

   Observation Rating Scale and a Teacher

   Questionnaire. Newton, MA: Educational

   Development Center, 1971. ERIC ED 058 160

36 *Published Proceedings of a Conference*

Treat such publications as you would a book, adding any pertinent information not included in the title:

Proceedings of the 1985 Oil Spill Conference. 25-

28 Feb. 1985. Los Angeles. Sponsored by

American Petroleum Institute, Environmental

Protection Agency, and the U.S. Coast

Guard. Washington: American Petroleum

Institute, 1985.

37 *Letters: Published/Unpublished*

Conrad, Joseph. "To Edward Garnett." 10 June

1896. In The Collected Letters of Joseph

Conrad. Ed. Frederick R. Karl and Laurence

Davies. Vol. 1. Cambridge: Cambridge UP,

1983.

When using unpublished letters from a collection, give the author, a description ("Letter to . . ."), the date, any identifying number or label, the name of the institution that houses the material, and its location. For example, suppose you want to quote an unpublished letter from John Steinbeck to Wanda Van Brunt that is in the Steinbeck Research Center at San Jose State University:

Steinbeck, John. Letter to Wanda Van Brunt.

13 Sept. 1948. Van Brunt Letters. Steinbeck

Research Center. San Jose State University,

San Jose, CA.

When citing a letter you have received personally, use the following format:

Shakespeare, William. Letter to the author.

22 July 1990.

38 *Interviews: Published/Unpublished*

```
Morrison, Toni.  Interview.  All Things

    Considered.  Natl. Public Radio.  KQED, San

    Francisco.  16 Feb. 1986.
Stryk, Lucien.  Interview.  American Poetry Review

    Mar.-Apr. 1990.  47-55.
```

When citing a personally conducted interview, give the name of the person interviewed, the kind of interview (personal or telephone), and the date:

```
Presley, Elvis.  Telephone interview.  1 Apr. 1992.
```

39 *Lecture*

Give the speaker's name, the title of address if there is one (in quotations), the meeting, the sponsoring organization, the location, and the date:

```
Cook, William W.  "Writing in the Spaces

    Left."  Opening General Sess.  CCCC

    Convention.  Cincinnati, 19 Mar. 1992.
```

Had there been no title, the citation would have read as follows:

```
Cook, William W.  Address.  Opening General

    Sess.  CCCC Convention.  Cincinnati, 19 Mar.

    1992.
```

When citing an on-campus lecture, give the name, the title if there is one, the location, and the date:

```
Klein, Jurgen.  "Dark Romanticism in Late 18th-

    Century British Literature."  San Jose State

    University, 23 Mar. 1992.
```

40 *Work of Art*

Give the artist's name, the title of the painting or sculpture (underlined), the institution where it is located, and the city:

Cezanne, Paul. The Aqueduct. Pushkin Museum,

Moscow.

Pissaro, Camille. Haymaking at Eragny. National

Gallery of Canada, Ottawa.

When the titles are not in English, it may be useful to place their translation in brackets:

Gauguin, Paul. Ea Haere Ia De ["Where are you

going?"]. Hermitage, St. Petersburg.

41 *Recording*

Begin with the composer, conductor, or performer (depending on who is cited first); then give the title (underlined), the artist (identified by *with*), and the catalog number. If the recording is on tape, indicate immediately after the title:

Bradbury, Ray. The Martian Chronicles: "There Will

Come Soft Rains; Usher II." Read by Leonard

Nimoy. Caedmon, TC 1466, 1975.

Hayden, Franz-Joseph. Five Concertos for Flute,

Oboe and Orchestra. Jean Pierre Rampal,

flute, and Pierre Pierlot, oboe. Cond. Roland

Douatte. Collegium Musicum de Paris.

Everest, SDBR 3465, 1979.

Shakespeare, William. Julius Caesar. Dir. Howard

Sackler. With Sir Ralph Richardson, Anthony

Quayle, Alan Bates, and Michael Gwynn.

Shakespeare Recording Society. Caedmon,

SRS-M-230, 1964.

Shostakovich, Dimitri. <u>Symphony No. 7 in C major,</u>

    <u>Op. 60</u>—the "Leningrad." Audiotape. Cond.

    Neeme Jarvi. Scottish National Orchestra.

    Chandos, ABTD 1312, 198.

Vonnegut, Kurt, Jr. <u>Kurt Vonnegut, Jr. Reads</u> Cat's

    Cradle. Caedmon, TC 1346, 1973.

42 *Film or Videotape*

Begin with the title (underlined), the director, the distributor, and the year; include any significant additional information (writer, performers, producer, and so on):

<u>A bout de souffle</u> [Breathless]. Dir. Jean-Luc

    Godard. With Jean-Paul Belmondo and Jean

    Seberg. Beauregard, 1960.

<u>Breathless</u>. Dir. Jim McBride. With Richard Gere

    and Valerie Kaprisky. Orion, 1983.

When citing the contribution of a particular individual (actor, composer, director, producer, screenwriter), begin with that person's name:

Godard, Jean-Luc, dir. <u>A bout de souffle</u>

    [Breathless]. With Jean-Paul Belmondo and

    Jean Seberg. Beauregard, 1960.

When citing educational filmstrips and videotapes, give the title (underlined), the medium, the producer, the publisher, the date, and the length:

<u>Alcohol and Drug Abuse</u>. Videocassette. Prod.

    Healthscope. American College of Physicians,

    1986. 25 min.

<u>Cathedral</u>. Videocassette. Prod. PBS Video.

    Unicorn Projects, 1985. 58 min.

43   *Live Performance*

For the performance of a play, opera, ballet, or concert, give the title, director, major performers, theater, city, and date. For a symphony orchestra, it is appropriate to open with the conductor:

```
Blomstedt, Herbert, cond.  San Francisco Symphony

     Orch.  Richard Strauss Program.  Davies Hall,

     San Francisco.  20 Feb. 1992.
```

44   *Radio or Television Program*

Give the title of the program (underlined), then the network, the local station and city, and the date of broadcast. When citing a specific episode, enclose it in quotation marks and place it before title:

```
"Keeper of the Deep."  20/20.  ABC.  KGO, San

     Francisco.  14 Feb. 1992.

"What Smells?"  Prod. and dir. Vishnu Methar.

     Writ. Amanda McConnell.  Nova.  PBS.  KTEH,

     San Jose.  13 Feb. 1992.
```

45   *Computer Software*

Give the author of the program, if any, the title (underlined), a descriptive label ("Computer software"), the distributor, and the year of publication:

```
Easy.  Release 1.5.  Computer software.  Micropro,

     1986.

Microsoft Word.  Version 5.5.  Computer software.

     Microsoft, 1990.
```

46   *Map or Chart*

List a map or a chart like an anonymous book, adding the necessary descriptive label:

```
Special Places of the World: New York City.  Map.

     Washington, DC: National Geographic Society,

     1990.
```

<u>Western States and Provinces</u>.   Map.   Falls Church:

   American Automobile Association, 1989.

47   *Cartoon*

Give the cartoonist's name, the title of the cartoon if any (in quotation marks), the descriptive label *Cartoon* (neither underlined nor in quotation marks), and the usual publication information:

Evans, Greg.   "Luann."   Cartoon.   <u>San Jose Mercury</u>

   <u>News</u> 22 Feb. 1992: 9C.

Explanatory Notes

Occasionally you may find it convenient—or necessary—to include explanatory material that will not fit gracefully into your text. In such instances you can use footnotes (at the bottom of the page) or endnotes (at the end of the text). To identify these notes, use the traditional system of raised numbers, consecutively numbered throughout the paper. In the text the numbers appear at the end of the sentence, after the period. The matching foot- or endnotes themselves are indented five spaces and double spaced.

Endnotes appear in a separate section between the end of the text and the Works Cited section. This section is headed by *Notes*, with a double line space between the title and the first entry. Neither foot- nor endnotes give full bibliographic documentation, but rather use the same parenthetical system as in the body of the text.

As researchers we use explanatory notes for two reasons: to list multiple citations too numerous to fit in the text, and to clarify or elaborate on remarks that we have made. Such commentary has some of the character of parenthetical material; it is related to what we are discussing, but its fuller treatment would constitute a digression. For example, in an article on the role of aristocracy and chivalry in the medieval romance, *Sir Gawain and the Green Knight*, Britton J. Harwood's first note elaborates on his allusion to the conflict between aristocratic and Christian ideals.[1] His second note (our major example) then qualifies the distinction between knights and nobility.[2]

Notes

[1] Some readers, for example, have maintained

that categories like free will and grace are

essential in Sir Gawain and the Green Knight . . .

[2] By attempting to discern a particular value, I do not mean to exaggerate either the legal differences between the English peerage in the late fourteenth century (some 70 families) and the knights (some 1,200–1,500 when the century began) or the space between them as status groups. By 1300, for example, knights were allowed coats of arms (Given–Wilson 65–66, 70).

Entries in Works Cited

Given–Wilson, Chris. The English Nobility in the Late Middle Ages. London: Routledge, 1987.

Harwood, Britton J. "Gawain and the Gift." Publications of the Modern Language Association 106 (1991): 483–95.

Glossary of Rhetorical and Stylistic Terms

The following are terms for devices that either do not appear in the text or that may profit from further definition and illustration.

Abstraction   The process of grouping things and qualities into ever broadening classes (from Eureka lemon, to lemon, to citrus, to fruit). The process by which we order, arrange, and find significance. Sometimes expressed as a "ladder of abstraction," a scale of related words mounting progressively from specific to general. The reverse process whereby we divide groups and classes into particulars, moving toward specificity, is called *concretion*.

Alliteration   Repetition of consonant sounds in adjacent words. A device so conspicuous that it must be used with restraint:

> Over tens of thousands of years, the ice sheets reached thicknesses of several kilometers; they planed, **scoured** and **scarred** the landscape as far south as central Europe.
> —"What Drives Glacial Cycles?" *Scientific American*, Jan. 1990

Anadiplosis   Beginning one clause or sentence with the same word or words that ended the previous one. A transition device to emphasize continuity.

> The trees thinned out to make **meadows**, and **the meadows** grew wider and fuller, and soon the meadows became open plains.   —Tim O'Brien, *Going After Cacciato*

Analogy   Similarities between things usually not thought of in connection with one another. Like *metaphor*, a way of thinking or seeing that goes beyond the surface, the obvious, the literal, and the predictable. To see what a skilled writer can make of an extended analogy, consult Paul Fussell's comparison of universities and the military (see the "Analogy" section in Chapter 2, p. 77). But sentence-level analogies also have their power:

Last week I tried to make eye contact with a tarantula. This was a huge specimen, all hairy and handsomely colored, with a body **as big as a hamster** and legs **the size of Bic pens**.
—David Quammen, "The Face of a Spider"

Anaphora   Repetition of the same word or words at the beginnings of successive phrases, clauses, or sentences. An intensifying device that calls attention to parallel structures (and ideas). In the following, a writer uses anaphora to express a young girl's fascination with a juggler:

She stood silently, **watching** the balls blur together and come apart again, **watching** them disappear in one hand and reappear in the other, **watching** them move so quickly that they seemed to flow like water.   —Lisa Goldstein, *The Red Magician*

Anthimeria   The use of one part of speech as another. Thus, Annie Dillard refers to certain days as "partly cloudies." Some examples become so commonplace that they drop their special character and enter our daily language (hence, we *hose* our driveways).

From time to time I stop in the middle of a small task and **glass** the horizon with binoculars.
—Gretel Ehrlich, "Time on Ice," *Harper's*, Mar. 1992

Antimetabole   A structural flip-flop in which words are repeated in successive clauses in reverse order:

The man was the job and the job was the man.
—Kurt Vonnegut, Jr., *Mother Night*

Asyndeton   As opposed to *polysyndeton*, a departure from the general punctuation of a series (A, B, *and* C), deleting the *and* before the final item. The effect is sometimes to make a series seem more rapid, abrupt; other times, it may make the final item seem more climactic:

Joan's gone back to the room and left me in the lobby to wait for Steve to join us for breakfast. He's a few minutes late, but I know he'll be here soon, is on his way, is even now parking his car.   —Stanley Elkin, "In Darkest Hollywood," *Harper's*, Dec. 1989

Audience   The readers to whom we address our writing. On the basis of two questions (What do they know? What do they want?), we make choices about style, arrangement, and detail. We may be familiar or formal or somewhere in between, we may approach them as insiders or outsiders, but we must shape our material for their acceptance. We can usually assume that our readers will meet us half way.

Clausal Modification   As opposed to single words (adjectives and adverbs) and *phrasal modification*. The use of a full adverbial or adjectival clause to present a detail *that could be expressed by* (expressible with) a phrase or a single word. Phrases and single words are more economical, but a clause has the clout of a full verb. When we write with numerous clausal modifiers, we create a style not only that seems formal and authoritative but also that is ponderous and time-consuming. (Compare: Numerous clausal modifiers make our prose formal and authoritative but also ponderous and time-consuming.) Modern writers are relying increasingly on shorter structures, the prepositional phrase especially.

Cliche   An expression worn out from overuse (*madder than a hornet, smooth as glass, the bottom line, back to square one*). Because they are ready-made and overused, the first things off the rack, it is the nature of cliches to be old hat, to fall on deaf ears, to be run into the ground. When they overpopulate our writing, we can be reasonably sure that our thinking has been conventional and stereotypic.

Clustering   A multidimensional method for both exploring and organizing ideas. You can cluster your own ideas, information you have collected, or words and images from something you have read. Clustering encourages and rewards connecting, finding relationships. To illustrate, the following is a cluster a student might develop to prepare for an exam on phrases:

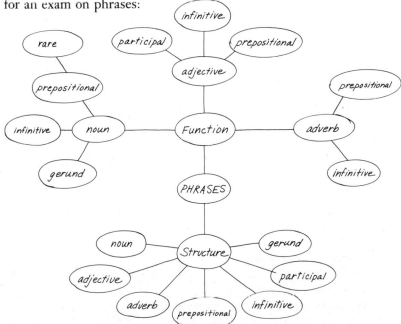

Coherence   Paragraphs and sequences of paragraphs are like the two-faced Roman god Janus (appropriately, the patron of beginnings and endings): they look forward and backward. Even as a paragraph advances a thought, looking forward, it builds on previous thoughts, looking back. The two faces of the paragraph are coherence and continuity. Coherence (or cohesiveness) pulls along what has already been said: continuity (or continuousness) does indeed *continue*, continue in the same direction and spirit.

Colloquial Language   A broad term covering everything from the slang we use in daily speech to the language of informal writing. Rhetorically, colloquial language sometimes enjoys connotations of honesty and spontaneity, narrowing the distance between writer and reader. At the same time, it can also seem haphazard and ill-considered, suggesting we have not taken much care. For most academic writing, we should use colloquial language sparingly (preferring "He became angry" to "He got mad," or "They have two children" to "They have two kids").

Connotation   As opposed to *denotation*. The emotional weight or associations of certain words. Connotative words are expressive, suggesting the user's evaluation of the subject. The difference between denotation and connotation is the difference between "He *visited* us" and "He *graced* us with his presence" or "He *inflicted* his presence on us."

Cumulative Sentence (Loose)   A sentence that begins with a main clause and adds trailing modifiers. Sometimes the trailing modifiers are parallel, all modifying the main clause in the same manner, adding to an accumulation of related details. The following example describes sportswriters awaiting a big fight.

> So there we were, hanging around, twiddling our thumbs, drinking Scotch, and telling stories, and trying to make copy out of nothing.   —James Baldwin, "The Fight: Patterson vs. Liston"

> main clause
> So there we were,
>   hanging around,
>   twiddling our thumbs,
>   drinking Scotch, and
>   telling stories, and
>   trying to make copy out of nothing.

Sometimes the trailing modifiers are subordinate, each one modifying the structure before, presenting an increasingly refined image, as in the following:

> **And we watched him* jump rope,** which he must do according to some music in his head, very beautiful and gleaming and far away, like a boy saint helplessly dancing and seen through the steaming windows of a storefront church.
> —"The Fight: Patterson vs. Liston"

main clause
And we watched him jump rope,
   which he must do according to some music in his head,
      very beautiful and
         gleaming and
         far away,
      like a boy saint helplessly dancing and
            seen through the steaming windows . . .

Cyberrhea   An affliction that strikes some word processor users; excessive frequency and looseness of productivity. Particularly virulent among those who have not discovered the fortifying virtues of revision.

Deadwood   A metaphor taken from orchardists (dead, nonbearing branches eventually threaten the life of a tree). A term for wordiness or padding. Words supplying detail that is either unnecessary or clearly implied:

> One problem that many college students have in school is expressing themselves in writing.

Compare:

> Many college students have difficulty writing.

Delayed Revelation   A popular technique for arousing the reader's curiosity, whether at the sentence, paragraph, or essay level. (See the section "Pronouns and Delayed Revelation" in Chapter 12, "The Rhetoric of Pronouns.") In the following, James Baldwin exploits the device to intensify a common allegation against writers:

> The charge has often been made against American writers **that they do not describe society, and have no interest in it**.
> —"The Discovery of What It Means to Be an American"

* former heavyweight boxing champion Floyd Patterson

Compare:

> The charge that they do not describe society, and have no interest in it, has often been made against American writers.

Denotation   The neutral, objective meaning of words. The power of words to signify apart from suggestions of evaluation. See also *connotation*.

Descriptive Verbs   Precise, concrete verbs as opposed to vague, general ones. The difference between *go* and *walk*, and between *walk* and *slog*, *strut*, *stomp*, or *stagger*.

Dialogue Guide   The phrase identifying the speaker of directly quoted words:

> "Aren't you carrying this a little far?" **Stephen asks**, sounding worried.   —Bobbie Ann Mason, "Residents and Transients"

See also *signal phrase*.

Drafting   After different forms of *prewriting*, the phase in the writing process when we begin formally to produce a draft. Writing blocks often begin with premature attempts to draft, to start before we have any useful notion of what to say or how to say it. The focus in this stage is on developing the tentative plan we found in prewriting, on completeness and organization rather than on refinement (the focus of *revision*). Many professional writers argue that their writing does not begin until they have a draft upon which to work.

Dynamic Verbs   Verbs that are kinetic, that move (or *bob* or *blink*), as opposed to static verbs like *be*.

Editing   Tidying up. The stage when writers clean up the surface features of their text: grammar, spelling, punctuation. The indispensable phase when we are making our work presentable, fit to go out in public, but also one that should be postponed until last.

Ellipsis   In documentation, the part we leave out of a quotation and whose absence we indicate with three spaced dots. In grammar, the omission of words whose presence must be "understood" in order for a structure to be complete.

> The light was yellow and smoky, the streets outside [were] unlit and sinister.
> —Robert Stone, "Havana Then and Now," *Harper's*, Mar. 1992

Epistrophe   Ending each item in a series with the same word or words. An emphatic device that dramatizes the verbal common denominator that unites a series of items.

> Too many doors opened into offices in which Mosbacher could see ordinary people bent over their work—people in shirtsleeves, minor **people**, small **people**, noisy **people**, unimportant **people**, poor **people**.
> —Lewis H. Lapham, "Notebook: Journey to the East," *Harper's*, Mar. 1992

To further understand the punctuation of Lapham's series, see *asyndeton*.

Exposition   Explanatory as opposed to descriptive or narrative writing. In narratives, awkward writers halt the action to fill in background information; skillful writers continue narrative momentum by integrating such material into their stories. Aside from such uses, exposition exists in its own right and often draws upon narration and description to complete its explanatory function. The following illustrates how a fiction writer introduces expository (or, in this case, background) information into a narrative:

> And when I turned my head to take a parting glance at **the tug which had just left us anchored outside the bar**, I saw the straight line of the flat shore joined to the stable sea, edge to edge, with a perfect and unmarked closeness, in one levelled floor half brown, half blue under the enormous dome of the sky.   —Joseph Conrad, "The Secret Sharer"

Compare:

> **A tug had left us anchored outside the bar.** When I turned to take a parting look at it, I saw . . .

Expressive Writing   As opposed to *representational*. Writing whose chief purpose is to reflect the feelings and judgment of the writer. Writer-centered, "I" writing. (See the section "Adjectives: Representational and Expressive" in Chapter 13, "The Rhetoric of Adjectives.")

Freewriting   A warm-up technique. Nonstop writing without immediate concern for organization or direction. A way to plunge into a subject and establish a flow, to wander in darkness while moving toward the light.

Hyperbole   Overstatement, exaggeration. A device often used comically but that has been nearly exhausted by the advertisement industry. A good reason for writers to cultivate *understatement*.

Hypotaxis   A style that uses explicit connecting words to identify the logical relationship between ideas (as opposed to *parataxis*—simple juxtaposition to suggest connection). "I was tired *so* I quit" as opposed to "I was tired; I quit." The pair of terms dramatize a major truism about writing: that it is a process of saying and not saying, of explicit and implicit meaning.

Inversion   A sentence that departs from the standard word order, often placing the subject after the verb:

pred   subj
On the airfield were grouped   the dignitaries who had been detailed to receive him officially.   —Lawrence Durrell, *Mountolive*

Ironic Capitalization   The use of capital letters to spell words and phrases that would ordinarily take lowercase letters. A device for expressing irony or contempt:

The final and most excruciating callowness of youth is what SF [science fiction] readers particularly prize: Big Ideas.
—Thomas M. Disch, "Big Ideas and Dead-End Thrills," *The Atlantic*, Feb. 1992

Jargon   At best, the specialized language of a profession or field. At worst, a deliberately inaccessible vocabulary confected to impress, intimidate, and obscure. (Why, for example, do hospitals call a newborn a *neonate*, a Latinate term that translates exactly as "newborn"?) Richard Weaver understood perfectly the motives for jargon:

If certain government policies were announced in the language of the barbershop, their absurdity might become overwhelmingly apparent.   —*The Ethics of Rhetoric*

Metaphor   A way of thinking, of understanding one thing in terms of another. As a figure of speech, a metaphor is a word whose meaning is not literal but imaginative and comparative. Take the following description of a Georgia cabin:

The walls, unpainted, are seasoned a rosin yellow. And cracks between the boards are black. **These cracks are the lips the night winds use for whispering. Night winds in Georgia are vagrant poets, whispering.**   —Jean Toomer, *Cane*

Metaphoric Verbs   The most common form of metaphors. Ultimately more subtle and flexible than their noun equivalents. Thus, when we are *starved* for affection, we *cultivate* friendships (which sounds better than *starting a friendship garden*, suggesting friends as carrots and turnips).

Metonymy   A figure of speech that substitutes for the name of a thing something that is suggested by it. For example, in some neighborhoods police are referred to as "the heat"; in others, attorneys and financial advisors are called "suits." Thus, in *Citizen Cohn* Nicholas von Hoffman describes the bribery of judges as "dropping packets of green bills into black robes" (308). The concept is most useful, however, in description. The most skillful writers use descriptive detail, surface particulars, that suggest the nature or character of the subject.

Mixed Metaphor   A place where the hand of a writer should never set foot.

News   In the broadest sense, our motive for writing. There are two kinds of news, news that informs and news that reminds. The first presents new information, something the reader does not know; the second rediscovers or "renews," reacquainting the reader with forgotten values. On the sentence level, the "news" is its specific theme or point, whether explicit or implicit, to which all the details are subordinate. An unfocused sentence has no clear news.

Nominal Style   Writing in which nouns are the principal news-carriers. As opposed to *verbal style* (in which verbs carry most of the news). The nominal style generally has more formality and surface authoritativeness. Its weight owes to so much meaning invested in static and often more polysyllabic nouns (*indication* versus *indicate*). Relying on verbs, the verbal style is more direct and lively. Verbs, after all, move.

Nominal	*Verbal*
causing 32 injuries	injuring 32
give a demonstration	demonstrate
give an indication	indicate

Sometimes, of course, we want to spend some time on an idea, linger over and draw it out for emphasis: "This will *give you an indication* of just how much . . ."

Onomatopoeia   The quality of words to echo the sounds of the things they name.

> I do remember the way the heater pipes **banged** and **rattled,**
> startling all of us out of sleep until we got so used to the
> sound that we automatically shut it out or raised our voices
> above the racket. —Judith Ortiz Cofer, "Silent Dancing"

Or, in *U.S.A.* John Dos Passos describes a character "carving out the
century with a *s*calpel so *k*een, so *c*omical, so exa*ct* . . ." The sharp,
abrupt, *alliterated* sounds imitate the precise act of cutting.

Outline   Something best kept simple, at least when used as a plan and
not a description. In *Writing for Story*, Jon Franklin, who believes in
outlines if they are kept under control, recommends a five-part, fifteen-
word outline for stories, but the same advice applies to essays. A good
working outline (when we use one) is general, tentative, provisional,
pointing a direction but not putting on blinders or committing us to
follow a predetermined path. It encapsulates the spirit of our writing,
gives us crude or general guidelines, but leaves us free to devise and
revise.

Oxymoron   The combination of mutually contradictory terms, like
bittersweet, jumbo shrimp, living death, surgical bombing, or *youth culture.*

Paragraph   The basic unit of written expression. See also *coherence.*

Parallelism   Structural repetition, compounding, multiplication, the
use of a series (if only of two items), often to convey a message about
multiplicity and variety. Parallel items can be connected with *and.*

> The landscape was a compensation too, for I liked its heaving
> grey and brown billows, dotted with corn-stacks, patched and
> striped by plough and stubble and green crops, and crossed by
> bridle tracks and lonely wandering roads.
> —Siegfried Sassoon, *Memoirs of an Infantry Officer*
>
> The landscape was a compensation too, for
> I liked its heaving grey and
>   brown billows,
>   dotted with corn-stacks,
>   patched and
>   striped by plough and
>   stubble and
>   green crops, and
>   crossed by bridle tracks and
>   lonely wandering roads.

Paraphrase   Restatement in our own words of someone else's (or even our own) ideas. A sentence-by-sentence paraphrase (using a dictionary) is an excellent way to penetrate the meaning of difficult passages. The practice also sharpens our powers of phraseology.

> *Original*   It is as unjust to reward the undeserving as it is to punish the innocent.
>
> *Paraphrase*   Unmerited reward is as unfair as unrewarded merit.

Paraphrase or restatement of an idea is also a form of revision. Sometimes the only way to cope with a difficult sentence is to restate its idea in entirely different words.

Parataxis   As opposed to *hypotaxis*. Simple juxtaposition of structures to suggest relationships that could be expressed openly with structure words. Thus, "I say to-may-toe and you say ta-mah-toe." The "and" is a neutral linker, not an indicator of relationship and thus dispensable. If we leave it out, we have the purest form of parataxis. Replace it with *but* or *whereas*, and we have an example of hypotaxis.

The distinction, if not the terminology, is useful for reminding us that writing alternates between open and implied meanings. As a result, reading is a little like playing connect-the-dots.

Periodic Sentence   As opposed to a *cumulative* or *loose* sentence. A sentence that does not disclose its complete meaning until the end. Structurally, a sentence that postpones completion of the main clause. Often a sentence with lengthy sentence anticipators, giving the main clause climactic power:

> Up from the skeleton stone walls, up from the rotting floor boards and the solid hand-hewn beams of oak of the pre-war cotton factory, **dusk came.**   —Jean Toomer, *Cane*
>
> The boy who was beaten at school, who went too much to church, who carried the fear of poverty all his life, but who nevertheless was filled with the memories of country pleasures; the young bank clerk who worked such long hours for so little money, but who danced, sang, played, flirted—**this naturally vigorous, sensuous being was killed in 1914, 1915, 1916.** I think the best of my father died in that war, that his spirit was crippled by it.   —Doris Lessing, "My Father"

Personification   Giving a quality, idea, or thing the attributes of living beings. Often an expressive device that transforms something abstract or lifeless into something living, reacting, sympathetic, as in Gertrude Stein's playful Valentine to conjunctions:

> Conjunctions have made themselves live by their work. They work and as they work they live and even when they do not work and in these days they do not always live by work still nevertheless they do live.   —"Poetry and Grammar"

Phrasal Modification   As opposed to *clausal modification*. Modifying details *presented in phrases* when they could be presented in clauses or, sometimes, single words. Phrases have more weight and rhythm than single words ("the web *of love*" versus "*love's* web"), but are usually less emphatic than clauses, which carry the full load of a predicate verb.

adv clause
When we look back in time and study old cultures and people, we are impressed that death has always been distasteful to man and will probably always be.
—Elisabeth Kübler-Ross, "On the Fear of Death"

part phrases
Looking back in time and studying old cultures and people, we are impressed . . .

Phrase   The basic structural unit of the sentence, more so even than words, which usually operate in phrases. One test of a phrase is that it can be replaced *structurally* with a single word, producing a much more general version of the original statement:

subj
Walking along woodland trails in the fall of the year is fun for
prep obj
someone like me who works with fungi.
—George Barron, "Jekyll-Hyde Mushrooms," *Natural History*, Mar. 1992
(*It* is fun for *me*.)

subj   prep phrase
The effect of the fall of Teotihuacan,   in about A.D. 750,

dir obj
provides   another indication that Mexican culture was emulated by, rather than imposed upon, the Maya.
—Nicholas M. Hellmuth, "Echoes of a Lost Colony," *Natural History*, Mar. 1992.
(*This, then*, provides *that*.)

Placement   As important as selection of the right words. Consider the contrasting messages of the following two sentences:

> **Women and men do not receive an equal education because outside the classroom women are perceived not as sovereign beings but as prey.**
> —Adrienne Rich, "Taking Women Students Seriously"
>
> **Because outside the classroom women are perceived not as sovereign beings but as prey,** women and men do not receive equal education.

One places effect before cause; the other, cause before effect. The first opens a paragraph that goes on to discuss how campus women must live in fear of various forms of sexual harassment and even outright assault. The second could go on to explain how the educations of men and women are unequal.

Plagiarism Unacknowledged borrowing of someone else's words or ideas. An offense that is both difficult to conceal and fatal to one's credibility.

Polyptoton A saturation technique. A form of repetition, one involving the use of words, usually different parts of speech, derived from the same root (*real, really, realize, reality*):

> **Deliberation** is good only because it decreases the number of things it is necessary to **deliberate** about.
> —Richard Weaver, *The Ethics of Rhetoric*

Because each part of speech carries its own kind of information, takes its own angle on reality, polyptoton has a peculiar power to bracket, surround, and generally encompass a subject.

Polysyndeton As opposed to *asyndeton*. Separating items in a series with conjunctions, usually *and*, sometimes *or*. An emphatic device that slows down a listing and calls more attention to individual items (*Bob and Carol and Ted and Alice*—movie title).

Prewriting A useful catch-all term for the informal exploratory writing that precedes the more formal *drafting*. It is a time to write spontaneously without fear of digressions or errors or inconsistencies, a time to pursue ideas to see where they will take us. The value of prewriting is that it liberates us from the responsibility of finding meaning and form too quickly. Prewriting can be a casual, nonthreatening warm-up, but also one latent with discovery and surprise.

Punctuation To writing what enunciation is to speech. Not mere mechanical conventions but the indication of traffic flow in a sentence.

Often the difference between gliding and staggering. Look how a carefully placed dash can smooth a sentence by an excellent writer:

> To have that sense of one's intrinsic worth which constitutes self-respect is potentially to have everything: the ability to discriminate, to love and to remain indifferent.
> —Joan Didion, "On Self-Respect"

> To have that sense of one's intrinsic worth which constitutes self-respect is potentially to have everything: the ability to discriminate—to love and to remain indifferent.

The context establishes that love and indifference are forms of discrimination, but the punctuation of the original sentence allows the momentary interpretation that there are three abilities: to discriminate, to love, and to remain indifferent. The dash gives the reader a clearer signal.

In some cases writers will use unconventional punctuation in order to create appropriate rhythms:

> Anybody leaving the sidewalk [in Paris] to go on or walking anywhere goes on at a certain pace and that pace keeps up and nothing startles them nothing frightens them nothing makes them go faster or slower nothing not the most violent or unexpected noise makes them jump, or change their pace or their direction.   —Gertrude Stein, *Paris France*

Notice when a punctuation mark does finally appear.

Representational Writing   Writing that strives as honestly as it can to be objective, to present the subject as it would appear to any careful and neutral observer. Writing that minimizes use of such devices of emotional coloration as connotative words, metaphors, and imaginative similes.

Revision   Where wise writers spend 90 percent of their time. The top-down process of smoothing out and polishing what we have written. We begin with confirming the shape and development of our work, then verify the sequence of our paragraphs and sentences. Then we examine the connections and transitions between ideas. We check to see if any sentences require clarifying or strengthening. Can we substitute a better word or a more effective structure? Should a phrase be moved from the end to the middle or beginning of a sentence? Are the right words in the right places?

Rhetoric   The art of making truth effective, as Aristotle put it. The calculated use of language, not to deceive but to do full justice to our ideas and properly dispose our audience.

Rhetorical Question   A question that, technically, the reader will not have the opportunity to answer. In writing, however, a way to challenge the reader and make convenient transitions.

Sentence Openers   Things other than subjects that open a sentence, from anticipators and inversion to "it" or "there" expletives, adverbs, and even coordinating conjunctions. Something to cultivate, if only to avoid the abrupt, choppy effect of starting every sentence with the subject (and thus create the impression that a paragraph is a sequence of separate statements). Notice how the following writer uses openers to fold three sentences into a single paragraph:

> **With each job description I read,** I felt a tightening of what I must call my soul. I found myself growing false to myself, acting to myself, convincing myself of my rightness for whatever was being described. **And** this is where I suppose life ends for most people, who stiffen in the attitudes they adopt to make themselves suitable for jobs and lives that other people have laid out for them.   —V. S. Naipaul, *A Bend in the River*

Series   A device of emphasis, a way to expand and elaborate on sentences. See also *parallelism*.

Signal Phrase   The prose equivalent of a *dialogue guide*; a phrase used to integrate a quotation into our text. For example, in *Style as Argument*, Chris Anderson introduces a quote from Tom Wolfe:

> In "The New Journalism," **Wolfe explains** that exclamation points, italics, and abrupt shifts help him give the illusion in his writing "not only of a person talking but of a person thinking" (22).

Simile   A comparison usually introduced by *like* or *as*. A way to describe.

> The water had become dense now, and thick; **like** an oatmeal soup that is slowly stirred into thickness over a slow fire.
> —Lawrence Durrell, *Mountolive*

Punctuation note: Following current practice, the simile should be set off by a comma, not a semicolon.

Static Verb As opposed to an action or *dynamic* or kinetic verb. A verb that leaves its subject motionless, usually a linking verb. As one journalist put it, weak verbs are to writing what rain is to a garden wedding.

Style The distinctive way a thing is done. In writing, anything that distinguishes our expression from that of others, or from what is ordinary and predictable. In rhetoric, the last persuasive touch.

Synonyms Words having nearly the same meaning, the key term being "nearly." True synonyms, words with identical meanings, are as rare as true identical twins. Words have almost as much individuality as people, and as with people, there are moments when only a certain one will do. Thus, a thesaurus or list of synonyms is like a photo album of people who look alike from a block away. The proper use of a thesaurus is to find a word that is on the tip of our tongue. A thesaurus should not be used as a writer's dating service, a list of attractive and interchangeable prospects.

Thesis Statement Or topic sentence. An explicit statement of the central idea of a paragraph, usually at the beginning. By one count, about half of all professional paragraphs have one; by other counts, the figure is lower.

Understatement As opposed to overstatement or *hyperbole*. A form of emphasis that invites the reader to supply the missing sentiment:

"He does not exactly smother me with his intimacy."
(Translation: He can't stand me.)

"No one would object if you decided to leave early."
(Translation: Please go away.)

Verbal Style As opposed to *nominal style*. Writing in which verbs rather than nouns carry most of the meaning ("investigated" versus "conducted an investigation"). Verbs being mobile and nouns being static, the verbal style is more energetic, animated, and even pictorial.

White Space The blank, unprinted area on a page. Useful because it frames and highlights the printed material containing our message. Something exploited creatively by those who write poetry, advertising copy, and effective paragraphs.

Appendix

Answers to Selected Exercises

The following are possible answers for selected exercises.

Chapter 6, pages 157–158

One possibility:

A long-secret document **was disclosed** today in an Irish newspaper **outlining concessions that the two main Protestant parties in Northern Ireland are willing to make in order to break a political impasse in the British province.**

Or:

Disclosed in an Irish newspaper today was a long-secret document outlining . . .

Chapter 15, pages 314–315

pack tightly	jam, squeeze, wedge
hold firmly	pin, grip
stop up	block, obstruct
find out	discover, learn
push down	depress
get away	escape, elude
look steadily	stare
walk about idly	stroll, saunter
tell about	advertise, disclose
go down	descend
lay open	expose, reveal, disclose
move quickly	speed, race, dash
read rapidly	skim

Chapter 16, pages 329–330

1 His coat was cut from a rather loud piece of horse robe with shoulders so wide that his neck stuck up out of it like **a celery stalk.**

2 He wore a blue uniform coat that fitted him the way **a stall fits a horse.**

3 She smelled the way **the Taj Mahal looks by moonlight.**

4 My brain felt like **a bucket of wet sand.**

5 He had a jaw like **a park bench.**

6 The belt broke like **a piece of butcher's string.**

7 My voiced sounded like **somebody tearing slats off a chicken coop.**

8 A few locks of dry white hair clung to his scalp, like **wild flowers fighting for life on a bare rock.**

9 I lit a cigarette. It tasted like **a plumber's handkerchief.**

10 Even on Central Avenue, not the quietest dressed street in the world, he looked about as inconspicuous as **a tarantula on a slice of angel food.**

Part 3, page 390

There are good reasons why fossil fuels are so popular: (1) they are accessible in one form or another in all regions of the world; (2) humankind has learned to exploit them efficiently and relatively cleanly to produce the energy services it needs, the relatively simple technology of controlled combustion providing energy for applications at nearly every scale; (3) they make excellent fuels for transportation—because they are portable and store a great deal of chemical energy and because the oxygen required for combustion is ubiquitous in the air; and (4) one form can readily be converted to another, say, from solid to liquid or gas, and the fuels are excellent feedstocks for chemicals and plastics.

Part 3, pages 415–416

The cycle of a vigorous city, one that maintains its vitality generation after generation, seems to run like this: first comes a period in which it generates diverse exports, in the process earning an increasing diversity and volume of imports; second, as export generating dies down, a significant explosion of import replacing (provided a critical mass of replaceable imports has piled up—otherwise there is merely a decline); third, a period in which potential new exports, often incorporating innovations, are generated in the city's now greatly enlarged and diversified internal economy; fourth, a period of vigorous export generating and of earning wide ranges and great volumes of new replaceable imports—in other words, a return to the first phase of the cycle and a preparation for repeating the second phase.

In some cities, at some times, the phases follow each other very rapidly; in others the changes occur slowly; but, rapid or slow, this is the cycle that keeps their economies going.

Part 3, pages 416–417

[1]To the uninitiated, it's hard to pin down just where Lakes Basin is. [2]You can attempt to triangulate its position using better-known locales. [3]It lies 2 hours northeast of Nevada City, an hour northwest of Lake Tahoe, and an hour south of the Feather River Gorge. [4]Still, even these calculations may leave the basin's location hazy.

[5]But that's the pleasure of this corner of California. [6]Finding it is as happily surprising as finding a forgotten $20 bill in your back pocket.

[7]Lakes Basin straddles the crest of the Sierra Nevada in Plumas and Sierra counties. [8]The Middle Fork of the Feather River runs to the north, the North Fork of the Yuba to the south. [9]Elevations range from 4,000 to 8,000 feet. [10]The pine- and fir-clad mountainscape was polished by ice-age glaciation, which is evident also in the chain of granite-set lakes that give the region its name.

[11]Another geological phenomenon first lured settlers here: gold. [12]A couple of years after the strikes at Sutter's Mill, argonauts began panning basin streams like Jamison Creek, then turned their attentions to hard-rock mining of nearby mountains like 7,447-foot Eureka Peak.

[13]By the 1870s, the Sierra Buttes Mining Company had dug some 65 miles of tunnels into the peak.[14]Gravity-powered trams hauled ore down to the Mohawk Mill's 60 stamps, each weighing 600 to 950 pounds. [15]Some 400 miners lived down in the company town of Johnsville.

[16]Today, that hard-won wealth is recalled at Plumas-Eureka State Park. [17]Exhibits explain the industrial alchemy that pulled ore from the mountain, then turned it to pure gold with "grizzlies" (sorters), "jaw crushers" (ore grinders), feeders, and amalgam plates. [18]There's a working model of a stamp mill, a blacksmith shop, a stable, and—dwarfing them all—the Mohawk Mill, a 150-foot-tall behemoth of sugar pine that looms almost as large and steeply sloped as the gold-rich mountain behind it. [19]It's being restored.

Index

Note: **Boldface** numbers indicate where key terms are introduced and/or defined in the text.